SEO

FOR

DUMMIES®

A Wiley Brand

6th Edition

W9-ATZ-330

SEO

FOR

DUMMIES®

A Wiley Brand

6th Edition

by Peter Kent

SEO For Dummies®, 6th Edition

Published by: **John Wiley & Sons, Inc.,** 111 River Street, Hoboken, NJ 07030-5774, www.wiley.com

Copyright © 2016 by John Wiley & Sons, Inc., Hoboken, New Jersey

Media and software compilation copyright © 2016 by John Wiley & Sons, Inc. All rights reserved.

Published simultaneously in Canada

No part of this publication may be reproduced, stored in a retrieval system, or transmitted in any form or by any means, electronic, mechanical, photocopying, recording, scanning or otherwise, except as permitted under Sections 107 or 108 of the 1976 United States Copyright Act, without the prior written permission of the Publisher. Requests to the Publisher for permission should be addressed to the Permissions Department, John Wiley & Sons, Inc., 111 River Street, Hoboken, NJ 07030, (201) 748-6011, fax (201) 748-6008, or online at http://www.wiley.com/go/permissions.

Trademarks: Wiley, For Dummies, the Dummies Man logo, Dummies.com, Making Everything Easier, and related trade dress are trademarks or registered trademarks of John Wiley & Sons, Inc., and may not be used without written permission. All trademarks are the property of their respective owners. John Wiley & Sons, Inc., is not associated with any product or vendor mentioned in this book.

LIMIT OF LIABILITY/DISCLAIMER OF WARRANTY: THE PUBLISHER AND THE AUTHOR MAKE NO REPRESENTATIONS OR WARRANTIES WITH RESPECT TO THE ACCURACY OR COMPLETENESS OF THE CONTENTS OF THIS WORK AND SPECIFICALLY DISCLAIM ALL WARRANTIES, INCLUDING WITHOUT LIMITATION WARRANTIES OF FITNESS FOR A PARTICULAR PURPOSE. NO WARRANTY MAY BE CREATED OR EXTENDED BY SALES OR PROMOTIONAL MATERIALS. THE ADVICE AND STRATEGIES CONTAINED HEREIN MAY NOT BE SUITABLE FOR EVERY SITUATION. THIS WORK IS SOLD WITH THE UNDERSTANDING THAT THE PUBLISHER IS NOT ENGAGED IN RENDERING LEGAL, ACCOUNTING, OR OTHER PROFESSIONAL SERVICES. IF PROFESSIONAL ASSISTANCE IS REQUIRED, THE SERVICES OF A COMPETENT PROFESSIONAL PERSON SHOULD BE SOUGHT. NEITHER THE PUBLISHER NOR THE AUTHOR SHALL BE LIABLE FOR DAMAGES ARISING HEREFROM. THE FACT THAT AN ORGANIZATION OR WEBSITE IS REFERRED TO IN THIS WORK AS A CITATION AND/OR A POTENTIAL SOURCE OF FURTHER INFORMATION DOES NOT MEAN THAT THE AUTHOR OR THE PUBLISHER ENDORSES THE INFORMATION THE ORGANIZATION OR WEBSITE MAY PROVIDE OR RECOMMENDATIONS IT MAY MAKE. FURTHER, READERS SHOULD BE AWARE THAT INTERNET WEBSITES LISTED IN THIS WORK MAY HAVE CHANGED OR DISAPPEARED BETWEEN WHEN THIS WORK WAS WRITTEN AND WHEN IT IS READ.

For general information on our other products and services, please contact our Customer Care Department within the U.S. at 877-762-2974, outside the U.S. at 317-572-3993, or fax 317-572-4002. For technical support, please visit www.wiley.com/techsupport.

Wiley publishes in a variety of print and electronic formats and by print-on-demand. Some material included with standard print versions of this book may not be included in e-books or in print-on-demand. If this book refers to media such as a CD or DVD that is not included in the version you purchased, you may download this material at http://booksupport.wiley.com. For more information about Wiley products, visit www.wiley.com.

Library of Congress Control Number: 2015951276

ISBN 978-1-119-12955-4 (pbk); 978-1-119-12960-8 (epub); 9-781-119-12974-5 (epdf)

Manufactured in the United States of America

10 9 8 7 6 5 4 3 2 1

Contents at a Glance

Table of Contents

Part IV: After You've Submitted Your Site..................... 283

Chapter 16: Using Link Popularity to Boost Your Position 285

Chapter 17: Finding Sites to Link to Yours.....................309

Introduction

● ●

*W*elcome to *SEO For Dummies,* 6th Edition. What on earth would you want this book for? After all, can't you just build a Web site and let your Web designer get the site into the search engines? Can't you simply pay someone $25 to register the site with thousands of search engines? I'm sure you've seen advertising stating, "We guarantee top-ten placement in a gazillion search engines!" and "We'll register you in 5,000 search engines today!"

Well, unfortunately, it's not that simple. (Okay, fortunately for me, because if it were simple, Wiley wouldn't pay me to write this book.) The fact is that search engine optimization is a little complicated. Not brain surgery complicated, but not as easy as "Give us 50 bucks, and we'll handle it for you."

The vast majority of Web sites don't have a chance in the search engines. Why? Because of simple mistakes. Because the people creating the sites don't have a clue what they should do to make the site easy for search engines to work with. Because they don't understand the role of links pointing to their site, and because they've never thought about keywords. Because, because, because. This book helps you deal with those becauses and gets you not just one, but dozens, of steps ahead of the average Web-site Joe.

About This Book

This book demystifies the world of search engines. You find out what you need to do to give your site the best possible chance to rank well in the search engines.

In this book, I show you how to

- ✔ Make sure that you're using the right keywords in your Web pages.

- ✔ Create pages that search engines can read and will index the way you want them to.

- ✔ Avoid techniques that search engines hate — things that can get your Web site penalized (knocked down low in search engine rankings).

- ✔ Build pages that give your site greater visibility in search engines.

- ✔ Get search engines and directories to include your site in their indexes and lists.

- ✔ Turn up the search engines' Local search results (you know, on the little map that often appears).

- ✔ Get into the product and shopping indexes.

- ✔ Encourage other Web sites to link to yours.

- ✔ Make the most of social networking and video.

- ✔ Keep track of how your site is doing.

- ✔ And plenty more!

Foolish Assumptions

I don't want to assume anything, but I have to believe that if you're reading this book, you already know a few things about the Internet and search engines. I presume that you

- ✔ Have access to a computer that has access to the Internet.

- ✔ Know how to use a Web browser to get around the Internet.

- ✔ Know how to carry out searches at the Web's major search engines, such as Google and Yahoo!.

Of course, for a book like this, I *have* to assume a little. This is a book about how to get your Web site to rank well in the search engines. I have to assume that you know how to create and work with a site or at least know someone who can create and work with a site. In particular, you (or the other person) know how to

- ✔ Set up a Web site.

- ✔ Create Web pages.

- ✔ Load those pages onto your Web server.

- ✔ Understand a little (not a lot) HTML (HyperText Markup Language), the coding used to create Web pages.

There are many ways to create Web sites these days. You may be creating the site by hand, writing the HTML directly—but probably not. These days, you're more likely to be using some kind of *content management* tool, a system that manages page creation for you, insulating you from the underlying HTML to a great degree; a tool such as WordPress or another "blogging" system, or Drupal, or an ecommerce system such as X-Cart, Volusion, or BigCommerce.

That's fine. Most such systems these days take SEO into consideration and provide tools to help you optimize your site (though not all do!). Still, you need to know at least a little about HTML; when I refer to a <TITLE> tag or meta tags, or whatever, you'll understand what I'm talking about. I don't go into a lot of complicated code in this book; this isn't a primer on HTML. But to do search engine work, you (or someone on your team) need to know what a <TITLE> tag is, for instance, and how to insert it into a page, either directly or using the content-management system's tools; how to recognize JavaScript (though not how to create or modify it); perhaps, depending on the tools you are using, how to open a Web page in a text editor and modify it; and so on. So a little basic HTML knowledge is handy to optimize a site for the search engines. If you need more information about HTML, take a look at *Beginning HTML5 and CSS3 For Dummies*, 5th Edition, by Ed Tittel and Chris Minnick (John Wiley & Sons, Inc.).

Icons Used in This Book

This book, like all *For Dummies* books, uses icons to highlight certain paragraphs and to alert you to particularly useful information. Here's a rundown of what those icons mean:

A Tip icon means I'm giving you an extra snippet of information that may help you on your way or provide some additional insight into the concepts being discussed.

The Remember icon points out information that is worth committing to memory.

The Technical Stuff icon indicates geeky stuff that you can skip if you really want to, although you may want to read it if you're the kind of person who likes to have the background info.

The Warning icon helps you stay out of trouble. It's intended to grab your attention to help you avoid a pitfall that may harm your Web site or business.

Beyond the Book

Don't forget to visit the Web sites associated with this book.

At www.SearchEngineBulletin.com, you find all the links in this book (so that you don't have to type them!). You'll also find additional useful information that didn't make it into the book.

There's a handy online Cheat Sheet with fingertip facts about search engine optimization. You can access it at

```
www.dummies.com/cheatsheet/seo
```

For Parts II through V, there are online articles that provide more information about the world of search engine optimization. You'll find them at

```
www.dummies.com/extras/seo
```

Occasionally, Wiley has updates to its technology books. If this book does have technical updates, they will be posted at

```
www.dummies.com/extras/seo
```

Part I
Getting Started with SEO

In this part . . .

✔ Understanding how search engines work

✔ Deciphering search results

✔ Connecting your pages to search engines

✔ Evaluating your competition

✔ Making your site friendly for visitors and search engines

✔ Visit `www.dummies.com` for great Dummies content online.

Chapter 1

Surveying the Search Engine Landscape

*Y*ou've got a problem. You want people to visit your Web site; that's the purpose, after all — to bring people to your site to buy your product, or find out about your service, or hear about the cause you support, or for whatever other purpose you've built the site. So you've decided you need to get traffic from the search engines — not an unreasonable conclusion, as you find out in this chapter. But there are *so many* search engines! You have the obvious ones — Google, AOL, Yahoo!, and Bing (formerly MSN) — but you've probably also heard of others: HotBot, Dogpile, Ask.com, Netscape, and EarthLink. There's also Lycos, InfoSpace, Mamma.com, WebCrawler, and many more. To top it all off, you've seen advertising asserting that for only $49.95 (or $19.95, or $99.95, or whatever sum seems to make sense to the advertiser), you, too, can have your Web site listed in hundreds, nay, thousands of search engines. You may have even used some of these services, only to discover that the flood of traffic you were promised turns up missing.

Well, I've got some good news. You can forget almost all the names I just listed — well, at least you can after you read this chapter. The point of this chapter is to take a complicated landscape of thousands of search sites and whittle it down into the small group of search systems that really matter. (Search sites? Search systems? Don't worry; I explain the distinction in a moment.)

If you really want to, you can jump to the "Where Do People Search?" section (near the end of the chapter) to see the list of search systems you need to worry about and ignore the details. But I've found that when I give this list to someone, he or she looks at me like I'm crazy because they know that some popular search sites aren't on the list. This chapter explains why.

Investigating Search Engines and Directories

The term *search engine* has become the predominant term for *search system* or *search site,* but before reading any further, you need to understand the different types of search, um, thingies that you're going to run across.

Although out on the Interwebs you will hear the term *search engine* a *lot*, perhaps almost exclusively, I like to sometimes use the term *search site*. Why? Because there are many search sites that either don't use search engines (they have directories instead, as I explain below) or get their search results from somewhere else.

Take, for instance, AOL.com (`http://www.aol.com/`). One might be forgiven for thinking that AOL.com is a search engine; after all, it has a big search box right at the top, and if you enter a phrase and press Enter, or click a colored SEARCH button, you get search results.

However, AOL doesn't own a search engine, despite the fact that you can search at the AOL site. (Indeed, *many* people *do* search at AOL, around 200 million times a month). Rather, AOL gets its search results from the Google search engine. Hence my desire to differentiate between search *sites* (places where you can search) and search *engines* (the systems that actually do all the work). It's an important distinction, as this chapter explains later.

Search sites, indexes, & engines

Let me quickly give you a few simple definitions:

- **Search Site:** A Web site where you can search for information on the Web.
- **Search Engine:** A system that collects pages from the Web, saves them in a massive database, indexes the information, and provides a mechanism for people to search through the data.
- **Search Index:** The index containing all the information that the engine collected and searches.
- **Search Directory:** A system that contains some basic information about Web sites, rather than about collected and indexed Web pages.

Index envy

Late in 2005, Yahoo! (www.yahoo.com) claimed that its index contained information for about 20 billion pages, along with almost 2 billion images and 50 million audio and video pages. Google (www.google.com) used to actually state on its home page how many pages it indexed — it reached 15 billion or so at one point — but decided not to play the "mine is bigger than yours" game with Yahoo! and removed the stat.

In 2015, Google reported that it had discovered *60* trillion pages, though not all were indexed; still, some reports claimed that, in 2014, Google had 65 billion pages in its index! Whatever the actual number is, just assume that it's more than you can shake the proverbial stick at. (Yahoo! doesn't even have a directory these days; rather, it uses the search-results index from Bing.)

Large search-index companies own thousands of computers that use software known as *spiders, searchbots,* or *robots* (or just plain *bots*) to grab Web pages and read the information stored in them. These systems use complex *algorithms* — calculations based on complicated formulae — to index that information and rank it in search results when people search. Google, shown in Figure 1-1, is the world's most popular search site.

Figure 1-1:
Google, the world's most popular search engine, produced these results.

Search directories

Before there were search engines, there were search directories. A *directory* is a categorized collection of information about Web sites. Rather than containing information *from* Web *pages,* it contains information *about* Web *sites.* In fact, before Google was even a twinkle in its fathers' eyes, Yahoo! directory was America's dominant search site; "The Google of the 1990s," as I've seen it described.

Directories are not created using spiders or bots to download and index pages on the Web sites in the directory; rather, for each Web site, the directory contains information, such as a title, description, and category, submitted by the site owner. The two most important directories, Yahoo! and Open Directory, have staff members who examine all the sites in the directory to make sure they're placed into the correct categories and meet certain quality criteria. Smaller directories often accept sites based on the owners' submission, with little verification.

The most significant search directories in recent years were owned by Yahoo! (`http://dir.yahoo.com`) and the Open Directory Project (affectionately known as DMOZ due to its original name — Directory Mozilla — and its domain name, `www.dmoz.org`; see Figure 1-2; the Open Directory Project actually is a volunteer-managed directory owned by AOL). However, search directories are simply nowhere near as important today as in the past. In 2011, in fact, Google gave up on its own directory; until then, `http://dir.google.com` led to a Google directory based on the Open Directory Project data.

And just weeks before I began work on this edition of *SEO For Dummies,* Yahoo! closed down its directory, barely informing the world. Can DMOZ be far behind? Especially as it's been a decade since one of its founders suggested that it really served no purpose? Probably not.

These directories are becoming pretty irrelevant to average users; most users don't know they even exist. Google dumped its directory, Yahoo! Directory just expired, and it's unclear whether the lights are on at DMOZ (it's very hard to get a site into that directory these days). In fact, there's a good chance that the only reason Yahoo! continued its directory as long as it did was the $299 annual fee it got from the companies submitting to it. (Just sayin'!)

However, directories *may* still be useful to your SEO efforts, Chapter 14 will address it.

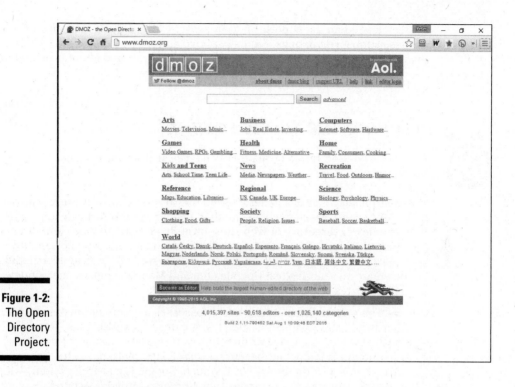

Figure 1-2:
The Open
Directory
Project.

Spidered Directories

I wasn't sure what to call these things, so I made up a name: *spidered directories.* A number of small search sites don't use spiders to examine the *full* contents of each page in the index. Rather, spiders grab a little background information about each page, such as titles, descriptions, and keywords. In some cases, this information comes from the meta tags pulled off the pages in the index. (I tell you about meta tags in Chapter 3.) In other cases, the person who enters the site into the index provides this information. These are a form of directory, but they are generally created programmatically rather than by site owners requesting inclusion. (Yahoo! Directory was, and DMOZ still is, perhaps, "hand built" by using data submitted by site owners.) A number of the smaller systems discussed in Chapter 14 are of this type.

Pay-per-click systems

Many search sites provide *pay-per-click* (PPC) listings. When you search at Google, for instance, you'll see results that come out of Google's main index, but also small text ads. Advertisers place these small ads into the PPC system, and when users perform their searches the results contain some of these sponsored listings, typically above and to the right of the free listings. Pay-per-click systems are discussed in an additional chapter posted at www.SearchEngineBulletin.com.

Keeping the terms straight

Here are a few additional terms that you'll see scattered throughout the book:

- ✔ **Search site:** This is a general term I use to refer to a Web site that provides search results; a Web site that lets you search through some kind of index or directory of Web sites, or perhaps both an index and directory. (In some cases, search sites known as *meta indexes* allow you to search through multiple indices.) Google.com, AOL.com, and EarthLink.com are all search sites. Dogpile.com and Mamma.com are meta-index search sites.

- ✔ **Search system:** This organization possesses a combination of software, hardware, and people that indexes or categorizes Web sites — the system builds the index or directory you search at a search site. The distinction is important because a search site might not actually own a search index or directory. For instance, Google is a search system — it displays results from the index that it creates for itself — but AOL.com and EarthLink.com aren't. In fact, if you search at AOL.com or EarthLink.com, you actually get Google search results.

  Google and the Open Directory Project provide search results to hundreds of search sites. In fact, most of the world's search sites get their search results from elsewhere (mostly Google these days); see Figure 1-3.

- ✔ **Search term:** This is the word, or words, that someone types into a search engine when looking for information.

- ✔ **Search results:** Results are the information (the results of your search term) returned to you when you go to a search site and search for something. As just explained, in many cases the search results you see don't come from the search site you're using, but rather from some other search system.

- ✔ **SERPs:** I don't use the term much, but you'll hear others in the business talking about the *serps*. It simply means *search engine results page,* the page that appears after you search.

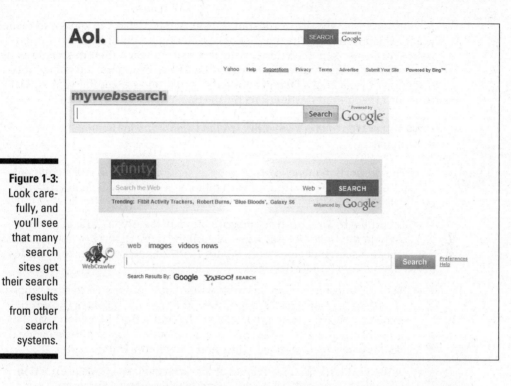

Figure 1-3: Look carefully, and you'll see that many search sites get their search results from other search systems.

✔ **Natural search results:** A link to a Web page can appear on a search results page two ways: The search engine may place it on the page because the site owner paid to be there (pay-per-click ads), or it may pull the page from its index because it thinks the page matches the search term well. These free placements are often known as *natural search results;* you'll also hear the term *organic search results* and sometimes even *algorithmic search results.*

✔ **Search engine optimization (SEO):** Search engine optimization (also known as *SEO*) refers to "optimizing" Web sites and Web pages to rank well in the search engines — the subject of this book, of course.

Why bother with search engines?

Why bother using search engines for your marketing? Because search engines represent the single most important source of new Web site visitors.

You may have heard that most Web site visits begin at a search engine. Well, this isn't true, though many people continue to use these outdated statistics because they sound good — "80 percent of all Web site visitors reach the site through a search engine," for instance. However, way back in 2003, that claim was finally put to rest. The number of search-originated site visits dropped below the 50 percent mark. Most Web site visitors reach their destinations by either typing a *URL* — a Web address — into their browsers and going there directly or by clicking a link on another site that takes them there. Most visitors *don't* reach their destinations by starting at the search engines.

However, search engines are still *extremely important* for a number of reasons:

- ✔ The proportion of visits originating at search engines is still significant. Sure, it's not 80 percent, but with billions of searches each month, it's still a lot of traffic.

- ✔ According to a report by comScore published early in 2015, Internet users in the United States were performing more than 21 billion searches at major search engines each month (with 29 percent of those searches coming from mobile devices).

- ✔ Many billions more searches are carried out in other search sites, such as map sites (MapQuest), video sites (YouTube), retail sites (Amazon, eBay, Craigslist), and so on. It's likely that more than 35 billion searches are performed in the United States each month, 2 to 3 searches every day for every man, woman, child, and baby in the United States.

- ✔ Of the visits that don't originate at a search engine, a large proportion are revisits — people who know exactly where they want to go. This isn't new business; it's repeat business. Most *new* visits come through the search engines — that is, search engines are the single most important source of *new* visitors to Web sites.

- ✔ It's also been well established for a number of years that most people researching a purchase begin their research at the search engines. (Except for those who don't. As I discuss in Chapter 15, many, perhaps most, product searches actually begin in sites such as Amazon, eBay, and Craigslist. But then, I think it's important to understand that these sites *are* search engines; they are, in effect, product-search engines.)

- ✔ Search engines represent an inexpensive way to reach people. Generally, you get more bang for your buck going after free search-engine traffic than almost any other form of advertising or marketing.

Here's an example. One client of mine, selling construction equipment to the tune of $10,000 a month, rebuilt his site and began a combined natural-search and paid-search campaign, boosting sales to around $500,000 a month in less than two years. It's hard to imagine how he could have grown his company, with relatively little investment, so quickly without the search engines!

Where Do People Search?

You can search for Web sites at many places. Literally thousands of sites, in fact, provide the ability to search the Web. (What you may not realize, however, is that many sites search only a small subset of the World Wide Web.)

However, *most* searches are carried out at a small number of search sites. How do the world's most popular search sites rank? That depends on how you measure popularity:

- ✔ Percentage of site visitors *(audience reach)*
- ✔ Total number of visitors
- ✔ Total number of searches carried out at a site
- ✔ Total number of hours visitors spend searching at the site

Each measurement provides a slightly different ranking. Although all provide a similar picture with the same sites generally appearing on the list, some search sites are in slightly different positions.

The following list shows the United States' top general search sites early in 2015, according to comScore:

Google sites: 65.4 percent

Microsoft sites (Bing): 19.7 percent

Yahoo! sites: 11.8 percent

Ask Network: 2.0 percent

AOL, Inc.: 1.2 percent

Remember that this is a list of search sites, not search systems. In fact, the preceding list shows *groups* of sites — the Microsoft entry, for instance, includes searches on Bing.com and MSN.com.

In some cases, the sites own their own systems. Google provides its own search results, for instance, but AOL doesn't. (AOL gets its results from Google.) Yahoo! gets its results from Bing, thanks to a Yahoo!/Microsoft partnership — known as the *Yahoo! and Microsoft Search Alliance* — that was implemented in August 2010. (Look for the little *Powered by Bing* notice at the bottom of Yahoo! search pages. It's been reported that Yahoo! wants out of the agreement—so it can go back to using Google search results!—but can't figure out how to break the 10-year contract with Microsoft.)

The fact that some sites get results from other search systems means two things:

✔ **The numbers in the preceding list are somewhat misleading.** They suggest that Google has 65.4 percent of all searches. But Google also feeds AOL its results — add AOL's searches to Google's, and you have 66.5 percent of all searches. Additionally, Google feeds search results to various other sites, increasing that number further. Microsoft feeds not just 19.7 percent of results but, when you add in the Yahoo! searches, powered by Microsoft, actually over 31.5 percent.

✔ **You can ignore some of these systems.** At present, and for the foreseeable future, you don't need to worry about AOL.com. Even though it's one of the world's top search sites (though admittedly still far behind Google, Yahoo!, and Bing), as long as you remember that Google feeds AOL, you need to worry about Google only. You don't really need to worry about Yahoo!, either; as long as Bing feeds Yahoo!, you can think of the two as essentially the same index.

Now reexamine the preceding list of the U.S.'s most important search sites and see what you can remove to get closer to a list of sites you care about. Check out Table 1-1 for the details.

Table 1-1	The Top Search Sites	
Search Site	*Keep It On the List?*	*Description*
Google.com	Yes	The big kid on the block. Lots of people search the Google index on its own search site, *and* it feeds many sites. Obviously, Google has to stay on the list.
Bing	Yes	Bing creates its own index, gets many searches, *and* feeds data to Yahoo!. So Bing is critical.
Yahoo.com	No	Yahoo! is obviously a large, important site, but it gets its search results from Bing, so as long as you're in the Bing index, you're in Yahoo!.
Ask.com (previously known as AskJeeves.com)	Yes	It has its own search engine and feeds some other systems — MyWay, Lycos, and Excite. Keep it in mind, though it's small and relatively unimportant compared to Google and Bing.
AOL.com	No	Fuggetaboutit — AOL gets search results from Google.

Based on the information in Table 1-1, you can whittle down your list of systems to three: Google, Bing, and Ask. The top two search systems are very important, accounting for 95 percent or more of all search results, with a small follower, Ask, which provides results to many smaller search sites.

There's one more system I'm tempted to add to these three systems, though: the Open Directory Project (www.dmoz.org). This directory system feeds data to hundreds of search sites, so if you can get listed in here, it's a great thing, and, in fact, in earlier editions of this book, I *have* included it. However, whether you actually *can* get listed these days is another matter, so I'm going to leave it off the list, though I look at it in more detail in Chapter 14.

To summarize, three important systems are left:

- ✔ Google
- ✔ Bing
- ✔ Ask

That's not so bad, is it? You've just gone from thousands of sites to three, and only the top two are critical. (The only reason Ask.com gets included on such lists is that even though it has a tiny share of the search market, there's nothing *below* it on the list that comes close.)

Now, some of you may be thinking, "Aren't you missing some sites? What happened to HotBot, Mamma.com, WebCrawler, Lycos, and all the other systems that were so well known a few years ago?" A lot of them have disappeared or have turned over a new leaf and are pursuing other opportunities.

For example, Northern Light, a system well known in the late 1990s, now sells search software. And in the cases in which the search sites are still running, they're generally fed by other search systems. WebCrawler, for instance, gets search results from Google and Yahoo!, which means, in effect, from Google and Bing.

AltaVista, the Web's first big search index, has been owned by Yahoo! for years, but now the domain merely redirects to Yahoo.com. The same goes for AllTheWeb (for the geeks among you who remember it) — another domain redirect to Yahoo.com. If the search site you remember isn't mentioned here, it's either out of business, being fed by someone else, or simply not important in the big scheme of things.

When you find a new search system, look carefully on the page near the search box, or on the search results page — perhaps at the bottom of the page in the copyright message — and you may find where the search results are coming from.

You'll also want to work with some other search systems, as you find out in Chapter 14. In some cases, you need to check out specialty directories and indexes related to the industry in which your Web site operates or submit your site to Web directories in order to build links back to your site. In addition, in Chapter 15, you find out about the product search sites — hugely important for those of you selling products. And in Chapter 20, I tell you about the video sites — YouTube, for instance, is the world's third most important search engine, after Google and Bing. However, the preceding systems — Google, Bing, and Ask.com — are the most important general-search systems. And again, only the first two are really critical.

Google alone provides almost 70 percent of all search results. Get your site into both Google and Bing , and you're in front of probably around 99 percent of all searchers. Well, *perhaps* you're in front of them. You have a *chance* of being in front of them, anyway, if your site ranks highly (which is what this book is all about).

Search Engine Magic

Go to Google and search for the term *personal injury lawyer*. Then look at the blue bar below the Google logo, and you see something like this:

```
About 42,800,000 results (0.48 seconds)
```

This means Google has found over 40 million pages that it believes match these three words in some way. Yet, somehow, Google has managed to rank the pages. It's decided that one particular page should appear first, and then another, and then another, and so on. (By the way, this has to be one of the wonders of the modern world: Search engines have tens of thousands of computers, evaluating a trillion pages or more, in a fraction of a second.)

How do they do it?

How on earth does Google do it? How does it evaluate and compare pages? How do other search engines do the same? Well, I don't know *exactly*. Search engines don't want you to know how they work (or it would be too easy to create pages that exactly match the criteria of the search system for any given search term, "giving them what they want to see"). But I can explain the general concept.

When Google searches for your search term, it begins by looking for pages containing the exact phrase. Then it starts looking for pages containing the words close together, and for synonyms; search for *dog* and Google knows you may be interested in pages with the word *canine*, for instance. (One Google source claims that synonyms come into play in around 70 percent of all searches.) Then it looks for pages that have the words scattered around. This isn't necessarily the order in which a search engine shows you pages; in some cases, pages with words close together (but not the exact phrase) appear higher than pages with the exact phrase, for instance. That's because search engines evaluate pages according to a variety of criteria.

Search engines look at many factors. They look for the words throughout the page, both in the visible page and in the nonvisible portions of the HTML source code for the page. Each time they find the words, they are *weighted* in some way. A word in one position is worth more than a word in another position. A word formatted in one way is worth more than a word formatted in another. (You read more about this in Chapter 7.) There's more, though. Search engines also look at links pointing to pages and use those links to evaluate the referenced pages: How many links are there? How many are from popular sites? What words are in the link text? You read more about this in Chapters 16 through 18.

Stepping into the programmers' shoes

There's a lot of conflicting information out there about SEO. Some of it's good, some of it's not so good, and some of it's downright wrong. When evaluating a claim about what search engines do, I sometimes find it useful to step into the shoes of the people building the search engines; I try to think about what would make sense from the perspective of the programmers who write the code that evaluates all these pages.

Consider this: Say, you search for *personal injury lawyer*, and the search engine finds one page with the term in the page's title (between the <TITLE> and </TITLE> tags, which you read more about in Chapters 3 and 7), and another page with the term somewhere deep in the page text. Which do you think is likely to match the search term better? If the text is in the title, doesn't that indicate that page is likely to be related in some way to the term? If the text is deep in the body of the page, couldn't it mean that the page isn't directly related to the term, but that it's related to it in some incidental or peripheral manner?

Considering SEO from this point of view makes it easier to understand how search engines try to evaluate and compare pages. If the keywords are in the links that point to the page, the page is likely to be relevant to those keywords; if the keywords are in headings on the page, that must be significant; if the keywords appear frequently throughout the page, rather than just once, that must mean something. Suddenly, it all makes sense.

By the way, in Chapter 9, I discuss things that search engines don't like. You may hear elsewhere all sorts of warnings that may or may not be correct. Here's an example: I've read that using a refresh meta tag to automatically push a visitor from one page to another will get your site penalized and may even get your site banned from the search engine. You've seen this situation: You land on a page on a Web site, and there's a message saying something like, "We'll forward you to page *x* in five seconds, or you can click <u>here</u>." The theory is that search engines don't like this, and they may punish you for doing this.

Now, does this make any sense? Aren't there good reasons to sometimes use such forwarding techniques? Yes, there are. So why would search engines punish you for doing it? They don't. They probably won't index the page that is forwarding a visitor — based on the quite reasonable theory that if the site doesn't want the visitor to read the page, the search engine doesn't need to index it — but you're not going to get punished for using it.

Remember that the search engine programmers aren't interested in punishing anyone; they're just trying to make the best choices between billions of pages. Generally, search engines use their "algorithms" to determine how to rank a page, and they try to adjust the algorithms to make sure "tricks" are ignored. But they don't want to punish anyone for doing something for which there might be a good reason, even if the technique could also be used as a trick.

What would the programmers do? I like to use this as my "plausibility filter" when I hear someone make some unusual or even outlandish claim about how search engines function.

Gathering Your Tools

You need several tools and skills to optimize and rank your Web site. I talk about a number of these in the appropriate chapters, but I want to cover a few basics before I move on. It goes without saying that you need:

- ✔ Basic Internet knowledge
- ✔ A computer connected to the Internet
- ✔ A Web site
- ✔ One of these three things:
  - Good working knowledge of HTML
  - Access to a geek with a good working knowledge of HTML
  - A Web-site creation tool that provides SEO functions that allow you to modify the site in the required manner

Certain changes need to be made to a Web site in order to optimize it properly; the Title tag needs to be changed, along with the Description meta tag, the headings need to use H1 tags, you need to be able to put keywords into the URL, and so on. This means that whoever does this work needs to understand what these things mean, and how to modify them. *Or* the tool you use to build your Web site has to provide a convenient way to allow you to change these elements. Some do, some don't (see the Part V Web Extra: *Ten Ways to Make WordPress (and Others) Search Engine Friendly*).

Teaching HTML and and how to upload pages to a Web site is beyond the scope of this book. If you're interested in finding out more, check out *HTML, XHTML, & CSS For Dummies*, by Ed Tittel and Jeff Noble, and *Creating Web Pages For Dummies,* 9th Edition, by Bud E. Smith (both published by John Wiley & Sons, Inc.).

✔ Web browser and SEO tools

All of the Big Three browsers (Chrome, Firefox, and Internet Explorer) have a bunch of SEO-related tools now, and even the next two browsers on the popularity list (Safari and Opera) have some, too, though probably not as many. Look in your browser's add-on library for tools such as these:

- *NoFollow:* Lots of tools indicate the presence of "nofollow" links (see Chapter 16).

- *Whois:* These tools retrieve information about the domain of the site you're viewing. Great for digging up info on competitors.

- *Firebug:* A fantastic little tool for examining the code underlying a Web page. Right-click a component on the page you're looking at, select Inspect Element, and you see a frame that shows you how the component was created. Designed for Firefox, but with a "lite" version that works in other browsers.

- *Google Global:* Handy if you want to see Google search results in different countries.

- *Compete Browser Extension:* Provides information, in the status bar, about the popularity of the site you are visiting, from Compete.com. (Alexa and Quantcast are two other well-known page-popularity services.)

- *PageRank:* Various tools display the Google PageRank of the page currently displayed in the browser (see Chapter 16).

- *SEO plug-ins:* Search the add-on library for the term *SEO,* and you'll find a number of add-ons that are collections of tools that provide access to all sorts of data. For instance, the WebRank Toolbar shows Google PageRank, along with Alexa, Compete, and Quantcast rankings. SEOQuake provides all sorts of things, such as the number of pages on the displayed Web site that are indexed by Google and Bing, the number of links pointing to the site according to those search engines, a link to Whois information, a link to a list of similar sites, Alexa rank and PageRank, and so on.

Geek or no geek

Many readers of this book are business people who don't plan to do the search engine work themselves (or, in some cases, realize that it's a lot of work and need to find someone with more time or technical skills to do the work). However, having read the book, they understand far more about search engines and are in a better position to find and direct someone else working on their site. As one reader-cum-client told me, "There's a lot of snake oil in this business," so his reading helped him understand the basics and ask the right questions of search engine optimization firms. (See the Part 4 Web Extra, *How to Pick an SEO Firm (Without Getting Burned!)*, for more information on that subject.)

Don't upgrade your browser as soon as there's a new version. Browsers often release new versions quicker than the add-on authors can keep up, so if you upgrade too soon, you'll find most of your add-ons are disabled.

Chapter 2

Search Results, Deconstructed

*B*efore I jump into the nitty-gritty of how to get your site ranked high in the search engines, you should look at what the term *search results* really means. All too often, people think of search results as a single *thing*, whereas, in fact, it's a combination of *different* things, and until you understand what those different things really are, you can't see the entire picture.

Different search terms will produce different search results. The results will always include information from the organic index, but whether or not results are included from the Local index, the Shopping index, the PPC index, and so on depends on the type of search made. Search for *pizza*, for instance, and you'll find information from the Local index, search for *first indian war of independence* and you won't. The search engines are trying to provide you with the best results, so they analyze the search terms to figure out what you're likely to be looking for. Are you looking for a local business? News? A video or image, perhaps?

The *search engine results pages* (SERPs) produced by major search engines seem to get more complicated year by year, and it's worth understanding where the information on the results pages actually comes from, which is what I look at in this chapter.

The Big Two: Organic and PPC

Search results are mostly dominated by two particular indexes: the *organic* or *natural search* results, and the *PPC* (Pay Per Click) search results. Take a look at Figure 2-1; I've marked the two areas.

PPC Results, from
Google AdWords

PPC Results, from Google
Product Listing Ads

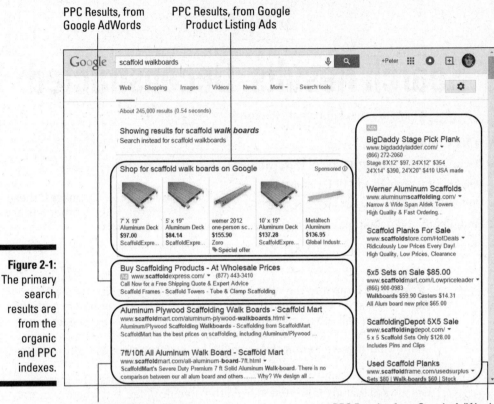

Figure 2-1:
The primary
search
results are
from the
organic
and PPC
indexes.

Organic Search Results

PPC Results, from Google AdWords

The organic-results index is created by *searchbots*. For instance, Google uses something called a *googlebot* to retrieve pages. It's common to talk about searchbots as if somehow they wander around the Web, moving from page to page through links between the pages, collecting the pages, and reading them. Of course what's really going on is that bots are programs, running on the search engine's servers, that send requests to Web servers asking for pages — just as your browser does when you click a link. When they receive the page, they read it, and then request the pages that the retrieved page links to.

By the way, the search results typically put ten results from the organic index into the search-results page, though, as you see later in this chapter, those results are often interspersed with other types of search results. (In some cases, in particular when adding *local* results to the page, the search engines may display a smaller number of organic-search results, perhaps seven or eight.)

The other major form of search result is the PPC (Pay Per Click) ad. Most search results today, including results from Google, Yahoo!, and Bing, include

PPC ads, ads that cost the advertiser nothing until someone clicks the ad, at which point the advertiser is charged a click fee (thus, "pay per click").

PPC ads are typically placed at the top of the search results (three or four results, sometimes five in Yahoo!, though some searches result in no ads) and in a column to the right of the main search results.

There are two important categories of PPC ads:

- Simple text ads
- "Shopping" or "product listing" ads that often contain images

Figure 2-1, for instance, shows several ads at the top with the images; these ads are from the Google Product Listings Ads index, while the other ads are from the Google AdWords index, which contains text ads.

It's sometimes unclear where the PPC ads end and the organic results begin — the three major search engines put a colored background under the ads at the top and a label that says *Ads* or *Sponsored Results*, but on many screens, the color is sometimes not, and the label is often missed among the general page clutter. Thus many users don't realize the distinction between organic results and PPC ads.

On the other hand, among people who *do* understand the distinction, there are various schools of thought: Some users never click the ads, some always click the ads and ignore the organic results, while others realize that the ads provide really good results for some searches and not-so-good results for others.

When people talk about search engine optimization, they're typically talking about the organic search results. When you optimize pages, for instance (see Chapters 3, 7, and 9), you're typically doing so in order to rank well in the organic index. In this book, though, I discuss other indexes, in particular the Local and Shopping indexes (see the next two sections). As for the simple text-based PPC ads, that subject isn't covered in this book.

Looking at Local Results

There's another type of search result that is incredibly important, with a huge presence in many search-results pages: Local results. Search Yahoo!, for instance, for the term *personal injury attorney,* and you may see something like Figure 2-2. These Local results can take up a lot of space, in particular in Google and Yahoo!, and often appear above organic search results (though below PPC ads) and thus are an important consideration for businesses that serve a particular geographic area. I look at this subject in Chapter 12.

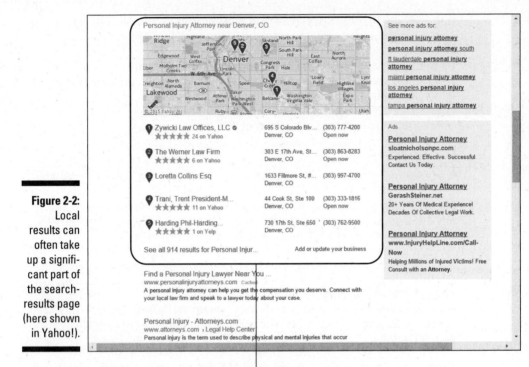

Personal Injury Attorney near Denver, CO

See more ads for:

personal injury attorney
personal injury attorney south
ft lauderdale **personal injury attorney**
miami **personal injury attorney**
los angeles **personal injury attorney**
tampa **personal injury attorney**

Ads

Personal Injury Attorney
sloatnicholsonpc.com
Experienced. Effective. Successful.
Contact Us Today.

Personal Injury Attorney
GerashSteiner.net
20+ Years Of Medical Experience!
Decades Of Collective Legal Work.

Personal Injury Attorney
www.InjuryHelpLine.com/Call-Now
Helping Millions of Injured Victims! Free
Consult with an **Attorney**.

① Zywicki Law Offices, LLC ⊘ 695 S Colorado Blv... (303) 777-4200
★★★★★ 24 on Yahoo Denver, CO Open now

② The Werner Law Firm 303 E 17th Ave, St... (303) 863-8283
★★★★★ 6 on Yahoo Denver, CO Open now

③ Loretta Collins Esq 1633 Fillmore St, #... (303) 997-4700
Denver, CO

④ Trani, Trent President-M... 44 Cook St, Ste 100 (303) 333-1816
★★★★★ 11 on Yahoo Denver, CO Open now

⑤ Harding Phil-Harding... 730 17th St, Ste 650 (303) 762-9500
★★★★★ 1 on Yelp Denver, CO

See all 914 results for Personal Injur... Add or update your business

Find a Personal Injury Lawyer Near You ...
www.personalinjuryattorneys.com Cached
A personal injury attorney can help you get the compensation you deserve. Connect with
your local law firm and speak to a lawyer today about your case.

Personal Injury - Attorneys.com
www.attorneys.com › Legal Help Center
Personal injury is the term used to describe physical and mental injuries that occur

Figure 2-2:
Local
results can
often take
up a signifi-
cant part of
the search-
results page
(here shown
in Yahoo!).

Local Search Results

Checking Out Shopping Results

It's often not hard for the search engines to figure out when someone is quite likely searching for a product he may be interested in buying. If someone searches for *shoes,* it's quite likely he's interested in buying a pair, either offline (that's where the Local results come in) or online (that's where the Shopping results come in). On the other hand, if someone searches on *shoe manufacturing victorian england,* it's unlikely that he's in the market for a pair.

The major search engines all maintain product indexes, totally separate from the organic or even the regular text-based PPC indexes. However, product results are typically a form of PPC advertising; you submit your products to the search engines' product listings, and get charged if anyone clicks on your listing in the search results. (Chapter 15 explains how to get your products into those indexes.)

When a search engine figures a searcher may be looking for product information, it inserts product results — typically with images — into the search-results page, as shown previously in Figure 2-1. Clicking the Shopping search results leads into the search engine's shopping area, where the searcher can find more information about these, and other, products.

Staying Current with News Results

Another significant search-result component is the News results. If the search engines think News results might be useful to you, based on your search — search for a politician or just about any country name, for instance — then you'll see News results embedded into the results page.

Again, these are from a completely different source; in fact, publishers have to apply to be included in the News results, shown in Figure 2-3. (Google has an established process and takes many sites; see `http://support.google.com/news/publisher`. Yahoo! and Bing are far more restrictive.)

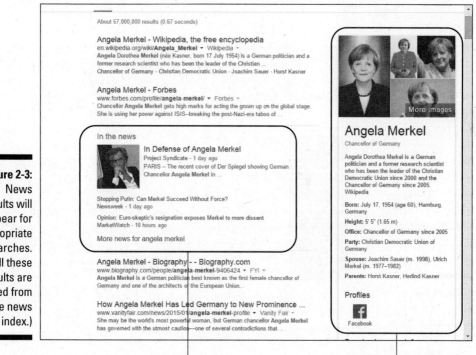

Figure 2-3: News results will appear for appropriate searches. (All these results are pulled from the news index.)

News Results

Detailed Information about a Famous Person

Notice also in Figure 2-3 that, on the right side, you can see more detailed results related to Angela Merkel. It's now common on Google and Yahoo! to see this kind of detailed result for searches on the names of famous people, such as politicians and celebrities. (As you can see in Figure 2-5, search engines may also display similar blocks of information for other things, such as famous locations.)

Viewing Video and Image Results

You've almost certainly seen video and image results in the search engines (see Figure 2-4). All three of the major search engines index Youtube.com (it's owned by Google). But they index other sites, too, such as Vimeo.com, Vevo.com, and Metcafe.com. If you want to try getting your videos into the search results, see Chapter 20.

As for images (see Figure 2-5), it's possible to encourage the search engines to rank your images high for particular keywords; I discuss that subject in Chapter 24.

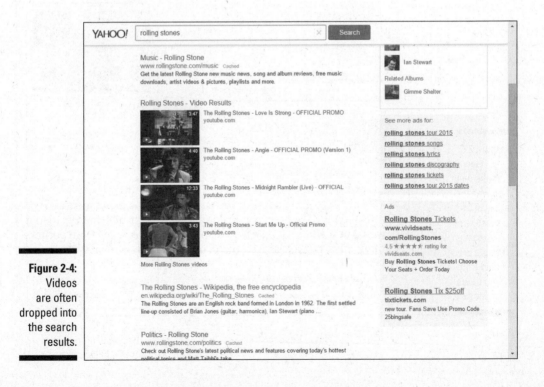

Figure 2-4:
Videos are often dropped into the search results.

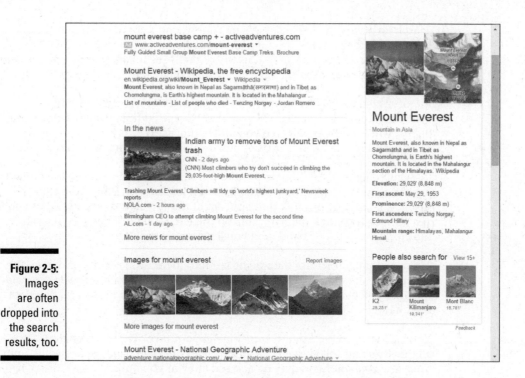

Figure 2-5:
Images
are often
dropped into
the search
results, too.

Getting Friendly with Social Results

In Chapter 19, you find out about the social networks and how to use them to your advantage. The three major search engines incorporate social-network results into the organic index; in other words, they index social-network sites just like any other site.

The different search engines use the data in different ways, and in different ways at different times; for instance, in the past Google has experimented with actually displaying a Twitter feed inside the search results, but decided it didn't work well. For a while, Google also displayed photos taken from authors' Google+ accounts next to their search results, but also gave up on that.

So *how* the data is used varies, but the social networks definitely are important not only in their own right, but also as a way to feed information into the search results. Check out Chapter 19 for more information.

Collecting Bits n' Pieces

Finally, the search engines often embed little "bits and pieces" into the search results, data totally separate from these other indexes. For instance, search for *sunrise 80209* in Google or Yahoo!, and right at the top of the search results you'll see the time of the next sunrise (see Figure 2-6). Try searching for *173 pounds in usd*, in any of the three major search engines, and you'll see the current exchange rate, British pounds to U.S. dollars.

All three also have calculators (try *(5674374 / 231) + (12987 * 7)*, for instance). Looking for a flight? Or movie? Google and Bing will both provide flights, while all three will give you movie times. (Try, say, *fly denver to los angeles* and the name of a current movie, along with a city and state name.)

Cooking tonight? Well, Google used to provide recipes, but at the time of writing had removed them. No problem, search for *lamb* on Bing, then click the <u>Also try: Lamb Recipes</u> link that appears at the top, and that's just what you'll get. Yahoo!, too; click the <u>More</u> link on the left, then click <u>Recipes</u>. Search Bing for a musician or band, and you'll get music results.

There are many forms of data being fed into the search results. (Some of the specialty results shown in the preceding examples use *rich snippets,* information that you can feed to the search engines if you know how to tag the data; see Chapter 7 for information.)

You may want to dig around sometime in your favorite search engine — try all the links and see where they go and read the Help pages to see what fancy tools are available. You may be amazed at what you find.

Figure 2-6: The search engines provide all sorts of weird and wonderful results.

Chapter 3

Your One-Hour, Search Engine–Friendly Web Site Makeover

. . . .

In This Chapter

▶ Finding your site in the search engines

▶ Choosing keywords

▶ Examining your pages for problems

▶ Getting search engines to read and index your pages

. . . .

A few small changes can make a *big* difference in your site's position in the search engines. So instead of forcing you to read this entire book before you can get anything done, this chapter helps you identify problems with your site and, with a little luck, shows you how to make a significant difference through quick fixes.

It's possible that you may not make significant progress in a single hour, as the chapter title promises. You may identify serious problems with your site that can't be fixed quickly. Sorry, that's life! The purpose of this chapter is to help you identify a few obvious problems and, perhaps, make some quick fixes with the goal of really getting something done.

Is Your Site Indexed?

It's important to find out whether your site is actually in a search engine or directory. Your site doesn't come up when someone searches at Google for *rodent racing*? Can't find it in Bing? Have you ever thought that perhaps it simply isn't there? In the next several sections, I explain how to find out whether your site is indexed in a few different systems.

Various browser add-ons, such as SEOQuake, automatically tell you the number of indexed pages when you visit a site.

Google

I'll start with the behemoth: Google. Here's the quickest and easiest way to see what Google has in its index. Search Google, either at the site or through the Google toolbar (see Chapter 1) for the following:

```
site:domain.com
```

Don't type the www. piece, just the domain name. For instance, say your site's domain name is *RodentRacing.com*. You'd search for this:

```
site:rodentracing.com
```

Google returns a list of pages it's found on your site; at the top, underneath the search box (or perhaps somewhere else; it moves around occasionally), you see something like this:

```
2 results (0.16) seconds
```

That's it — quick and easy. You know how many pages Google has indexed on your site and can even see which pages.

Well, you *may* know. This number is not always accurate; Google will show different numbers in different places. The number you see in the first page of search results may not be the same as the number it shows you on, say, the tenth page of search results, nor the same as the number it shows you in the Google Webmasters Console (see Chapter 13). Still, it gives you a general idea (usually *reasonably* accurate) of your indexing in Google.

Here's another way to see what's in the index — in this case, a particular page in your site. Simply search for the URL: Type, or copy and paste, the URL into the Google search box and press Enter. Google should return the page in the search results (if it's in the index).

You can also click the little green down triangle at the end of the URL in the search results and select Cached to see the copy of the page that Google has actually stored in its cache (see Figure 3-1). If you're unlucky, Google tells you that it has nothing in the cache for that page. That doesn't necessarily mean that Google hasn't indexed the page, though.

This is Google's cache of http://www.dummies.com/biz.html. It is a snapshot of the page as it appeared on May 16, 2015 02:28:44 GMT. The current page could have changed in the meantime. Learn more
Tip: To quickly find your search term on this page, press Ctrl+F or ⌘-F (Mac) and use the find bar.

Text-only version

DUMMIES B2B
Making Business Easier

Services   Case Studies   Contact Us   877-409-4177

We've written
For Dummies books for
these companies...

Google   Coca-Cola
IBM

And we can make one for
you too!

Find Out How

Content Designed to Engage, Inspire, and Drive Sales
From e-books and videos to mobile apps and sponsorships, we'll help you connect with more customers.
See All of Our Partnership Services

Figure 3-1:
A page
stored in
the Google
cache.

A *cache* is a temporary storage area in which a copy of something is placed. In this context, the search engine cache stores a Web page that shows what the search engine found the last time it downloaded the page. Google, Bing, and Yahoo! keep a copy of many of the pages they index, and they all also tell you the date that they indexed the cached pages. (Bing currently also uses a little green triangle, just like Google, at the end of the URL; click that to see the Cached page link pop up. Yahoo! currently puts a Cached link in gray text immediately after the URL in the search results.)

You can also go directly to the cached page on Google. Type the following into the Google search box:

```
cache:http://yourdomain.com/page.htm
```

Replace *yourdomain.com* with your actual domain name, and *page.htm* with the actual page name, of course. When you click Search, Google checks to see whether it has the page in its cache.

What if Google doesn't have the page? Does that mean your page isn't in Google? No, not necessarily. Google may not have gotten around to caching it. Sometimes Google grabs a little information from a page but not the entire page.

You can search for a Web site at Google another way, too. Simply type the domain name into the Google search box and click Search. Google returns that site's home page at the top of the results, generally followed by more pages from the site.

Yahoo! and Bing

And now, here's a bonus. The search syntax I used to see what Google had in its index for RodentRacing.com — `site:rodentracing.com` — not only works on Google but also Yahoo! and Bing. That's right, type the same thing into any of these search sites and you see how many pages on the Web site are in the index (though doing this at Yahoo!, of course, gets you the Bing results because they share the same index).

Open Directory Project

You might also want know whether your site is listed in the Open Directory Project (`www.dmoz.org`; assuming that the site still functions when you read this). This is a large directory of Web sites, actually owned by AOL although volunteer run; it's potentially important, because its data is "syndicated" to many different Web sites, providing you with many links back to your site. (You find out about the importance of links in Chapter 16.) If your site isn't in the directory, it should be (if possible; getting it in there can be quite difficult).

Just type the domain name, without the `www.` piece. If your site is in the index, the Open Directory Project will tell you. If it isn't, you should try to list it; see Chapter 14.

Taking Action If You're Not Listed

What if you search for your site in the search engines and can't find it? If the site isn't in Google or Bing, you have a huge problem. (If the site isn't in the Open Directory Project, see Chapter 14.) Or perhaps your home page, or maybe one or two pages, are indexed, but nothing else within your site is indexed. There are two basic reasons your site isn't being indexed in the search engines:

✔ **The search engines haven't found your site yet.** The solution is relatively easy, though you won't get it done in an hour.

✔ **The search engines have found your site but, for several possible reasons, can't or won't index it.** This is a serious problem, though in some cases you can fix it quickly.

These are the specific reasons your site may not be indexed, in order of likelihood, more or less:

✔ There are no links pointing to the site, so the search engines don't know the site exists.

✔ The Web server is unreliable.

✔ The robots.txt is blocking search-engine access to the site.

✔ The robots meta tag is blocking pages individually.

✔ You bought a garbage domain name.

✔ The site is using some kind of navigation structure that search engines can't read, so they can't find their way through the site.

✔ The site is creating dynamic pages that search engines choose not to read (this is quite rare today).

✔ You have a "canonical" tag referencing another Web site (very unlikely, though possible if you are inheriting the site from someone else).

No links

The single most common reason that search engines don't index sites is that they don't know the sites exist. I frequently work with clients whose sites, we discover, are not indexed; when I examine the incoming links, I find that. . .there aren't any.

The search engines "crawl" the Web, following links from site to site to site. If there are no links from other Web sites, pointing to your site, the search engines will never find your site.

You may have heard that you can "submit" your site to the search engines, and you should definitely do that; *not* by using "submission services," but by submitting an XML sitemap through the Google and Bing Webmaster accounts (see Chapter 13 for the details). But this may not be enough. Even if the search engines know your site exists — because you told them it does — if they see *no* links from other sites, they may not care. In fact, if no other site cares enough to link to your site, why should the search engines care? If you have no links from other sites to yours, the search engines may not index it, or they may take their sweet time getting around to it, or perhaps they'll index a little piece of it but not much.

So, the solution is simple; get some links right away! Ask all your friends, colleagues, and family members to link to it, from whatever Web sites and social-network accounts they have. Then read Chapters 16 and 17 to learn about links.

Unreliable Web Server

Another reason that search engines may not index a site is that the site is on an unreliable Web server. If your site keeps crashing — or if it's unavailable when the search engines come by to crawl it — they *can't* crawl it. Or maybe they won't, because even if they *can* get in now and then, they don't want unreliable sites listed in the search results. That's "bad user experience."

So check your site. Is it incredibly slow to load, or is it down a lot of the time? You might even sign up with a site-checking service such as `www.pingdom.com` or `https://uptimerobot.com` (the former has a free trial, the latter has a free, reduced-service account).

robots.txt is blocking your site

Enter this URL into your browser (replacing *domain* with your actual domain name) and press Enter: `www.domain.com/robots.txt`.

If a simple text file loads into your browser, you're looking at the robots.txt file. (If you see a server error instead, move onto the next issue. You don't have a robots.txt file.)

The robots.txt file provides instructions to "robots" — search as search engines' search bots — about what areas of your site can and cannot be indexed. If you see a line that says *Disallow*, read Chapter 21 to find out how robots.txt works. It's common to block some areas of the site, but sometimes people make mistakes in robots.txt and accidentally block crawling.

robots meta tags are blocking pages

It's also possible that individual robot meta tags are blocking specific pages — perhaps all your pages. Check out your pages to see if robots tags are causing problems:

1. **Open the source code of your Web pages.**

   In the three primary browsers — Chrome, Firefox, and Internet Explorer — type Ctrl-U (Command-U on the Mac, sometimes) or right-click and select either View Page Source or View Source.

2. **Search the page for the text *robots*.**

   If your pages are using robots meta tags, you'll see something like *<META NAME="robots"*.

3. **If you don't find this tag in your pages, fuggedaboutit.**

4. **If you do find a robots meta tag in your pages, see Chapter 21 for information on figuring out problems.**

Bad domain name

Did you recently buy a domain name? It's possible that you purchased a domain name that had previously been blocked by the search engines because a previous owner was using the domain used for various nefarious — "spammy" — practices, attempting to trick the search engines but getting caught. (I talk about these practices in Chapters 9 and 21.)

Firstly, if nobody has ever used the domain name before, then the name can't be bad; you can use a service such as `www.domainhistory.net` or `www.domaintools.com` to see the domain name's history and find out whether it's been used before.

If the domain previously has been in use, how do you know if it has problems? How do you know if the site has been penalized by the search engines? There is *simply no easy answer to this question*, as the search engines don't have a public list of spammy sites. Google says there are indications of problems that you can look for, but no definitive answer:

- If you are buying a domain name that is currently in use, and the site has links pointing to it but is not indexed, that's a bad sign.

- If the old site is not up and running — perhaps you are buying an old expired domain name — go to `www.archive.org` and search the Wayback Machine to see what the Web site on that domain name looked like at various times in the past. Does it look "spammy"? It is an ugly site with little real value or real content, perhaps promoting get-rich-quick schemes, online gambling, pharmaceuticals or the like? Does it have a lot of what looks like auto-generated content, perhaps really clumsily written? Did it use a lot of SEO tricks (see Chapter 9)? Those are big problems.

- Search for the domain name and see what people on the Web are saying about the domain name. Are people complaining about it, stating that it uses SEO tricks? Obviously, another problem.

If you think this is a possible problem, I suggest you Google the phrase *matt cutts buy domain spam still rank youtube* and see the Matt Cutts video on this issue (I talk a little about Matt Cutts in Chapter 23). It *may* be possible to "revive" a "damaged" domain name, though you're probably better off just getting another domain name!

Unreadable navigation

Problems with navigation structures are much less common than they used to be, because search engines today are far better at reading Web pages than they were in the early days. Still, just in case . . .

A site may have perfectly readable pages, with the exception that the *searchbots* — the programs search engines use to index Web sites — can't negotiate the site navigation. The searchbots can reach the home page, index it, and read it, but they can't go any further.

Why can't the searchbots find their way through? The navigation system may have been created using JavaScript, and because search engines mostly ignore JavaScript, they don't find the links in the script. Look at this example:

```
<SCRIPT TYPE="javascript" SRC="/menu/menu.js"></SCRIPT>
```

In many sites, this is how navigation bars are placed into each page: Pages call an external JavaScript, held in menu.js in the menu subdirectory. Search engines may not read menu.js, in which case they'll never read the links in the script. And it's not just JavaScript; problems can be caused by putting navigation in Flash and Silverlight (Adobe's and Microsoft's animation formats).

However, these days Google *does* read and execute JavaScript, and does a good job with Flash, too, so this sort of thing is unlikely to be a problem. (Google states that they don't do so well with Silverlight.)

But it's not all about Google. As recently as May 2015, Bing had these statements in its Webmaster guidelines:

> Don't bury links to content inside JavaScript . . . don't bury links in Javascript/flash/Silverlight; keep content out of these as well . . . avoid housing content inside Flash or JavaScript — these block crawlers from finding the content . . . The technology used on your website can sometimes prevent Bingbot from being able to find your content. Rich media (Flash, JavaScript, and so forth) can lead to Bing not being able to crawl through navigation, or not see content embedded in a web page.

Of course, there are other search engines, not as big as Google and Bing but worth keeping happy nonetheless.

If you think your navigation system may be causing problems, try these simple ways to help search engines find their way around your site, whether or not your navigation structure is hidden:

✔ **Create more text links throughout the site.** Many Web sites have a main navigation structure and then duplicate the structure by using simple text links at the bottom of the page. You should do the same.

✔ **Add an HTML sitemap page to your site.** This page contains links to most or all of the pages on your Web site. Of course, you also want to link to the sitemap page from those little links at the bottom of the home page.

✔ If working with Flash, use sIFR (Scalable Inman Flash Replacement), which combines Flash with search-engine readable text.

Dealing with dynamic pages

This is another case in which things are much better today than in the past. In the past, *dynamic* sites often had problems getting indexed — that is pages with long, complicated URLs that are being created on the fly when a browser requests them. The data is pulled from a database, pasted into a Web page template, and sent to the user's browser. The long, complicated URL is a database query requesting the data; for example, product information that should be placed into a page, like this:

```
http://yourdomain.com/products/index.html?&DID=18&CATID=13&ObjectGroup_ID=79
```

Search engines often wouldn't index such pages, for a variety of reasons explained in Chapter 9.

Such URLs are unlikely to be a problem these days, but there's still a really good reason for not using URLs like this: It would be better, from an SEO perspective, to have keywords in your URLs, rather than database-query nonsense. There's a way to do that, using *URL rewriting,* which I explain in Chapter 7.

Another problem is caused by *session IDs* — URLs that are different every time the page is displayed. Look at this example:

```
http://yourdomain.com/buyAHome.do;jsessionid=07D3CCD4D9A6A9F3CF9CAD4F9A728F44
```

Each time someone visits this site, the server assigns a special ID number to the visitor. That means the URL is never the same, so Google probably won't index it. In fact, Google used to recommend that sites not use session IDs (there are technical alternatives). It's still probably a good idea today to avoid ssession IDs, if possible.

Search engines may choose not to index pages with session IDs. If the search engine finds links that appear to have session IDs in them, it quite likely will not index the referenced page, in order to avoid filling the search index with duplicates.

The Canonical tag

This problem is probably quite rare, though does happen now and then. There's something called the *canonical* tag, which looks like this:

```
<link rel="canonical" href="https://yourdomain.com/rodents/blue-mice.html"/>
```

This tag is used in situations in which a Web site might deliver the same content using different URLs; articles in a blog might appear in multiple sections, content might be delivered with session IDs, content might be syndicated onto other Web sites, and so on.

So the canonical tag tells the search engines, "This is the original URL for this page; don't index the page you're looking at, index this other one." Clearly, a misplaced canonical tag can cause pages to not get indexed.

Picking Good Keywords

Getting search engines to recognize and index your Web site can be a problem, as the first part of this chapter makes clear. Another huge problem — one that has little or nothing to do with the technological limitations of search engines — is that many companies have no idea what *keywords* (the words people are using at search engines to search for Web sites) they should be using. They try to *guess* the appropriate keywords, without knowing what people are really using in search engines.

I explain keywords in detail in Chapter 6, but here's how to do a quick keyword analysis:

1. **Point your browser to** `https://adwords.google.com/select/KeywordToolExternal`.

   Log into your Google account (yes, you'll need a Google account). You see the Google AdWords Keyword Planner. AdWords is Google's PPC (pay per click) division.

2. **In the top search box, type a keyword you think people may use to search for your products or services and then click Search.**

3. **Click the Get Ideas button at the bottom.**

   The tool returns a list of keywords, showing you how often that term and related terms are used by people searching on Google and partner sites (see Figure 3-2). Click between the Ad Group Ideas and Keyword Ideas to see different groupings of keywords

Figure 3-2:
The Google AdWords Keyword Planner provides a quick way to check keywords.

You may find that the keyword you guessed is perfect. Or you may discover better words, or, even if your guess was good, find several other great keywords. A detailed keyword analysis almost always turns up keywords or keyword phrases you need to know about. I often speak with clients whose sites rank really well for the chosen keywords, but they are totally unaware that they are missing some other, very popular, terms; it's a common problem.

Don't spend a lot of time on this task right now. See whether you can come up with some useful keywords in a few minutes and then move on; see Chapter 6 for details about this process.

Examining Your Pages

Making your Web pages "search engine–friendly" was probably not uppermost in your mind when you sat down to design your Web site. That means your Web pages — and the Web pages of millions of others — may have a few problems in the search engine–friendly category. Fortunately, such problems are pretty easy to spot; you can fix some of them quickly, but others are more troublesome.

Using frames

To examine your pages for problems, you need to read the pages' source code. Remember, I said you'd need to be able to understand HTML! To see the source code, choose View➪Source or View➪Page Source in your browser. (Or use a tool such as Firebug, an add-on designed for Firefox but available, in a lite form, for other browsers. See www.getfirebug.com.)

When you first peek at the source code for your site, you may discover that your site is using frames. (Of course, if you built the site yourself, you already know whether it uses frames. However, you may be examining a site built by someone else.) You may see something like this on the page:

```
<HTML>
<HEAD>
</HEAD>
    <FRAMESET ROWS="20%,80%">
        <FRAME SRC="navbar.html">
        <FRAME SRC="content.html">
    </FRAMESET>
<BODY>
</BODY>
</HTML>
```

When you choose View➪Source or View➪Page Source in your browser, you're viewing the source of the *frame-definition document,* which tells the browser how to set up the frames. In the preceding example, the browser creates two frame rows, one taking up the top 20 percent of the browser and the other taking up the bottom 80 percent. In the top frame, the browser places content taken from the navbar.html file; content from content.html goes into the bottom frame.

Framed sites don't index well. The pages in the internal frames get *orphaned* in search engines; each page ends up in search results alone, without the navigation frames with which they were intended to be displayed. The good news is that framed sites now are rare; they were very popular at the turn of the century, but seem to have fallen out of favor. Still, I run into them now and then.

Framed sites are bad news for many reasons. I discuss frames in more detail in Chapter 8, but here are a few quick fixes:

✔ Add TITLE and DESCRIPTION tags between the <HEAD> and </HEAD> tags. (To see what these tags are and how they can help with your frame issues, check out the next two sections.)

✔ Add <NOFRAMES> and </NOFRAMES> tags between the <BODY> and </BODY> tags and place 200 to 300 words of keyword-rich content between the tags. The NOFRAMES text is designed to be displayed by browsers that can't work with frames, and search engines will read this text, although they won't rate it as highly as normal text (because many designers have used <NOFRAMES> tags as a trick to get more keywords into a Web site, and because the NOFRAMES text is almost never seen these days, because almost no users have browsers that don't work with frames).

✔ In the text between the <NOFRAMES> tags, include a number of links to other pages in your site to help search engines find their way through.

✔ Make sure every page in the site contains a link back to the home page, in case it's found "orphaned" in the search index.

Looking at the TITLE tags

TITLE tags tell a browser what text to display in the browser's title bar and tabs, and they're very important to search engines. Quite reasonably, search engines figure that the TITLE tags may indicate the page's title — and, therefore, its subject.

Open your site's home page and then choose View ⇨ Source in your browser to see the page source. A window opens, showing you what the page's HTML looks like. Here's what you should see at the top of the page:

```
<HTML>
<HEAD>
<TITLE>Your title text is here</TITLE>
```

Here are a few problems you may have with your <TITLE> tags:

✔ **They're not there.** Many pages simply don't have <TITLE> tags. If they don't, you're failing to give the search engines one of the most important pieces of information about the page's subject matter.

✔ **They're in the wrong position.** Sometimes you find the <TITLE> tags, but they're way down in the page. If they're too low in the page, search engines may not find them.

✔ **There are *two* sets.** Now and then I see sites that have two sets of <TITLE> tags on each page; in this case, the search engines will probably read the first and ignore the second.

✔ **Every page on the site has the same <TITLE> tag.** Many sites use the exact same tag on every single page. Bad idea! Every <TITLE> tag should be different.

✔ **They're there, but they're poor.** The <TITLE> tags don't contain the proper keywords.

Your `TITLE` tags should be immediately below the `<HEAD>` tag and should contain useful keywords. Have 40 to 60 characters between the `<TITLE>` and `</TITLE>` tags (including spaces) and, perhaps, repeat the primary keywords once. If you're working on your Rodent Racing Web site, for example, you might have something like this:

```
<TITLE>Rodent Racing Info. Rats, Mice, Gerbils, Stoats,
        All Kinds of Rodent Racing</TITLE>
```

Find out more about keywords in Chapter 6 and titles in Chapter 7.

Examining the DESCRIPTION tag

The `DESCRIPTION` tag is important because search engines may index it (under the reasonable assumption that the description describes the contents of the page) and, in many cases, use the `DESCRIPTION` tag to provide the site description on the search results page. Thus you might think of the `DESCRIPTION` tag as serving two purposes: to help with search rank and as a "sales pitch" to convince people viewing the search-results page to click your link. (Google says it doesn't use the tag for indexing, but it's still important because Google will often display the tag contents in the search-results page.)

Open a Web page, open the HTML source (select View⇨Source from your browser's menu), and then take a quick look at the `DESCRIPTION` tag. It should look something like this:

```
<META NAME="description" CONTENT="your description goes here">
```

Sites often have the same problems with `DESCRIPTION` tags as they do with `<TITLE>` tags. The tags aren't there, are hidden away deep down in the page, are duplicated, or simply aren't very good.

Place the `DESCRIPTION` tag immediately below the `<TITLE>` tags (see Figure 3-3) and create a keyworded description of up to 250 characters (again, including spaces). Here's an example:

```
<META NAME="description" CONTENT="Rodent Racing - Scores, Schedules, Everything
        Rodent Racing. Mouse Racing, Stoat Racing, Rats, Gerbils -
        Everything You Need to Know about Rodent Racing and Caring for
        Your Racers.">
```

Sometimes Web developers switch the attributes in the tag, putting the `CONTENT=` before the `NAME=`, like this:

```
<META CONTENT="your description goes here" NAME="description">
```

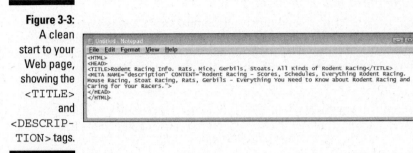

I'm sure the order of the attributes isn't important for Google or Bing, but I *have* seen it confuse some smaller systems in the past. There's no real reason to switch the order of the attributes so I'd recommend not doing it.

Giving search engines something to read

You don't necessarily have to pick through the HTML code of your Web page to evaluate how search engine–friendly it is. You can find out a lot just by looking at the Web page in the browser. Determine whether you have any text on the page. Page *content* — text that search engines can read — is essential, but many Web sites don't have any page content on the front page and often have little or none on interior pages. This is often a problem for e-commerce sites, which all too frequently have nothing more than a short blurb for each product they are selling, ending up with a content-light site.

Here are some potential problems:

- Having a (usually pointless) Flash intro on your site
- Creating a totally Flash-based site
- Embedding much of the text on your site into images, rather than relying on readable text
- Banking on flashy visuals to hide the fact that your site is light on content
- Using the wrong keywords (Chapter 6 explains how to pick keywords.)

If you have these types of problems, they can often be time consuming to fix. (Sorry, you may run over the one-hour timetable by several weeks.) The next several sections detail ways you might overcome the problems.

Eliminating Flash and Silverlight

Huh? What's Flash? You've seen those silly animations when you arrive at a Web site, with a little *Skip Intro* link hidden away in the page. Words and pictures appear and disappear, scroll across the pages, and so on. These are Adobe Flash (formerly Macromedia Flash) files, or perhaps Microsoft Silverlight files.

I suggest that you kill the Flash intro on your site. They don't *hurt* your site in the search engines (unless, of course, you're removing indexable text and replacing it with Flash), but they don't help, either, and I rarely see a Flash intro that actually serves any purpose. In most cases, they're nothing but an irritation to site visitors. (The majority of Flash intros are created because the Web designer likes playing with Flash.) And a site that is nothing but Flash — no real text; everything's in the Flash file — is a disaster from a search engine perspective. (Indeed, since I've been writing this book Flash intros have fallen out of favor to a great degree, but they're still out there.)

If you're really wedded to your Flash intro, though — and there are occasionally some that make sense — there *are* ways to use Flash and still do a good job in the search engines; see Chapter 9 for information on the SWFObject method. Just don't expect Flash on its own to work well in the search engines.

Replacing images with real text

If you have an image-heavy Web site, in which all or most of the text is embedded onto images, you need to get rid of the images and replace them with real text. If the search engine can't read the text, it can't index it.

It may not be immediately clear whether text on the page is real text or images. You can quickly figure it out a couple of ways:

- ✔ Try to select the text in the browser with your mouse. If it's real text, you can select it character by character. If it's not real text, you simply can't select it — you'll probably end up selecting an image.

- ✔ Right-click the text, and if you see menu options, such as Save Image and Copy Image, you know it's an image, not text.

Using more keywords

The light-content issue can be a real problem. Some sites are designed to be light on content, and sometimes this approach is perfectly valid in terms of design and usability. However, search engines have a bias for content — that is, for text they can read. (I discuss this issue in more depth in Chapter 11.) In general, the more text — with the right keywords — the better.

Using the right keywords in the right places

Suppose that you do have text, and plenty of it. But does the text have the right keywords? The ones discovered with the Google AdWords Keyword Planner earlier in this chapter? It should.

Where keywords are placed and what they look like is also important. Search engines use position and format as clues to importance. Here are a few simple techniques you can use — but don't overdo it!

✔ Use keywords in folder names and filenames, and in page files and image files.

✔ Use keywords near the top of the page.

✔ Place keywords into <H> (heading) tags.

✔ Use bold and italic keywords; search engines take note of these.

✔ Put keywords into bulleted lists; search engines also take note of this.

✔ Use keywords multiple times on a page, but don't use a keyword or keyword phrase too often. If your page sounds really clumsy through over-repetition, it may be too much.

You can avoid over-repetition by using synonyms.

Ensure that the links between pages within your site contain keywords. Think about all the sites you've visited recently. How many use links with *no* keywords in them? They use buttons, graphic navigation bars, short little links that you have to guess at, *click here* links, and so on. Big mistakes.

Some writers have suggested that you should never use *click here* because it sounds silly and people know they're supposed to click. I disagree, and research shows that using the words can sometimes increase the number of clicks on a particular link. However, for search-engine purposes, you should rarely, if ever, use a link with only the words *click here* in the link text; you should include keywords in the link.

To reiterate, when you create links, include keywords in the links wherever possible. For example, on your rodent-racing site, if you're pointing to the scores page, don't create a link that says *To find the most recent rodent racing scores, click here* or, perhaps, *To find the most recent racing scores, go to the scores page.* Instead, get a few more keywords into the links, like this: *To find the most recent racing scores, go to the rodent racing scores page.* That tells the search engine that the referenced page is about *rodent racing scores.*

Getting Your Site Indexed

So your pages are ready, but you still have the indexing problem. Your pages are, to put it bluntly, just *not in the search engine!* How do you fix that problem?

For the Open Directory Project, you have to go to dmoz.org and register directly, but before doing that, you should read Chapter 14. With Google, Bing, and Ask.com, the process is a little more time consuming and complicated.

The best way to get into the search engines is to have them *find* the pages by following links pointing to the site. In some cases, you can ask the search engines to come to your site and pick up your pages. However, if you ask search engines to index your site, they probably won't do it. And if they *do* come and index your site, doing so may take weeks or months. Asking them to come to your site is unreliable.

So how do you get indexed? The good news is that you can often get indexed by some of the search engines *very* quickly.

Find another Web site to link to your site, right away. I'm not talking about a full-blown link campaign here, with all the advantages I describe in Chapters 16 and 17. You simply want to get search engines — particularly Google, Bing, and Ask.com — to pick up the site and index it. Call friends, colleagues, and relatives who own or control Web sites, and ask them to link to your site; many people have blogs these days, or even social-networking pages they can link from. Of course, you want sites that are already indexed by search engines. The searchbots have to follow the links to your site.

When you ask friends, colleagues, and relatives to link to you, specify what you want the links to say. No *click here* or company name links for you. You want to place keywords into the link text. Something like *Visit this site for all your <u>rodent racing needs - mice, rats, stoats, gerbils, and all other kinds of rodent racing</u>*. Keywords in links are a powerful way to tell a search engine what your site is about.

After the sites have links pointing to yours, it can take from a few days to a few weeks to get into the search engines. With Google, if you place the links right before Googlebot indexes one of the sites, you may be in the index in a few days. I once placed some pages on a client's Web site on a Tuesday and found them in Google (ranked near the top) on Friday. But Google can also take several weeks to index a site. The best way to increase your chances of getting into search engines quickly is to get as many links as you can on as many sites as possible.

You should also create an XML sitemap, submit that to Google and Bing, and add a line in your `robots.txt` file that points to the sitemap so that search systems — such as Ask.com — that don't provide a way for you to submit the sitemap can still find it. You find out all about that in Chapter 13.

Chapter 4

Beating the Competition — Planning a Powerful Search Engine Strategy

Search engine optimization is getting tougher all the time. Not because the techniques are any harder than they used to be (although in a sense, they are — after all, the tricks people used to employ don't work as they did; see Chapter 9), but because it's getting so much more competitive. As more and more people learn about SEO, more and more of your competitors are doing a better and better job at SEO, so it gets harder and harder to compete for those top spots.

There's a lot to learn about generating traffic from search engines, and sometimes it's hard to see the forest for the trees. As you discover in this book, there are page-optimization and link strategies and index submissions and directory submissions and electronic press releases and blogs and this and that — it goes on and on. Before you jump right in, I need to discuss the big picture (to give you an idea of how all this fits together) and help you decide what you should do and when (to help you plan your strategy). In this chapter, I show you how a search engine campaign works overall.

Don't Trust Your Web Designer

Let me start with a warning: Don't rely on your Web designer to manage your SEO project. In fact, I know that many of you are reading this book because you did just that and have realized the error of your ways.

Here's one of the more egregious cases I've run across. The owner of a small e-commerce store came to me for help. He had paid a Web-design firm $5,000 to build his site, and before beginning, he had asked the firm to make sure that the site was search engine–friendly. Unfortunately, that means different things to different people, and to the design firm, it didn't mean much. The site it built definitely was *not* optimized for search engines. The owner asked the firm what it was planning to do about the search engines. It told him *that* would cost him another $5,000.

This unusual case is worse than most, but the first part — that your Web-design firm says it will handle the search engines and then doesn't — is *very* common. When I hire a Web designer to build a site for me, I explain exactly what I want. And you should do the same. (Thus, this book can help you even if you never write a line of HTML code.)

The problem is twofold:

- ✔ Web designers pretty much *have* to say they understand search engines, because all their competitors are saying it.

- ✔ Many Web designers think they *do* understand, but typically, it's at an "add some meta tags and submit to the search engines" level. It won't work.

Sorry, Web designers. I don't want to be rude, but this is a simple fact, attested to by many, many site owners out there. I've seen it over and over again. Not trusting your Web designer or team — even if it claims it knows what it's doing — is probably the first step in your search engine strategy!

Big doesn't always equal better

By the way, don't imagine that just because you're working with a large Web-design team with extensive programming experience, such a team understands search engines. In fact, the more sophisticated design teams are sometimes the ones that get into the most trouble, building complex sites that simply won't work well with search engines. I consult with companies big and small, so I've advised large design teams made up of very good programmers. I can assure you that large, sophisticated teams often know as little about SEO as the independent Web designer who's been in business a few months.

Understanding the Limitations

You've probably received spam e-mails guaranteeing top-ten positions for your Web site in the search engines. You've probably also seen claims that you'll be ranked in hundreds or thousands of search engines. Most of this is nonsense — background noise that creates an entirely false picture. As one of my clients put it, "There's a lot of snake oil out there!" Here are the facts.

Sometimes, it's easy to get a very high position in the search systems. For instance, a client wanted to be positioned in Google for six important key phrases. I built some pages, ensured that Google knew where those pages were (find out how to do this in Chapter 13), and waited. In just four days, the client didn't just have a top-ten position or even just a number-one position, but the top *two* positions for five of the six key phrases. But this situation is very unusual. More commonly, the game takes much more work and much more time.

Typically, getting a high position isn't that easy. You try a couple of techniques, but they don't seem to work. So you try something else, and maybe you achieve a little success. Then you try another thing. Search engine optimization can often be *very* labor intensive, and you may not see results for weeks, and more likely, months.

The degree of work required depends on the competitiveness of the keywords you're going after. Some keywords are incredibly competitive: *mortgage, insurance, attorney, real estate,* and so on are highly competitive, with millions of people wanting some of the action. Other phrases are very easy — such as *rodent racing,* for instance. If you're in the rodent-racing business, you're in luck because you can probably rank right at the top very easily!

Although how search engines function is based on science, search engine optimization is more art than science. Why? Because the search engine companies don't want you to know exactly how they rank sites. You have to just experiment. Ranking a site can be very difficult and tremendously laborious. After all, why should it be easy? There is huge competition, so it *can't* always be easy. If it were easy for your site, then it would be easy for your competitors' sites, wouldn't it? And, after all, there can only ever be one number one.

Eyeing the Competition

Some search terms are incredibly competitive. That is, many, many sites are competing for the top positions. Other search terms are far less competitive. How can you tell just how competitive your search terms are? Let me show you a few ways to figure it out:

- **Search for your terms.** This *is not* a terribly good method for those of you looking to build an SEO strategy, but it is so commonly recommended that I want to explain it anyway. Go to Google and search for a few of your terms. (I discuss keywords in more detail in Chapter 6.) For instance, search for *zofran attorney,* and Google reports, under the search box:

   ```
   About 195,000  results
   ```

   This tells you that nearly 200,000 pages in the Google index match the search terms. Actually, most of these pages don't match well. Most of the pages don't actually have the term *zofran attorney.* Rather, they have the words *zofran* and *attorney* scattered around the page. It's common for journalists to use this search method to make some point or other — to prove the popularity of a particular subject, for instance — without realizing that it makes no sense.

- **Search for your terms by using quotation marks.** Type search terms in quotation marks, like this: "*zofran attorney.*" This time, Google searches for the exact phrase and comes back with a different number. When I searched, it came back with 1,030 because Google ignores all the pages with the words scattered around the page, and returns only pages with the exact phrase.

Here's the problem with these two techniques: Although they show you how commonly used the words are, they don't show you how well the pages are optimized. Remember, you're not competing against every page with these terms; you're really competing with pages that were optimized for search engines. There may be millions of pages with the term, but if none of them have been optimized, you can take your newfound SEO knowledge, create your own optimized pages, and have a good chance of ranking well.

Getting a "gut feel" for the competition

So here's another quick technique I like to use — a simple way to get a feel for competitiveness in a few seconds. Search for a term and then scan down the page looking for the number of

✔ **PPC ads on the page:** For instance, in Figure 4-1 you see Bing search results for the phrase *personal injury attorney*. As you look down the page, you see three PPC ads at the top of the page and then more ads all the way down the right side of the page. Lots of PPC ads indicate lots of interest in the phrase. If people are spending money on PPC ads, many are also probably spending money on SEO.

✔ **Lots of local results:** Google, Yahoo!, and Bing interpret some searches as *local* results; as explained in Chapter 12, in such cases the search engines try to figure out *where* you are and then display information about businesses in your local area. The phrase *personal injury attorney* is definitely one that all three major search engines regard as *local*.

✔ **Bold and highlighted words on the page:** You also notice that Google bolds the words that you searched for. All the major search sites do this. Lots of bold words often mean well-optimized pages.

✔ **Bold words in the links (page titles):** Bold words in each page result's link indicate that someone has been optimizing the pages. The links are the page titles, so the more bold text you see as you scan down, the more often site owners have been placing the keywords into the <TITLE> tags and the more competitive the search terms are likely to be. (At the time of writing Google is not bolding terms in the titles. It has in the past; perhaps it will again in the future.)

✔ **Complete phrases on the page:** The *more frequently* you see the full phrase you searched for, the more competitive the terms are likely to be. If the search engine returns mostly pages with the words scattered around, it's not very competitive.

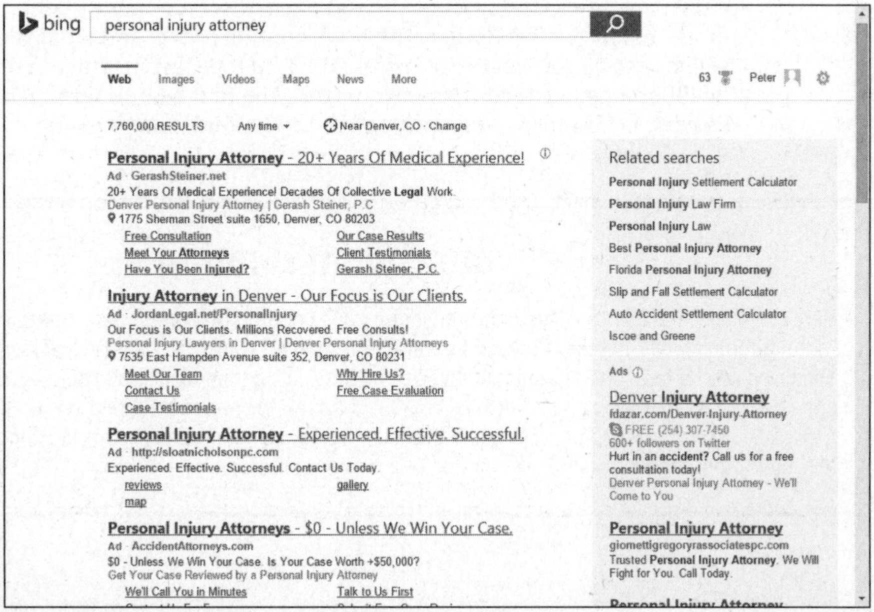

Figure 4-1: Searching for *personal injury attorney* brings up lots of bold text.

Here's another example. Search Bing for *rodent racing*. What do you see? Something similar to Figure 4-2. First, notice the absence of PPC ads; apparently, nobody's willing to *pay* to rank high for this term!

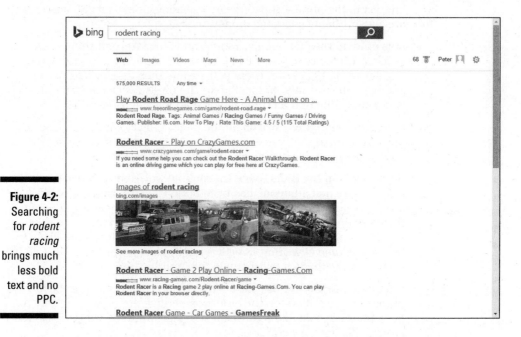

Figure 4-2:
Searching for *rodent racing* brings much less bold text and no PPC.

Next, notice relatively little bold or highlighted text on the page, and none of the page titles (the links at the top of each search result) contain the full phrase *rodent racing*. Rather, the titles contain *rodent* and what the search engine sees as related terms; *racer* and *road rage*, for instance. You can see the difference between these two pages. The first search term, *personal injury attorney,* is far more competitive than the second, *rodent racing*.

Get your rodent running

Here's an example of how quickly a page can rank for an uncompetitive phrase. I created a page optimized for the term and posted it to my Web site (`http://Rodent-Engineering. PeterKentConsulting.com`). Within a few days, the page was ranked number one on Google for *rodent engineering* and has remained there for several years. There you have an example of how quickly things can happen for noncompetitive terms. (In the real world, for competitive terms, things are far more difficult.)

How important is competitiveness? When targeting search terms that aren't very competitive, you may be able to create a few optimized pages and rank well. In very competitive areas, though, creating a few nicely optimized pages isn't enough. You *must* have links pointing to the site (perhaps many of them), and you may also need a large number of pages. In some really competitive areas, it may take hundreds, if not thousands, of links.

Why is my competitor ranking so high?

I get this question all the time. A client points out a competitor's site and asks why the competitor ranks so high. "His site is not even as well optimized as mine, yet he's still above me!" I often hear. And now and then I hear something like, "This guy was nowhere five months ago, and now his site is higher than mine!"

The answer to the "why is my competitor ranking higher" question is almost always that the competitor has done a better job at creating links. So if you are in this situation, do a link analysis on the competitor. (See Chapter 17 for information on how to do that.) You'll see how many links that site has, what keywords are being used in its links, and what sort of sites it's getting links from. It's all useful information, and information that will give you an idea at how much link work you have to do.

Going Beyond Getting to #1

Everyone wants to rank #1 for the top keywords. Lawyers want to rank #1 for *attorney* or *lawyer*. Real estate agents want to rank #1 for *real estate*. Shoe stores want to rank #1 for *shoes,* and so on.

But what does being #1 achieve? You're trying to get the right people to visit your Web site, not to get any particular position, right? Getting ranked in search engines is merely a way to generate that qualified traffic to your site. People often assume that to generate traffic, they have to get the #1 position for the top keywords. That's not the case. You can generate plenty of traffic to your site without ever getting to #1 for the most popular phrases. And in many cases, the traffic arriving at your site will be better — the visitors will be more appropriate for your site. To draw the best types of visitors for your site, you have two things to understand: *highly targeted keyword phrases* and the *search tail.*

Highly targeted keyword phrases

If your keywords are very competitive, look for keywords that aren't so sought after:

✔ **Go local.** One common strategy is, of course, to focus on local keywords. If you're a real estate agent, don't target *real estate.* Instead, target real estate in your area: *Denver realtor, Chicago real estate, Dallas homes for sale,* and so on.

✔ **Focus on more specialized search terms.** A realtor might target traffic on keywords related to commercial real estate or condos, for instance.

✔ **Incorporate spelling mistakes.** Some realtors target the very common misspelling *realator,* for instance. This technique isn't as effective as it once was, because the search engines adjust for spelling mistakes, but it may still work to some degree.

Understanding the search tail

Specialized search terms are hidden away in the search *tail.* The *search tail* is an important concept to understand. Although the first few top keywords may get far more searches than any other search, when you look at the total number of searches, the top terms actually account for only a small percentage of the searches.

Look at Table 4-1 for search terms taken from Wordtracker, a great little tool that shows what search terms people are typing into search engines. I searched for *video games,* and Wordtracker returned 300 results containing that term. I don't have room for 300, so I've shown the first few.

Table 4-1	Search Terms for *Video Games*		
		Searches/Day	Cumulative Searches
1	video games	9,132	9,132
2	music video games	859	9,991
3	adult video games	621	10,612
4	used video games	269	10,881
5	video games xbox	240	11,121
6	video games playstation 2	237	11,358

		Searches/Day	Cumulative Searches
7	violent video games	230	11,588
8	online video games	229	11,817
9	sex video games	209	12,026
10	free video games	194	12,220
11	history of video games	186	12,406
12	xxx video games	151	12,557
13	video games game cube	145	12,702
14	trade video games	134	12,836
15	violence in video games	128	12,964
16	cheap video games	128	13,092
17	nude video games	103	13195
18	video poker games	101	13,296

Look at the Searches/Day column. It starts at 9,132 searches per day for *video games,* but immediately drops to 859 for *music video games.* By the time you get to the eighteenth search term, it's down to just 101 searches a day. Position 300 gets only 7 searches a day. This fact leads people to focus on the top phrases, where, it appears, most of the searching is going on.

However, look at the Cumulative Searches column. As you go down the list, you see the total of all searches from position one down to the current position. The first 18 keyword phrases account for 13,296 searches a day, of which 9,132 — 69 percent — are the top phrase *video games.* As you continue down, the cumulative number continues growing, of course. By the time you reach 300, the cumulative number has risen to 18,557, of which only 49 percent is the top phrase.

As you can see from the numbers in Table 4-1 and Figure 4-3, there's this long "tail"; the searches tail off. Wordtracker gave me only the first 300 search phrases; certainly thousands more contain the phrase *video games.*

For each phrase, Wordtracker gave an estimate of how often the phrase is searched upon every day. And even in these first 300 searches, most are *not* for the term *video games* but are for phrases *containing* the term *video games.*

There's more, of course. What if you look, for instance, for the term *computer games*? How about *online games*? How about searching for the term *online video games*? You get a completely different set of 300 keyword phrases from Wordtracker.

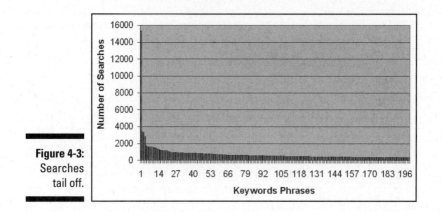

Figure 4-3:
Searches
tail off.

Thus, if you get matched only with the exact phrase *video games,* you're missing 49 percent of the first 300 phrases, many of which — perhaps most — would be useful to you. Add the thousands of other related phrases, and the primary term becomes less and less important.

REMEMBER

It's essential that you understand that most of the action is not at the top; it's in the search tail! This means two things:

✔ Even if you can't rank well for a primary term, there's still plenty of room to play.

✔ If you focus *only* on a primary term, you're missing most of the action.

However, consider for a moment local search results (see Chapter 12). Small businesses that need to be listed in the local results may still want to target the primary keywords, for two reasons.

✔ Because you're up against a smaller number of competitors locally than you would be for a national search, with a little effort you can often rank well for the primary terms.

✔ Locally, there will be far fewer searches for a term than nationally, so you may need to target the primary terms to get a reasonable amount of traffic.

Controlling Search Engine Variables

You have control over five basic variables, and a sixth that waits for no man. Everything in this book fits somewhere into one of these six categories:

✔ Keywords

✔ Content

> ✔ Page optimization
>
> ✔ Submissions
>
> ✔ Links
>
> ✔ Time

Everything you do will be with the intention of affecting in some way one of the first five variables, and as you work, the sixth, time, will keep on ticking. Here's a quick summary of each.

Keywords

As you read in Chapter 6, keywords are incredibly important. They're the very foundation of your search engine strategy. Keywords target searchers. You place keywords in your pages and in links pointing to your pages as bait to attract people to your site. Pick the wrong keywords and you're targeting the wrong people.

Content

Content, from a search engine perspective, really means text, and as you read in Chapter 11, you need content, and a lot of it. Search engines index words, and you want them to index the keywords you're interested in. The more words you have on your site — the more pages of text content — the more times your keywords can appear.

Think of a page of content as a ticket in the lottery: The more pages you have, the more lottery tickets you have. One common SEO strategy is to build huge sites, hundreds of thousands of pages, with vast amounts of text with keywords scattered through. Because of the nature of the search tail explained earlier in this chapter, each page has a chance to match a search now and then. The site has hundreds of thousands of lottery tickets. (However, it is important to keep in mind here that SEO is more than just creating massive amounts of content. This example is just an illustration of a common technique used in SEO strategies.)

You can play the content game a couple of ways:

> ✔ Create thousands of pages and hope that some of the text matches searches now and then.
>
> ✔ Create pages optimized for specific phrases that you know are used frequently.

Page optimization

Content is just a start. Content has to be placed onto the pages in the correct way; the pages must be *optimized* to get the most out of the keywords. As you read in Chapters 3 and 7, you must place the words onto the pages in the correct places and formats.

If a search engine finds the relevant keywords on your page, that's good. If it finds the keywords in the right places on the page, that's a really powerful thing that differentiates your page from your competitors'.

Submissions

In some ways, *submissions* — submitting information to the search engines; telling them where your pages can be found; and asking them, in effect, to come to your site and index it — aren't as important as many people imagine. This may be one of the biggest scams in the business (a business replete with scams!) — the idea that you have to *submit* your pages to thousands of search engines, when in fact, up until mid-2005, it really didn't matter much. You could submit, but the search engines would quite likely ignore the submission; links are what really counted. (Companies selling search-engine-submission services — *"Submit your site to a thousand search engines!"* — have, fortunately, all but disappeared; the exception is for local search, in which submissions actually *are* valid in some circumstances. See Chapter 12.)

However, in 2005, Google introduced a new concept, the *XML sitemap,* and was quickly followed by Yahoo! and Bing. This sitemap file is placed into your Web site's root directory containing a list of links to all your pages so that the search engines can more easily find them.

The way to get indexed is by making sure that the search engines find links to your site; but you should also provide Google, and Bing (no need to worry about Yahoo!, because its data comes from Bing) with the XML sitemap to help those search engines find their way around your site. Read more about working with the XML sitemap in Chapter 13.

Links

Links pointing to your Web site are incredibly important in a competitive keyword market. If you're targeting *rodent engineering,* you probably don't need to worry too much about links (although every site needs at least some incoming links — links pointing to your site from other sites). But if you have lots of competition vying for your keywords, you won't win without links.

Links are so important, in fact, that a page can rank in the first position in any of the three major search engines even if the page doesn't have the keywords that have been searched for — as long as links pointing to the page have the keywords. I explain links with keywords in Chapter 17. The more competitive your area, the more important links become.

Time and the Google sandbox

Finally, the one factor you have little control over. You really have control over time only in the sense that the sooner you get started, the older your search-engine project becomes. Age is critical because the older the site, the more credibility the search engines give it.

There's something known as the *Google sandbox* or *aging delay.* (Some people will tell you that these are actually two different types of time-related effects.) The idea is that when Google first finds your site, it puts it into a sandbox; it may index it, but it won't necessarily rank it well to begin with. It may take months before the site comes out of the sandbox. (People talk about the *Google sandbox,* but it's likely that, in theory at least, other search engines have something similar.) That's the theory, anyway.

There's a lot of debate about the effect of age; some say it's critical, and that for about eight months your site hasn't a chance of ranking well (I'm not in that camp), and others say that although search engines may take age into account to some degree, it's by no means an overwhelming factor (that's where I sit).

My belief is that if there are time-related weighting mechanisms, even a sandbox of some kind, they are not as powerful as many in the business claim. I've seen sites move upward in the search results very quickly. Time is certainly an issue; it takes time for the search engines to index your pages, it takes time for you to create links to your site, it takes time for the search engines to find the links, and so on. But having seen sites move quickly in some circumstances, I don't worry too much about the "sandbox."

It comes down to this: The longer your domain has been registered, the better, and the longer your site has been up, the better. So you have control over this essential factor in just one way: The sooner you get started, the better. Register your domain name as soon as possible. Get a site, even a few pages, posted as soon as possible, and get links pointing from other sites to your site as soon as you can. Get new content posted as soon as possible. The sooner you start, the sooner you'll start ranking well.

Reading history

I don't know exactly how Google handles all this, of course, but you can be fairly sure that Google uses some kind of historical data to help rank pages. In fact, there's even a patent application submitted in the names of various Google employees (although, strangely, without Google's name itself on the patent) that discusses the idea of using historical data. (A long, complicated URL takes you to the patent, so I've provided the link at www.searchenginebulletin.com.) This document is wonderful bedtime reading if you're looking for a way to get to sleep — without drugs. You won't find an explanation of how Google ranks Web pages, but you will find a lot of interesting possibilities.

Determining Your Plan of Attack

Now you know what you're facing. As you read in Chapter 1, you can more or less forget those thousands of search sites and focus on a handful. And, as I explain in this chapter, you have six essential factors to play with: keywords, content, page optimization, links, submissions, and time.

Forget about time — all I'll say is, get started right away! As for the other factors, how do you proceed? It depends to some degree on your budget and the competitiveness of the area you're working in.

- **Do a keyword analysis.** Regardless of competition or budget, you have to do one. Would you study for an exam without knowing what the exam is about? Would you plan a big meal and then send an assistant to the grocery store without explaining what you need? If you don't do a keyword analysis, you're just guessing; you will definitely fail to pick all the right keywords. See Chapter 6 for the lowdown on how to do this analysis.

- **Create readable pages.** If you want your site to appear, you have to create pages that the search engine spiders or bots can read. You may be surprised to hear that millions of pages on the Web cannot be read by search engines. For the lowdown on determining whether your pages are being read, see Chapter 3; to find out how to fix the problem if they're not, see Chapters 7 and 9.

- **Create keyworded pages.** Having readable pages is just a start. Next, you have to put the keywords into the pages — in the right places and in the right format. The more keyworded pages, the better, too. See Chapters 7 and 11 for details.

✔ **Consider Local.** If your business sells locally, rather than Web-wide, you really should read Chapter 12 to find out what you need to do to your site to get it to rank when people search locally.

✔ **Get listed in the search engines.** When your pages are ready to be indexed, you need to do two things:

  • Let the search engines know where those pages are.

  • Get the search engines to include the pages in their indexes and directories.

  See Chapters 13 and 14 for the details.

✔ **Get other sites to link to your site.** Check out Chapters 16 through 18 to find out how the number and type of links pointing to your site affect your rank.

The preceding strategies are the basics, but you may want — or even need — to go further. I cover these additional techniques in detail later:

✔ **Register with other places.** You may also want to register at specialized sites that are important for your particular business. See Chapter 18.

✔ **Register with the shopping indexes.** If you're selling a product, it's a good idea to register with the product indexes. In fact, most product searches are probably not even carried out through the general search engines, so you really need to read Chapter 15.

But there's more. If you're in a very competitive market, you may want to really push two techniques:

✔ **Create large amounts of content.** Make hundreds, perhaps thousands, of pages of content. (It may take a major effort, of course, and months, even years, to make it work.)

✔ **Go after links in a big way.** You may need hundreds, perhaps thousands, of links to rank well if your competitors have done the same.

In some cases, you may also want to consider the following techniques:

✔ **Social networking:** Twitter, LinkedIn, Facebook, Google+, MySpace, and so on. Social networking can be a powerful marketing technique for some businesses. See Chapter 19.

✔ **Video:** You can use video in various ways to bring visitors to your site, too, and in some cases to help push your site up in the search ranks. See Chapter 20 for information.

Look Away a Few Minutes

People in the SEO business tend to focus, not surprisingly perhaps, on the search engines. For all the reasons discussed in Chapter 1 — not least the tens of billions of searches carried out at the major search engines each month — SEO people get tunnel vision and sometimes forget there's a wider world out there.

I believe that an essential part of any search-engine campaign is to spend at least a little time thinking about where your prey are when they're *not* at the search engines. Where are the people you are seeking hanging out when they are not at Google, Yahoo!, Bing, or some other search site?

What is online marketing about? (Any marketing, really.) It's about *position* and *messaging*. It's about getting a persuasive message (about why someone should hire you, buy your product, donate money, or whatever) in front of the right people. The search engines can be a critical component of such a plan, but they are rarely the only component. And, in fact, as search marketing becomes more competitive, marketers need to look more closely for opportunities to get in front of people on the Web in various other places.

Essentially, you should think about where your prospects are and how to reach them where they are. For instance, say that you're an attorney. Where are your potential clients? Well, it's true that many people search Google, Bing, et al for attorneys. But many are going other places (or searching at a major search engine and *then* ending up elsewhere). They are going to sites such as Avvo.com, Nolo.com, LawInfo.com, Lawyers.com, and so on. So the question then becomes, can you reach people through *those* sites? There's a lot of experimentation required.

Sometimes you can buy your way in to those sites; that doesn't mean, however, that every deal is a good deal — it's a very common complaint in the legal industry that site *x* or site *y* costs a lot and provides little in return. On the other hand, there *are* often affordable opportunities. For instance, in the legal business many attorneys have found answering questions on Avvo. com to be very effective. In fact, *community marketing* (what I've been calling social networking for years longer than the term *social networking* has been in common use) is often a good way to go; an example is one of my clients, selling auto-parts for a particular sports car model, who is very well known in the community related to those sports cars — the forums in which owners get together and chat about their vehicles.

Here's another example: Tens of thousands of businesses use Craigslist to market their services. I know people with active, profitable business who do *nothing* but promote through Craigslist. SEO is important, but don't be blinded to other opportunities. Stop and think for a while: Where are your prospects going, and how can you reach them?

Two Things to Remember

Before I leave this chapter, I want to tell you about two things that are really worth remembering.

The first is that the ideal situation is to have a site that is so useful or cool or wonderful in some way that people *naturally* link to it. That's really what search engines are looking for, and much of what is done in the SEO field is intended to *simulate* this situation. People find ways to create links to their Web site to make the search engines *think* that the site is so useful or cool or wonderful in some way that thousands of people are linking to it. Of course, the real thing is better than the simulated thing, but quite frankly it's very difficult to pull off. If you're selling ball bearings, just how useful or cool or wonderful can you make your site? There's a limit to anyone's imagination, after all, so you may have to play the simulation game — but keep in mind what the search engines *really* want.

The other thing I want you to know is that a site's position in the rankings has a tendency to bounce around in the search engine field. Your site probably won't be on an arrowlike upward trajectory, constantly improving in its search engine position — rather, it goes up, and it goes down. Here's an example.

I have a client selling industrial equipment who really wanted to rank well for two particular terms (among many others); I'll say phrase A and phrase B. Well, for a long time he was ranked pretty well, near the top of the search results, for both phrases. Then, sometime in the summer of 2007, things got "all shook up." Not just his site but thousands of sites. Google changed something and continued changing that something over a period of weeks, and people found their search results dropping and then rising and then dropping again. Talk about a roller coaster . . . .

Phrase A dropped like a stone. Once at position #3, it disappeared: It wasn't in the first 100 search results. It was gone for several days and then suddenly reappeared for a few days. Then it disappeared again — in fact, it did this several times, bouncing up and down, sometimes near the very top of the search results and then completely unfindable. Meanwhile, through all this, phrase B remained rock solid, moving up and down, as search results tend to, among the first five results.

Then phrase B disappeared, too, and played the same game for a while. Then both bounced around, and finally everything settled down and both phrases ended up back where they were in the first place. Today, phrase A is in position #2 (right behind Wikipedia), and phrase B is in position #4; in both cases, the site ranks ahead of *all* the competitors. (In the second case, the phrase has another meaning, and most of the sites ahead of my client are government and education sites, which are often hard to beat.)

Now, this sort of fluctuation is terribly frustrating, frightening even. If your business depends on a high rank, any day your rank drops is a bad day! (You can level these fluctuations by getting traffic to your site in other ways, by the way, through PPC advertising, for instance, or affiliate marketing.)

When you drop in the rank, it's tempting to blame yourself (or your SEO consultant); you figure that whatever you last did to the site, that's what caused the problem. But it's very hard to correlate any particular action with a particular increase or decrease in search engine rank. Often when a rank drops, it's because of something that Google has done, not anything you've done. Perhaps Google decides that a certain type of link — reciprocal or paid links (see Chapter 17) — should no longer be of much value. Or perhaps it gives more weight to a particular page tag, or to another form of link. You may have changed something completely different, see your site drop, assume it's because of the action you took, and be totally unaware of the real cause of the drop. In the preceding example, my client decided that he was being punished for creating links in Craigslist.com back to his site — then, later, being punished for *not* creating links in Craigslist.

Sometimes you just have to wait and let the situation settle down and *keep on keeping on!* Keep on creating well-optimized content, and keep on creating links (and various, different types of links) back to your site. This stuff really does work; you just have to work at it.

On the other hand, it *is* possible to get on the wrong side of the search engines; perhaps you have done something that the search engines object to. That's a subject you can find out about in Chapter 20.

This chapter provides an overview of the search engine battle you're about to join. It's time to jump in and make it all happen, so Chapter 5 explains what search engines really like to see: Web sites that people on the Internet believe are really useful.

Chapter 5

Making Your Site Useful and Visible

In This Chapter

▶ Understanding the basic rule of Web success

▶ Knowing why search engines like content

▶ Making your site work for visitors and search engines

*O*bviously, it's important to create Web pages that search engines will read and index, pages that you hope will rank well for important keywords. But if you're going to build a Web site, you need to step back and figure out what purpose the site should serve and how it can accomplish that purpose.

Learning from Amazon

Creating a *useful* site is the key. Even if your sole aim is to sell a product online, the more useful the site is to visitors (and, for the same matter, the more user-friendly your site), the more successful it's likely to be. Take Amazon.com, for instance. It certainly wasn't the first online retailer of books and music, or any of the other products it offers. But one of Amazon's real strengths is that it doesn't just sell products; it's a really *useful* site, in many ways:

✔ It provides tons of information about the products it sells. The information is useful even if you don't buy from Amazon.

✔ You can save information for later. If you find a book you're interested in but don't want to buy right now, save it in your Wishlist and come back next month, next year, or five years from now.

✔ You can read sample chapters, look at tables of contents, listen to snippets of music, and so on.

✔ You can read product reviews from both professional reviewers and consumers.

Would Amazon be so successful if it just provided lists of the products it sells, instead of offering visitors a veritable cornucopia of useful stuff? Absolutely not.

Having done a little consulting work for Amazon, I've spent some time looking at the site from an SEO perspective, and what interests me are the many ways in which Amazon drops keywords into their pages. As you discover elsewhere in this book, keywords on Web pages are a huge part of SEO — and Amazon's pages are scattered with keywords. Take a look at the books pages, for instance, and you'll find the following:

✔ **Editorial Reviews:** These are descriptions of the book by the publisher, stacked full of keywords related to the subject covered by the book.

✔ **Customer Reviews:** When someone reviews a book about, say, Search Engine Optimization, they tend to use words related to the subject, such as *websites*, *SEO*, *programming*, *PHP*, *sitemaps*, *link bait*, and so on.

✔ **Customer Discussions:** Amazon also has discussion groups for virtually every product it sells. And when people talk about a product, they're going to use keywords that are related to that product.

✔ **Popular Highlights:** For Kindle books, text from the book that has been highlighted by readers.

✔ **Statistically Improbable Phrases:** These are unusual phrases that appear in the book, which makes them great keywords, of course.

✔ **Capitalized Phrases (CAPs):** A CAP is a list of capitalized phrases in the book (often very relevant keywords).

✔ **Tags customers associate with this product:** The tag list is essentially a list of keywords that other customers associate with the book.

✔ **Books on Related Topics:** Other books will often have titles containing relevant keywords.

However, many of these features (and the other useful features on Amazon product pages) were added *without* SEO in mind. Amazon added most of these things to make the site *useful* — SEO was an afterthought. Reviews, for instance, certainly do add keywords to the page, but they also help buyers make a decision (and can dramatically increase *conversion rates* — that is, converting shoppers to buyers). So creating a useful site often serves two purposes: It generates traffic through non–search engine channels, *and* it helps your site rank well in search engines.

Consider this: The more useful your site is, the greater the chance of success. The more useful or interesting your site, the more people will talk and blog about it, the more they are likely to link to it from social-networking sites (see Chapter 19), the more likely journalists are to write about it, the more likely it is to be mentioned on radio or TV, the more people will link to it from their Web sites, and so on. Search engine marketing and non–search engine marketing are both important because both forms of Web site promotion can lead to more links pointing to, and more traffic arriving at, your site. And, as you find out in Chapter 16, links to your site are critical to search engine success.

With all these byproducts of having a useful Web site in mind, this chapter focuses on the basics about what you need to do to create a successful Web site.

Revealing the Secret But Essential Rule of Web Success

Here's a simple rule to success on the Web:

Make your site useful and then tell people about it.

That's not so complicated, really. Figure out how your site can be useful and then find as many ways as possible to let people know about it. You'll use search engines, of course, but you should be using other methods, too. Remember, search engines are not the only way to get people to your site. In fact, many Web sites have succeeded without using search engines as their primary method of attracting visitors.

Amazon — Success sans search

It's unlikely that search engines were a large factor in Amazon's success; Amazon grew rapidly mainly because of the enormous press attention it received, beginning in 1994. Today, a huge amount of Amazon's traffic is *direct;* people already know the Amazon brand and go straight to the site, or they go through the hundreds of thousands of Amazon affiliate sites. On the other hand, you've probably noticed that Amazon does remarkably well in the search results for many, many product searches.

Many successful companies have done little or nothing to promote themselves through search engines, yet they still turn up at the top when you search for their products or services. Why? Because their other promotions have helped push them higher in the search engines by creating thousands (even tens or hundreds of thousands) of links to them around the Internet.

The evolving, incorrect "secret"

Over the last couple of decades, a number of popular ideas about what makes a successful Web site have been bandied around, and all are wrong to some degree. Here are some of those dated secrets to successful Web sites:

- ✔ **Links:** When the Web began booming in 1994, it was all about *links*. You would hear in the press that the secret to a successful Web site was linking to other sites.

- ✔ **Cool:** Then people started saying that the secret of success was to make your site *cool*. Cool sites were more entertaining and more likely to attract repeat visitors.

- ✔ **Community:** Then people started talking about *community;* yeah, that's the ticket! The secret to a successful Web site was creating a community where people could meet and chat with each other.

- ✔ **Content:** Then around 2000, people discovered that the secret was *content*. By putting more stuff, particularly textual information, on your site, you could be more successful.

- ✔ **Blogging:** At some point, it was decided that the real secret was having a blog on your site.

- ✔ **MySpace, Facebook, and Twitter:** Later, the secret became having associated MySpace, Facebook, and Twitter accounts. (Remember MySpace!?)

REMEMBER

Specific, one-size-fits-all secrets to success never make sense.

The most harmful of the preceding ideas was that your site had to be cool. This silly idea led to the expenditure of billions of dollars on useless but pretty Web sites, most of which (thankfully!) have since disappeared. Unfortunately, some of the *it's-all-about-cool* crowd is still in the Web business and still convincing companies to spend money on ridiculous, wasteful things, such as Flash intros for their Web sites.

Uncovering the real secret

Ready to hear the real secret of site-creation success? Your Web site has to be *useful.* The problem with the secrets I mention in the preceding section is that they're too specific, leading people to build sites that were in many cases inappropriate.

Sure, outgoing links are important to directory sites, but they're much less important to the vast majority of Web sites. If you own an entertainment site, you may want to make it cool and entertaining. Certainly, community can be an effective tool, but not every site has to have it. Content is very important, too — especially from a search engine perspective — but many successful Web sites don't have much content. (I talk in more detail about content in the next section because it's a special case.)

As for MySpace, at one point it was common knowledge that "if you want to do business online you *have* to have a MySpace site." You don't hear that often today, and it was nonsense back then. Today, you hear a lot about Twitter and Facebook, and while they can be very important, not all Web sites can incorporate a successful Twitter and Facebook strategy.

I've been writing this since 1997: *Forget cool; think useful.*

When you're planning your Web site, think about what kinds of folks you want to attract to the site. Then try to come up with ideas about what features and information might be *useful* to them. Your site may end up with a lot of link pages, providing a directory of sorts for people in your industry. Or maybe you really need a cool and entertaining site. Or, if you decide to use discussion groups and chat rooms as a way to build community and pull the crowds into your site, that's fine. Or maybe you decide to create a huge repository of information to attract a particular type of customer. That's okay, too. Maybe your target audience hangs out in MySpace; if so, perhaps you do need a MySpace page . . . and Facebook and Twitter accounts, too. Maybe you do *all* these things. But the important first step is to think about what you can do to make your site more useful, and not be distracted by the hype.

Showing a bias for content

Content is a special case. Search engines are biased toward ranking content-heavy Web sites well for a couple of reasons:

✔ Search engines were originally academic research tools designed to find *text information.* Search engines mostly index text — *content.*

✔ Search engines need something to base their judgments on. When you type a term into a search engine, it looks for the words you provided. So a Web site built with few words is at a disadvantage right from the start.

As you discover elsewhere in this book — such as in the discussion of PageRank in Chapter 16 — search engines do have other criteria for deciding if a Web site matches a particular search (most notably the number and type of links pointing to the site). But search engines still have a huge bias toward textual content.

Unfortunately, this bias is often a real problem. The real world simply doesn't work the way search engines see it. Here's an example: Suppose your business rents very expensive, specialized photographic equipment. Your business has the best prices and the best service of any company renting this equipment. Your local customers love you, and few other companies match your prices, service, or product range. So you decide to build a Web site to reach customers elsewhere and ship rentals by UPS and FedEx.

Search engines base your rank partly on the number and type of keywords in your pages.

To rank well, a competitor has added a bunch of pages about photography and photographic equipment to its site. To compete, you have to do the same. Do your customers care? No, they just want to find a particular piece of equipment that fills their need, rent it, and move on quickly. All the additional information, the content that you've added, is irrelevant to them. It's simply clutter.

This is a common scenario. I once discussed the content issue with a client who was setting up a Web site at which people could quickly get a moving-service quote. The client wanted to build a clean, sparse site that allowed customers to get the quote within a couple minutes. "But we don't want all that stuff, that extra text, nor do our clients!" he told me, and he had a good point.

You can't ignore the fact that search engines like content. However, you can compete in other ways. One of the most important ways is getting links from other sites, as you discover in Chapter 16. Search engines like to see links on other sites pointing to your site. Sites that have hundreds or thousands of other sites linking to them often rank well. But they still need at least *some* content for the search engines to index. And the best situation is to have lots of useful content with lots of incoming links.

Making Your Site Work Well

I've been writing about site design for almost twenty years, and I'm happy to say that many of the rules of good site design just happen to match what search engines like. And many of the cool tricks that designers love cause problems with search engines. So I want to quickly review a few tips for good site design that will help both your site visitors and the search engines to work with your site.

Limiting multimedia

Much multimedia used on the Web is pointless because it rarely serves a useful purpose to the visitor. It's there because Web designers enjoy working with it and because many people are still stuck in the old "you've got to be cool" mindset.

Look at the world's most successful Web sites (with the exception of sites such as YouTube.com, of course, which are all about multimedia), and you'll find that they rarely use multimedia — Flash animations and video, for example — for purely decorative purposes. Look at Amazon: Its design is simple, clean, black text on white background, with lots of text and very little in the way of animations, video, or sound (except, for instance, where it provides music samples in the site's CD area and videos demonstrating products). Amazon uses multimedia to serve a purpose, not as decoration. Look at Yahoo!, Google, CNN, or eBay — they're not cool; they just get the job done.

You can employ multimedia on a Web site in useful ways. I think it makes a lot of sense to use Flash, for instance, to create demos and presentations. However, Flash intros are almost *always* pointless, and search engines don't like them because Flash intros don't provide indexable content. Anytime you get the feeling it would be nice to have an animation, or when your Web designer says you should have some animation, slap yourself twice on the face and then ask yourself this: Who is going to benefit — the designer or the site visitor? If that doesn't dissuade you, have someone else slap you.

Using text, not graphics

A surprising number of Web sites use graphics to place text onto pages. Many pages *appear* to have a lot of text, but when you look closely, you see that every word is in an image file. Web designers often employ this technique so that all browsers can view their carefully chosen fonts. But search engines don't read the text in the images they run across, so this page provides *no* text that can be indexed by search engines. Although this page may contain lots of useful keywords (you find out all about keywords in Chapter 6), the search engines read nothing. From a usability perspective, the design is bad, too, because all those images take longer to download than the equivalent text would take.

As an SEO friend likes to say, "Google likes black text on a white background." In other words, search engines like *simple.* The more complicated your Web pages are, the harder it is for search engines to read and categorize them. (Okay, this isn't as true as it used to be. Still, lots of complicated technology can get in the way of indexing.)

You must strike a compromise between employing all the latest Web-design technology and tools and ensuring that search engines can read your pages. From a search engine perspective, in fact, one step behind probably isn't enough!

Don't be cute

Some sites do everything they can to be cute. The Coca-Cola site was a classic example of this a few years ago, though it finally got the message and changed. The site had icons labeled *Tour de Jour, Mind Candy, Curvy Canvas, Netalogue,* and so on. What do these things mean? Who knows? Certainly not the site visitor.

This sort of deranged Web design is far less common now than it used to be, but you still see it occasionally — particularly in sites designed by hip Web-design firms. One incredibly irritating technique is the hidden navigation structure. The main page contains a large image with hotspots on it. But it's unclear where the hotspots are, or what they link to, until you point at the image and move the mouse around. This strikes me as the Web-design equivalent of removing the numbers from the front of the homes in a neighborhood. You can still figure out where people live; you just have to knock on doors and ask.

Sweet and sickly cuteness doesn't help your site visitors find their way around and almost certainly hurts you with the search engines.

Making it easy to move around

Web design is constantly getting better, but it still surprises me that designers sometimes make it difficult for visitors to move around a Web site.

Think carefully about how your site is structured:

- ✔ Does it make sense from a visitor's standpoint?
- ✔ Can visitors find what they need quickly?

> ✔ Do you have *dangling* or *orphaned* pages — pages where a visitor can't find a link to get back into your main site? Search engines don't like dangling pages. And consider what happens if someone on another site links directly to the page: Visitors can get to the page through those links, but then can't get to the rest of your site.

Providing different routes

People think differently from each other, so you need to provide them with numerous avenues for finding their way around your site. And by doing so, you're also giving more information to search engines and ensuring that search engines can navigate your site easily.

Here are some different navigational systems that you can add to your site:

> ✔ **Sitemap:** This page links to the different areas of your site, or even, in the case of small sites, to every page in the site. See www.peterkent consulting.com/sitemap.htm as an example.

> ✔ **Table of Contents or Index page:** You can sort the page thematically or alphabetically.

> ✔ **Navigation bars:** Most sites have navigation bars these days.

> ✔ **Navigation text links:** These are little links at the bottom of your pages, or along the sides, that can help people find their way around — and help the search engines, too.

Using long link text

It's a proven fact that Web users like *long link text* — links that are more than just a single word and actually describe where the link takes you. Usability testing shows that long link text makes it much easier for visitors to find their way around a site. It's not surprising, if you think about it; a long link provides more information to visitors about where a link will take them.

Unfortunately, many designers feel constrained by design considerations, forcing all navigation links, for instance, to conform to a particular size. You often see buttons that have enough room for only ten or so characters, forcing the designer to think about how to say complicated things in one or two words.

Long links that explain what the referenced page is about are a great thing, not only for visitors, but also for search engines. By using keywords in the links, you're telling the search engines what the referenced pages are about.

You also have a problem if all the links on your site are on image buttons. Search engines can't read images, so image buttons provide no information about the referenced page. You can't beat a well-keyworded text link for passing information about the target page to the search engines.

Don't keep restructuring

Try to ensure that your site design is good before you get too far into the process. Sites that are constantly being restructured have numerous problems, including the following:

- Links from other Web sites into yours get broken, which is bad for potential visitors as well as for search engines (or, more precisely, bad for your position in the search engines because they won't be able to reach your site through the broken links).

- If you don't restructure carefully, all the pages you have indexed in the search engines may be lost, so you have to start over from the beginning — and it may take weeks or months to get fully reindexed.

- Anyone who has bookmarked your page now has a broken bookmark.

On the other hand, you can resolve these problems through the use of a 301 redirect; see Chapter 24 for information.

It's a good idea to create a custom 404 error page, which is displayed in your browser if the server is unable to find a page you've requested. (Ask your Web server administrator how to create this page; the process varies among servers.) Create an error page with links to other areas of the site, perhaps even a sitemap, so that if visitors and searchbots can't find the right page, at least they'll be able to reach some page on your site.

Editing and checking spelling

Check your pages for spelling and editing errors. Error-free pages not only make your site appear more professional but also ensure that your valuable keywords are not wasted. If potential visitors are searching for *rodent racing,* for example, you don't want the term *rodint racing* in your Web pages. (Except, that is, if you are trying to catch traffic from oft-misspelled keywords, which I discuss in Chapter 6.)

Ugly doesn't sell

Before I move on, I really have to cover this, um, sensitive subject, because I've run into a lot of people wasting money on SEO that would be better spent on Web design.

You see, I often get e-mails from people saying that they've had their site up "for months now, and haven't sold a thing; can you take a look and tell me why?" I type the URL into my browser, wait for the page to load, and I'm then knocked out of my chair by the unadulterated grotesqueness of the page. (I now keep a pair of very heavily shaded sunglasses — polarized, UV-filtered, glare-protected glacier glasses — for these very cases. If I get a feeling about the site I'm about to see, on go the glasses.)

I don't get it. I know some people are colorblind, but are some ugly blind? Can't they *see* the ugliness? During my phone-consulting sessions, I'll sometimes have to load my client's site into a browser window, load a competitor's site into another window, and ask the client, "Now which site would you rather buy from?" (For example, the site in Figure 5-1 or the site in Figure 5-2?)

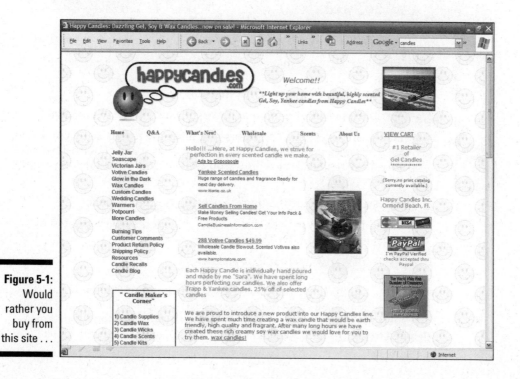

Figure 5-1:
Would rather you buy from this site . . .

Figure 5-2:
. . .or this
one?

Here's the fact: Ugly doesn't sell. By *ugly*, I mean a range of problems:

- Awful color combinations that just don't work
- Terrible typeface choices that make the pages close to unreadable
- Combinations of fonts and colors that make the text close to unreadable — such as white text on black backgrounds (no, it's *not* cool; ask yourself, why do virtually all the world's top Web sites use black text on a white background?)
- Cutesy backgrounds that look . . . cutesy, not professional
- Incredibly clunky images that look as though they were created by an amateur in front of the TV one evening
- Messy page layouts that look amateurish

I sometimes help clients build Web sites, but I know my limitations. I'm not a graphic designer and don't pretend to be one; I'll build sites but find an expert to do the graphic design. Way too many people out there have decided to play graphic designer. If you're not one, don't try to act like one.

Having said that, be careful with graphic designers. Too many people in the Web business build beautiful pages that aren't particularly functional, and some of them like to use every graphic design tool in the box, making your site beautiful but unusable.

This is not merely a matter of aesthetics. In fact, I'm not saying that you need a beautiful Web site — just a professional-looking site. The fact is, sites that look unprofessional, as though they were built by a couple of guys who just learned HTML last week after they got home from work in the evenings, have trouble converting visitors to buyers. Would you buy from a site that looks as though it were built by one-handed gnomes? Well, if you wouldn't, why would other people? They don't.

By the way, I do understand that many small businesses have money issues; they can't afford a top professional designer. But there is actually no direct correlation between good Web design and dollars. It's possible to pay very little and get a decent site or to pay a lot and get garbage.

If, thanks to budgetary considerations — you're stone cold broke and plan to pay the designer with food and beer — you have to use Cousin Joe, the fireman, to create your site, or perhaps your sophomore daughter, Jenny (I've seen both situations), and if Joe or Jenny has, let's say, less-than-adequate design skills, what do you do? Buy some templates! Search online for *Web page templates* and then spend a few hours looking for something nice. Even if you have the slimmest of budgets and have to use a nondesigner to create your site, you still shouldn't settle for bad design.

There's a level below which you must not go. Remember the phrase, "The kingdom was lost for the want of a nail"? Or, "Penny smart, pound foolish"? Well, no amount of search engine optimization will make up for bad Web design. You might have the best SEO in the world and rank #1 for all your keywords — but if your visitors land on a dreadful site, all is for naught.

Panda — Google Endorses Good Design

Starting early in 2011, Google began making major updates to its search algorithm using the code name *Panda*. This multistage update has continued to this day, as Google keeps getting better at figuring out design issues. (The algorithm is reportedly named after a Google engineer, Navneet Panda.)

Google's Panda update is an important step in an attempt to weed out Web sites that people are unlikely to appreciate and to downgrade Web sites that people don't find useful or that are irritating in some way. Google is now not just trying to rank sites based on whether the information someone is searching for is present, but whether that information is presented in a way that people are likely to find acceptable.

Google had a *quality-rating panel* — a group of real users — look at sites and say what they liked and what they didn't. Then Google's programmers "coded" that, so Google's programs could examine Web pages and decide whether or not people would like them.

What sorts of things have an effect? One thing I know for sure, because Google has publicly stated this, is that Google now looks at page-layout issues and in particular advertising placement. Too many ads, in the wrong places, and your site will be downgraded.

You've seen sites that are overwhelmingly ads, right? You land on a page, and have to dig your way through ads to get to the content. Well, you don't like it, other people don't like it, and now Google doesn't like it. As Matt Cutts said on Google's Inside Search blog (http://insidesearch.blogspot. com/2012/01/page-layout-algorithm-improvement.html):

". . . we've heard complaints from users that if they click on a result and it's difficult to find the actual content, they aren't happy with the experience. Rather than scrolling down the page past a slew of ads, users want to see content right away. So sites that don't have much content "above-the-fold" can be affected by this change. If you click on a website and the part of the website you see first either doesn't have a lot of visible content above-the-fold or dedicates a large fraction of the site's initial screen real estate to ads, that's not a very good user experience. Such sites may not rank as highly going forward."

So suddenly, user experience has become much more important. No longer can you worry about merely using the search engines to get people to your site and forget about how people like your site when they get there. Of course, that was always a bad strategy, but it's even worse now, because Google is now in effect pre-approving sites, removing sites that are great matches for a searcher's search terms yet that it believes the searcher won't like when he arrives.

A few years ago, a client asked me to help him get more search-engine traffic to his site because he wasn't making enough sales. But that wasn't his problem; his site was dreadful, ugly and unprofessional. I redesigned the Web site, and a few days after the launch, my client called and said, "I don't know what you did in the search engines, but my phone is ringing off the hook!" In fact, I had not yet done anything much related to SEO; his site already had enough traffic to make the phone ring off the hook. I just had to make the site friendlier — not to search engines, but to real people. So it's always been a good idea to review your Web site from the perspective of a visitor arriving at the site. It's just good business sense.

Today, it's even more important. You need to look at your site from the viewpoint of your visitors and potential customers, think about what they want to see and consider whether they would like the site. Is your site ugly? Is it cluttered with ads? Is it hard to find one's way around the site? Or is your site interesting, useful, and engaging? Will visitors want to stick around? Or will they almost immediately click the Back button? Today, after Panda, Web site *usability* has become an SEO issue every bit as much as keyword placement and linking always were.

Note, by the way, that this is not just a Web-page issue, but a sitewide issue. Google will examine your pages and then decide whether your *site* is nice or nasty. You may have some really good pages on your site, but if the overall site is not liked, even the good pages may not do well in the search results.

So, what sort of specifics should you look for?

- ✔ **Advertising:** Advertising placement is important. Do you have too many ads *above the fold* (high up on the page)? Does the advertising overwhelm the content?

- ✔ **Light on content:** Pages with lots of navigation links and sitewide template components, but not a lot of content, may be a problem.

- ✔ **Duplication:** If your site contains lots of pages that are essentially duplicates (the same content reworked with different keywords), you may have a problem.

- ✔ **Garbage content:** Is the content on your pages essentially garbage? Badly written text purely created to hold keywords? If Google can't figure it out now, it will be able to soon.

- ✔ **Hard to read:** Are your Web pages hard to read? Perhaps the font is too small, or you use huge blocks of dense text, which are really hard for people to deal with (break them up into smaller chunks of text, add some whitespace and perhaps some images, and narrow the column!). Or perhaps you use light-color text on a dark background (long known to discourage people from reading). Such problems are disliked by real people and thus likely to end up in Google's Panda.

- ✔ **Design issues:** Remember, Panda is ongoing; now that Google has started considering user experience on the Web site, it will continue evolving the mechanisms it uses. I'm betting that eventually (maybe already), *ugly* will become a problem.

However, please don't over-extrapolate. Don't think you need a multimillion dollar budget and months of usability testing to compete in the search engines. A little commonsense about site usability goes a long way.

Keep It Fresh (Perhaps)

Finally, a quick word on freshness. Late in 2011, Google announced that it was modifying its algorithm to take content age into account more frequently. As is common in the SEO business, there was talk about how "everything had changed" and dire predictions that in order to compete, every Web site would have to be continually updated. It's nonsense.

What Google was up to was simply recognizing that for *some* searches, *freshness* is essential. That's just commonsense, and Google was simply announcing that it was planning to do a better job of finding recent content when someone searched, for instance, for information on news, sporting events, celebrities, and the like. So that means if your Web site is related to the type of information that is likely to require up-to-date information, you'd better provide it. It *doesn't* mean that pizza parlors and sites related to Egyptology will have to update their content every day in order to stay ranked.

Part II
Building Search Engine-Friendly Sites

Visit www.dummies.com/extras/seo for great Dummies content online.

In this part . . .

- ✔ Identifying powerful keywords
- ✔ Attracting search engines
- ✔ Applying markup
- ✔ Removing obstacles
- ✔ Adding valuable content
- ✔ Optimizing local searches
- ✔ Visit www.dummies.com/extras/seo for great Dummies content online

Chapter 6

Picking Powerful Keywords

· ·

· ·

I was talking with a client some years ago who wanted to have his site rank well in the search engines. The client is a company with annual revenues in the millions of dollars, in the business of, oh, I don't know . . . staging rodent-racing events. (I've changed the details of this story a tad to protect the guilty.)

I did a little research and found that most people searching for rodent-racing events use the keywords *rodent racing*. (Big surprise, huh?) I took a look at the client's Web site and discovered that the words *rodent racing* didn't appear anywhere on the site's Web pages.

"You have a little problem," I said. "Your site doesn't use the words *rodent racing,* so it's unlikely that any search engine will find your site when people search for that."

"Oh, well," was the client's reply, "our marketing department objects to the term. We have a company policy to use the term *furry friend events.* The term *rodent* is too demeaning, and if we say we're racing them, the animal rights people will get upset."

This is a true story; well, except for the bit about rodent racing and the furry friends thing. But, in principle, it happened. This company had a policy not to use the words that most of its potential clients were using to search for it.

This is an unusual example, in which a company knows the important keywords but decides not to use them. But, in fact, *many* companies build Web sites only to discover later that the keywords their potential clients and visitors are using are not in the site. How is that possible? Well, I can think of a couple of reasons:

- ✔ Most sites are built without any regard for search engines. The site designers simply don't think about search engines or have little background knowledge about how search engines work.

- ✔ The site designers *do* think about search engines, but they guess, often incorrectly, what keywords they should be using.

I can't tell you how the client and I resolved his problem because, well, we didn't. (Sometimes company politics trump common sense.) But in this chapter, I explain how to pick keywords that make sense for your site, as well as how to discover what keywords your potential site visitors are using to search for your products and services.

Understanding the Importance of Keywords

When you use a search engine, you type in a word or words and click the Search button. The search engine then looks in its index for those words.

Suppose that you typed *rodent racing*. Generally speaking, the search engine looks for

- ✔ Pages that contain the exact phrase *rodent racing*

- ✔ Pages that don't have the phrase *rodent racing* but do have the words *rodent* and *racing* in close proximity

- ✔ Pages that have the words *rodent* and *racing* somewhere, though not necessarily close together

- ✔ Pages with word stems; for instance, pages with the word *rodent* and the word *race* somewhere in the page

- ✔ Pages with synonyms, such as, perhaps, *mouse* and *rat*

- ✔ Pages that have links pointing to them, in which the link text contains the phrase *rodent racing*

- ✔ Pages with links pointing to them with the link text containing the words *rodent* and *racing*, although not together

Don't get too hung up on whether it's *keywords* or *keyword*. The term *keyword* from the search perspective simply means whatever a searcher types into a search box, whether it's just one word or ten. Thus, when I talk about a keyword or choosing keywords, I'm not talking only about single words; I'm also talking about *keyword phrases*.

The process is actually a lot more complicated. The search engine doesn't necessarily show pages in the order I just listed — all the pages with the exact phrase, and then all the pages with the words in close proximity, and so on. When considering ranking order, the search engine considers (in addition to hundreds of secret criteria) whether the keyword or phrase is in

- Bold text
- Italicized text
- Bulleted lists
- Text larger than other text on the page
- Heading text (<H> tags)

Furthermore, in recent years the search engines are working hard to understand what people really want. Google's Hummingbird algorithm, for example, was a major rewrite of how Google analyzed search queries and returned results. One of the major goals was to further improve the way Google understands "conversational search." That is, Google wants to be able to understand such searches as "the best place in Denver to buy a smart phone" or "where can I buy hiking gear in Dallas?"

The goal is to help users by presenting better search results that understand at a deeper level what people are looking for and what kind of results match well.

Despite the various complications, however, one fact is of paramount importance: If a search engine can't relate your Web site to the words that someone searches for, it has no reason to return your Web site as part of the search results.

Thus, picking the right keywords is critical. As Woody Allen once said, "Eighty percent of success is showing up." If you don't play the game, you can't win. And if you don't choose the right keywords, you're not even showing up to play the game. If a specific keyword or keyword phrase (or perhaps a synonym) doesn't appear in your pages (or in links pointing to your pages), your site *will not* appear when someone enters those keywords into the search engines. For instance, say you're a technical writer in San Diego, and you have a site with the term *technical writer* scattered throughout. You will *not* appear in search results when someone searches for *technical writer san diego* if you don't have the words *San Diego* in your pages. You simply will not turn up (*unless* you are listed in the local search results, or you've given Google some reason to believe your site is related in some way to those "local" keywords *San Diego*, a subject I deal with in Chapter 12).

 Understanding how to search helps you understand the role of keywords. Check out the bonus chapter I've posted at www.SearchEngineBulletin. com to find the different ways you can search by using search engines in general and Google in particular.

Thinking Like Your Prey

It's an old concept: You should think like your prey. Companies often make mistakes with their keywords because they choose based on how they — rather than their customers — think about their products or services. For example, lawyers talk about *practice areas*, a phrase ordinary people — lawyers' clients — almost never use. You have to stop thinking that you know what customers call your products. Do some research to find out what clients really do call your products and services.

The starting point of any great SEO strategy is a thorough keyword analysis. Check to see what people are actually searching for on the Web. You'll discover that some words you were sure people would use are rarely searched, and you'll also find that you've missed a lot of common terms. Sure, you may get some of the keywords right; however, if you're spending time and energy targeting particular keywords, you may as well get 'em all right.

The term *keyword analysis* has several meanings:

- ✔ When I use it, I'm referring to what I'm discussing in this chapter — analyzing the use of keywords by people searching for products, services, and information.

- ✔ Some people use the term to mean *keyword-density* analysis — finding out how often a keyword appears in a page. Some of the keyword analysis tools that you run across are actually keyword-density analysis tools.

- ✔ The term also refers to the process of analyzing keywords in your Web site's access logs.

Starting Your Keyword Analysis

Perform a *keyword analysis* — a check of what keywords people use to search on the Web — or you're wasting your time. Imagine spending hundreds of hours optimizing your site for a keyword you think is good, only to discover that another keyword or phrase gets two or three times the traffic. How would you feel? Sick? Stupid? Mad? Don't risk your mental health — do it right the first time.

Identifying the obvious keywords

Begin by typing the obvious keywords into a text editor or word processor. Type the words you've already thought of, or, if you haven't started yet, the ones that immediately come to mind. Then study the list for a few minutes. What else can you add? What similar terms come to mind? Add them, too.

When you perform your analysis, you'll find that some of the initial terms you think of aren't searched very often, but that's okay. This list is just the start.

Looking at your Web site's access logs

Take a quick look at your Web site's access logs (often called *hit logs*). You may not realize it, but most logs show you the keywords that people used when they clicked a link to your site at a search engine. (If your logs don't contain this information, you probably need another program.) Write down the terms that are bringing people to your site. Also, you can use your Google Webmaster account to gather this information; see Chapter 13. (Unfortunately, Google often doesn't provide keywords these days when forwarding traffic to Web sites; other search engines generally do.)

Examining competitors' keyword tags

You probably know who your competitors are — you should, anyway. Go to their sites and open the source code of a few pages by following these steps:

1. **Choose View ⇨ Source from the browser's menu bar.**

2. **Look in the** `<META NAME="keywords">` **tag for any useful keywords.**

Often, the keywords are garbage or simply not there, but if you look at enough sites, you're likely to come up with some useful terms you hadn't thought of.

Brainstorming with colleagues

Talk to friends and colleagues to see whether they can come up with some possible keywords. Ask them something like, "If you were looking for a site where you could find the latest scores for rodent races around the world, what terms would you search for?" Give everyone a copy of your current keyword list and ask whether they can think of anything to add. Usually, reading the terms sparks an idea or two, and you end up with a few more terms.

Looking closely at your list

After you've put together your initial list, go through it looking for more obvious additions. Don't spend too much time on this; all you're doing here is creating a preliminary list to run through a keyword tool, which figures out some of these things for you.

Obvious spelling mistakes

Scan through your list and see if you can think of any obvious spelling mistakes. Some spelling mistakes are incredibly important, with 10, 15, or 20 percent (sometimes even more) of all searches containing the misspelled word. For example, about one-fifth of all Britney Spears–related searches are misspelled — spread out over a dozen misspellings. I'm not commenting on the intellect of Britney Spears fans; it's just a name that could be spelled several ways.

The word *calendar* is also frequently misspelled. The following estimates provided by a keyword tool show how often *calendar* is searched for each day in its various permutations:

> *calendar:* 10,605 times
>
> *calender:* 2,721
>
> *calander:* 1,549
>
> *calandar:* 256

Thirty percent of all searches on the word *calendar* are misspelled. (Where do I get these estimates, you're wondering? You find out later in this chapter in the "Using a Keyword Tool" section.)

If the traffic from a misspelling is significant, you may want to create a page on your site that uses that misspelling. Some sites contain what I call "Did You Mean" pages, such as the one shown in Figure 6-1. Some sites contain pages with misspellings in the <TITLE> tags, which can work very well. These don't have to be pages that many people see. After all, the only people who will see the misspelled titles in a search results page are those who misspelled the words in the first place.

One nice thing about misspellings is that competitors often miss them, so you can grab the traffic without much trouble. Don't underestimate the effectiveness of this technique.

"But Google recognizes spelling mistakes, doesn't it?" I can hear you thinking. Yes, it does, and it handles them in a couple of ways. In some cases, when Google is pretty sure that it was a spelling mistake, it goes ahead and searches for the assumed correct spelling and puts a line like this near the top of the page:

```
Showing results for free currency converter. Search
            instead for free currancy converter
```

On the other hand, sometimes Google isn't so sure, and it displays a couple of entries that have the assumed correct spelling, followed by another few entries that are misspelled. So misspellings aren't as useful as they used to be, but they're still worth addressing in some situations.

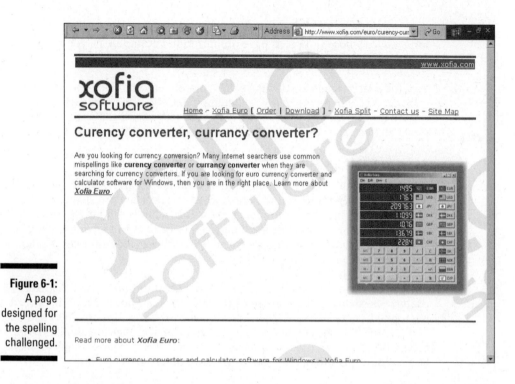

Figure 6-1:
A page designed for the spelling challenged.

Synonyms

Sometimes similar words are easily missed. If your business is home related, for instance, have you thought about the term *house*? Americans may easily overlook this word, using *home* instead, but other English-speaking countries use the word *house* more often. Add it to the list because you may find quite a few searches related to it. Also, as I mentioned earlier, the major search engines also consider synonyms when analyzing Web pages; if the page contains the word *canine*, it might also assume the page matches — to some degree — *dog* (or perhaps *dentistry*?).

You might even use a thesaurus to find more synonyms. However, I show you some keyword tools that run these kinds of searches for you; see the section "Using a Keyword Tool," later in this chapter.

Split or merged words

You may find that although your product name is one word — *RodentRacing*, for instance — most people are searching for you by using two words, *rodent* and *racing*. Remember to consider your customer's point of view.

Also, some words are employed in two ways. Some people, for instance, use the term *knowledgebase*, while others use *knowledge base*. Which is more important? Both should be on your list, but *knowledge base* is used around four to five times more often than *knowledgebase*. If you optimize your pages for *knowledgebase* (I discuss page optimization in Chapter 7), you're missing out on around 80 percent of the traffic!

Yes, the search engines still figure out a match, but matching the search term exactly is better than just matching it closely. Don't believe me? Search Google or Bing for *knowledgebase*, then *knowledge base*; different results, right? Similar on Google, though still different; quite different on Bing.

Singulars and plurals

Go through your list and add singulars and plurals. Search engines *understand* plurals and often return plural results when you search for a singular term and vice versa, but they still treat singulars and plurals differently, and sometimes this can mean the difference between ranking at #1 and not ranking at all. For example, searching on *rodent* and *rodents* provides different results; again, similar, but definitely different.

So, it's important to know which term is searched for most often. A great example is to do a search on *book* (165,000 U.S. searches per month, according to the Google keyword tool, which I discuss later in this chapter) and *books* (246,000 searches per day) in Google. The searches are similar at the top on Google (both present Amazon, Barnes and Noble, and Google Books), less so lower down the page, and with more differences on Bing.

Don't worry about upper- versus lowercase letters. You can use *rodent* or *Rodent* or *RODENT*, for example. Most search engines aren't case sensitive. If you search for *rodent* (probably 90 percent of all searches are in lowercase), all the major search engines will find *Rodent* or *RODENT* — or *rODENT* or *ROdent,* for that matter.

Hyphens

Do you see any hyphenated words on your list that could be used without the hyphen, or vice versa? Some terms are commonly used both ways, so find out what your customers are using. Here are two examples:

- ✔ Google reports that the term *e-commerce* is used far more often than *ecommerce*.
- ✔ The dash in *e-mail* is far less frequently used, with *email* being by far the most common term.

Find hyphenated words, add both forms to your list, and determine which is more common, because search engines treat them as different searches.

Geo-specific terms

Is geography important to your business? Are you selling shoes in Seattle or rodents in Rochester? Don't forget to include terms that include your city, state, other nearby cities, and so on. (See Chapter 12 for more on this topic.)

Your company name

If you have a well-known company name, add that to the lis
mutations you can think of (for example, Microsoft, MS, MS

Other companies' names and product names

If people are likely to search for companies and products similar to yours, add those companies and products to your list. That's not to say you should use these keywords in your pages (you can in some conditions, as I discuss in Chapter 7), but it's nice to know what people are looking for and how often they're looking.

Using a Keyword Tool

After you've put together a decent keyword list, the next step is to use a keyword tool. This tool enables you to discover additional terms you haven't thought of and helps you determine which terms are most important — which terms are used most often by people looking for your products and services.

Both free and paid versions of keyword tools are available. Both the major PPC (Pay Per Click) advertising systems — Google AdWords and the Yahoo! Bing Network — provide free keyword-analysis tools. You need a Google account to get into the former, and a Microsoft account to get to the latter, but you don't need to actually spend any money on PPC to get to these tools.

✔ Google Adwords Keywords Planner: `https://adwords.google.com/KeywordPlanner`

✔ Bing Keywords Research Tool: http://www.bing.com/toolbox/keywords

Using the free Google keyword tool

To get to the Google Adwords Keywords Planner go to `https://adwords.google.com/KeywordPlanner` (or search for *google keyword planner* and click the link that appears).

If you already have an AdWords account, you'll go straight to the Planner (once logged into your Google account). If you don't have an AdWords account, unfortunately you'll have to go through the steps to set one up, which is a bit of a nuisance but worth the few minutes it will take; again, you don't have to actually spend money. (If you are already in your AdWords account, select the Keyword Planner from the Tools menu.)

You have to log in with a Google account, and provide some basic information to set up an AdWords account, but you won't have to spend a lot of time, and you won't need to pay anything or create an advertising campaign; you'll go straight to the Keyword Planner.

When you first view the Google Keyword Planner, you see a page like the one shown in Figure 6-2. You have several choices:

- ✔ *Search for new keyword and ad group ideas:* You enter one or more keywords, and the system tells you how often people search for those terms *and* find more terms, keywords that Google thinks are related.

- ✔ *Get search volume for a list of keywords or group them into ad groups*: This option allows you to enter or upload a list of keywords. Google will tell you how often those terms are searched for, but won't find additional terms.

- ✔ *Get traffic forecasts for a list of keywords:* This is more useful for PPC campaigns; Google estimates how many clicks you might get, and what they would cost, if you were advertising.

- ✔ *Multiple keyword lists to get new keyword ideas:* You enter two lists of keywords, and Google provides possible useful combinations

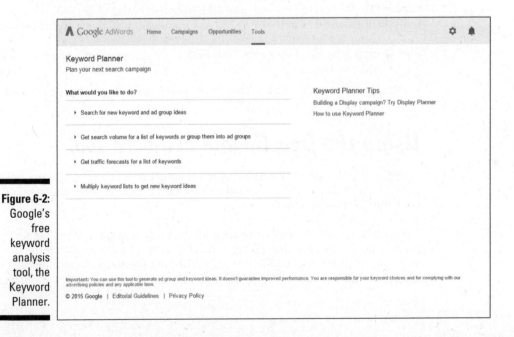

Figure 6-2:
Google's free keyword analysis tool, the Keyword Planner.

Again, this is really a PPC advertising tool, so some of the features are definitely related to advertising; for instance, where Google talks of "ad groups," it referrs to the idea of breaking an advertising campaign into different sub campaigns, in effect — different ad groups — with each ad group having different keywords and associated ads, and perhaps different criteria such as bid prices and time ranges.

The following example shows the first of the options preceding options; if you have time, check out the others as you may find other useful features. When you click the first option, you see the page open up to show you the options shown in Figure 6-3:

✔ Type a keyword phrase into the Your Product or Service box or type multiple keyword phrases if you like, each on a separate line.

✔ Type the domain name of a Web site into the Your Landing Page box. Google will find keywords that it believes are related to this site.

✔ Select a category from the Your Product Category text box.

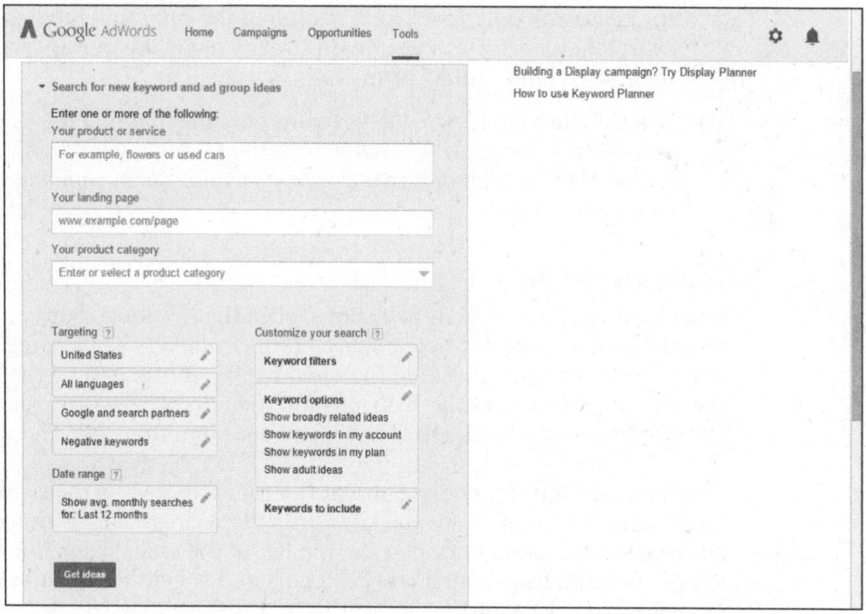

Figure 6-3:
The Keyword Planner provides sophisticated options and filters to help you get exactly what you need.

In effect, you're telling Google to look through its database of searches — actual keywords typed in by real searchers on its Web site and partner sites — to find searches that it thinks may be related to your keyword phrase, the Web site you entered, or the category you picked. Now, below these text boxes you'll find a number of options that will help you narrow down your keyword list. You can

✔ Limit the keywords to searches within particular geographic regions. You can specify one or more countries, or even locations within countries, such as states, provinces, Nielsen DMAs (Designated Market Areas), or even specific cities.

✔ Choose whether the keywords come from searches on Google.com *and* its search partners (primarily AOL.com), or just from Google.com.

✔ Enter negative keywords; that is, keywords that, if present in a keyword phrase, will cause Google to exclude the phrase from the list.

✔ Provide a date-range.

By default, you're given the average number of searches each month over the last year. This tool also allows you to ask for data from two date ranges so you can compare them.

✔ Ask Google to omit keywords from the returned list if the number of monthly searches is over or under a specified value, and based on certain advertising metrics (the amount of competition for the keywords, the bid price, and the impression share).

✔ Define how broadly Google finds possible keywords for you. You can ask for keywords that are closely related to the ones you have entered, only search among keywords you are already using in your advertising, and include or omit "adult" terms.

✔ Ask Google to only provide keyword phrases that include a specific keyword. For example, if you enter *shoe* then Google would only show you keywords that include the term *shoe*; *running shoe*, *climbing shoe*, *shoe store*, and so on.

Begin your search

When you've made all your selections, click the Get Ideas button, and Google finds keywords related to your search term. In the case of a category search, Google finds keywords related to that category. In the case of the Web site search, Google looks at the Web site and then finds keywords related to the site. Whichever method you choose, you see something like Figure 6-4.

This example starts with the chart at the top. This shows the search volumes, month by month, for the keywords that Google has returned. But notice the little menu button at the top left of the chart; click this button to open a menu from which you can choose to see different kinds of data related to your keywords:

✔ A month-by-month breakdown of mobile searches

✔ An overall breakdown showing the percentage of desktop and laptop computers, mobile devices, and tablets

✔ Regional breakdowns

✔ Some PPC-related data

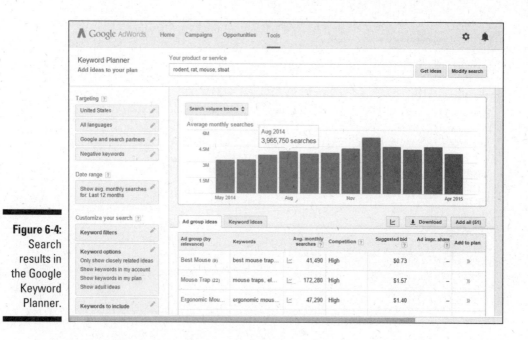

Figure 6-4:
Search
results in
the Google
Keyword
Planner.

But let's get to the actual keywords. Below the chart you see two tabs:

✔ Ad Group Ideas, the default view, shows you a list of potential ad groups.

This is a PPC system, so it's suggesting how you might create different ad campaigns, with different keywords and ads in each one. But that's okay, because even from an "organic-search" point of view this stuff can be useful, giving you different groups of keywords you might want to target.

For each ad group, you'll see some of the keywords in the group:

• The average number of searches for all the keywords in the group

• How competitive (from a PPC standpoint) the keywords are

More PPC-related information (suggested bid and ad-impression share), which I'm going to ignore and you don't need to worry about if you're focusing on SEO

Click on a group name; the Planner shows you the same information, but for each individual keyword in the group.

✔ Click the Keyword Ideas tab, and you see all the keywords that the Planner found, but they aren't divided into ad groups (see Figure 6-5). The box at the top shows information about the keywords entered into the system; the box below shows the Keyword Planner's suggestions.

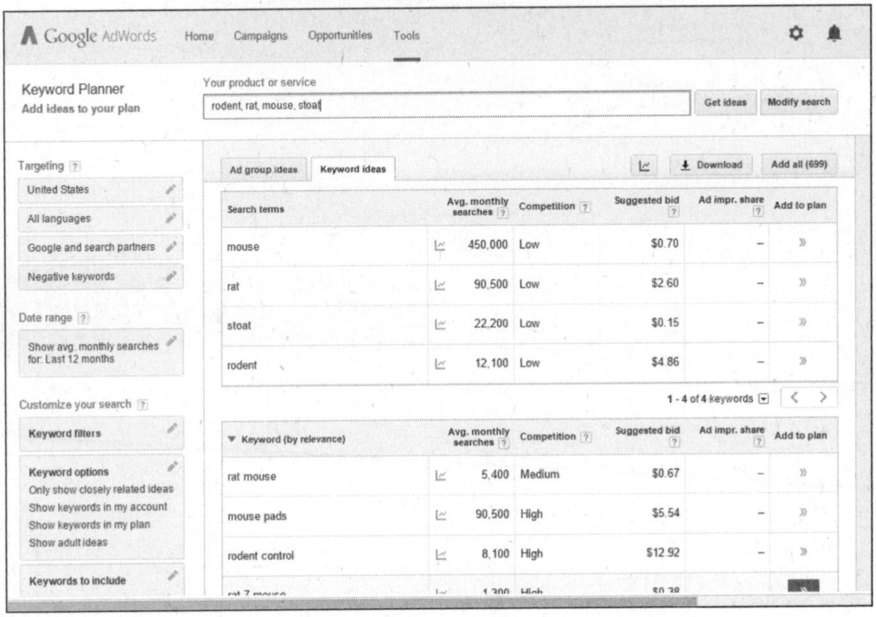

Figure 6-5:
The results
under the
Keyword
Ideas tab;
I clicked
the Toggle
Chart but-
ton to make
more space
by removing
the chart
from the
top.

A few quick tips about using the Keywords Tool:

✔ Point at the little graph icon on a keyword line (next to the Avg. Monthly Searches number) to display a chart showing the distribution of searches month-by-month.

✔ Click the column headings to sort by keyword "relevance."

Google sorts the keywords according to how relevant it believes they are to the ones you specified; in order of monthly searches; into High, Medium, and Low competition groups.

✔ Click the Toggle Chart button (the little button with a pictograph of a chart on it, on the same line as the tabs) to remove the chart, making more room for the keywords.

✔ Enter more keywords into the Your Product or Service text box at the top and click Get Ideas to retrieve more keywords.

The Google keyword tool is great. I keep a button on my browser's book-marks toolbar to take me there whenever I feel a sudden urge for more keywords. Note that you can download the list of keywords, or selected key-words, into a spreadsheet (see the Download button, top left of the table), which is very handy for saving keyword analyses. However, Google doesn't have some of the sophisticated keyword-analysis features that other, com-mercial keyword-analysis tools have . . . so I look at that subject later in this chapter.

Using the free Bing Ads keywords tool

The Bing PPC system (*Bing Ads*; formerly, the *Yahoo! Bing Network*) also provides a free keywords-research tool, although you have to set up a PPC account before you can get to it (go to www.bing.com/toolbox/keywords). However, this tool isn't as sophisticated as the Google tool, and usually returns fewer keyword suggestions.

Still, if you want to play with it, log into your Bing Ads account and select Research Keywords from the Tools menu; you'll see something like Figure 6-6. From the Keywords drop-down list box near the top, you can choose either

- Find Keywords Related to a Word or Phrase; enter one or more keywords or keyword phrases, each on a separate line.

- Find Keywords on a Website; enter a Web site's URL, of course.

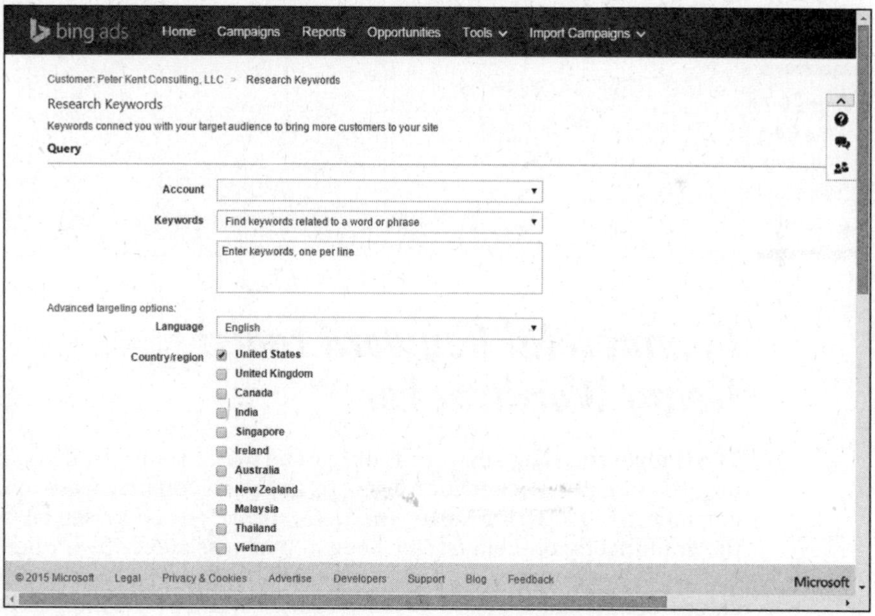

Figure 6-6: The Bing Ads PPC Keyword Analysis tool, after clicking the Advanced Targeting Options link.

As with the Google tool, you can also specify various options; click the Advanced Targeting Options link to see them. You can select the language, country, the type of device on which the keywords are used, and the maximum number of suggestions for each keyword you entered.

When you enter your keywords and click Search, the tool returns with suggestions; it shows how often the terms were searched for in the last month, along with a variety of PPC-related information (see Figure 6-7). As with Google, you can export this information to a CSV file, which can be opened in a spreadsheet program.

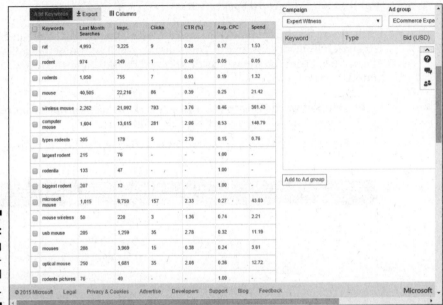

Figure 6-7: The Bing Ads keyword tool results.

Commercial keyword tools: Using Wordtracker

The Google and Bing keyword tools can be very useful, but if you're planning to go really deep in your keyword analysis, you may want to use a commercial tool. Wordtracker (www.wordtracker.com; see Figure 6-8) is the granddaddy of them all (it's been in business since 1998, when Google had barely begun operating), and is one of the most popular and sophisticated commercial keyword analysis tools. Owned by a company in London, England, Wordtracker has access to data from a couple of large metacrawlers, and a large British ISP. A *metacrawler* is a system that searches multiple search engines for you. For example, type a word into Dogpile's search box (www.dogpile.com), and the system searches at Google, Yahoo!, Bing, and Ask.com. It also works with SEMRush, a company that gathers competitive data about Web sites and Web traffic in various ways, including using the SEOQuake browser plug-in.

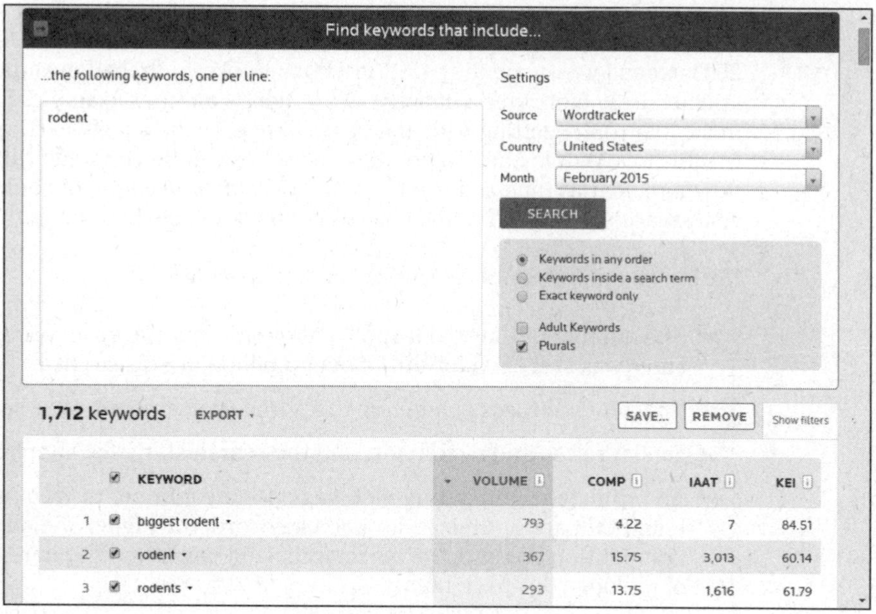

Find keywords that include...

...the following keywords, one per line:

rodent

Settings

Source | Wordtracker
Country | United States
Month | February 2015

SEARCH

○ Keywords in any order
○ Keywords inside a search term
○ Exact keyword only

☐ Adult Keywords
☑ Plurals

1,712 keywords   EXPORT ▾   SAVE... REMOVE   Show filters

		KEYWORD	▾ VOLUME ⓘ	COMP ⓘ	IAAT ⓘ	KEI ⓘ
1	☑	biggest rodent ▾	793	4.22	7	84.51
2	☑	rodent ▾	367	15.75	3,013	60.14
3	☑	rodents ▾	293	13.75	1,616	61.79

Figure 6-8:
Wordtrack-
er's "Find
Keywords"
screen.

Wordtracker's database has information about literally billions of searches, and the Wordtracker system allows you to dig through this database. Ask Wordtracker how often someone searched for the term *rodents,* and it tells you that it was searched for (at the time of writing) 112 times over the last month in the United States, but that the term *rodent* is far more popular, with 639 searches. (Those numbers don't sound like much, especially when compared to numbers that you'll find through Google. But Wordtracker is working with a smaller database than Google is. In any case, what really counts are the relative numbers; you want to know which keywords are more popular than others.)

Wordtracker also allows queries using the Google keyword tool to get Google's information, too (though the data is modified slightly).

Remember that certain searches are seasonal: *pools* in the summer, *heaters* in the winter, and so on. In the past, Wordtracker had only the last 100 days of information, so it wasn't representative of a full year for some terms. Now, however, Wordtracker has data going back a couple of years (depending on what plan you sign up for, you can view data from the last three months, six months, or all the data), so some terms may be diluted; *christmas tree decoration*, over a full year, is less popular a term than it would be if you searched through data from just November and December. However, one of the options is to specify which month.

Also, some searches may be influenced by the media and current events. While searches for *paris hilton* were very high in November and December 2003, when I wrote the first edition of this book . . . oh, bad example, they're still absurdly high, unfortunately. Okay, here's another example. Early on in a catastrophe getting wide media coverage, such as a big earthquake or trouble in a Middle Eastern country, searches can be very high (although nowhere near as high as for *paris hilton* or *kim kardashian*, of course). But such searches drop off quickly when media coverage has waned.

Here's what information Wordtracker can provide:

- The number of times in a specified month that the exact phrase you enter was searched for out of over 3 billion or so searches

- How often phrases *containing* the phrase you entered were searched for

- Similar terms and synonyms, and the search statistics about these terms

- An estimate of competing Web pages — the number of Web pages it found that are optimized for each keyword; the higher the number in the Competition column, the more optimized pages and the harder the task of ranking your page highly

- A *Keyword Effectiveness Index* (KEI) rating for each keyword. It's an amalgam of both the popularity of the term and how much competition there is for the term; a high number means a popular term with relatively little competition.

- An *In Anchor and Title* (IAAT) value, another competitiveness indicator. It shows how many Web pages have the term in both the page's Title tag and in the anchor text (see Chapter 16) of at least one link pointing to the page.

You can download the list of keywords you find in a CSV file that you can quickly open in your spreadsheet program (such as Microsoft Excel).

By the way, here's another reason that some search numbers sound very low on Wordtracker; only 2,219 searches for *true detective,* for example. *Primary* terms often are low because most searches are not for primary terms; many searches are for *lera lynn true detective, true detective season 2, true detective season 2 trailer song, true detective streaming,* and many other phrases. Although individual phrases may seem to have low numbers, these combined phrases often add up to a very large number. (Remember the search tail.)

On the face of it, Wordtracker may seem much the same as the Google tool, but it does have some additional features that help you manage your keyword lists. It allows you to set up *projects* (each Web site might be an individual project, for instance), and, within each project, multiple lists (each list could be a particular keyword focus). Then you can search for keywords and save the lists into your projects.

You can also filter the search in various ways: show only keywords above or below search-volume levels, show only keywords with IAAT or KEI values in a particular range, show only keywords that are in the form of a question (*are rabbits rodents?*), and so on. You can mix this up, too. For example, you can ask Wordtracker to show you only keywords that are in the form of a question, with a KEI value above 75 and an IAAT value below 400 (see Figure 6-9). This shows you question-type keywords that aren't very competitive — that is, for which you may have a good chance of ranking well. You can apply these filters while you are searching for keyword ideas, or apply them within the keyword lists you've saved within your projects, so you can extract specific groups of keywords.

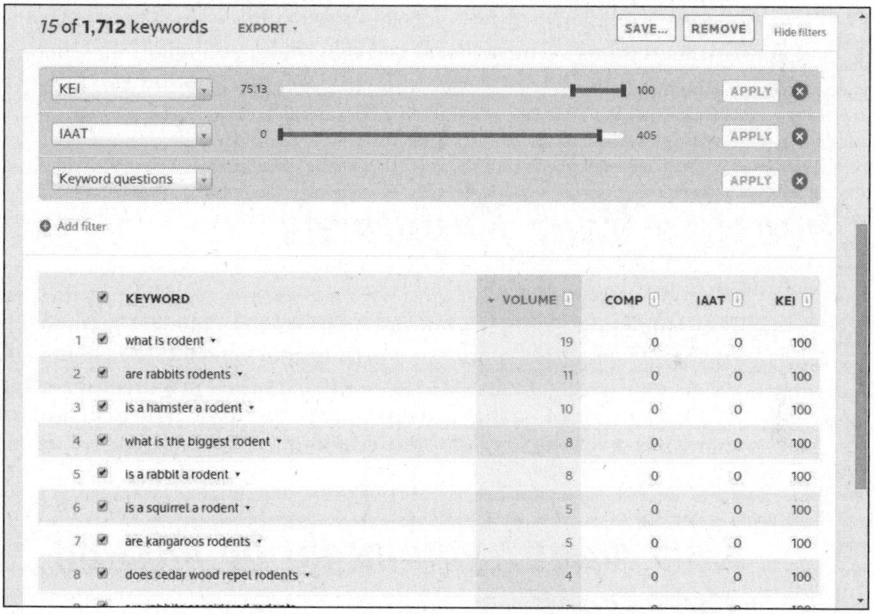

Figure 6-9:
Wordtracker
provides
filters to help
you discover
keyword
opportuni-
ties.

Wordtracker is well worth the price, ranging from $27 a month to $99 a month. Anyone heavily involved in the Web and search engines can easily get addicted to this tool.

Yet more keyword tools

Wordtracker is by no means the only keyword analysis tool on the market. If you're a real keyword junkie, just do a search for *keyword analysis* or *keyword tool*; you'll find plenty to keep you busy. In particular, these are popular, well-known systems:

- Moz: `https://moz.com/tools`
- Keyword Discovery: `www.keyworddiscovery.com`
- KeywordSpy: `www.keywordspy.com`
- SpyFu: `www.SpyFu.com`
- SEMRush: `www.SemRush.com`

There are also various keyword tools, such as `UberSuggest.org`, that do simple keyword look ups based on search engine "suggestions" (the text that the search engines show a searcher while he or she is typing keywords into the search box). These aren't the real thing; you might use them as a brainstorming tool, but they won't provide the information you need in order to make decisions about which keywords you plan to target.

Choosing Your Keywords

When you've finished working with a keyword tool, look at the final list to determine how popular a keyword phrase actually is. You may find that many of your original terms are not worth bothering with. My clients often have terms on their preliminary lists — the lists they put together without the use of a keyword tool — that are virtually never used. You also find other terms near the top of the final list that you hadn't thought about.

Cam again? You might be missing the target

Take a look at your list to determine whether you have any words that may have different meanings to different people. Sometimes, you can immediately spot such terms.

One of my clients thought he should use the term *cam* on his site. To him, the term referred to *Complementary and Alternative Medicine*. But to the vast majority of searchers, *cam* means something different. Search Wordtracker on the term *cam*, and you come up with phrases such as *web cams, web cam, free web cams, live web cams, cam, cams, live cams, live web cams,* and so on. To most searchers, the term *cam* refers to *Web cams* — cameras used to place pictures and videos online. The phrases from this example generate a tremendous amount of competition, but few of them would be useful to my client. That's okay, though, because very few people who *are* interested in Complementary and Alternative Medicine use the term *cam* anyway.

Ambiguous terms

A client of mine wanted to promote a product designed for controlling fires. One common term he came up with was *fire control system*. However, he discovered that when he searched on that term, most sites that turned up don't promote products relating to stopping fires. Rather, they're sites related to fire control in the military sense — weapons-fire control.

This kind of ambiguity is something you really can't determine from a system that tells you how often people search on a term, such as Wordtracker. In fact, spotting such terms is hard even when you search to see what turns up when you use the phrase. If a particular type of Web site turns up when you search for the phrase, does that mean that people using the phrase are looking for that type of site? You can't say for sure, though such a search can often tip you off that you're working with an ambiguous term.

Very broad terms

Look at your list for terms that are incredibly broad. You may be tempted to go after high-ranking words, but make sure that people are really searching for your products when they type in the word.

Suppose that your site is promoting *degrees in information technology*. You discover that around 40 people search for this term each day, but approximately 1,500 people a day search on *information technology*. Do you think many people searching on *information technology* are really looking for a degree? Probably not. Although the term generates 40,000 to 50,000 searches a month, few of these returns will be your targets.

Here are a couple of reasons to forego a term that's too broad:

- ✔ **Tough to rank.** It's probably a very competitive term, which means ranking well on it would be difficult.
- ✔ **Relevance is elsewhere.** You may be better off spending the time and effort focusing on another, more relevant term.

Picking combinations

Sometimes it's a good idea to target terms lower on your list rather than the ones up top because the lower terms *include* the higher terms.

Suppose that you're selling an e-commerce system and find the following list in Wordtracker, with the most popular term at the top:

```
ecommerce
e-commerce
shopping cart
shopping carts
shopping cart software
ecommerce solutions
ecommerce software
ecommerce software solution
e-commerce solutions
e-commerce software
shopping carts and accessories
```

The term *e-commerce* is probably not a great term to target because it's very general and has a lot of competition. But lower on the list is the term *e-commerce solutions*. This term is a combination of two keyword phrases: *e-commerce* and *e-commerce solutions*. If you target *e-commerce solutions* and optimize your Web pages for that term, you're also optimizing for *e-commerce*.

Notice also the term *ecommerce* (which search engines regard as different from *e-commerce*) and the term a little lower on the list, *ecommerce software*. A term even lower encompasses both of these terms — *ecommerce software solution*. Optimize your pages for *ecommerce software solution,* and you've just optimized for three terms simultaneously.

The keyword analysis procedure I describe in this chapter provides you with a much better picture of your keyword landscape. In contrast to the majority of Web site owners, you'll have a good view of how people are searching for your products and services.

Chapter 7

Creating Pages That Search Engines Love

In This Chapter

▶ Getting your site read

▶ Understanding the importance of mobile-friendly sites

▶ Knowing what search engines see

▶ Exploring keyword concepts

▶ Creating Web pages

*I*n this chapter, you find out how to create Web pages that search engines *really* like — pages that can be read and indexed and that put your best foot forward. Before you begin creating pages, I recommend that you read not only this chapter but also Chapter 9 to find out how to avoid things that search engines hate. There are a lot of ways to make a Web site work, and just as many ways to break it, too. Before you get started creating your pages, you should be aware of the problems you may face and what you can do to avoid them.

I'm assuming that you or your Web designer understand HTML and can create Web pages. I focus on the most important search engine–related things you need to know while creating your pages. It's beyond the scope of this book to cover basic HTML and Cascading Style Sheets. On the other hand, many content-management systems (CMS) do a really good job of optimizing for the search engines. These are automated Web-page-creation systems, such as WordPress, Drupal, and Joomla. But there are so many of these systems, I can't possibly cover that particular subject.

Thus I talk in terms of HTML; you'll have to translate into the particular features and options of the CMS you happen to be using. For instance, I'm going to discuss how you can put keywords into <IMG> tags using the ALT attribute; if you're using a CMS, you'll need to figure out how that particular system allows you to add that text when inserting an image (if it does, and most these days do).

Preparing Your Site

When you're creating a Web site, the first thing to consider is *where* to put your site. By that, I mean the Web server and the domain name.

Finding a hosting company

Although many large companies place their Web sites on their own Web servers, most small companies don't. They shouldn't do so, in fact, because there's simply no way a small business can manage a Web server anywhere near as cheaply and reliably as a good hosting company can do it. Rather, a hosting company rents space on its servers to other businesses.

You need to consider many issues when selecting a hosting company, most of which aren't directly related to the search engine issue. From an SEO perspective, you need to be able to upload pages directly to your site, as most hosts allow, or use a search-engine-friendly CMS system that either the hosting company provides or you install. I can't help much with that; you'll have to do some research on the system you are considering to see whether it's truly search-engine friendly (see Part V Web Extra, *Ten Ways to Make WordPress (and Others) Search Engine Friendly*).

As you learned in Chapter 3, it's also important that the hosting company you use is *reliable*. The servers must work virtually all the time and deliver pages quickly. Slow, unreliable servers can hurt your search-engine rankings. Most hosting companies these days are reasonably reliable, but not all.

Picking a domain name

Search engines read *uniform resource locators (URLs),* looking for keywords in them. For instance, if you have a Web site with the domain name `rodent-racing.com` and someone searches Google for *rodent racing*, Google sees *rodent-racing* as a match; because a dash appears between the two words, Google recognizes the individual words in the domain name. If, however, you run the words together (*rodentracing*), Google doesn't regard the individual words as individual words; it sees them as part of the same word. That's not to say that Google can't find text *within* words — it can, and you sometimes see words on the search results pages partially bolded when Google does just that — but when ranking the page, Google doesn't regard the word it found inside another word as the same as finding the word itself.

To see this concept in action, use the *allinurl:* search syntax at Google. Type *allinurl:rodent,* for example, and Google finds URLs that contain the word *rodent* (including the directory names and filenames).

So, putting keywords into the domain name and separating keywords with dashes provides a small benefit. Another advantage to adding dashes between words is that you can relatively easily come up with a domain name that's not already taken. Although it may seem as though most of the good names were taken long ago, you can often come up with some kind of keyword phrase, separated with dashes, that's still available. Furthermore, search engines don't care which first-level domain you use; you can use *.com,* *.net, .biz, .tv,* or whatever; it doesn't matter.

Now, having said all that, let me tell you my philosophy regarding domain names. In the search engine optimization field, it used to be very popular to use dashes and keywords in domain names, but in most cases, the lift provided by keywords in domain names is relatively small; in fact, while the search engines clearly read keywords in domain names, they give much less value to them than they have in the past. Rather, you should consider other, more important factors when choosing a domain name:

- ✔ **A domain name should be short, easy to spell, and easy to remember.** It should also pass the *radio test.* Imagine that you're being interviewed on the radio and want to tell listeners your URL. You want something that's instantly understandable without having to be spelled. You don't want to have to say "rodent dash racing dash events dot com"; it's better to say "rodent racing events dot com."

- ✔ **In almost all cases, you should get the *.com* version of a domain name.** If the *.com* version is taken, do *not* try to use the *.net* or *.org* version for branding purposes! People remember *.com,* even if you say *.org* or *.net* or whatever. So, if you're planning to promote your Web site in print, on the radio, on TV, on billboards, and so on, you need the *.com* version.

Domain confusion

Several years ago, I recommended that a nonprofit client of mine register the *.com* version of its domain name. (The client had been using *.org* for years.) During the few hours that the *.com* domain was not yet pointing to its site, but instead was pointing to the domain registrar's site, the nonprofit received several calls from people trying to get to its Web site. These people wanted to let the company know that something was wrong with its server because its domain name was pointing to the wrong place. For years, the company printed all its materials using *.org;* it had never printed anything with *.com* because it didn't own that domain name; however, people were still trying to get to the *.com* version, a perfect example of what I call *domain confusion.*

A classic example is a situation involving Rent.com and Rent.net. These two different Web sites were owned by two different companies. Rent.net spent millions of dollars on advertising; every time I saw a Rent.net ad on a bus, I had to wonder how much of the traffic generated by these ads actually went to Rent.com! (The Rent.net domain name is no longer in use — it now points to Move.com — and Rent.com is. I don't think that's a coincidence!)

Are keyworded domain names worth the trouble? Because the lift provided by keywords in the domain name may be rather small — and, in fact, putting too many keywords into a name can *hurt* your placement — you should probably focus on a single, brandable domain name (a *.com* version).

Be careful about using a domain-forwarding service for Web sites that you want to turn up in search engines. Many domain registrars allow you to simply forward browsers to a particular site: A user types *www.domain1.com*, and the registrar forwards the browser to *www.domain2.com*, for instance. Such forwarding systems may use frames (discussed in Chapter 9), which means that search engines don't index the site properly, or do not use 301 redirects to implement the forward as they should for SEO purposes (see Chapter 24 for more information on 301 redirects).

Mobile readiness and "Mobilegeddon"

In 2015, Google introduced another important concept for Webmasters to worry about: mobile readiness. By this point, a huge proportion of Web site visits, for a wide range of site types, were coming from mobile devices. For example, when I checked the site analytics for a heavy industrial client of mine in early 2015, I found that 29 percent of the traffic came from small mobile devices (smart phones), with another 13 percent from tablets. It isn't just the younger Internet users or the more technically adept that are moving to mobile. Across the board, a huge proportion of site visits now comes from mobile devices.

However, some sites see much higher percentages. Google has said that it expects overall search queries on mobile devices to exceed desktop searches (within the United States) — perhaps by the time you read this.

That's been true for some time, but what put the SEO world in a tizzy was when Google started talking about how it was going to start taking into consideration how a site would display on a mobile device, and factor that into ranking for when a search was carried out from such a device. (In an example of typical SEO-world drama, this change was labeled by many as *Mobilegeddon*.)

That is, if your site doesn't display well on a smart phone, it might not rank as well when someone searches from a smart phone. (Not surprisingly, there's no effect on regular-size devices; in fact, laptops aren't considered mobile devices from this perspective, and tablets are explicitly excluded by Google from this issue — it's the smart phone searches that are the SEO problem).

So, what's it mean to you? If you're about to build a new site, you really should plan to build a mobile-friendly site; that's easier than you might imagine, as many recent versions of CMS tools can do this for you automatically. If you already have a site . . . well, that's a problem; it might take a lot of work to rebuild.

However, most Web sites aren't mobile friendly; thus, many of your competitors probably don't have mobile friendly sites, limiting the "damage." Long term, this could cause your business serious problems.

There are essentially three ways to make a site mobile friendly:

- ✔ **Responsive Design:** This uses sophisticated HTML to automatically change the layout of a site's Web pages to suit the particular device on which it is being displayed. It's probably the most popular method these days.

  Google recommends responsive design.

- ✔ **Dynamic Serving:** With this method, you have two versions of your Web site: one for smart phones, and another for larger devices. The Web server decides which version to send when a page is requested.

- ✔ **Separate URLs:** In this case, you have two versions of your site. The server directs the user to the most appropriate site, on a different URL, depending on the device.

If I go any further, it will be way beyond the scope of this book, but here are a couple of pages to show you more:

- ✔ Google's information on making your site mobile friendly:

  `https://developers.google.com/webmasters/mobile-sites`

- ✔ Google's test tool; enter a Web page URL and Google will tell you whether it's mobile friendly:

  `https://www.google.com/webmasters/tools/mobile-friendly`

HTTPS

Google is now encouraging Web sites to *go HTTPS*. HTTPS means *HyperText Transfer Protocol over SSL* (or *over TLS*), or maybe *HyperText Transfer Protocol Secure*. Let's not get too geeky here; essentially, when your Web browser uses HTTPS to communicate with a Web server, the communication is encrypted. Believe it or not, even the NSA can't read the communications if they're intercepted. It's HTTPS that's being used by ecommerce sites when you send your credit-card information to make a purchase; you've probably seen `https://` for a URL in the browser Location bar, or a little lock icon indicating the user of HTTPS. (In fact, it isn't all about encryption of communications, it's also about authentication and data integrity; I'll leave you delve into the details if you're interested.)

In 2014, Google launched its *HTTPS Everywhere* program, a program aimed at getting the *entire Web* to go HTTPS. In other words, not just financial transactions should use HTTPS, but *everything* going across the Web should use it. I won't go into detail about why; you can search for *http everywhere* to learn more.

However, as part of this program, Google has decided to start using whether or not a page is being delivered across an HTTPS connection as part of the ranking algorithm. Before you get worried, right now it doesn't count for much. Here's what Google said when it first announced this:

> . . .*we're starting to use HTTPS as a ranking signal. For now it's only a very lightweight signal — affecting fewer than 1% of global queries, and carrying less weight than other signals such as* high-quality content — *while we give webmasters time to switch to HTTPS. But over time, we may decide to strengthen it, because we'd like to encourage all website owners to switch from HTTP to HTTPS to keep everyone safe on the web.*

The writing's on the wall. Anyone beginning a new Web site probably should take this into consideration from the start, and owners of existing sites might want to consider adding HTTPS soon. It isn't hugely complicated, but it's a bit geeky, and beyond the scope of this book. You can find more information here:

```
https://support.google.com/webmasters/answer/6073543
```

Seeing Through a Search Engine's Eyes

What a search engine sees when it loads one of your pages isn't always the same as what your browser sees. To understand why, you need to understand how a Web page is created. See Figure 7-1 and read this quick explanation:

1. A user types a URL into his browser or clicks a link, causing the browser to send a message to the Web server asking for a particular page.

2. The Web server grabs the page and quickly reads it to see whether it needs to do anything to the page before sending it.

3. The Web server compiles the page, if necessary.

   In some cases, the Web server may have to run ASP or PHP scripts, for instance, or it may have to find an *SSI (server-side include),* an instruction telling it to grab something from another page and insert it into the one it's about to send.

4. After the server has completed any instructions, it sends the page to the browser.

5. When the browser receives the page, it reads through the page looking for instructions and then, if necessary, further compiles the page.

6. When the browser is finished, it displays the page for the user to read.

   Here are a few examples of instructions the browser may find inside the file:

   - **<SCRIPT> tags containing JavaScript scripts or references to scripts stored in other files:** The browser then runs those scripts.

   - **Cascading Style Sheets (CSS):** These instructions tell the browser how the page — in particular, the text on the page — should be formatted.

   - **References to images or other forms of media:** After the browser finds these references, it pulls them into the page.

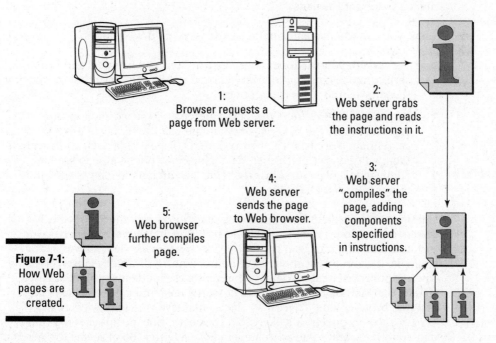

1:
Browser requests a page from Web server.

2:
Web server grabs the page and reads the instructions in it.

3:
Web server "compiles" the page, adding components specified in instructions.

4:
Web server sends the page to Web browser.

5:
Web browser further compiles page.

Figure 7-1:
How Web pages are created.

Scripting

ASP and *PHP* scripts are little programs that are written into Web pages. The scripts are read by a program working in association with the Web server when a page is requested. The searchbots see the results of these scripts because the scripts have been run by the time the Web server sends the page. *Server-side includes (SSIs)* are simple statements placed into the HTML pages that name another file and, in effect, say to the Web server, "Grab the information in this file and drop it into the Web page here." Again, the searchbots see the information in the SSI because the Web server inserts the information before sending the Web page.

So that's what happens normally when Web pages are created. But what about *searchbots,* the programs used by search engines to index pages? Well, in the past, they worked differently. When a searchbot requested a page, the server did what it would normally do — construct the page according to instructions and send it to the searchbot. But the searchbot didn't follow all the instructions in the page — it just read the page. For example, it wouldn't run scripts in the page, and it wouldn't use the Cascading Style Sheet information to format the page.

Thus, you can use two kinds of instructions to build Web pages:

✔ **Server-side instructions:** These instructions, such as ASP and PHP scripts and SSI instructions, are carried out by the server before sending the information to the searchbots.

✔ **Browser-side (or *client-side*) instructions:** These instructions are embedded into the Web page and, in the past, generally ignored by searchbots. For instance, if you created a page with a navigation system built with JavaScript, the search engines may not be able to read it. Some people even used browser-side instructions to *intentionally* hide things from search engines.

But things are different today; the only question is how much. Google, for instance, now does read browser-side scripting. It can read JavaScript, for instance, allowing it to read content inserted into pages using scripts. For example, it can read Facebook page content, much of which is inserted using JavaScript browser side. Today's searchbots are much more sophisticated than in the past. But that doesn't necessarily mean they'll read everything inserted browser side. There's an almost limitless variety of ways to use scripts and stylesheets; it's likely that the searchbots decipher some things and not others, and some search engines do a better job of seeing the results of browser-side scripts than others.

My belief is that if you want to make sure that something is definitely seen by the search engines, place it into the page server side. Yes, Google can read Facebook pages, but that doesn't necessarily mean it'll spend the time to figure out the scripts on *your* pages.

These concepts are very important:

Server side = visible to searchbots

Browser side = sometimes not visible to searchbots

Understanding Keyword Concepts

Here's the basic concept of using keywords: You put keywords into your Web pages in such a manner that search engines can find them, read them, and regard them as significant.

Your keyword list is probably very long, perhaps hundreds of keywords, so you need to pick a few to work with. (If you haven't yet developed a keyword list, refer to Chapter 6 for details.) The keywords you pick will be either

- Words near the top of the list that have many searches.

- Words lower on the list — in the "long tail — that may be worth targeting because you have relatively few competitors for those keywords.

It's often easy to create pages that rank well for the keywords at the bottom of your list because they're unusual terms that don't appear in many Web pages. However, they're at the bottom of your list because *people don't often search for them!* Therefore, you have to decide whether it's worthwhile to rank well on a search term that's searched for only once or twice a month.

Picking one or two phrases per page

You optimize each page for one or two keyword phrases. By *optimize,* I mean that you create the page in such a manner that it has a good chance of ranking well for the chosen keyword phrase or phrases when someone uses them in a search engine.

You can't optimize a page well for more than one keyword phrase at a time. For example, the <TITLE> tag is one of the most important components on a Web page, and the best position for a keyword is at the beginning of that tag. Clearly, you can place only one phrase at the beginning of the tag. (However, sometimes, as you find out in Chapter 6, you can combine keyword phrases — for example, optimizing for *rodent racing scores* also, in effect, optimizes for *rodent racing.*)

Have primary and secondary keyword phrases in mind for each page you're creating, but also consider all the keywords you're interested in working into the pages. For instance, you might create a page that you plan to optimize for the phrase *rodent racing,* but you also have several other keywords that you want to scatter around your site: *rodent racing scores, handicap, gerbil, rodentia, furry friend events,* and so on. Typically, you pick one main phrase for each page and incorporate the other keyword phrases throughout the page, where appropriate.

Place your keyword list into a word processor, enlarge the font, and then print the list and tape it to the wall. Occasionally, while creating your pages, glance at the list to remind yourself which words you need to weave into your pages.

Checking prominence

The term *prominence* refers to where the keyword appears — how prominent it is within a page component (the body text, the `<TITLE>` tag, and so on). A word near the top of the page is more prominent than one near the bottom; a word at the beginning of a `<TITLE>` tag is more prominent than one at the end; a word at the beginning of the `DESCRIPTION` meta tag is more prominent than one at the end; and so on.

Prominence is good. If you're creating a page with a particular keyword or keyword phrase in mind, make that term prominent — in the body text, in the `<TITLE>` tag, in the `DESCRIPTION` meta tag, and elsewhere — to convey to search engines that the keyword phrase is important in this particular page. Consider this title tag:

```
<TITLE>Everything about Rodents - Looking after Them, Feeding Them, Rodent
        Racing, and More.</TITLE>
```

When you read this tag, you can see that *Rodent Racing* is just one of several terms the page is related to. The search engine comes to the same conclusion because the term is near the end of the title, meaning that it's probably not the predominant term. But what about the following tag?

```
<TITLE>Rodent Racing - Looking after Your Rodents, Feeding Them, Everything You
        Need to Know</TITLE>
```

Placing *Rodent Racing* at the beginning of the tag places the stress on that concept; search engines are likely to conclude that the page is mainly about rodent racing.

Watching density

Another important concept is *keyword density*. When a user searches for a keyword phrase, the search engine looks at all pages that contain the phrase and checks the *density* — the ratio of the search phrase to the total number of words in the page.

Suppose that you search for *rodent racing* and the search engine finds a page that contains 400 words, with the phrase *rodent racing* appearing 10 times — that's a total of 20 words. Because 20 is 5 percent of 400, the keyword density is 5 percent.

Keyword density is important, but you can overdo it. If the search engine finds that the search phrase makes up 50 percent of the words in the page, it may decide that the page was created purely to grab the search engine's attention for that phrase and thus decide to ignore it. On the other hand, if the density is too low, you risk having the search engines regard other pages as more relevant for the search.

You can get hung up on keyword density, and some people use special tools to check the density on every page. This strategy can be very time consuming, especially for large sites. You're probably better off eyeballing the density in most cases.

Here's my general rule: If the phrase for which you're optimizing appears an awful lot, you've overdone it. If the text sounds clumsy because of the repetition, you've overdone it.

Placing keywords throughout your site

Suppose that someone searches for *rodent racing,* and the search engine finds two sites that use the term. One site has a single page in which the term occurs; the other site has dozens of pages containing the term. Which site does the search engine think is most relevant? The one that has many pages related to the subject, of course.

In many cases, you're not likely to grab a top position by simply creating a single page optimized for the keyword phrase. You may need dozens, perhaps hundreds, of pages to grab the search engines' attention (with plenty of links between pages and from other sites back to yours — which you find out about in Chapters 16 through 18).

Creating Your Web Pages

When you're creating your Web pages, you need to focus on two essential elements:

✔ The underlying structure of the pages

✔ The text you plunk down on the pages

The next sections fill you in on what you need to look out for.

Naming files

Search engines get clues about the nature of a site from its domain name as well as from the site's directory and file structure. The added lift is probably not large, but every little bit counts, right? You might as well name directories, Web pages, and images by using keywords.

For example, rather than create a directory named /events/, you could name it /rodent-racing-events/. Rather than have a file named gb123.jpg, you can use a more descriptive name, such as rodent-racing-scores.jpg. Don't have too many dashes in the file and directory names, though, because overdoing it may cause search engines to ignore the name.

You should separate keywords in a name with dashes, but *not* with underscores, despite what your Web designer may tell you. In the olden days, Google regarded underscores as *part* of the word, and dashes as separators (as a space, in effect; for obscure technical reasons, you should never put actual spaces in folder and filenames).

Years ago, rumors spread around the SEO community that Google had changed this behavior, and that it now treated underscores and dashes as the same thing. However, the last really reliable comment on this issue that I have been able to find (from Matt Cutts; see Chapter 23) is that Google never actually made this change, though they had considered it. (Ironically, it was a perhaps misinterpreted comment from Matt that started the rumor.)

So it seems that Google still (most likely) regards *rodent_racing*, for instance, as a single word, but *rodent-racing* as two words. Other search engines may operate differently; for instance, Bing probably treats both symbols the same, and likely always has. Thus, I still recommend dashes — hyphens — for several reasons:

✔ It's what Google recommends, and if it's good enough for Google, it's good enough for me.

✔ Some search engines may still have problems with underscores; most likely, Google still does.

✔ There was never any real reason for using underscores anyway, despite what many geeks seemed to think.

It isn't a huge deal, but in the world of SEO, every little optimization element counts. So don't let anyone tell you that you *should* be using underscores rather than dashes in file and directory names — it's simply not true!

Creating directory structure

First, let me explain a common belief in the SEO business: It may be a good idea to keep a *flat* directory structure in your Web site — that is, keep your pages as close to the root domain as possible, rather than have a complicated multilevel directory tree. Create a directory for each navigation tab and keep all the files in that directory.

Many observers believe that search engines downgrade pages that are lower in the directory structure. This effect is probably small, but the theory is that you're better off using a structure with fewer sublevels than with more. For instance, the first page that follows, according to this theory, would be weighted more highly than the second page:

```
http://www.domainname.com/page.html
```

```
http://www.domainname.com/dir1/dir2/dir3/dir4/page.html
```

However, a flat directory structure is probably not terribly important. Matt Cutts of Google (see Chapter 23) claims that the directory structure doesn't matter to Google, the single most important search engine, of course. And sometimes it's nice to use a directory structure to add a few keywords to the URL to tell the search engines what the page is about. For instance, you might have the following in a real estate site:

```
http://www.domain.com/real-estate/colorado-homes-for-sale/denver-county/
            lakewood.html
```

Don't use too many hyphens, though; a few here and there are okay (I have three in the second directory name), but overdoing it might cause problems.

Viewing TITLE tags

Most search engines use the site's <TITLE> tag as the link and main title of the site's listing on the search results page, as shown in Figure 7-2.

`<TITLE>` tags tell a browser what text to display in the browser's title bar and are very important for search engines as well. Searchbots read page titles and use that information to determine what the pages are about. If your `<TITLE>` tags have a keyword between them, search engines naturally assume that the word must have something to do with the content or purpose of the Web page.

The `<TITLE>` tag is one of the most important components as far as search engines are concerned. However, these tags are often wasted because so many sites don't bother placing useful keywords in them. Titles are often generic: *Welcome to Acme, Inc.*, or *Acme Inc. – Home Page*. Such titles are not beneficial for search engine optimization.

This is the page's URL

This text comes from between the page's `<TITLE></TITLE>` tags

This text is often the page's meta description text

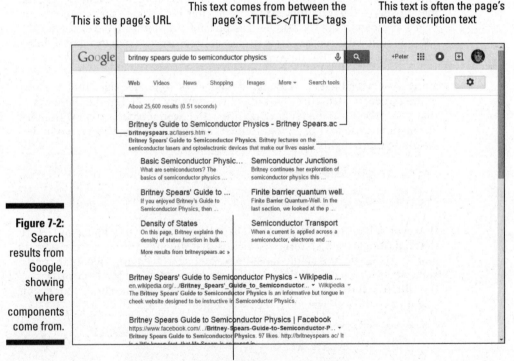

Figure 7-2:
Search results from Google, showing where components come from.

These are "sitelinks"; see Chapters 13 and 24

I searched at Google for *intitle:welcome* to find out how many pages have the word *welcome* in their `<TITLE>` tags. The result? Around 198 million! Around 125 million have *welcome to* in the title (*allintitle:"welcome to"*). Interestingly, these numbers are far lower than they were a few years ago, perhaps indicating evolving ideas related to Web design and SEO.

Having *Welcome to* as the first words in your title is a waste of space — only slightly more wasteful than your company name! Give the search engines a really strong clue about your site's content by using a keyword phrase in the <TITLE> tags. Here's how:

1. **Place your** <TITLE> **tags immediately below the** <HEAD> **tag.**

2. **Place 40 to 60 characters between the** <TITLE> **and** </TITLE> **tags, including spaces.**

3. **Put the keyword phrase you want to focus on for this page at the beginning of the** <TITLE> **tag.**

   If you want, you can repeat the primary keywords once. Limit the number of two-letter words and very common words (known as *stop words*), such as *as, the,* and *a,* because search engines ignore them.

Here's a sample <TITLE> tag:

```
<TITLE>Rodent Racing Info. Rats, Mice, Gerbils, Stoats, All Kinds of Rodent
       Racing</TITLE>
```

(By the way, I am aware that a stoat is not, strictly speaking, a rodent, but it looks quite rodenty to me, and I'm sure someone races them.)

Although the title tag is used as the link on the search-results page, it will be truncated if it's too long. On Google, for instance, depending on spacing between words, the title may be truncated to around 50 to 55 characters and have an ellipsis (. . .) displayed at the end of the line — that is, *Rodent Racing Info. Rats, Mice, Gerbils, Stoats, All Kinds of Rodent Racing* may be displayed as *Rodent Racing Info. Rats, Mice, Gerbils, Stoats, All. . .* — so make sure you get the important words that you want to be visible on the search-results page into those first 55 or so characters.

Also, use title case (capitalizing the initial letter of each word, as in *Rodent Racing Info. Rats, Mice, Gerbils, Stoats, All Kinds of Rodent Racing,* not *Rodent racing info. rats, mice, gerbils, stoats, all kinds of rodent racing*). Title case is much easier for people to read as they scan down the page.

The <TITLE> tag and often the DESCRIPTION tag (explained in the next section) appear on the search results page, so both these tags should contain text designed to encourage people to visit your site.

Using the DESCRIPTION meta tag

Meta tags are special HTML tags that you can use to carry information, which browsers or other programs can then read. When Internet search engines were first created, Webmasters included meta tags in their pages to make it easy for search engines to determine what the pages were about. Search engines also used these meta tags when deciding how to rank the page for different keywords.

The DESCRIPTION meta tag describes the Web page to the search engines. Search engines use this meta tag in two ways:

✔ They read and index the text in the tag and, in some circumstances, use it to figure out a page's relevance to a search term. (Google claims it *doesn't* use the tag for page ranking, but other search engines may.)

✔ In many cases, they use the text verbatim in the search results page. That is, if your Web page is returned in the search results page, the search engine may grab the text from the DESCRIPTION tag and place it under the text from the <TITLE> tag so that the searcher can read your description.

Now, this process can vary between search engines, and over time for the same search engine. Until sometime in 2007, in most cases, Google *didn't* use the text from the DESCRIPTION meta tag in its search results page. Rather, Google grabbed a block of text where it found the search keywords on the page and then used that text in the results page. However, these days it will often use the DESCRIPTION tag text if it finds the searched-for words in the description. If it doesn't, or if it finds only some of the searched for words, it may grab text from within the page content and display that instead. The DESCRIPTION meta tag is pretty important, so you should definitely use it. Think of it as serving two purposes:

✔ It's a page-ranking tool, helping, in *some* search engines, the page to rank higher on the search-results page.

✔ It's a sales pitch, seen by people viewing the search engine's search-results page; it should encourage people to click the link.

As is the <TITLE> tag, the DESCRIPTION may be truncated; in Google search results, the text will be truncated to around 150 characters. For instance, here's the description-tag text from CNN.com:

```
Find the latest breaking news and information on the top stories, weather,
business, entertainment, politics, and more. For in-depth coverage, CNN provides
             special reports, video, audio, photo galleries, and interactive
             guides
```

And here's how it appears in the Google search results:

```
Find the latest breaking news and information on the top stories, weather,
business, entertainment, politics, and more. For in-depth coverage, CNN provides
... .
```

So if you want part of the text to be seen, make sure it appears before that 150th-or-so character. You can have a longer description and get a few more keywords in there (though Google doesn't use it for ranking, so you won't be helping your position, at least with that search engine), but don't make it too long; perhaps 220 or 230 characters maximum, including spaces (the preceding CNN description is 225). Place the DESCRIPTION tag immediately below the <TITLE></TITLE> tags tags. Here's an example:

```
<META NAME="description" CONTENT="Rodent Racing - Scores, Schedules,
Everything Rodent Racing. Mouse Racing, Stoat Racing, Rat Racing, Gerbil Racing.
The Web's Top Rodent Racing Systems and Racing News">
```

As with the <TITLE> tag, title case is also a good thing; title case makes the DESCRIPTION text easier to read. Duplicating your most important keywords once is okay, but don't overdo it, or you'll upset the search engines. *Don't*, for instance, do this:

```
<META NAME="description" CONTENT="Rodent Racing, Rodent Racing,
Rodent Racing, Rodent Racing, Rodent Racing, Rodent Racing, Rodent Racing,
Rodent Racing, Rodent Racing, Rodent Racing">
```

Overloading your DESCRIPTION (or any other page component) with the same keyword or keyword phrase is known as *spamming* (a term I hate, but hey, I don't make the rules), and trying such tricks may get your page penalized; rather than *help* your page's search engine position, it may cause search engines to omit it from their indexes.

I also recommend avoiding sentences in your Description tag; rather, try to get the important words in front of people, conveying important information very quickly. Users generally scan search-results pages, looking at each search result for no more than about a second before moving to the next. If you provide a sentence for them to dig through . . . they won't. For instance, consider these two descriptions:

```
Enjoy the experience of finding clearance shoes, clothing, and accessories at
the very best prices. You'll find fashions from Acme, athletic gear from Widget,
comfortable shoes from Thingamibob
```

```
Clearance Shoes, Clothing, Accessories - Very Best Prices - Fashions: Acme -
Athletic Gear: Widget - Comfortable Shoes: Thingamibob
```

These two pieces of text convey exactly the same information, but it's much quicker and easier for the searcher to understand the second example than the first. You should consider your DESCRIPTION tag to be not only a search engine component but also a sales tool. Remember that much of the tag — perhaps the first 150 to 160 characters — will quite likely be seen in the search results, so you want to use text that encourages people to click the link — text that helps your links stand apart from the others on the page. An example is a compelling sales message or your phone number, which helps build credibility by ensuring that people recognize that it's a real site and not some search engine spam result! (Using a phone number also has the effect of making your listing stand out a little; the eye "trips" over changes in the pattern, such as numbers and capitalized words.) You might also want to think about your site's Unique Selling Proposition (USP). What makes your site special compared to others — a huge selection? Free shipping? Remember, this is a sales pitch to get people to click, so think about how you can do that.

Tapping into the KEYWORDS meta tag

The KEYWORDS meta tag was originally created as an indexing tool — that is, a way for the page author to tell search engines what the page is about by listing (yep) keywords. Although quite important many years past, this meta tag isn't so important these days. Some search engines may use it, but many don't, and even those that do use it don't give it much value. (Google and Bing almost certainly don't use it. Ask.com may, but again, it doesn't give it much weight.) Still, you might as well include the KEYWORDS meta tag. You do have a list of keywords, after all.

Don't worry too much about the tag — it's not worth spending a lot of time over. Here are a few points to consider, though:

- **Limit the tag to 10 to 12 words.** Originally, the KEYWORDS tag could be very large, up to 1,000 characters. These days, many in the optimization business are wary of appearing to be spamming search engines by stuffing keywords into any page component, and thus recommend that you use short KEYWORDS tags.

- **You can separate each keyword with a comma and a space.** However, you don't have to use both — you can have a comma and no space, or a space and no comma.

- **Make sure that most of the keywords in the tag are also in the body text.** If they aren't, the tag probably won't do you any good. Many people also use the KEYWORDS tag as a good place to stuff spelling mistakes that are commonly searched.

- **Don't use a lot of repetition.** You shouldn't do this, for instance: *Rodent Racing, Rodent Racing, Rodent Racing, Rodent Racing, Rodent Racing, Rodent Racing,* or even *Rodent Racing, Rodent Racing Scores, Rodent Racing, Gerbils, Rodent Racing Scores, Rodent Racing. . . .*

✔ **Don't use the same** KEYWORD **tag in all your pages.** You can create a primary tag to use in your first page and then copy it to other pages and move terms around in the tag.

Here's an example of a well-constructed KEYWORD tag:

```
<META NAME="keywords" CONTENT="rodent racing, racing rodents, gerbils, mice,
            mouse, raceing, mouse, rodent races, rat races, mouse races,
            stoat, stoat racing">
```

But again, don't waste much time on this tag. It's really not important at all.

Using other meta tags

What about other meta tags? Sometimes if you look at the source of a page, you see all sorts of meta tags, as shown in Figure 7-3 (in bold to make seeing them easier). Meta tags are useful for various reasons, but from a search engine perspective, you can forget most of them. (And most meta tags really aren't of much use for any purpose.)

```
<meta name="resource-type" content="document">
<meta http-equiv="pragma" content="no-cache">
<meta name="revisit-after" content="1">
<meta name="classification" content="Arts and Crafts">
<meta name="description"
content="New York Alive! Photographs is an online gallery containing dozens of signed, original, custom-printed black and white photographs of New York City, its landmarks, buildings, neighborhoods, people, and places.  Buy original images for home or office direct from the photographers.">
<meta name="keywords"
content=" New York City, New York, New York NY, NYC, skyline, landmarks, buildings, Manhattan, Brooklyn, neighborhood, neighbourhood, neighborhoods, neighbourhoods, photography, fine, fine art, art, artist, artists, artistic, arts, photo, photographic, photographs, photograph, photographer, photographers, pictures, black, black and white, white, images, imagery, image, gallery, galleries, virtual, online, on-line, exhibits, exibits, exhibition, exhibitions, exhibit, contemporary, Central Park, Greenwich Village, Soho, Wall Street, Statue of Liberty, Harlem, Washington Heights, Lower East Side, Ethnic, Empire State Building, Flatiron, Flat Iron, Building, Chrysler, Brooklyn Bridge, Wall Street, New York Stock Exchange, Chinatown, Little Italy, Yankees, people">
<meta name="robots" content="ALL">
<meta name="distribution" content="Global">
<meta name="rating" content="General">
<meta name="copyright" content="(c) Naomi Diamant, 2000. All rights reserved.">
<meta name="author" content="Abacus Consultants">
<meta http-equiv="reply-to" content="abacusconsultants@yahoo.com">
<meta name="language" content="English">
<meta name="doc-type" content="Public" ">
<meta name="doc-class" content="Completed">
<meta name="doc-rights" content="Copywritten Work">
```

Figure 7-3: Examples of meta tags you generally don't need.

You've heard about DESCRIPTION and KEYWORDS meta tags, but also of relevance to search engine optimization — though not always useful — are the REVISIT-AFTER and ROBOTS meta tags:

- ✔ REVISIT-AFTER tells search engines how often to reindex the page. Save the electrons; don't expect search engines to follow your instructions. Search engines re-index pages on their own schedules.

- ✔ ROBOTS blocks search engines from indexing pages. (I discuss this topic in detail in "Blocking searchbots," later in this chapter.) But many Web authors use it to *tell* search engines to index a page. Here's an example:

```
<META NAME="robots" CONTENT="ALL">
```

This tag is a waste of time. If a search engine finds your page and wants to index it, and hasn't been blocked from doing so, it will. And if the search engine doesn't want to index the page, it doesn't. Telling the search engine to do so doesn't make a difference.

There are also a few special Google meta tags:

```
<META NAME="googlebot" CONTENT="nosnippet">
```

This meta tag tells Google not to place a description under a search result's link. This tag also has the effect of removing the page from Google's *cache* (the saved version of an indexed Web page; you see <u>Cached</u> links by entries in the search-results page).

Here's another example:

```
<META NAME="googlebot" CONTENT="noarchive">
```

This meta tag tells Google not to place a copy of the page into the cache. (The nosnippet tag incorporates the noarchive command.) If you have an anal corporate attorney on staff who doesn't like the idea of Google storing a copy of your company's information on its servers, you can tell Google not to. There's also the NOINDEX tag, which tells Google not to index the page, and the NOFOLLOW tag, which tells it not to follow links from that page.

Including image ALT text

You use the <IMG> tag to insert images into Web pages. This tag can include the ALT= attribute, which means *alt*ernative text. ALT text was originally displayed if the browser viewing the page couldn't display images. ALT text is also used by programs that "speak" the page (for individuals without sight). In many browsers, ALT text also appears in a little pop-up box when you hold your mouse over an image for a few moments.

ALT attributes are also read by search engines. Why? Because these tag "attributes" offer another clue about the content of the Web page, by providing a description of what the image is. How much do ALT tags help? Perhaps not so much these days, because some Web designers have abused the technique by stuffing ALT attributes with tons of keywords. But using ALT attributes can't hurt (assuming that you *don't* stuff them with tons of keywords, but rather simply drop in a few here and there) and may even help push your page up a little in the search engine rankings (and can also help the specific image rank for those keywords in Image Search results).

You can place keywords in your ALT attributes like this:

```
<IMG SRC="rodent-racing-1.jpg" ALT="Rodent Racing - Ratty Winners of our Latest
          Rodent Racing Event">
```

It's definitely a good idea to use ALT attributes on image links, by the way. Doing so gives Google an idea of what the page referenced by the link is about.

Adding body text

You need text in your page. How much? More than a little, but not too much. Maybe 200 to 400 words is a good range. Don't get hung up on these numbers, though. If you put an article in a page and the article is 1,000 words, that's fine, and some pages may not have much text at all. But in general, when building a page that you want people to find in the search engines, a number in the 200 to 400 word range is good. That amount of content allows you to really define what the page is about and helps the search engine understand what the page is about.

Keep in mind that a Web site needs content in order to be noticed by search engines. (For more on this topic, see Chapter 11.) If the site doesn't have much content for the search engine to read, the search engine will have trouble determining what the page is about and may not properly rank it. In effect, the page loses points in the contest for search engine ranking. Certainly, placing keywords in content is not all there is to being ranked in search engines; as you find out in Chapters 16 through 19, for instance, linking to the pages is also very important. But keywords in content are very significant, so search engines have a natural bias toward Web sites with a large amount of content.

This bias toward content could be considered very unfair. After all, your site may be the perfect fit for a particular keyword search, even if you don't have much content in your site. In fact, inappropriate sites often appear in searches simply because they have a lot of pages, some of which have the right keywords.

Suppose that your rodent-racing Web site is the only site in the world at which you can buy tickets for rodent-racing events. Your site doesn't provide a lot of content because rodent-racing fans simply want to be able to buy tickets and nothing more. However, because your site has less content than other sites, it is at a disadvantage to sites that have lots of content related to rodent racing, even if these other sites aren't directly related to the subject. (On the other hand, if rodent-racing fans throughout the world decide that your site is *the* one on which to buy tickets, and enough of them link to you, you can still rank well regardless of how much page content you have.)

You can't do much to confront this problem, except to add more content (or create a lot of links)! You can find some ideas on where to get content in Chapter 11 and read all about links in Chapters 16 through 19.

Creating headers: CSS versus <H> tags

Back when the Web began, browsers defined what pages looked like. A designer could say, "I want body text here and a heading there and an address over there," but the designer had no way to define what the page actually looked like. The browser decided. The browser defined what a header looked like, what body text looked like, and so on. The page might appear one way in one browser and another way in a different browser.

These days, designers have a useful tool available to them: *Cascading Style Sheets (CSS)*. With CSS, designers can define exactly what each element should look like on a page.

Now, here's the problem. HTML has several tags that define headers: <H1>, <H2>, <H3>, and so on. These headers are useful in search engine optimization because when you put keywords into a heading, you're saying to a search engine, "These keywords are so important that they appear in my heading text." Search engines pay more attention to them, weighing them more heavily than keywords in body text.

But many designers have given up on using the <H> tags and rely solely on CSS to make headers look the way they want them to. The plain <H> tags are often rather ugly when displayed in browsers, so designers don't like to use them. <H> tags also cause spacing issues; for example, an <H1> tag always includes a space above and below the text contained in the tag.

However, there's no reason you can't use both <H> tags *and* CSS. You can use style sheets in two basic ways:

✔ Create a style class and then assign that class to the text you want to format.

✔ Define the style for a particular HTML tag.

Many designers do the former; they create a style class in the style sheet, as in the following example:

```
.headtext { font-family: Verdana, Arial, Helvetica, sans-serif; font-size: 16px;
            font-weight: bold; color: #3D3D3D }
```

Then they assign the style class to a piece of text, like this:

```
<DIV CLASS="headtext">Rodent Racing for the New Millennium!</div>
```

In this example, the headtext class makes the text appear the way the designer wants the headings to appear. But, as far as search engines are concerned, this is just normal body text.

A better way is to define the <H> tags in the style sheets, as in the following example:

```
H1 {
font-family: Verdana, Arial, Helvetica, sans-serif;
font-size: 16px;
font-weight: bold;
color: #3D3D3D
 }
```

Now, whenever you add an <H1> tag to your pages, the browser reads the style sheet and knows exactly which font family, size, weight, and color you want. It's the best of both worlds — you get the appearance you want, and search engines know it's an <H1> tag. (Note to Web designers who don't want to listen: Don't take my word for it. Even Google recommends that you use <H> tags.)

I have heard, in the last year or so, some in the SEO industry stating that H1 tags don't matter anymore; in one case, because the H1 tags don't help much, and putting the tags in a larger font seems to help just as much. My response? Again, Google recommends you use H tags, so until I hear someone at Google stating otherwise, that's the way I'd go. And as you can use CSS to format the H tags to look any way you want . . . why *shouldn't* you use H tags?

Formatting text

You can also tell search engines that a particular word might be significant in several other ways. If the text is in some way different from most of the other text in the page, search engines may assume that it has been set off for some reason, that the Web designer has treated it differently because it *is* in some way different and more significant than the other words.

Here are a few things you can do to set your keywords apart from the other words on the page:

- ✔ Make the text **bold.**
- ✔ Make the text *italic.*
- ✔ Use Title Case (uppercase the First Letter in Each Word and lowercase the other letters in the word).
- ✔ Put the keywords in bullet lists.

For each page, you have a particular keyword phrase in mind; this is the phrase for which you use the preceding techniques.

Another way to emphasize the text is to make a piece of text larger than the surrounding text. (Just make sure that you do this in a way that doesn't look tacky.) For example, you can use <H> tags for headers but also use slightly larger text at the beginning of a paragraph or for subheaders.

Creating links

Links in your pages serve several purposes:

- ✔ They help searchbots find other pages in your site.
- ✔ Keywords in links tell search engines about the pages that the links are pointing at.
- ✔ Keywords in links also tell search engines about the page containing the links.

You need links into — and out of — your pages. You don't want *dangling* or *orphan* pages — pages with links into them but no links out. All your pages should be part of the navigation structure. It's also a good idea to have links within the body text, too.

Search engines read link text for not only clues about the page being referred to but also hints about the page containing the link. I've seen situations in which links convinced a search engine that the page the links pointed to were relevant for the keywords used in the links, even though the page didn't contain those words. The classic example was an intentional manipulation of Google, late in 2003, to get it to display George Bush's bio (www.whitehouse.gov/president/gwbbio.html) when people searched for the term *miserable failure.* This was done by a small group of people using links in blog pages. Despite the fact that this page contained neither the word *miserable* nor the word *failure,* and certainly not the term *miserable failure,* a few dozen links with the words *miserable failure* in the link text were enough to trick Google.

(After several years, Google put a stop to the *miserable failure* situation, but the principle still works. I discuss this Googlebomb in Chapter 16.)

So when you're creating pages, create links on the page to other pages and make sure that other pages within your site link back to the page you're creating, using the keywords you placed in your <TITLE> tag.

Don't create simple Click Here links or You'll Find More Information Here links. These words (also called *anchor text)* don't help you. Instead, create links like these:

> For more information, see our *rodent-racing scores page*.
>
> Our *rodent-racing background page* provides you with the information you're looking for.
>
> Visit our *rat events* and *mouse events* pages for more info.

Links are critical. In Chapters 16 through 19, you find out about another aspect of links: getting links from other sites to point back to yours.

Using other company and product names

Here's a common scenario: Many of your prospective visitors and customers are searching online for other companies' names or for the names of products produced or sold by other companies. Can you use these names in your pages? Yes, but be careful *how* you use them.

Many large companies are aware of this practice, and a number of lawsuits have been filed that relate to the use of keywords by companies other than the trademark owners. Here are a few examples:

- ✔ A law firm that deals with Internet domain disputes sued Web-design and Web-hosting firms for using its name, Oppedahl & Larson, in their KEYWORDS meta tags. These firms thought that merely having the words in the tags could bring traffic to their sites. The law firm won. Duh! (Didn't anyone ever tell you not to upset large law firms?)

- ✔ Playboy Enterprises sued Web sites that were using the terms *playboy* and *playmates* throughout their pages, site names, domain names, and meta tags to successfully boost their positions. Not surprisingly, Playboy won.

- ✔ Insituform Technologies, Inc. sued National Envirotech Group after discovering that Envirotech was using its name in its meta tags. Envirotech lost. The judge felt that using the name in the meta tag without having any relevant information in the body of the pages was clearly a strategy for misdirecting people to the Envirotech site.

So, yes, you can get sued. But then again, you can get sued for anything. In some instances, the plaintiff loses. Playboy won against a number of sites, but lost against former playmate Terri Welles. Playboy didn't want her to use the terms *playboy* and *playmate* on her Web site, but she believed she had the right to, as a former Playboy Playmate. A judge agreed with her. The real point of the Terri Welles case is that nobody owns a word, a product name, or a company name. They merely own the right to use it in certain contexts. Thus, Playboy doesn't own the word *playboy* — you can say "playboy," and you can use it in print. But Playboy owns the right to use the word in certain contexts and to stop other people from using it in those same contexts.

If you use product and company names to mislead or misrepresent, you could be in trouble. But legally speaking, you can use the terms in a valid, nonfraudulent manner. (Again, this doesn't necessarily protect you from getting sued.) For instance, you can have a product page in which you compare your products to another, named competitor. That's perfectly legal. No, I'm not a lawyer, but I'm perfectly willing to play one on TV, given the opportunity. And I would bet that you won't be seeing the courts banning product comparisons on Web sites.

If you have information about competing products and companies on your pages, used in a valid manner, you can also include the keywords in the `<TITLE>`, `DESCRIPTION`, and `KEYWORDS` tags, as Terri Welles did:

```
<META NAME="keywords" CONTENT=" terri, welles, playmate, playboy, model, models,
          semi-nudity, naked, censored by editors, censored by editors,
          censored by editors, censored by editors, censored by editors,
          censored by editors, censored by editors, censored by editors">
```

And there's nuthin' Playboy can do about it.

What's ironic is that firms are being sued for putting other companies' names and brand names in their `KEYWORDS` tags, when it has little or no influence on search engine rank these days.

Creating navigation structures that search engines can read

Your navigation structure needs to be visible to search engines. As I explain earlier in the section "Seeing Through a Search Engine's Eyes," some page components may be invisible to search engines. For instance, a navigation structure created with JavaScript may not be deciphered by some search engines. If the only way to navigate your Web site is with the JavaScript navigation, you could have a problem; some search engines may not be able to find their way around your site. (As discussed in Chapter 3, Google's pretty good at reading JavaScript these days; some other search engines may not be.)

Here are a few tips for search engine–friendly navigation:

- ✔ If you use JavaScript navigation or another technique that could be invisible (which is covered in more detail in Chapter 8), make sure that you have a plain HTML navigation system, too, such as basic text links at the bottom of your pages.

- ✔ Even if your navigation structure is visible to the search engines, you may want to have these bottom-of-page links as well. They're convenient for site visitors and provide another chance for the search engines to find your other pages, provide more keywords on the page, and provide more keyworded links to other pages.

  Yet another reason for bottom-of-page, basic text navigation: If you have some kind of image-button navigation, you don't have any keywords in the navigation for the search engines to read.

- ✔ Add a sitemap page and link to it from your main navigation. It provides another way for search engines to find all your pages.

- ✔ Whenever possible, provide keywords in text links as part of the navigation structure.

Blocking searchbots

You may want to block particular pages, or even entire areas of your Web site, from being indexed. Here are a few examples of pages or areas you may want to block:

- ✔ Pages that are under construction
- ✔ Areas of the site that you don't really want indexed by the search engines
- ✔ Pages with information intended for internal use (you should probably password-protect that area of the site, too, of course)

In the past, many Webmasters have also blocked directories in which they stored scripts and CSS style sheets. However, Google recommends that you do *not* do this, as Google actually does read and interpret scripts and style sheets these days.

Using the ROBOTS meta tag or the `robots.txt` file, you can tell search engines to stay away. The meta tag looks like this:

```
<META NAME="robots" CONTENT="noindex, nofollow">
```

This tag does two things: *noindex* means "Don't index this page" and *nofollow* means "Don't follow the links from this page."

To block entire directories on your Web site, create a text file called `robots.txt` and place it in your site's root directory — which is the same directory as your home page. When a search engine looks at a site, it generally requests the `robots.txt` file first; that is, it requests `http://www.domainname.com/robots.txt`.

The `robots.txt` file allows you to block specific search engines and allow others, but Webmasters rarely do so. In the file, you specify which search engine (user agent) you want to block and from which directories or files. Here's how:

```
User-agent: *
Disallow: /includes/
Disallow: /scripts/
Disallow: /info/scripts/
Disallow: /staff.html
```

Because `User-agent` is set to *, all searchbots are blocked from `www.domainname.com/includes/`, `www.domainname.com/scripts/`, `www.domainname.com/info/scripts/` directories, and the `www.domainname.com/staff.html` file. (If you know the name of a particular searchbot that you want to block, replace the asterisk with that name.)

Be careful with your `robots.txt` file. If you make incomplete changes and end up with the following code, you've just blocked all search engines from your entire site:

```
User-agent: *
Disallow: /
```

In fact, this technique is sometimes used nefariously; I know of one case in which someone hacked into a site and placed the `Disallow: /` command into the `robots.txt` file — and Google dropped the site from its index!

Google now has a nice little `robots.txt` test tool in its Webmasters Console; see Chapter 13 for more information.

Chapter 8

Using Structured Data Markup

*S*tructured data markup is a way to mark your data to provide contextual information to the searchbots. In effect, you're telling the search engines that "this is a photograph of a recipe, and this is our company logo, and this is a phone number," and so on.

HTML is a basic markup language that tells browsers what to do with information; how to display it on the page, essentially. But structured data markup goes one step further and tells the searchbots *what the data actually is or means*, so the search engines can use the data in various ways.

Both Google and Bing use structured data markup. You can find information about each search engine's implementation at these links:

```
http://support.google.com/webmasters/bin/answer.py?hl=en&answer=99170
```

```
www.bing.com/webmaster/help/marking-up-your-site-with-structured-data-3a93e731
```

Structured data markup lets you code information, such as the following:

- ✔ Company information
- ✔ Articles
- ✔ Events
- ✔ Local businesses
- ✔ Music
- ✔ Navigation breadcrumb trails
- ✔ Offers

- ✔ Organizations
- ✔ People
- ✔ Products
- ✔ Recipes
- ✔ Restaurants
- ✔ Reviews
- ✔ Software
- ✔ Videos

Right now, Google uses the data in several ways. It uses it to create

- ✔ Rich snippets
- ✔ Knowledge Graphs (large information boxes related to a person, location, company, and so on)
- ✔ Actions (such as playing music or streaming video direct from the search results)
- ✔ Reviews (Google collects together reviews — such as movie reviews — and displays them in the search results)

Bing also uses the data in similar ways, creating "rich snippets" and more advanced forms of data presentation in search results. Rich snippets? Let's look at that next.

Creating Rich Snippets

A *rich snippet* is a term for extended information that's displayed in search results. For instance, look at the Bing result in Figure 8-1; notice the rating information provided and the address? This information is provided to Bing by Citysearch using structured data markup. How? In the page, Citysearch has provided this code:

```
<p id="coreInfo.address" class="placeAddress block"
itemscope itemtype="http://schema.org/PostalAddress"
itemprop="address">
<span class="street-address" itemprop="streetAddress">811
SW 2nd St</span>,
<span class="locality"
itemprop="addressLocality">Tulia</span>,
<span class="region" itemprop="addressRegion">TX</span>
<span itemprop="postalCode">79088</span>
```

```
<div class="rating scoreCard fullBlock relative "
itemscope itemtype="http://schema.org/AggregateRating"
itemprop="aggregateRating">
<div class="currentScore">
<span class="average highScorecard" id="score.value"
itemprop="ratingValue">100</span><span
class="scoreCardPercent highScorecard"
id="score.percent">%</span>
<meta content="100" itemprop="bestRating" />
<meta content="0" itemprop="worstRating" />
<span class="voteCount">
<span class="votes"><span id="score.count"
itemprop="ratingCount">1</span> Vote</span>
```

I've bolded a few areas so you can find things. First, notice the itemtype URLs: `http://schema.org/PostalAddress` and `http://schema.org/AggregateRating`. These URLs point to pages that describe the code needed.

On the PostalAddress page we find, for instance, that the information that appears after the streetAddress "itemprop" is (and this won't surprise you) a street address; the information after addressLocality is a "locality," such as a city name; and the information after postalCode is the address's postal or zip code.

You can also find, on the `http://schema.org/AggregateRating` page, that the ratingValue itemprop represents a value showing "the rating for the content," and the ratingCount value is the total number of ratings. Thus, Citysearch has managed to pass to the search engines information that they can now use in some way, because they actually know what the information *is*.

Figure 8-1:
A Bing
search
result
showing
a "rich
snippet"
created
using
structured
data
markup.

Pizza Hut in Tulia, TX | Citysearch
www.citysearch.com › Tulia › Restaurants › Pizza ▾
★★★★★ Rating: 100% · 1 rating · 811 SW 2nd St, Tulia, TX 79088
This national chain is a household name, thanks to its deep-dish and stuffed-crust pies. –
In Short Kid-friendly eat-in restaurants and small takeout shops alike ...

Here's another example. Search Bing for, say, *lamb recipes* and Bing formats the page especially for recipes (see Figure 8-2). You'll notice a few things: The search results contain both pictures and ingredient lists, and you can click on a recipe and get extended information (such as Ingredients and Directions). Bing can provide these rich snippets, thanks to special codes embedded in the HTML, known as *structured data markup*, that identify each piece of information to the search engine; Bing can extract the information, store it in a manner that it understands the data, and display it in the search results.

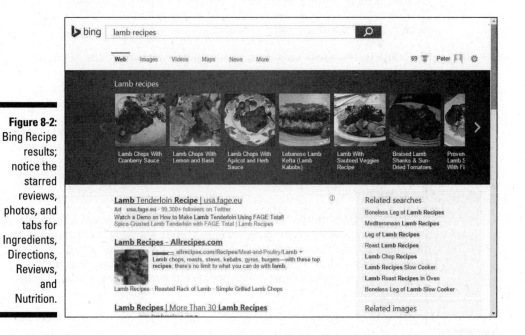

Figure 8-2: Bing Recipe results; notice the starred reviews, photos, and tabs for Ingredients, Directions, Reviews, and Nutrition.

Here, for instance, are a few pieces of code that I pulled from a FoodNetwork.com recipe. (I've removed a few pieces of code to focus on the important bits.) First, here's the photograph displayed in the search results:

```
<img class="photo" height="120" width="160"
src="http://img.foodnetwork.com/FOOD/2004/04/28/ee2e01_leg_of_lamb_med.jpg">
```

The `class="photo"` piece identifies this as the photograph of the dish. In the next piece of code, Food Network is identifying the author of the recipe; yep, the `class="author"` is the relevant code:

```
<p class="author">Recipe courtesy Emeril Lagasse, 2004</p>
```

Here you can see various ingredients (which the search engine will then parse to pull out the primary terms that it places into the snippet on the search results page: *garlic*, not *8 cloves garlic, minced*):

```
<li class="ingredient">1 leg of lamb, bone in (about 6 to 7 1/2 pounds</li>
<li class="ingredient">1/4 cup fresh lemon juice</li>
<li class="ingredient">8 cloves garlic, minced</li>
<li class="ingredient">3 tablespoons chopped fresh rosemary leaves</li>
```

Simple, eh? Well, not entirely. It can take some figuring out, but if you have specialty data, such as the preceding listed types, you should spend some time reading up on this stuff.

Google claims that coding data like this doesn't help with ranking, but I don't understand how that can be correct. If Google is trying to provide recipes with all the nice rich snippets (for instance, if your recipe doesn't contain the structured data), Google can't use your data to create rich snippets. I have to assume your recipe doesn't make it onto the search-results page. (At the time of writing, Google wasn't providing Recipe results, though its rich-snippets information claims that they do; maybe they'll be back soon.) As for Bing, using this data *does* help with rankings, in some cases. Clearly, if Bing can't find the structured data markup, then your recipe doesn't appear up top in that recipe bar, for instance.

Furthermore, using structured data markup helps listings stand out in the search results, making them more likely to be seen and clicked upon.

Pick Your Data Format

You may have noticed that I show two different coding methods above; the first was the Microdata markup (`http://www.schema.org`), and the second was something called microformats markup (`http://microformats.org/`). There are other ways to mark up code: RDFa, JSON-LD, and Open Graph, a markup designed by Facebook to help it recognize data that it finds in Web pages.

There are two different things to consider here: the *vocabulary* used, and the *markup method* used. For instance, schema.org publishes a vocabulary for hundreds of different "classes" or data types (most aren't supported by the search engines, but who knows what the future brings). In addition to the vocabularies listed earlier in this chapter, there are vocabularies for video games, exercise plans, maps, sports events, bus trips, train reservations, and even for actions (such as the action of eating and the action of wearing).

For example, for an article placed into a Web page, you can define the various elements of the article by using such terms as articleBody, articleSection, wordCount, author, and so on.

However, somehow you have to code your pages using this vocabulary — you have to *mark up* your data — and that can be done in various ways. A great way to see this in action is to spend some time digging around on schema.org, where you'll find these hundreds of vocabularies. In many cases, you see examples of each one employed by using three formats: Microdata, RDFa, and JSON-LD.

So which data format do you use? Well, Google prefers JSON-LD; on the other hand, Google doesn't currently support JSON-LD markup for all data types, so read Google's latest information (see the link earlier in this chapter) to figure out whether JSON-LD is supported for your data.

For data types with no JSON-LD, Google recommends Microdata or RDFa. They certainly used to support microformats, but seem to be recommending these other three formats right now.

Bing doesn't seem to care. Currently, Bing states that "It's entirely up to you to decide which of the supported specifications best fits your data." However, it doesn't appear to support JSON-LD. If you like, you can use JSON-LD for the data that Google prefers it; if it's a component for which Bing also reads structured data markup, also use one of the Bing approved formats (there's no reason you can't use JSON-LD *and* microdata, for instance).

Providing Knowledge Graph Information

You've probably seen the Google Knowledge Graph. This is a block of information displayed in response to a search about a well-known company, organization, place, person, or other "entity"; you can see an example in Figure 8-3. Google has tools that gather this information from various places, but they also allow companies and people to submit their own information for the Knowledge Graph, using structured data markup. Currently, you can submit logos, contact numbers, and social profile links to Google.

For example, the following code is JSON-LD code providing links to social profiles (Google will place the appropriate social-network icons into the Knowledge Graph box):

```
<script type="application/ld+json">
{ "@context" : "http://schema.org",
  "@type" : "Organization",
  "name" : "Acme, Inc.",
```

```
    "url" : "http://www.acmeincdomain.com",
    "sameAs" : [ "http://www.facebook.com/acmeprofile",
        "http://www.twitter.com/acmeprofile",
        "http://plus.google.com/acmeprofile"]
}
</script>
```

Figure 8-3:
Microsoft's
Knowledge
Graph.

Getting Help

If you have one of the data types that the search engines use, you really should look into using structured data markup; use the Google and Bing links earlier in the chapter to visit their help pages and find out what they currently support. You may also want to spend some time on Schema.org learning about the vocabulary and the Microdata and JSON-LD markup methods.

There may be a way to short circuit some of the work, using Google's Data Highlighter tool. You'll find this in your Google Webmasters account (click Search Appearance, then select Data Highlighter; see Chapter 13). You'll enter a URL, and Google will show you your page. You'll then select components on the page and (using a drop-down list box that appears,) select the appropriate data type. Google will then show you other pages on your site; you'll be able to see how well Google recognizes the data types you defined.

The problems with the Data Highlighter are twofold:

✔ You need a pretty consistent format to make it work.

   That isn't a problem for most template-based CMS systems, which account for a large percentage of sites these days.

✔ It's no help with Bing. You're just telling Google what the data is. You aren't actually changing the code.

However, Google also provides other handy tools to help with markup:

✔ **Markup Helper:** This tool helps you tag your data (using the Microdata format); provide a URL or paste HTML, and Google displays the Web page. You can then highlight a piece text; a drop-down list box appears, from which you select the appropriate data type. Google provides you with the finished HTML code to use. You'll find a link under Other Resources in your Google Webmaster account (Chapter 13), or you can go there directly:

   ```
   www.google.com/webmasters/markup-helper
   ```

✔ **The Structured Data Testing Tool:** Enter a URL, or paste code, and the tool reports back what it found, including errors. You'll find a link under Other Resources in your Google Webmaster account (Chapter 13), or you can go there directly:

   ```
   https://developers.google.com/structured-data/testing-tool
   ```

✔ **The Structured Data Dashboard:** You can find this in your Google Webmasters account (click the Search Appearance menu, then the Structured Data option; see Chapter 13). The console will show you the data that Google has found in your pages, and also report any errors it has found.

Chapter 9

Avoiding Things That Search Engines Hate

In This Chapter

▶ Working with frames and iframes

▶ Creating a readable navigation system

▶ Avoiding problems with Flash and Silverlight

▶ Reducing page clutter

▶ Dealing with dynamic Web pages

*I*t is possible to look at your Web site in terms of its search engine friendliness. (Chapter 7 of this book does just that.) It is equally possible, however, to look at the flip side of the coin — the things people often do that hurt their Web site's chance of ranking high within the search engines, and in some cases even making their Web sites invisible to search engines.

This tendency on the part of Web site owners to shoot themselves in the foot is very common. In fact, as you read through this chapter, you're quite likely to find things you're doing that are hurting you. Paradoxically, serious problems are especially likely for sites created by mid- to large-size companies using sophisticated Web technologies.

Steering you clear of major design potholes is what this chapter is all about. Guided by the principle *First Do No Harm*, the following sections show you the major mistakes to avoid when setting up your Web site.

Dealing with Frames

Frames were very popular a few years ago, but they're much less so these days, I'm glad to say. A *framed* site is one in which the browser window is broken into two or more parts, each of which holds a Web page (see Figure 9-1).

Figure 9-1:
A framed
Web site;
each frame
has an indi-
vidual page.
The scroll
bar moves
only the
right frame.

Frame 1 contains
navigational links.

Frame 2 contains
content pages.

From a search engine perspective, frames create the following problems:

- **Search engines index individual pages, not framesets.** Each page is indexed separately, so pages that make sense only as part of the frameset end up in the search engines as independent pages — *orphaned* pages, as I like to call them. (Jump to Figure 9-2 to see an example of a page, indexed by Google, that belongs inside a frameset.)

- **You can't point to a particular page in your site.** This problem may occur in the following situations:

  - *Linking campaigns (see Chapters 16 through 18):* Other sites can link only to the front of your site; they can't link to specific pages.

  - *Pay-per-click campaigns:* If you're running a *pay-per-click (PPC)* campaign, you can't link directly to a page related to a particular product.

  - *Indexing products by shopping directories (see Chapter 15):* In this case, you need to link to a particular product page.

TECHNICAL STUFF

Refraining

Here's how Google currently describes how they work with frames, in their Webmaster help files:

"Frames can cause problems for search engines because they don't correspond to the conceptual model of the web. In this model, one page displays only one URL. Pages that use frames or iframes display several URLs (one for each frame) within a single page. Google tries to associate framed content with the page containing the frames, but we don't guarantee that we will.

Search engines index URLs — single pages, in other words. By definition, a framed site is a collection of URLs, and search engines therefore can't properly index the pages.

The HTML Nitty-Gritty of Frames

Here's an example of a *frame-definition,* or *frameset,* document:

```
<HTML>
<HEAD>
</HEAD>
<FRAMESET ROWS="110,*">
<FRAME SRC="navbar.htm">
<FRAME SRC="main.htm">
</FRAMESET>
</HTML>
```

This document describes how the frames should be created. It tells the browser to create two rows, one 110 pixels high and the other * high — that is, it occupies whatever room is left over. The document also tells the browser to grab the navbar.htm document and place it in the first frame — the top row — and place main.htm into the bottom frame.

Search engines these days can find their way through the frameset to the navbar.htm and main.htm documents, so Google, for instance, indexes those documents.

But suppose the pages *are* indexed. Pages intended for use inside a frameset are individually indexed in the search engine. In Figure 9-2, you can see a page that I reached from Google — first (on the left) in the condition that I found it and then (on the right) in the frameset it was designed for.

I found this page indexed in Google . . .   . . . it really belongs in this frame.

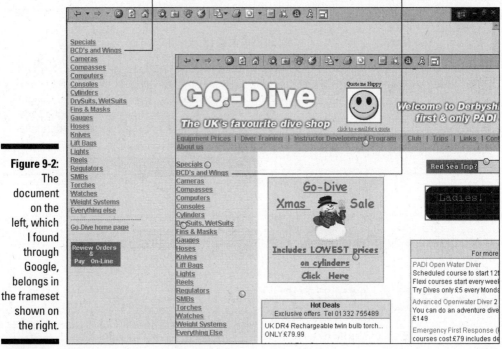

Figure 9-2:
The document on the left, which I found through Google, belongs in the frameset shown on the right.

This is not a pretty sight — or site, as it were. But you can work around this mess by doing the following:

✔ Provide information in the frame-definition document to help search engines index it.

✔ Ensure that all search engines can find their way through this page into the main site.

✔ Ensure that all pages loaded into frames contain TITLE tags, meta tags, and navigation links.

✔ Make sure that pages are opened in the correct frameset.

However, frames are so rarely used these days — and in fact not included in the most recent HTML specification, although they are supported by most browsers — that I think that's all I'll say about frames.

Handling iframes

An *iframe* is an inline floating frame, far more common these days than regular frames. You can use an iframe to grab content from one page and drop it into another, in the same way that you can grab an image and drop it into the page. The tag looks like this:

```
<iframe src ="page.html">
</iframe>
```

I think iframes can be very useful now and then, but you should be aware of the problems they can cause. In particular, search engines index the main page and the content in an iframe separately, even though to a user they appear to be part of the same page. As with regular frames, the iframed document can be orphaned in the search results. As shown earlier in the discussion of frames, Google states that it *tries* to deal with iframes properly, but can't guarantee it. You may want to add links at the bottom of the iframe content, in case someone stumbles across it when it's orphaned.

Here's another reason *not* to use frames and iframes: because you can achieve a similar effect using CSS (Cascading Style Sheets).

Fixing Invisible Navigation Systems

Navigation systems that were invisible to search engines were once a very common problem, but much less so these days because searchbots are so much smarter. Still, some search engines are smarter than others, and some navigation systems may cause problems with some systems, but you can deal with a navigation-system problem very easily.

In Chapter 7, I explain the difference between *browser-side* and *server-side* processes, and this issue is related. A Web page is compiled in two places — on the server and in the browser. If the navigation system is created "on the fly" in the browser, it may not be visible to a search engine.

Examples of such systems include those created by using

- JavaScripts
- Adobe Flash animation format
- Microsoft's Silverlight animation format
- Java applets

So do you need to worry about these issues? I say you don't, unless you know for sure you are having problems; if, for instance, the search engines aren't indexing your Web site, despite the fact that you have more than just one or two links pointing to the site (I discuss this issue in detail in Chapter 3), one question you should ask yourself is how the navigation system was created. If it's just basic HTML links, you don't have a problem; move on. If the navigation system is built into the JavaScript, then there *might* be a problem. That's unlikely to be a problem with Google, as it reads JavaScript quite well; Bing, however, still warns Webmasters that it may not be able to read JavaScript (and that affects Yahoo!, of course, as Bing feeds results to Yahoo!). If the site is being indexed by Google but not Bing, and your navigation structure is within JavaScript, maybe that's the problem.

As for Adobe Flash, Google generally reads Flash pretty well; again, Bing states it may not be able to find links in Flash. Both search engines still state they have problems with this format.

What about Java applets? I assume that if your navigation is built into an applet, the search engines *can't* see the links. But using Java applets for navigation is pretty rare.

Some other more obscure format? Assume that search engines can't read it.

Fixing the problem

But let's say you think you have this problem: One or more search engines are having problems finding their way through your site, because you're using some format other than HTML for your navigation system. Or perhaps you just want to be conservative, and make sure you don't have problems. What do you do?

The fix is easy: Just, to quote Bing, "implement a down-level experience which includes the same content elements and links as your rich version does. This will allow anyone ([including] Bingbot) without rich media enabled to see and interact with your website."

Let me translate the geekspeak. By "down-level," they mean simply use add links in a simpler format (that is, HTML). Add a secondary form of navigation that duplicates the top navigation.

You can duplicate the navigation structure by using simple text links at the bottom of the page, for instance, or perhaps in a navigation bar on the side of the page. If you have long pages or extremely cluttered HTML, you may want to place small text links near the top of the page, perhaps in the leftmost column, to make sure that search engines get to them.

Flush the Flash Animation

Adobe Flash animation is a very useful tool. But you should be aware of the SEO problems related to using it.

Many Web designers place fancy Flash animations on their home pages just to make them look cool. Often these animations serve no purpose beyond making site visitors wait a little longer to see the site. (This design flaw is falling out of favor, but you still see it here and there.) Major search engines can now read and index Flash content (albeit not always well — Bing warns that it might not be able to read it), but Flash animations often don't contain any useful text for indexing. So, if you built your entire home page — the most important page on your site — by using Flash, the page is worthless from a search engine perspective.

Some designers even create entire Web sites using Adobe Flash (generally because they are Flash designers, not Web designers). Do this, and your site will almost certainly *not* do well in search results.

However, there are ways around the problem, by providing alternate content. In effect, you're placing the code containing the Flash near the top of your HTML and then follow it with basic HTML that will be seen by browsers without Flash enabled and will be read by the search engines.

I'm no Flash expert, but one solution I'm aware of is the use of SWFObject, which is a method for embedding Flash content into Web pages using JavaScript. SWFObject includes the ability to define an alternate-content element and put the HTML text into a `<div>` tag of the same name as that element. Search for *swfobject* for details. Site visitors will see the Flash, but searchbots will see the alternate content.

Using SWFObject sounds remarkably like *cloaking* (see the section "Using Session IDs in URLs," later in this chapter, and Chapter 10 for more detail). However, Google is aware of SWFObject and even recommends it.

(By the way, many home-page Flash animations automatically forward the browser to the next page — the *real* home page — after they finish running. If you really have to have a Flash intro, make sure that you include a clearly visible Skip Intro link somewhere on the page.)

Flash has many good uses, and search engines *can* index Adobe Flash files . . . but generally not well. And here's the proof. Ask yourself how often you find Flash files, or pages that are mostly Flash components, at the top of the search results. The answer is virtually *never*. I've received a lot of criticism over the years from fans of Flash, and they sometimes point me to documents (generally on the Adobe Web site), talking about how well Flash files work with the search engines. Sure, those files can be indexed, but they almost certainly will not rank well. Furthermore, they may on occasion be orphaned — that is, the search engine may provide a link in the search results to the Flash file itself, rather than the page containing the file. A much better strategy is to provide alternate HTML content on the page, using a method such as the SWFObject script I describe earlier.

Use Flash when necessary, but *don't* rely on it for search engine indexing.

Waiting for Silverlight (to Disappear)

Microsoft's answer to Flash was Silverlight, released in 2007. One occasionally runs across Silverlight applications here and there, but it never quite caught on, and is unlikely to be used much in the future for two main reasons. Many browsers either don't, or soon won't, support Silverlight, and Microsoft has ended development.

So, you're unlikely to run into problems with Silverlight. But if your site *does* use Silverlight, you should understand that the problems are the same as with Flash, but much worse.

Anything in the Silverlight animation probably isn't being indexed by the search engines.

Avoiding Embedded Text in Images

Many sites use images heavily. The overuse of images is often the sign of an inexperienced Web designer — in particular, one who's quite familiar with graphic design tools (perhaps a graphic artist who has accidentally encountered a Web project). Such designers often create entire pages, including the text, in a graphical design program and then save images and insert them into the Web page.

The advantage of this approach is that it gives the designer much more control over the appearance of the page — and is often much faster than using HTML to lay out a few images and real text.

Putting text into graphics has significant drawbacks, though. Such pages transfer across the Internet much more slowly, and because the pages contain no real text, search engines don't have anything to index. And don't believe the "Google is magic" hype; Google does *not* read text in the images it finds online and is unlikely to do so for a number of years yet.

I don't see this happening anywhere near as much as it did in the past. A decade ago I had a *pro bono* client, a nationally recognized ballet theatre that, I discovered, had a Web site that was nothing but images. These days, this kind of thing is much rarer, though I still run across sites with significant portions created using images. It's a shame to see blocks of text, full of useful keywords, that aren't doing the site any good in the search engines because they're images.

Reducing the Clutter in Your Web Pages

This is another of those "this used to be pretty important . . . probably not so much these days" things.

It used to be that simple was good; cluttered was bad, because the more cluttered your pages, the more work it is for search engines to dig through them. What do I mean by *clutter?* I'm referring to everything in a Web page that is used to create the page but that is not actual page content.

For instance, one of my clients had a very cluttered site. The HTML source document for the home page had 21,414 characters, of which 19,418 were characters other than spaces. However, the home page didn't contain a lot of text: 1,196 characters, not including the spaces between the words.

So, if 1,196 characters were used to create the words on the page, what were the other 18,222 characters used for? They were used for elements such as these:

- ✔ **JavaScripts:** 4,251 characters
- ✔ **JavaScript event handlers on links:** 1,822 characters
- ✔ **The top navigation bar:** 6,018 characters
- ✔ **Text used to embed a Flash animation near the top of the page:** 808 characters

The rest is the normal clutter that you always have in HTML: tags used to format text, create tables, and so on. The problem with this page was that a search engine had to read 18,701 characters (including spaces) *before it ever reached the page content.* Of course, the page didn't have much content, and what was there was hidden away below all that HTML.

This clutter above the page content meant that some search engines might not reach the content. But is this important today? Probably not so much. On the other hand, there are several things you can do to unclutter your pages that are good for other reasons, such as page loading speeds, so why not? (In my preceding client example. I was able to remove around 11,000 characters without much effort.)

Use external JavaScripts

You don't need to put JavaScripts inside a page. JavaScripts generally should be placed in an *external file* — a tag in the Web page calls a script that is pulled from another file on the Web server — for various reasons:

- ✓ **They're safer outside the HTML file.** That is, they're less likely to be damaged while making changes to the HTML.
- ✓ **They're easier to manage externally.** Why not have a nice library of all the scripts in your site in one directory?
- ✓ **The download time is slightly shorter.** If you use the same script in multiple pages, the browser downloads the script once and caches it.
- ✓ **They're easier to reuse.** You don't need to copy scripts from one page to another and fix all the pages when you have to make a change to the script. Just store the script externally and change the external file to automatically change the script in any number of pages.
- ✓ **Doing so removes clutter from your pages!**

Creating external JavaScript files is easy: Simply save the text between the `<SCRIPT></SCRIPT>` tags in a text editor and copy that file to your Web server (as a `.js` file — `mouseover_script.js`, for instance).

Then add an `src=` attribute to your `<SCRIPT>` tag to refer to the external file, like this:

```
<script language="JavaScript" type="text/javascript"
          src="/scripts/mouseover_script.js"></script>
```

Use external CSS files

If you can stick JavaScript stuff into an external file, it shouldn't surprise you that you can do the same thing — drop stuff into a file that's then referred to in the HTML file proper — with Cascading Style Sheet (CSS) information. For reasons that are unclear to me, many designers place huge amounts of CSS information directly into the page, despite the fact that the ideal use of a style sheet is generally *external*. One of the original ideas behind style sheets was to allow you to make formatting changes to an entire site very quickly.

If you want to change the size of the body text or the color of the heading text, for example, you make one small change in the CSS file and it affects the whole site immediately. If you have CSS information in each page, though, you have to change each and every page. (Rather defeats the object of CSS, doesn't it?)

Here's how to remove CSS information from the main block of HTML code. Simply place the targeted text in an external file — everything between and including the `<STYLE></STYLE>` tags — and then call the file in your HTML pages by using the `<LINK>` tag, like this:

```
<link rel="stylesheet" href="site.css" type="text/css">
```

Move image maps to the bottom of the page

An *image map* (described in detail later in this chapter) is an image that contains multiple links. One way to clean up clutter in a page is to move the code that defines the links to the bottom of the Web page, right before the `</BODY>` tag. Doing so doesn't remove the clutter from the page — it moves the clutter to the end of the page, where it doesn't get placed between the top of the page and the page content. That makes it more likely that the search engines will reach the content.

Avoid the urge to copy and paste from MS Word

That's right. Don't copy text directly from Microsoft Word and drop it into a Web page. You'll end up with *all sorts* of formatting clutter in your page!

Here's one way to get around this problem:

1. **Save the file as an HTML file.**

   Word provides various options to do this, but you want to use the simplest: Web Page (Filtered).

2. **In your HTML-authoring program, look for a Word-cleaning tool.**

   Word has such a bad reputation that some HTML programs have tools to help you clean the text before you use it. Dreamweaver has such a tool, for instance (Clean Up Word HTML).

Managing Dynamic Web Pages

Chapter 7 explains how your standard, meat-and-potatoes Web page gets assembled in your browser so that you, the surfer, can see it. But you can assemble a Web page in more than one way. For example, the process can go like this:

1. The Web browser requests a Web page.

2. The Web server sends a message to a database program requesting the page.

3. The database program reads the URL to see exactly what is requested, compiles the page, and sends it to the server.

4. The server reads any instructions inside the page.

5. The server compiles the page, adding information specified in server-side includes (SSIs) or scripts.

6. The server sends the file to the browser.

Pages pulled from databases are known as *dynamic pages,* as opposed to normal *static pages,* which are individual files saved on the hard drive. The pages are dynamic because they're created on the fly, when requested. The page doesn't exist until a browser requests it, at which point the data is grabbed from a database by some kind of program — a CGI, ASP, or PHP script, for instance, or from some kind of content-management system — and dropped into a Web page template and then sent to the browser requesting the file.

Dynamic pages often caused problems in the past. Even the best search engines often didn't read them. Of course, a Web page is a Web page, whether it was created on the fly or days earlier. After the searchbot receives the page, the page is already complete, so the searchbots *could* read them if they wanted to, but sometimes, based on what the page URL looked like, they choose not to. So it isn't the page itself that's the problem; static or database, the final Web page is the same thing. It's the structure of the URL that's the problem, because the search engines can look at the URL and recognize that the page is a dynamic page.

Search engine programmers discovered that dynamic pages were often problem pages. Here are a few of the problems that searchbots were running into while reading dynamic pages:

- ✔ Dynamic pages often have only minor changes in them. A searchbot reading these pages may end up with hundreds of pages that are almost exactly the same, with nothing more than minor differences to distinguish one from each other.

✔ Search engines were concerned that databased pages might change frequently, making search results inaccurate.

✔ Searchbots sometimes get stuck in the dynamic system, going from page to page to page among tens of thousands of pages. On occasion, this happens when a Web programmer hasn't properly written the link code, and the database continually feeds data to the search engine, even crashing the Web server.

✔ Hitting a database for thousands of pages can slow down the server, so searchbots often avoided getting into situations in which that is likely to happen.

✔ Sometimes URLs can change (I talk about session IDs a little later in this chapter), so even if the search engine indexed the page, the next time someone tried to get there, it would be gone, and search engines don't want to index dead links.

All these problems were more common a few years ago, and, in fact, the major search engines are now far more likely to index databased pages than they were back then. Databased pages may still limit indexing by some search engines, though in particular, URLs with very long, complicated structures.

Understanding dynamic-page URLs

What does a dynamic-page URL look like? Go deep into a large ecommerce site; if it's a product catalog, for instance, go to the farthest subcategory you can find. Then look at the URL. Suppose that you have a URL like this:

```
http://www.yourdomain.edu/march/rodent-racing-scores.php
```

This URL is a normal one that should have few problems. It's a static page — or at least it looks like a static page, which is what counts. (It *might* be a dynamic, or databased, page, but there's no way to tell from the URL.) Compare this URL with the next one:

```
http://www.yourdomain.edu/march/scores.php?prg=1
```

This filename ends with `?prg=1`. This page is almost certainly a databased dynamic page; `?prg=1` is a *parameter* that's being sent to the server to let it know which piece of information is needed from the database. This URL is okay, especially for the major search engines, although a few smaller search engines may not like it; it almost certainly won't stop a searchbot from indexing it. It's still not very good from a search engine perspective, though, because it doesn't contain good keywords.

Now look at the following URL:

```
http://yourdomain.com/march/index.html?&DID=18&CATID=13&ObjectGroup_ID=79
```

Now the URL is getting more complicated. It contains three parameters: `DID=18`, `CATID=13`, and `ObjectGroup_ID=79`. These days, Google will probably index this page; at one point, a number of years ago, it likely wouldn't have.

Today, I wouldn't worry much about dynamic-page URLs not being indexed, unless yours are particularly complicated. However, there's another good reason for not using dynamic-page URLs: They generally don't contain useful keywords, and the URL is an important place to put keywords. If a search engine sees _rodent-racing_ in a URL, that's a really good signal to the search engines that the page is in some way related to racing rodents, rather than, say, dental surgery or baseball.

What does Google say? Its _SEO Starter Guide_ (see Chapter 23) says "Creating descriptive categories and filenames for the documents on your website can not only help you keep your site better organized, but it could also lead to better crawling of your documents by search engines." Elsewhere, a document about dynamic URLs discourages Webmasters from changing them, while in another document it states "rewriting dynamic URLs into user-friendly versions is always a good practice when that option is available to you."

So, despite the document _discouraging_ changing URLs, I believe there are real advantages to doing so, and Google has itself stated this. In addition, many in the SEO business agree; "rewriting" URLs (explained in the following section) is common practice.

Fixing your dynamic Web page problem

If you do have problems, how do you make search engines read your state-of-the-art dynamic Web site? Here are a few ideas:

- ✔ **Find out whether the database program has a built-in way to create static HTML.** Some ecommerce systems, for instance, spit out a static copy of their catalog pages, which is intended for search engines. When visitors click the Buy button, they're taken back into the dynamic system. Google has even on occasion recommended this process; however, this is probably not a process used very frequently nowadays.

- ✔ **Modify URLs so that they don't look like they're pointing to dynamic pages.** You can often help fix the problem by removing characters such as ?, #, !, *, %, and & and reducing the number of parameters to one. For the specifics, talk with the programmer responsible for the database system.

✔ **Use a URL rewrite trick — a technique for changing the way URLs look.**
Different servers have different tools available; the `mod_rewrite` tool,
for instance, is used by the Apache Web server (a very popular system),
and ISAPI Rewrite can be used on Windows servers. *Rewriting* is a process
whereby the server can convert fake URLs into real URLs. The server
might see, for instance, a request for a page at

```
http://yourdomain.com/march/rodent-racing-scores.html
```

The server knows that this page doesn't exist and that it really refers to,
perhaps, the following URL:

```
http://yourdomain.com/ showprod.cfm?&DID=7&User_ID=2382175&st=6642&st2=
        45931500&st3=-43564544&topcat_id=20018&catid=20071&objectgro
        up_id=20121.
```

✔ In other words, this technique allows you to use what appear to be
static URLs yet still grab pages from a database. Furthermore, the URLs
then contain nice keywords, which is an SEO advantage. This topic is
complicated, so if your server administrator doesn't understand it, it
may take him a few days to figure it all out; for someone who understands URL rewriting, however, it's fairly easy and can take just a few
hours to set up.

If you want to find out more about URL rewriting, simply search for *url
rewrite,* and you'll find tons of information.

Using Session IDs in URLs

Just as dynamic Web pages can throw a monkey wrench into the search
engine machinery, session IDs can make search engine life equally interesting. A *session ID* identifies a particular person visiting the site at a particular
time, which enables the server to track which pages the visitor looks at and
which actions the visitor takes during the session.

If you request a page from a Web site — by clicking a link on a Web page, for
instance — the Web server that has the page sends it to your browser. Then
if you request another page, the server sends that page, too, but the server
doesn't know that you're the same person. If the server needs to know who
you are, it needs a way to identify you each time you request a page. It does
that by using session IDs.

Session IDs are used for a variety of reasons, but their main purpose is
to allow Web developers to create various types of interactive sites. For
instance, if developers have created a secure environment, they may want
to force visitors to go through the home page first. Or, the developers may
want a way to resume an unfinished session. By setting cookies containing

the session ID on the visitor's computer, developers can see where the visitor was in the site at the end of the visitor's last session. (A *cookie* is a text file containing information that can be read only by the server that set the cookie.)

Session IDs are common when running software applications that have any kind of security procedure (such as requiring a login), that need to store variables, or that want to defeat the browser cache — that is, ensure that the browser always displays information from the server, never from its own cache. Shopping cart systems typically use session IDs — that's how the system can allow you to place an item in the shopping cart and then go away and continue shopping. It *recognizes* you based on your session ID.

A session ID can be created in two ways:

✔ Store it in a cookie.

✔ Display it in the URL itself.

Some systems are set up to store the session ID in a cookie but then use a URL session ID if the user's browser is set to not accept cookies. (Relatively few browsers, perhaps 1 or 2 percent, don't accept cookies.) Here's an example of a URL containing a session ID:

```
http://yourdomain.com/index.jsp;jsessionid=07D3CCD4D9A6A9F3CF9CAD4F9A728F44
```

The `07D3CCD4D9A6A9F3CF9CAD4F9A728F44` piece of the URL is the unique identifier assigned to the session.

If a search engine recognizes a URL as including a session ID, it probably doesn't read the referenced page because each time the searchbot returns to your site, the session ID will have expired, so the server will do one of the following:

✔ **Display an error page rather than the indexed page or perhaps display the site's default page (generally the home page).** In other words, the search engine has indexed a page that isn't there if someone clicks the link in the search results page.

✔ **Assign a new session ID.** The URL that the searchbot originally used has expired, so the server replaces the ID with another one and changes the URL. So, the spider could be fed multiple URLs for the same page.

Even if the searchbot reads the referenced page (and sometimes it does), it may not index it. Webmasters sometimes complain that a search engine entered their site, requested the same page over and over, and left without indexing most of the site. The searchbot simply got confused and left.

Or, sometimes the search engine doesn't recognize a session ID in a URL. One of my clients had hundreds of URLs indexed by Google, but because they were all long-expired session IDs, they all pointed to the site's main page.

These are all worst-case scenarios, as the major search engine's searchbots do their best to recognize session IDs and work around them. Furthermore, Google recommends that if you are using session IDs, you use the canonical directive to tell the search engines the correct URL for the page. For instance, let's say you're using session IDs, and your URLs look something like this:

```
http://www.youdomain.com/product.php?item=rodent-racing-gear
         &xyid=76345&sessionid=9876
```

A search engine might end up with hundreds of URLs effectively referencing the same page. So, you can put the <link> tag in the <head> section of your Web pages to tell the search engines the correct URL, like this:

```
<link rel="canonical" href="http://www.yourdomain.com/product.php?item= rodent-
         racing-gear " />
```

Session ID problems are rarer than they once were; in the past, fixing a session ID problem was like performing magic: Sites that were invisible to search engines suddenly become visible! One site owner in a search engine discussion group described how his site had never had more than 6 pages indexed by Google, yet within a week of removing session IDs, Google had indexed over 600 pages.

If your site has a session ID problem, there are a couple of other things you can do, in addition to using the canonical directive:

- ✔ **Rather than use session IDs in the URL, store session information in a cookie on the user's computer.** Each time a page is requested, the server can check the cookie to see whether session information is stored there. (Few people change their browser settings to block cookies.) However, the server shouldn't *require* cookies, or you may run into further problems.

- ✔ **Get your programmer to omit session IDs if the device requesting a Web page from the server is a searchbot.** The server delivers the same page to the searchbot but doesn't assign a session ID, so the searchbot can travel throughout the site without using session IDs. (Every device requesting a page from a Web server identifies itself, so it's possible for a programmer to send different pages according to the requestor.) This process is known as *user agent delivery,* in which user agent refers to the device — browser, searchbot, or other program — that is requesting a page.

The user agent method has one potential problem: In the technique some-times known as *cloaking,* a server sends one page to the search engines and another to real site visitors. Search engines generally don't like cloaking because some Web sites try to trick them by providing different content from the content that site visitors see. Of course, in the context of using this technique to avoid the session-ID problem, that's not the intent; it's a way to show the *same* content that the site visitor sees, so it isn't true cloaking. However, the (very slight) danger is that the search engines may view it as cloaking if they discover what is happening. (I don't believe that the risk is big, though some people in the SEO business will tell you that it is.) For more on cloaking, see Chapter 10.

Fixing Bits and Pieces

Forwarded pages, image maps, and special characters can also cause prob-lems for search engines.

Forwarded pages

Search engines don't want to index pages that automatically forward to other pages. You've undoubtedly seen pages telling you that a page has moved to another location and that you can click a link or wait a few seconds for the page to automatically forward the browser to another page. This is often done with a REFRESH meta tag, like this:

```
<meta http-equiv="refresh" content="0; url=http://yourdomain.com">
```

This meta tag forwards the browser immediately to *yourdomain*.com. Quite reasonably, search engines don't like these pages. Why index a page that doesn't contain information but instead forwards visitors to the page *with* the information? Why not index the target page? That's just what search engines do.

If you use the REFRESH meta tag, you can expect search engines to ignore the page (unless it's a very slow refresh rate of over ten seconds, which is specified by the number immediately after content=). But don't listen to the nonsense that you'll hear about your site being penalized for using refresh pages: Search engines don't index the page, but there's no reason for them to penalize your entire site. (On the other hand, there's an old trick using JavaScript in which the search engines are shown one page, but the visitor is instantly forwarded to another page with different content; the theory is that the search engines won't see the JavaScript redirect, so they'll index the heavily keyworded initial page and not realize users are going to a different one. Search engines don't appreciate that, and often catch it these days! As noted earlier, Google especially is quite good at reading JavaScript.)

Image maps

An *image map* is an image that has multiple links. You might create the image like this:

```
<img name="main" src="images/main.gif" usemap="#m_main">
```

The `usemap=` parameter refers to the map instructions. You can create the information defining the *hotspots* on the image — the individual links — by using a `<MAP>` tag, like this:

```
<map name="m_main">
<area shape="rect" coords="238,159,350,183" href="page1.html">
<area shape="rect" coords="204,189,387,214" href=" page2.html">
<area shape="rect" coords="207,245,387,343" href=" page3.html">
<area shape="rect" coords="41,331,155,345" href=" page4.html">
<area shape="rect" coords="40,190,115,202" href=" page5.html">
<area shape="rect" coords="42,174,148,186" href=" page6.html">
<area shape="rect" coords="40,154,172,169" href=" page7.html">
<area shape="rect" coords="43,137,142,148" href=" page8.html">
<area shape="rect" coords="45,122,165,131" href=" page9.html">
<area shape="rect" coords="4,481,389,493" href=" page10.html">
<area shape="rect" coords="408,329,588,342" href=" page11.html">
        <area shape="rect" cords="410,354,584,391" href=" page12.html">
        </map>
```

There was a time when search engines wouldn't read the links, but that time is long gone; major search engines now read image maps, though some smaller ones may not. A more important problem these days is that links in images don't provide the benefit of keywords that search engines can read. The solution is simple: Use additional simple text links in the document.

Special characters

The issue of using special characters is a little complicated. Currently Google seems to handle special-character searches well. Search for *rôle* and for *role*, and you'll get different results. Try the test at Bing, and you'll get almost the same result both times.

Consider, then, that when people search, they don't use special characters. They simply type the search term with the keyboard characters in front of them. Almost nobody would search for *shakespearean rôles*; people would search for *shakespearean roles* (even if they realized that the word role has an accented *o*). Thus, if you use the word rôle, your page won't match searches for *role*.

My general advice is to avoid special characters when possible, particularly in really SEO-valuable fields such as the `<Title>` tag and `DESCRIPTION` meta tag.

Chapter 10

Dirty Deeds, Done Dirt Cheap

. . . .

In This Chapter

▶ Examining the principles of tricking search engines

▶ Understanding how you can hurt your site

▶ Looking at doorway pages, redirects, cloaking, and more

▶ Understanding how you may be penalized

. . . .

*E*veryone wants to fool the search engines — and the search engines know it. That's why search engine optimization is such a strange business — a hybrid of technology and, oh, I dunno . . . industrial espionage, perhaps? Search engines don't want you to know exactly how they rank pages because if you did, you would know exactly how to trick them into giving you top positions.

Now for a bit of history. When this whole search engine business started out, search engines just wanted people to follow some basic guidelines — make the Web site readable, provide a <TITLE> tag, provide a few keywords related to the page's subject matter, and so on — and then the search engines would take it from there.

What happened, though, is that Web sites started jostling for position. For example, although the KEYWORDS meta tag seemed like a great idea, so many people misused it (by repeating words and using words that *weren't* related to the subject matter) that it eventually became irrelevant to search engines. Eventually, the major search engines stopped giving much weight to the tag or just ignored it altogether.

Search engines try to hide their methods as much as they can, but it sometimes becomes apparent what the search engines want, and at that point, people start trying to give it to them in a manner the search engines regard as manipulative. This chapter discusses which things you should avoid doing because you risk upsetting the search engines and getting penalized — potentially even getting booted from a search engine for life!

Tricking Search Engines

Before getting down to the nitty-gritty details about tricking search engines, I focus on two topics: why you need to understand the dangers of using dirty tricks and what the overriding principles behind tricking the search engines are based on.

Deciding whether to trick

Should you use the tricks in this chapter, and if not, why not? You'll hear several reasons for not using tricks. The first, ethics, is one I don't belabor because I'm not sure that the argument behind this reason is very strong. You'll hear from many people that the tricks in this chapter are unethical, that those who use them are cheating and are one step on the evolutionary ladder above pond scum (or one step below pond scum, depending on the commentator).

Self-righteousness is in ample supply on the Internet. Maybe these people are right, maybe not. I do know that many people who try such tricks also have great reasons for doing so and are not the Internet's equivalent of Pol Pot or Attila the Hun. They're simply trying to put their best foot forward in a difficult technical environment.

Many people have tried search engine tricks because they invested a lot of money in Web sites that turn out to be invisible to search engines. These folks can't afford to abandon their sites and start again. (See Chapter 9 for a discussion of why search engines sometimes can't read Web pages.) You can, and rightly so, point out that these folks can deal with the problem in other ways, but that just means the people involved are misinformed, not evil. The argument made by these tricksters might go something like this: *Who gave search engines the right to set the rules, anyway?*

One could argue that doing pretty much anything beyond the basics is cheating. Over the past few years, I've heard from hundreds of people who have put into action many of the ideas in this book, with great results. So if smart Webmasters armed with a little knowledge can push their Web sites up in the ranks above sites that may be more appropriate for a particular keyword phrase, yet are owned by folks with less knowledge . . . is that fair?

Also, consider that the search engines have actually (although unintentionally) *encouraged* the use of some dirty tricks. For example, the search engines don't like people to buy links (see Chapter 17). Yet the search engines have *encouraged* the purchasing of links, by *rewarding* the purchasing of links. *Buying links worked!* (And, some would argue, still works today.) So business man X looks at competitor Y and sees how well Y's Web site is ranking, and then discovers that Y ranked the site by purchasing links. Well, what is business man X supposed to think?

Ethics aside, the really good reason for avoiding egregious trickery is that it may have the opposite effect and *harm* your search engine position. A corollary to that reason is that other, legitimate ways exist to get a good search engine ranking. (Unfortunately, they're often more complicated and time consuming.)

Figuring out the tricks

The idea behind most search engine tricks is simple: to confuse the search engines into thinking that your site is more appropriate for certain keyword phrases than they would otherwise believe. You do this generally by showing the search engine something that the site visitor doesn't see.

Search engines want to see what site visitors see, yet they know they can't. It will be a long time before search engines will be able to see and understand the images in a Web page, for instance. Right now, they can't even read text in the images, although that could be possible at some point. (Recent patents suggest that this is something Google is working on now — but I bet it will still be years before Google tries to read all the text it finds in the average Web site's images, if it ever does.) But to view and understand the images as a real person sees them? Britney Spears could well be president of the United States before that happens.

The search engine designers have started with this basic principle:

> *What the search engine sees should be what the user sees* except for certain things it's not interested in — images, for instance — and certain technical issues that are not important to the visitor (such as the DESCRIPTION meta tag, which <H> tag has been applied to a heading, and so on).

Here's one other important principle: *The text on the page should be there for the benefit of the site visitor, not the search engines.*

Ideally, search engine designers want Web designers to act as though search engines don't exist. (Of course, this is *exactly* what many Web designers have done and the reason that so many sites rank poorly in search engines!) Search engine designers want their programs to determine which pages are the most relevant for a particular search query. They want you — the Web designer — to focus on creating a site that serves your visitors' needs and let search engines determine which site is most appropriate for which searcher. At least that was the original theory. Over the years, the search engines realized that total ignorance of SEO simply wasn't going to happen. Now they provide basic SEO advice.

Still, what search engines definitely don't want is for you to show one version of a page to visitors and another version to search engines because you feel that version is what the search engine will like most.

Do these tricks work?

Tricks do work, at least in some circumstances for some search engines. On the other hand, over time, search engines have become better and better at spotting the more obvious tricks; you don't find crudely keyword-stuffed pages and pages with hidden text ranking well very often these days, for instance, though only a few years ago you did.

Could you use sophisticated tricks and rank first for your keywords? Perhaps, but your rank may not last long, and the penalty it could incur can last for a long time. (In most cases, the pages will simply drop in rank as the search engines apply an algorithm that recognizes the trick, but in some cases, a search engine could decide to remove all pages from a particular site from the index; see Chapter 21 for a discussion of this disaster.)

These tricks can be dangerous. You may get caught in one of several ways:

- ✔ A search engine algorithm may discover your trickery, and your page or your entire site could be dropped from the search engine.

- ✔ A competitor might discover what you're doing and report you to the search engines. Google has stated that it prefers to let its algorithms track down cheaters and uses reports of search engine spamming to tune these algorithms, but Google will take direct action in some cases; in fact, it does employ a team of people to examine suspected "spam" sites.

- ✔ Your trick may work well for a while, until a major search engine changes its algorithm to block the trickery — at which point your site's ranking will drop like a rock.

If you follow the advice from the rest of this book, you'll surpass 80 percent of your competitors. You don't *need* tricks.

Concrete Shoes, Cyanide, TNT — An Arsenal for Dirty Deeds

The next few sections take a look at some search engine tricks employed on the Web.

Keyword stacking and stuffing

You may run across pages that contain the same word or term, or maybe several words or terms, repeated again and again, often in hidden areas of the page (such as the KEYWORDS tag), though also sometimes visible to visitors. This is one of the earliest and crudest forms of a dirty deed, one that search engines have been aware of for years and are pretty good at finding these days. It's rare to find crudely keyword-stacked pages ranking well in the search results anymore.

Take a look at Figure 10-1. The Web designer has repeated the word *glucosamine* numerous times, each one in a hyperlink to give it a little extra oomph. I found this page in Google a few years ago by searching for the term *glucosamine glucosamine glucosamine*; more recently, the same search phrase didn't pull up anything nearly as crude as this page.

Look at this tactic from the search engine's perspective. Repeating the word *glucosamine* over and over isn't of any use to a site visitor, so it's understandable why search engine designers don't appreciate this kind of thing. This sort of trick rarely works these days, so sites doing this are also becoming less abundant.

Figure 10-1:
The person creating this page stacked it with the word *glucosamine.*

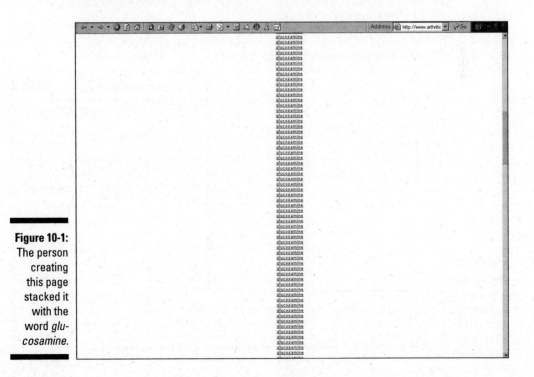

The terms *keyword stacking* and *keyword stuffing* are often used interchangeably, though some people regard keyword stuffing as something a little different — placing inappropriate keywords inside image ALT attributes and in hidden layers. (The term *keyword stacking* is far less common these days.)

Hiding (and shrinking) keywords

Another old (and very crude) trick is to hide text; that is, to hide it from the site visitor but make it visible to the search engine, allowing you to fill a simple page with keywords for the sake of search engine optimization. (Remember that search engines don't want you to show them content that isn't also visible to the site visitor.)

This trick, often combined with keyword stuffing, involves placing large amounts of text into a page and hiding it from view. For instance, take a look at Figure 10-2. I found this page in Google some time ago. It has hidden text at the bottom of the page.

If you suspect that someone has hidden text on a page, you can often make it visible by clicking inside text at the top of the page and dragging the mouse to the bottom of the page to highlight everything in between. You can also look in the page's source code.

There's a big space at the bottom of this page . . .

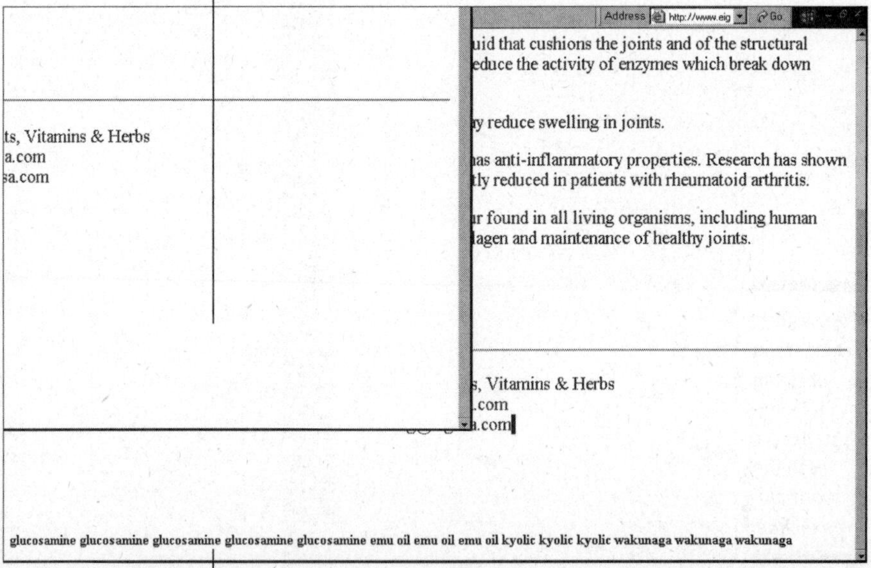

		uid that cushions the joints and of the structural educe the activity of enzymes which break down
		y reduce swelling in joints.
ts, Vitamins & Herbs a.com sa.com		as anti-inflammatory properties. Research has shown tly reduced in patients with rheumatoid arthritis.
		ar found in all living organisms, including human lagen and maintenance of healthy joints.
		s, Vitamins & Herbs .com a.com

glucosamine glucosamine glucosamine glucosamine glucosamine emu oil emu oil emu oil kyolic kyolic kyolic wakunaga wakunaga wakunaga

Figure 10-2:
This text is
hidden at
the bottom
of the page.

. . . but if you drag the cursor down from the end of the text, you'll see the hidden text.

How did this designer make the text disappear? At the bottom of the source code (choose View ⇨ Source), I found this:

```
<FONT SIZE=7 COLOR="#ffffff"><H6>glucosamine glucosamine glucosamine glucosamine
        glucosamine emu oil emu oil emu oil kyolic kyolic kyolic wakunaga
        wakunaga wakunaga</H6></FONT>
```

Notice the `COLOR="#ffffff"` piece; `#ffffff` is hexadecimal color code for the color white. The page background is white, so — abracadabra — the text disappears.

Surprisingly, I still see this trick employed now and then. In fact, I sometimes get clients who have a sudden inspiration — "Hey, couldn't we just put a bunch of keywords into the site and make it the same color as the background?" they ask, as if they have discovered something really clever. I have to explain that it's the oldest trick in the book.

My opinion of this crude trick goes like this:

- ✔ **It may help.** The trick actually *can* work, though not nearly as often as it used to.

- ✔ **It might not hurt.** You still find pages using this trick, so clearly the search engines don't always find it.

- ✔ **. . . but it might.** But search engines *do* discover the trick, frequently, and may penalize your site for doing it. The page may get dropped from the index, or you may have your entire site dropped.

- ✔ **So why do it?** It's just way too risky . . . and unnecessary, too.

Here are some other tricks used for hiding text from the visitor while still making it visible to the search engine:

- ✔ **Placing text inside** `<NOFRAMES>` **tags:** Some designers do this even if the page isn't a frame-definition document. I've seen this method work, too, but not in recent years.

- ✔ **Placing text inside** `<NOSCRIPT>` **tags:** `<NOSCRIPT></NOSCRIPT>` tags are used to put text on a page that can be read by browsers that don't work with JavaScript. Some site owners use them to give more text to the search engines to read, and from what I've seen, the major search engines often do read this text, or at least they did a few years ago. However, the text inside these tags probably isn't given as much weight as other text on a page, and over time will probably be given less and less weight. (However, I recently read an experiment from 2015 showing that Google *still* indexes the text in `NOSCRIPT` tags.)

- ✔ **Using hidden fields:** Sometimes designers hide words in a form's hidden field (`<INPUT TYPE="HIDDEN">`). I doubt whether this does anything to help, anyway.

✔ **Using hidden layers:** Style sheets can be used to position a text layer underneath the visible layer or outside the browser. This trick is quite common and probably hard for search engines to figure out.

Some Web designers still stuff keywords into a page by using a very small font size. This trick is another one that search engines may look for and penalize.

Here's another variation: Some Web designers make the text color *just a little different* from the background color to make it hard for someone reading the page to see. The text is effectively invisible, especially if it's at the bottom of the page preceded by several blank lines. Search engines can look for ranges of colors to determine whether this trick is being employed.

And remember, it's not just the search engines looking, it's your competitors, too. They might just report you. (See the section "Paying the Ultimate Penalty," later in this chapter.)

Hiding links

A variation on the old hidden-text trick is to hide links. As you discover in Chapters 16 through 18, links provide important clues to search engines about the site's purpose. They also provide a way for search engines to discover pages. Thus, some Web designers create links that are specifically for search engines to find but are not intended for site visitors. Links can be made to look exactly like all the other text on a page or may even be hidden on punctuation marks — visitors are unlikely to click a link on a period, so the link can be made "invisible," allowing a search engine to discover a page that the site visitor will never see. Links may be placed in transparent images or invisible layers, in small images, or in `<NOFRAMES><NOSCRIPT>` tags or may be hidden in any of the ways discussed previously for hiding ordinary text.

When I think about tricks like this, though, I think, "What's the point?" There are so many legitimate things you can do in SEO, why bother with something like this?

Duplicating pages and sites

If content with keywords is good, then twice as much content is better, and three times as much is better still, right? Some site developers have duplicated pages and even entire sites, making virtual photocopies and adding the pages to the site or placing duplicated sites at different domain names.

Sometimes called *mirror pages* or *mirror sites,* these duplicate pages are intended to help a site gain more than one or two entries in the top positions. If you can create three or four Web sites that rank well, you can dominate the first page of the search results.

Some people who use this trick try to modify each page just a little to make it harder for search engines to recognize duplicates. But search engines have designed tools to find duplication and often drop a page from their indexes if they find it's a duplicate of another page at the same site. Duplicate pages found across different sites are often okay, which is why content syndication can work well if done right (see the discussion of duplicate content in Chapter 11), but entire duplicate sites are something that search engines frown on.

On the other hand, one strategy that works well, and is not necessarily a "dirty trick," is to create multiple sites. A company selling widgets, for instance, may have a primary site, with information about all its widgets, plus secondary sites; one focused on widgets for use during the summer, another for winter widgets, and a third for travel-size widgets. I've seen this strategy used very successfully, often resulting in multiple Page 1 search results.

Page swapping and page jacking

Here are a couple of variations on the duplication theme:

- ✔ **Page swapping:** In this now little-used technique, one page is placed at a site and then, after the page has attained a good position, it's removed and replaced with a less optimized page. One serious problem with this technique is that major search engines often reindex pages very quickly, and it's impossible to know *when* the search engines will return.

- ✔ **Page jacking:** Some truly unethical search engine marketers have employed the technique of using other peoples' high-ranking Web pages, in effect stealing pages that perform well for a while. This is known as *page jacking.*

Doorway and Information Pages

A *doorway page* is created solely as an entrance from a search engine to your Web site. Doorway pages are sometimes known as *gateway pages* and *ghost pages.* The idea is to create highly optimized pages that are picked up and indexed by search engines and that, with luck, rank well and thus channel traffic to the site.

Search engines hate doorway pages because they break one of the cardinal rules: They're intended for search engines, not for visitors. The sole purpose of a doorway page is to channel people from search engines to the real Web site.

One man's doorway page is another man's *information page* — or what some people call *affiliate pages, advertising pages,* or *marketing pages.* The difference between a doorway page and an information page is, perhaps, that the information page is designed for use by the visitor in such a manner that search engines will rank it well, whereas the doorway page is designed in such a manner that it's utterly useless to the visitor because it's intended purely for the search engine; in fact, originally doorway pages were stuffed full of keywords and duplicated hundreds of times.

Crude doorway pages don't look like the rest of the site, having been created very quickly or even by some kind of program. Doorway pages are part of other strategies. The pages used in redirects and cloaking (discussed in the next section) are, in effect, doorway pages.

Where do you draw the line between a doorway page and an information page? That's a question I can't answer here; it's for you to ponder and remains a matter of debate in the search engine optimization field. If a client asks me to help him in the search engine race and I create pages designed to rank well in search engines but in such a manner that they're still useful to the visitor, have I created information pages or doorway pages? Most people would say that I created legitimate information pages.

Suppose, however, that I create lots of pages designed for use by the site visitor — pages that, until my client started thinking about search engine optimization, would have been deemed unnecessary. Surely these pages are, by *intent,* doorway pages, aren't they, even if one could argue that they're useful in some way?

Varying degrees of utility exist, and I know people in the business of creating "information" pages that are useful to the visitor in the author's opinion only! Also, a number of search engine optimization companies create doorway pages that they simply *call* information pages.

Still, an important distinction exists between the two types of pages, and creating information pages is a widely used strategy. Search engines don't know your intent, so if you create pages that appear to be useful, are not duplicated dozens or hundreds of times, and don't break any other rules, they'll be fine.

Here's a good reality check. Be honest: Are the pages you just created truly of use to your site visitors? If you submitted these pages to Yahoo! Directory or the Open Directory Project for review by a human, would the site be accepted? If the answer is no, the pages probably aren't informational. The "trick," then,

is to find a way to convert the pages you created for search engine purpo[se]
into pages that are useful in their own right — or for which a valid argument,
at least, for utility can be made.

Using Redirects and Cloaking

Redirecting and cloaking serve the same purpose. The intention is to show
one page to the search engines but a completely different page to the site
visitor. Why do people want to do this? Here are a few reasons:

- If a site has been built in a manner that makes it invisible to search
  engines, cloaking allows the site owner to deliver indexable pages to
  search engines while retaining the original site.

- The site may not have much textual content, making it a poor fit for the
  search engine algorithms. Although search engine designers might argue
  that this fact means that the site isn't a good fit for a search, this argument clearly doesn't stand up to analysis and debate.

- Each search engine prefers something slightly different. As long as
  search engines can't agree on what makes a good search match, why
  should they expect site owners and developers to accept good results in
  some search engines and bad results in others?

I've heard comments such as the following from site owners, and I can understand their frustration: "Search engines are defining how my site should work
and what it should look like, and if the manner in which I want to design my
site isn't what they like to see, that's not my fault! Who gave them the right to
set the rules of commerce on the Internet?!"

What might frustrate and anger site owners more is if they realized that for
years, one major search engine *did* accept cloaking, as long as you paid for
it. Yahoo!'s Submit Pro program was in effect just that, a way to feed content
into the search engine directly but display different content to site visitors.
So cloaking is a crime, but until fairly recently, and for a decade or so, one
search engine said, "Pay us, and we'll help you do it." (Is that a fee, a bribe, or
a protection-racket payment?)

Understanding redirects

A *redirect* is the automatic loading of a page without user intervention. You
click a link to load a Web page into your browser, and within seconds, the
page you loaded disappears, and a new one appears. Designers often create
pages designed for search engines — optimized, keyword-rich pages — that

redirect visitors to the real Web site, which is not so well optimized. Search engines read the page, but visitors never really see it.

Redirects can be carried out in various ways:

- ✔ By using the REFRESH meta tag. This is an old trick that search engines discovered long ago; most search engines don't index a page that has a REFRESH tag that quickly bounces the visitor to another page.

- ✔ By using JavaScript to automatically load another page within a split second.

- ✔ By using JavaScript that's tripped by a user action that is almost certain to occur. You can see an example of this method at work in Figure 10-3, a page I found long ago (the trick isn't that common these days). The large button on this page has a JavaScript mouseover event associated with it; when users move their mice over the image — as they're almost certain to do — the mouseover event triggers, loading the next page.

You're unlikely to be penalized for using a redirect. But a search engine may ignore the redirect page. That is, if the search engine discovers that a page is redirecting to another page, it simply ignores the redirect page and indexes the destination page. Search engines reasonably assume that redirect pages are merely way stations on the route to the real content.

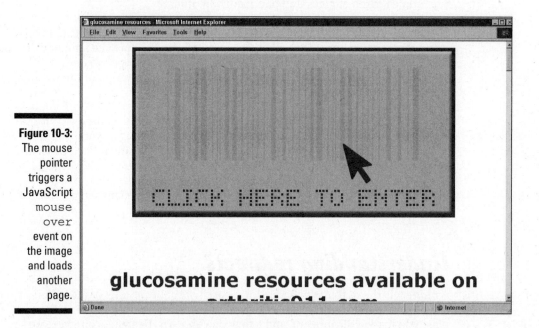

Figure 10-3:
The mouse pointer triggers a JavaScript mouse over event on the image and loads another page.

Examining cloaking

Cloaking is a more sophisticated trick than using a redirect and harder for search engines to uncover than a basic REFRESH meta tag redirect. When browsers or searchbots request a Web page, they send information about themselves to the site hosting the page — for example, "I'm Version 11 of Internet Explorer," or "I'm Googlebot." The cloaking program quickly looks in its list of searchbots for the device requesting the page. In addition, a cloaking program also has a list of IP numbers that it knows are used by searchbots; if the request comes from a matching IP number, it knows it's a searchbot.

So, if the device or IP number isn't found in the list of searchbots, the cloaking program tells the Web server to send the regular Web page, the one intended for site visitors. But if the device name or IP number *is* listed in the searchbot list — as it would be for Googlebot, for instance — the cloaking program sends a *different* page, one that the designer feels is better optimized for that particular search engine. (The cloaking program may have a library of pages, each designed for a particular search engine or group of engines.)

Here's how the two page versions differ:

- **Pages provided to the search engine:** Often much simpler; created in a way to make them easy for search engines to read; have lots of heavily keyword-laden text that would sound clumsy to a real person.

- **Pages presented to visitors:** Often much more attractive, graphics-heavy pages, with less text and more complicated structures and navigation systems.

Search engines don't like cloaking. Conservative search engine marketers steer well clear of this technique. Here's how Google defines cloaking:

> *The term "cloaking" is used to describe a Web site that returns altered Web pages to search engines crawling the site.*

Well, that's pretty clear — cloaking is cloaking is cloaking. But, wait a minute:

> *In other words, the Web server is programmed to return different content to Google than it returns to regular users, usually in an attempt to distort search engine rankings.*

Hang on: These two definitions aren't describing the same concept. The phrase "in an attempt to distort" is critical. If I "return altered pages" without intending to distort rankings, am I cloaking? Here's more from Google:

> *This can mislead users about what they'll find when they click on a search result. To preserve the accuracy and quality of our search results, Google may permanently ban from our index any sites or site authors that engage in cloaking to distort their search rankings.*

Notice a few important qualifications: *altered pages . . . usually in an attempt to distort search engine rankings . . . cloaking to distort their search engine rankings.*

This verbiage is ambiguous and seems to indicate that Google doesn't totally outlaw the use of cloaking; it just doesn't like you to use cloaking to cheat. Some would say that using cloaking to present to Google dynamic pages that are otherwise invisible, for instance, or that are blocked from indexing perhaps by the use of session IDs (see Chapter 9), would be an acceptable practice. And here's another very common use for "cloaking"; many, many sites display different content depending on the location of the person viewing the page (they use IP location to do this; see Chapter 12). Thus, they show different content to different people, including "searchbots."

And here's another form of "valid cloaking." As discussed in Chapter 9, SWFObject is a JavaScript that intentionally displays something different to the search engines; it shows a Flash animation to the visitor, but alternate text to browsers that don't read Flash and to searchbots. Google is aware of SWFObject and indeed has announced that it reads the script, so this sounds like a form of legitimate cloaking.

So there are many legitimate uses for cloaking. However, as I've pointed out, many in the business advise that you never use cloaking in any circumstance, just in case Google *thinks* your purpose is to "distort search engine rankings." My theory is that in most cases it's fine, unless your purpose may be unclear, in which case there's a risk that Google may misinterpret your aims.

Tricks Versus Strategies

When is a trick not a trick but merely a legitimate strategy? I don't know, but I'll tell you that there are many ways to play the SEO game, and what to one man is a trick might to another be the obvious thing to do.

Here's an example: creating multiple Web sites. One client has *two* Web sites ranking in the top five on Google for his most important keyword. (No, I can't tell you what the keyword is!) Another client at one point had around seven of the top ten results for one of his critical keywords; several of the links pointed to his own Web sites, and several pointed to his products positioned on other people's Web sites.

Now, this is definitely a trick: Build a bunch of small Web sites that point links back to your "core" site and then link all those sites from various places. The aim (and it can sometimes work if it's done correctly) is to boost the core site by creating many incoming links, but in many cases the "satellite" sites may also rank well. I've seen this technique work; I've also seen it fail miserably.

Is this a trick, though — building stand alone sites with the intention of seeing which ones will rank best? And doing so not merely as a way to create links to a core site but as a way to see what works best for search engines? I don't know. I'll leave it for you to decide.

Link Tricks

I look at on-page tricks in this chapter, but there's another category, off-page tricks, or *link trickery* — that is, creating what amounts to fake links pointing to your site, links that only exist for the purpose of pushing your site up in the search engines. In fact, link trickery is far more common these days than on-page tricks. You can find out more about links in Chapters 16 to 19 and about the most egregious link trick — buying links — in Chapter 17.

Paying the Ultimate Penalty

Just how much trouble can you get into by breaking the rules? The most likely penalty isn't really a penalty. It's just that your pages won't work well with a search engine's algorithm, so they won't rank well.

You can receive the ultimate penalty, though: having your entire site booted from the index. Here's what Google has to say about it:

> We investigate each report of deceptive practices thoroughly and take appropriate action when abuse is uncovered. At minimum, we will use the data from each spam report to improve our site ranking and filtering algorithms. The result of this should be visible over time as the quality of our searches gets even better.

Google is describing what I just explained — that it tweaks its algorithm to downgrade pages that use certain techniques. But:

> In especially egregious cases, we will remove spammers from our index immediately so they don't show up in search results at all. Other steps will be taken as necessary.

One of the dangers of using tricks, then, is that someone — perhaps your competitors — might report you, and if the trick is bad enough, you get the boot. Where do they report you? Google provides a form (at www.google. com/webmasters/tools/spamreport) and it's accessible through the Webmaster account (see Chapter 13). Bing used to provide an easily accessible form, but now has hidden it away with a long convoluted URL; you can get to it through here: http://j.mp/1NLNY3r.

Note, by the way, that a report titled *Most SEOs Don't Report Competitors to Google* on SEORoundtable.com found that 28 percent of respondents to a survey stated that they *had* reported competitors for using spam techniques. That may not be most, but it's still almost a third. Yes, this really does happen.

What do you do if you think you've been penalized? You can find out in Chapter 21.

Chapter 11

Bulking Up Your Site — Competing with Content

In This Chapter
▶ Creating content yourself
▶ Understanding copyright
▶ Finding free material
▶ Paying for content

Content is an extremely important factor in getting a high ranking in the search engines. *Content* is a geeky Web term that means, in the broadest sense, "stuff on your Web site." A *content-rich* Web site is one that contains lots of information for people to see, read, and use.

For search engines, content has a more narrow definition: words, and lots of 'em. So if you're interested in search engine optimization, you should concentrate on the *text* part of your Web site's content (the right text, of course, using the keywords you find out about in Chapter 6). You don't need to worry about pictures, video, or sound — at least as far as the search engines are concerned — because those forms of content generally don't help you get higher rankings. (Which is not to say that these things don't have a place in a search-engine strategy — see Chapter 20 for information on using video, for instance — but it does mean that when you're talking about getting Web pages ranked, it's mostly the text that counts.) You don't need Flash animations, either, because although some search engines index them, they don't index well; how often do you find a Flash page ranking highly in the search results? As explained in Chapter 9, if you do use Flash extensively, you should also use alternate text for the search engines to read.

What you should be concerned about is text — words that the search engines can read. Now, it's not *always* necessary to bulk up your site by adding textual content — in some cases, it's possible to get high search engine rankings with a small number of keyword-laden pages. If that's your situation, congratulations. Sit back and enjoy the fruits of your rather minimal labors and skip this chapter. But if you don't find yourself in that happy situation, you need this chapter.

You may find that your competitors have Web sites stacked full of content. They have scores of pages, perhaps even hundreds of pages — or hundreds of thousands — full of text that is nicely laden with all the juicy keywords you're interested in. That's tough to compete with.

This is a critical issue, something that is often a real challenge for site owners. This chapter describes a slew of shortcuts to free and low-cost content, such as government materials, marketing and technical documents from manufacturers, and even something called *copyleft*.

Creating Content Three Ways

You can compete in the search engines in several different ways: Create a few well-optimized pages, get lots of links into your site, target keywords that competitors have missed, and put masses of content on your site. (Chapter 4 has more on these "basic" strategies.) In some cases, when going up against a well-entrenched competitor, you may have no choice but to fight on several fronts. You may find that you *must* do something to stack your site with content.

Evaluate competing sites to help you determine at what point you should stop adding content. Compare your site to competitors that rank well in search engines. The major search engines also use link popularity to rate Web pages. If you're sure that your site has more well-optimized pages than those competing sites, it may be time to stop adding content. You may want to focus instead on getting links to your site. (For more on that subject, check out Chapters 16 to 18.)

I've got some bad news and some good news about creating content:

- ✔ **The bad news:** The obvious way to create content — writing it yourself or getting someone else to write it for you — is a huge problem for many people. Most people find writing difficult, and even if they find it easy, the results are often less than appealing. Perhaps you know someone who can write well, and you can convince this person to write a few paragraphs for you. But are your powers of persuasion sufficient to get you 10, 20, or 50 pages? What about 500 or 5,000? You can always pay someone for content, but the problem with paying is that it costs money.

✔ **The good news:** You can use some shortcuts to create content. Tricks of the trade can help you quickly bulk up your Web site (even if your writing skills match those of a dyslexic gerbil and your funds make the Queen of England's bikini budget look large in comparison). Note, though, that these tricks involve using *someone else's content.*

Here are three different ways to get content for your site:

✔ Write your own content.

✔ Convince (pay, force, bribe) someone else to create your content.

✔ Find existing content from somewhere else.

Writing Your Own Stuff

The obvious way to create content, for many small-site owners anyway, is to start writing articles. That's not a terrible idea in many cases. Thousands of sites rank well using content from the sites' owners.

If you use the write-it-yourself approach, keep the following points in mind:

✔ **Writing content is time consuming, even for good writers.** You may want to evaluate whether you can devote the time to writing and maintaining your own content and then allocate time in your schedule to do so.

✔ **Many people are *not* good writers.** Not only is the writing process time consuming, but the results are also often sad.

✔ **If you *do* write your own stuff, pleeze spill chuck it.** Then have it edited by someone who has more than a third-grade education and then spill chuck it again.

Do *not* rely on a word processor's grammar checker. This tool is worse than useless for most writers. Grammar checkers are of benefit only to those what already has a good grasp of grammar.

What will you write about? The obvious topic, of course, is your product or service (assuming that your site is selling something). The more you can say about each item you sell, the better. That should keep you busy for a while, but eventually, most businesses find that they have written all they can about their products, and they still don't have a large site, so the next few sections present a few other ideas.

Summarizing online articles

Here's a quick way to get keywords onto your page:

1. **Use the search engines to track down articles related to your subject area.**

2. **Create a library area on your Web site in which you link to these articles.**

3. **For each link, write a short, keyword-laden summary of what the article is all about.**

The advantage to this kind of writing is that it's fairly quick and easy.

You may want to include the first few sentences of the article. This strategy comes under the gray area of copyright fair use. What really counts is what the article's owner thinks. In most cases, if you contact the article's owner (and you don't *have* to contact that person), the owner is happy to have you summarize the article, excerpt a small portion of it, and link to her site. Most people recognize that *this process is good for them!* However, occasionally you find someone who just doesn't get it and creates a fuss. Just remove the link and move on.

By the way, a number of highly popular and successful blogs (in particular, celebrity and news blogs) are based on this very concept — that is, summarizing other people's work. The fancy term is *content curation*; if you think this might work for you, search for the term to learn more.

You may want to approach the owners of the sites you're linking to and ask them to add a link back to your site. See Chapter 17 for more information.

Reviewing Web sites and products

Similar to how you summarize, you can link to useful Web sites and write short (yes, keyword-laden) reviews of each one.

You can also write short (um, keyword-laden) reviews of products related to the subject matter covered by your site. An additional benefit of such a program is that eventually people may start sending you free stuff to review. There are many successful sites — earning money mainly from advertising — based solely on this concept, such as PopGadget.net and Engadget.com, and a number of companies that promote businesses by finding bloggers to review products; search for the terms *influencer marketing* and *blogger outreach* to learn about this form of marketing.

Convincing Someone Else to Write Content

You may find that having articles written (by others) specifically for your site is rather appealing, for two reasons. First, someone else does the work, not you. Second, if it doesn't turn out well, someone else (not you) gets blamed.

One approach, assuming that you can't force someone to write for you, is to pay someone. Luckily (for you), writers are cheap. For some reason, people often have a bizarre vision of a glamorous writing life that's awaiting them. (It has been over 20 years since I wrote my first bestseller, and I'm still waiting for the groupies to turn up.) So you may be able to find someone locally to write for you for $10 or $12 an hour, depending on where you live and how well you lie. Or, maybe you can find a high school kid who can string together a few coherent words and is willing to work for less.

If you work for a large corporation, you may be able to convince a variety of people to write for you — people who may assume that it's actually part of their jobs (again, depending on how well you lie). Spread the work throughout various departments — marketing, technical support, sales, and so on — and it may turn into a decent amount of content. Still, you can use quicker and easier ways to get content, as described in the next section.

If you pay someone to write for you, draw up a simple contract saying that the work is a work for hire and that you're buying all rights to it. Otherwise, you don't own it and can use it for only limited purposes that are either stated in the contract or are more or less obvious. If you ask someone to write an article for your Web site and you don't get a contract giving you full rights, you can't later decide to syndicate the article on other sites or in newsletters. (Chapter 17 has more information on this syndication stuff.) Worse, perhaps, is that without a contract the writer has the legal right to sell the work to other Web sites. (This happens a lot, by the way.) If an employee writes the material for you on company time, the work is generally considered a work for hire and company property. However, if you have a very small company with an informal employment relationship and the writing is outside the scope of the employee's normal work duties, you should request that the employee sign a contract.

A huge (politically incorrect) business has grown up over the past few years: overseas outsourced SEO work, specifically (regarding this chapter's subject) the outsourcing of articles written for SEO purposes. If you hire an Indian writer or a Chinese writer, for example, you may find that the writing, um, doesn't sound quite *right*. In fact, some of this work is truly dreadful. On the other hand, you can find people in these countries (and in other, less obvious nations, such as South Africa) who can write very well and can produce articles for your site for around $10 to $20 apiece. If you want to try this method, you can find writers on sites such as Elance.com, Naukri.com, Guru.com, and oDesk.com.

There are also companies that will manage content for you. They'll work with you to develop a content plan and write the content. Search for the terms *content creation* and *content marketing* and you'll find lots of options. For instance:

- **Brafton:** www.brafton.com
- **IdeaLaunch:** www.idealaunch.com

Using OPC (Other People's Content)

Writing or hiring is the slow way to create content. Using someone else's content — that's the quick way. See the following list of quick content sources for your site (I explain the details later in this chapter):

- **Product information:** Contact the manufacturer or distributor of the products you sell on your site for marketing and sales materials, technical documentation, and so on.

- **Web sites and e-mail newsletters:** Contact the owners of other sites and e-mail newsletters and ask whether you can use their work.

- **Government sources:** Check U.S. government Web sites for free materials.

- **Content-syndication sites:** A number of sites provide free content for the asking.

- **"Advertorial" services:** Companies such as ARAcontent (www.aracontent.com) provide free articles, often known by the term *advertorials* (because they are generally ads posing as editorial content — advertorial firms don't actually use the term *advertorial*, of course). These companies provide both print and Web content.

- **Traditional syndication services:** Numerous companies sell syndicated materials you can use on your site.

- **Open content and copyleft:** This unusual new movement is probably based on the old Internet maxim "Information wants to be free."

- **Search pages:** You can search at a site to generate a search results page with your favorite keywords.

✔ **Press releases:** You may be able to find press releases related to your area of business. They're copyright free, and you can use them as you want. (Of course, you should make sure that they're not from competitors.)

✔ **A Q&A area on your site:** This is a way to serve your site visitors *and* get keywords onto the site.

✔ **Forums or message boards:** With forums and message boards on your site, your visitors create the keywords for you. This is a very powerful concept, by the way; in fact, it's a basic building block for many online businesses. There are many very successful businesses that are purely based on letting other people create the content through the "community." (Ever heard of Facebook?)

This list gives you a good idea of the sources of content, and the "Hunting for Other People's Content" section, later in this chapter, explores how you find, evaluate, and procure content from these sources.

Before I show you how to help yourself to someone else's content, I need to warn you about a critical legal issue: copyright law. You must have a working knowledge of copyright restrictions so that you can properly evaluate whether (and how) it's appropriate to use the content you find. The next section gives you an overview of what you need to know, and the additional free chapter at http://SearchEngineBulletin.com goes into excruciating detail, in case you're curious.

Understanding Copyright — It's Not Yours!

I'm continually amazed at how few people understand copyright — even people who should know better.

When I speak to clients about adding content to a Web site, I sometimes hear something like this: "How about that magazine article I read last week? Let's put that up there!" Or maybe, "Such and such a site has some great information — let's use some of that." That's called *copyright infringement*. It's against the law, and although serious harm is unlikely to befall you in most cases, you *can* get sued or prosecuted. Plus, it's just, well, not very nice. (That's the perspective of a writer who has found his work stolen on a number of occasions.)

Let me quickly summarize copyright law so that you have a better idea of what you can and can't use on your site:

- ✔ As soon as someone creates a work — writes an article, writes a song, composes a tune, or whatever — copyright is automatic. There's no need to register copyright; the creator owns the copyright whether or not it has been registered. Most copyright works, in fact, aren't registered, which is a good thing. If they were, the Library of Congress, which houses the Copyright Office and stores copyright registrations, would be the size of Alabama.

- ✔ If you don't see a copyright notice attached, it doesn't mean that the work's copyright isn't owned by someone. Current copyright law doesn't require such notices.

- ✔ If someone owns the copyright, that person has the right to say what can be done with, um, copies. Therefore, you generally can't take an article you find in a newspaper, magazine, or Web site and use it without permission. (There are exceptions, which you find out about in a moment.)

- ✔ In the United States, certain kinds of copyright infringement are felonies. You may not only get sued but also prosecuted.

- ✔ If you don't know whether you have the right to use something, assume that you *don't.*

- ✔ You can't just rewrite an article. *Derivative works* are also protected. If the result is clearly derived from the original, you could be in trouble.

- ✔ Copyright has to be expressly assigned. If you hire me to write an article for your Web site and I don't sign a contract saying that you own all rights or that the work was a work for hire, you only have the right to place it on your Web site. I still have the right to use the article elsewhere.

A number of exceptions can prove *very* important when you're gathering content, so listen closely:

- ✔ **If it's really old, you can use it.** Copyright eventually expires. Anything published before 1923, for instance, is free for the taking. Some things *after* that date are expired, too — most materials published before 1950 are probably in the public domain — but it gets complicated. Search for *copyright flowchart* to find charts that may help you figure it out.

- ✔ **If the "guvmint" created it, you can use it.** The U.S. government spends millions of dollars creating *content.* This content is *almost* never copyright-protected.

✔ **If it's donated, you can use it.** Authors often *want* you to use their materials. If they have given the public permission to use it, you can use it.

✔ **It's only fair.** Copyright law has a *fair use* exception that allows you to use small parts of a work, without permission, under particular conditions.

I strongly suggest that you read the free chapter at `http://SearchEngine Bulletin.com` to get the details on copyright and make sure that you beg or borrow, but not steal, other people's work.

Hunting for Other People's Content

I list different types of other people's content and warn you about copyright earlier in this chapter. Now it's time to get out there and grab tons of content. You're about to find some great places to look.

Keywords

When you're out on your content hunt, remember that the purpose is to find *keywords* to add to your site. You can do that in several ways:

✔ **Find content with the keywords already in it.** You want content that has at least *some* of your keywords, though you'll often find that it's not enough.

✔ **Add keywords to the content you get.** In some cases, you shouldn't edit the content because you're expected to use the content without changes. In other cases, you may be allowed to modify the content. You can, for instance, modify *open content* (described later in this chapter), and some syndicators allow it. As syndicator Featurewell says, "Clients can make minor edits to stories and photos, provided they do not modify or change the meaning, tone or general context of the articles . . . ." Thus, you can replace a few words here and there with your keywords, as long as the article still makes sense and retains the same tone and context.

✔ **"Chunk up" the article.** Break it into smaller, Web-friendly pieces and separate each piece with a heading (containing keywords, of course).

Newspapers often modify content they buy. A syndicated column you read in New York may be different from the same column run in a paper in Los Angeles, because newspapers cut and modify for space reasons or because they don't like the way something is worded.

When adding content, you're generally interested in adding pages with a variety of keywords sprinkled throughout. Remember, if you have a rodent-racing site, you want lots of pages with the words *rodent, racing, race, event, mouse, rat,* and so on.

Product information

Does your Web site sell products that you buy from a wholesaler or manufacturer? If so, contact your source and find out what materials are available: brochures, spec sheets, technical documentation, or user manuals. Take a look at anything the manufacturer has available. (I have one client who built an entire retail Web site around the idea of scanning and posting brochure content from wholesalers. It's a multimillion dollar business now.)

In many cases, the material may be available in Adobe Acrobat PDF files. You can post these files on your site within seconds, and they will be indexed by the major search engines, including Google. However, such files generally don't rank well in the search engines, so the ideal approach is to also convert the work to HTML files.

In fact, you may want to convert PDF files to Web pages for several reasons:

✔ Web pages load more quickly than PDF files.

✔ After a file is converted, you can link from the document into your site, whereas a PDF file itself becomes *orphaned* in the search result — a file with no indication of, or link to, the site it comes from.

✔ You can insert keywords into the <TITLE>, DESCRIPTION, and KEYWORDS tags, and stress keywords by putting them in bold, italic, and <H> tags.

✔ You can add links to other pages within your site.

✔ You can do more keywording in Web pages, adding headers, side navigation, footer links, and so on.

Just *how* do you convert PDF files? If you own Adobe Acrobat, you can try to use that program, though you may not like the results. Search for *pdf to html converter* to find other converters. None of these tools is perfect, so you may have some clean-up work to do on the PDF files.

Web sites and e-mail newsletters

The Web is so full of content that it's about to sink. (Well, not your site, obviously, or you wouldn't be reading this chapter.) Why not grab a few articles you like from other sites or from the e-mail newsletters you subscribe to? In fact, you may want to go hunting to find articles for this very purpose.

If you ask nicely, many people are happy to let you use their content. In fact, as I explain in Chapter 17, many people use content-syndication as a strategy for site promotion. They *want* people to use their stuff, as long as the sites that are using the material provide *attribution* (clearly state where the material is from and who wrote it) and then provide a link back to the site of origin.

Asking for permission is quite easy: Simply contact the owner of the article you saw on a site or in a newsletter and ask whether you can use the article. I did this on one occasion and, within *10 minutes,* received a positive response. Within 16 minutes, I had an article on my site that was loaded with keywords and that ranked very highly in the search engines in its own right. (I realized that the author's page ranked #3 for one of my critical keywords. Thus, within minutes, I had a page that had the potential to rank very highly for some important keywords.)

When you talk to the article's owner, make sure that you praise the article. (After all, you do like it, or you wouldn't be asking. Too much good content is out there to be using garbage.) Also, clearly state that you will provide the owner's bio at the bottom of the article and a link back to the owner's site. (Right now, maybe you're thinking, *but isn't that duplicate content?* Yes, it may be, but I get to that subject a little later in this chapter.)

If you own your own site, you have it easy: You can simply save the e-mail response from the article's author as evidence of permission to use the article. If you're working for a large corporation with a legal department, however, you have a bigger problem: Your lawyers, working under the principle of "common sense is dead," will expect you to have the article's author sign a 32-page document providing permission, declaring that he has the right to give permission, and signing over exclusive and lifetime rights to the article and any spin-off toys or clothing derived from it, in this or any other universe. (I didn't make up that universe bit, by the way; I took it from a very real publishing contract.) Sorry, I don't know how to help you here. (I would tell you to just remember what Shakespeare said — "First thing we do, let's kill all the lawyers" — except that I'm sure my publisher's legal department would get upset, and I actually do quite a bit of work in the legal business so I guess I shouldn't complain . . . .)

Where can you find these articles? Search for Web sites that are likely to have the type of information you need. (You'll want to avoid sites that are directly competing.) Keep your eyes open for blogs and newsletters.

Try searching for a combination of one of your keyword phrases and the words *article* and *newsletter* — for instance, *rodent racing article* and *rodent racing newsletter.*

How do you know who owns the copyright to the article? Here's a quick general rule: If the article has an attribution attached to it, contact that person. For instance, many e-mail newsletters are either written by a single person (in which case you contact him) or have a variety of articles, each one with an author bio and an e-mail address (in which case you contact the author, not the newsletter itself). In many cases, the author has given the newsletter one-time rights and still owns the copyright.

Some mechanisms used for syndicating content make it hard for search engines to read the syndicated content! So, you need to make sure that you use the right technique. See "Content-syndication sites," later in this chapter, for more information.

Government sources

I love government sources because they're *huge,* with a surprising range of information. In general, documents created by the U.S. federal government are in the public domain. Under the terms of Title 17 United States Code section 105, works created by U.S. government departments do not have copyright protection.

However, you should be aware of some important exceptions:

- ✔ The government may still hold copyrights on works that have been given to the government — bequests or assignments of some kind.
- ✔ The law is a U.S. law, making U.S. government works copyright free. Most other governments hold copyrights on their works.
- ✔ In some cases, works that nongovernmental agencies create on behalf of the government may not be protected by copyright — the law isn't clear.
- ✔ Works created by the National Technical Information Service (NTIS; www.ntis.gov) may have a limited, five-year copyright protection.
- ✔ The United States Postal Service is exempt from these regulations. The Postal Service can have copyright protection for its works. (It doesn't want people printing their own stamps!)

✔ In some cases, the government may publish works that were originally privately created works. Such documents may still be copyright protected.

Even with these exceptions, vast quantities of juicy government content are available. Now, don't think, "Oh, there probably aren't any government documents related to *my* area!" Maybe; maybe not. Where do you think all the tax billions go? The money can't *all* go to defense, bridges to nowhere, and studies of crustaceans on treadmills!. And yet it has to be spent somehow, so some of it goes to creating vast amounts of Web content!

You can place this content directly on your Web site. You'll find the content in Web pages or Adobe Acrobat PDF files; as discussed earlier in this chapter, you'll probably want to convert PDF files to HTML.

You will find not only useful documents for your purposes (text-heavy documents that search engines can read) but also other materials that may be useful for your site, such as videos.

Here are a few good places to find government materials:

✔ **FedWorld:** www.fedworld.gov

✔ **Government Printing Office:**

  • *Catalog of U.S. Government Publications:* http://catalog.gpo.gov/

  • *Federal Digital System:* http://www.gpo.gov/fdsys

✔ **Library of Congress — Government Web Resources:** http://lcweb. loc.gov/rr/news/extgovd.html

✔ **CIA's Electronic Reading Room:** www.foia.cia.gov

Or, just try this search syntax: *site:.gov your keywords*. For instance, typing *site:.gov rodent racing* tells the search engine to search within .gov domains only for *rodent racing*. (A lot of search results are returned for that search, though, surprisingly, nothing is returned when you search for *site:.gov "rodent racing".*)

Content-syndication sites

In the "Web sites and e-mail newsletters" section, earlier in this chapter, I discuss the idea of finding Web pages or e-mail newsletter articles you like and asking the owners for permission to use them. Well, here's a shortcut: Go to content-syndication sites.

Content-syndication sites are places where authors post their information so that site owners or newsletter editors can pick it up and use it for free. Why? Because you agree to place, in return, a short blurb at the bottom of the article, including a link back to the author's Web site.

Should you use these sites? Perhaps, if you can find something relevant that is of high quality. I would search for the article (try using `Copyscape.com`) to make sure it doesn't appear a thousand times elsewhere, though (a few times is okay; again, I discuss duplicate content later).

Here are a few places to get you started in the wonderful world of content-syndication:

- **Article Dashboard:** `www.articledashboard.com`
- **EZineArticles.com:** `www.ezinearticles.com`
- **GoArticles.com:** `www.goarticles.com`
- **The Open Directory Project's List of Content Providers:** `www.dmoz.org/Business/Publishing_and_Printing/Publishing/Services/Free_Content`

There are scores of these syndication libraries, so you'll have plenty of choice. (You'll find a lot of duplicates, though.)

Some Web sites have their own *syndication areas* — libraries from which you can pick articles you want to use. Also, see Chapter 17, where I talk about syndicating your own content and point you to other syndication sites.

Make sure that when you grab articles from a content-syndication site you're not using a competitor's article! All these articles have links back to the author's site, so you don't want to be sending traffic to the enemy.

Geeky stuff you must understand

I have to get into a little technogeeky information now, I'm afraid. I hate to do it, but if you don't understand this topic, you may be wasting your time with content-syndication.

Many syndication systems use a simple piece of JavaScript to allow you to pull articles from their sites onto yours. For instance, take a look at this code I pulled from a site that syndicates news articles:

```
<script src="http://farmcentre.com/synd/synd.jsp?id=cfbmc"> </script>
```

This piece of code tells the Web browser to grab the `synd.jsp` file from the `farmcentre.com` Web site. That file uses JavaScript to insert the article into the Web page. Articles or other forms of content can be automatically embedded in other ways, too, such as using `<iframe>` tags.

The problem is that the search engines may not read the JavaScript that's pulling the content into your site, as I explain in Chapter 9. They *can* read JavaScript, and sometimes do. Google, for instance, can read content placed into Facebook pages. Have you noticed that as you scroll down a Facebook page, the page grows? This is done using all sorts of scripts (look at the source code; you won't see much content, but plenty of scripting). Google can read the content that is pulled by the scripts.

Does that mean it will do the same for *your* pages? Will Bing? I don't know, but my advice is not to risk it. If you want to ensure that the search engines read your content, avoid placing it onto the page using JavaScript.

So the risk of using JavaScript to drop content into your site is that the coding gets ignored. The syndicated article you wanted to place into the Web page *never gets placed into the page that the searchbot reads!* All the time and energy you spent placing content is wasted.

As for `<iframe>` tags, search engines follow the link that's used to pull the page into the frame and view that content as though it were on the origin Web site, leading to the orphan problems discussed in Chapter 9.

This whole geeky topic strikes me as quite humorous, really. Thousands of people are syndicating content or using syndicated content, mostly for search engine reasons. People syndicating the content want to place their links on as many Web pages as possible, for two reasons:

- ✔ Readers will see the links and click them.
- ✔ The search engines will see the links and rank the referenced site higher.

Also, people using the syndicated content are doing so because they want content, stuffed with good keywords, for search engines to read.

And in many cases, both the syndicators and the people using syndicated content are wasting their time because search engines aren't placing the content, seeing the keywords, or reading the links!

To make sure the content you use works for you, follow the suggestions in this list:

- ✔ **Don't use browser-side inclusion techniques.** That includes JavaScript and iframes.

✔ **Use server-side inclusion techniques.** That includes server includes, PHP, and ASP. If you're not sure whether a technique is server side or browser side, ask a knowledgeable geek — you want an inclusion technique that loads the content into the page *before* it's sent to the browser or searchbot.

✔ **Use manual inclusion techniques.** That is, copy and paste the content into your pages directly. Plenty of content relies on manual inclusion, and you may even get content owners who are using automatic-inclusion techniques to agree to let you manually copy their content.

As long as you're aware of syndicated content's pitfalls and how to avoid them, it's quite possible to find syndicated content and make it work so that you reap the search engine benefits of having that content on your site.

A *hosted-content service* hosts the content on its site along with a copy of your Web site template so that the content appears to be on your site (unless you look in the browser's Location or Address bar, where you see the company's URL). The problem with these services is that search engines are unlikely to pick up the content because they see the same articles duplicated repeatedly on the same domain. Google, for instance, will probably keep one set and ignore duplicates. (Also, see the section "A Word about Duplicated Content," later in this chapter.) And in any case, the content isn't on your site, it's on the host site!

The problem with automatic updates

Another problem with content-syndication sites involves *automatic updates*, which allow a content owner to change the content immediately. For example, sites that provide weekly or monthly syndicated newsletters often use automatic updates. The content provider can use this technique to update the content on dozens or hundreds of sites by simply changing the source file. The next time a page is loaded on one of the sites with the syndicated content, the new information appears.

But if you're adding content for keyword purposes, automatic updating may not be such a good thing. If you find an article with lots of nice keywords, it could be gone tomorrow. Manual inclusion techniques ensure that the article you placed remains in place and also allow you to, for instance, break the article into chunks by adding keyword-laden headings. (Although it's hard to say whether a site owner who uses automatic updating is likely to let you use manual inclusion, plenty of content is out there.)

Traditional syndication services

Content-syndication is nothing new — it has been around for a hundred years. (I just made up that statement, but it's probably true.) Much of what you read in your local newspaper isn't written by the paper's staff; it comes from a syndication service.

Some syndication services sell content for your site. In general, this material should be better than free syndicated content. However, much of the free stuff is pretty good, too, so you may not want to pay for syndicated material until you exhaust your search for free content. (This content is often fed to Web sites using RSS feeds, so see the upcoming section "RSS syndication feeds.")

Here are a few places you can find commercial syndicated material:

- **Featurewell:** `www.featurewell.com`
- **Brafton:** `www.brafton.com`
- **Moreover:** `www.moreover.com`
- **StudioOne:** `www.studioonenetworks.com`
- **Universal uclick:** `www.universaluclick.com`
- **YellowBrix:** `www.yellowbrix.com`
- **The Open Directory Project list of content providers:** `www.dmoz.org/News/Media/Services/Syndicates`

Specialty syndication services provide content for particular industries. For example, AKZO Media (`www.akzomedia.com`) provides content for the real estate industry.

RSS syndication feeds

RSS is one of those geeky acronyms that nobody can define for certain. Some say it means *really simple syndication;* others believe that it means *rich site summary* or *RDF site summary.* What it stands for doesn't really matter. All you need to know is that RSS is an important content-syndication tool.

RSS systems comprise two components:

- An RSS *feed,* or a source of content of some kind
- An RSS *aggregator* or *news reader,* or a system that drops the information from the feed into a Web page

For example, all top search engines provide RSS feeds of their news headlines, at least for personal or noncommercial use. You can install an RSS aggregator on your site and point it to an RSS news feed. The page will then contain recent searches on news headlines. (Google allows you to use the feed to place Google News into your site, although it also states that you can't use the news feed "to increase traffic to your site.")

The big advantage of RSS feeds is that you define the keywords you want to have sent to your site. Tell the feed that you want feeds related to rodent racing, and, naturally, content is fed back to you with the keywords rodent racing in it, along with lots of other, related keywords.

What you need, then, is an aggregator that you can install into your Web site. Aggregators range from fairly simple to quite complicated — and that's assuming you have some technical abilities in the first place. (If you don't, there's no range; they're all complicated!) RSS feeds can be integrated both browser side and server side. Again, you probably need server-side integration to make sure the search engines read the inserted content.

Also, often RSS feeds merely pass a link to material on another site, in which case you don't benefit much. Make sure that you're getting useful content passed to your site. (Many content-syndication companies use RSS feeds to distribute their work.)

To find RSS feeds, keep your eyes open for RSS or XML symbols and other indicators showing that an RSS feed is available — many blogs, for instance, provide RSS feeds. You can see examples of these icons in Figure 11-1.

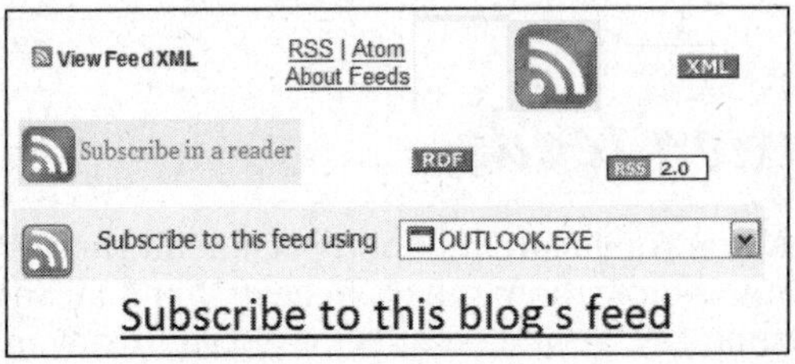

Figure 11-1:
Look for these sorts of icons and links to indicate that an RSS feed is available.

However, you must remember that just because you find an RSS feed available doesn't mean that you can put it into your site without permission. In fact, many blog owners provide feeds so that their readers can view the blogs in a personal RSS reader; you can, for instance, subscribe to RSS feeds within Microsoft Outlook, Internet Explorer, and a Yahoo! or Google account. Before you use a feed, read the feed license agreement or, if you can't find it, contact the owner.

In contrast to the automated syndication techniques I mention earlier in this chapter (under *Content-syndication sites*), which use JavaScript and other browser-side systems for inserting content, RSS aggregators for Web pages often use *server-side* techniques, so the content is inserted into the Web page *before* the search engines see it. That's what they call in the search engine business *A Good Thing*. (Some also provide browser-side widgets to do the work, which isn't so good.)

If you decide that you want to go ahead with RSS, you need an aggregator. Try searching for *news aggregator*, *feed aggregator*, or *rss aggregator*.

Open content and copyleft

Have you heard of *open-source software?* This type of software is created through the contributions of multiple individuals who agree to allow pretty much anyone to use the software, at no charge. Another movement that doesn't get quite the same attention as open-source software is the *open-content* or *creative commons* movement. Open content is free and available for your use.

Open content relies on the concept known as *copyleft*. Under copyleft, the owner of a copyrighted work doesn't release it into the public domain. Instead, she releases the work for public modification, with the understanding that anyone using the work must agree to not claim original authorship and to release all derivative works under the same conditions.

This was an exciting concept a few years ago, though it seems to be fading. The home page of the Open Content Alliance site (www.opencontentalliance. org) hadn't been updated for five years when I checked it recently, for instance. Still, you might want to check out these sites to see if you can find anything useful:

- ✔ **Creative Commons:** www.creativecommons.org
- ✔ **The Open Directory Project's open content page:** http://dmoz.org/ Computers/Open_Source/Open_Content
- ✔ **Wikipedia List of Wikis** (many contain articles with some form of open-content license): http://en.wikipedia.org/wiki/List_of_wikis

Watch for competitors' information. Some companies use open content as a way to get their links onto the Web.

Search results pages

The great thing about search results pages is that they have the exact keywords you define, liberally scattered throughout. When you conduct a search in a search engine — whether you're searching Web sites, a directory of magazine articles, or news headlines — what does the search engine return? Matches for your keywords.

RSS provides one way to insert searches — in particular, searches of news headlines — into your pages. Even though the page's content changes continually, you don't have to worry about the content changing to a page that doesn't contain your keywords, because the content is a reflection of the keywords you provide. You may also be able to find search pages that you can manually copy and paste. Sites that contain large numbers of articles and a search function may be good candidates. Run a search; then, copy the results and paste them into a Web page.

Make sure that the links in the search results still work and that they open the results in a new window. (You don't want to push people away from your site.)

Press releases

The nice thing about press releases is that you can use them without permission. The purpose of a press release is to send it out and see who picks it up. You don't need to contact the owner of the press release, because you already have an implied agreement that you can simply post the release wherever you want (unchanged and in its entirety, of course).

You may be able to find press releases that have the keywords you want, are relevant to your site in some way, and are not released by competitors. For instance, if you're in the business of running rodent-racing events, companies selling rodent-racing harnesses and other gear aren't direct competitors and may well have press releases you can use.

Where do you find these press releases? Try searching for *press releases* at a search engine. Combine the search term with some keywords, such as *rodent racing press release*. You can also find them at press release sites, such as these:

- ✔ **EmailWire:** www.emailwire.com
- ✔ **Free-Press-Release.com:** www.free-press-release.com
- ✔ **Hot Product News:** www.hotproductnews.com

- ✔ **I-Newswire.com:** `http://i-newswire.com`
- ✔ **M2PressWIRE:** `www.presswire.net`
- ✔ **Online Press Releases:** `www.onlinepressreleases.com`
- ✔ **OpenPR.com:** `www.openpr.com`
- ✔ **PR Newswire:** `www.prnewswire.com`
- ✔ **PR Web:** `www.prweb.com`
- ✔ **PR.com:** `www.pr.com`
- ✔ **PressBox.co.uk:** `www.pressbox.co.uk`
- ✔ **PRLeap:** `www.prleap.com`
- ✔ **PRLog.org:** `www.prlog.org`
- ✔ **TransWorldNews.com:** `www.transworldnews.com`

You can even subscribe to press release services so that you get relevant press releases sent to you as soon as they're published.

Q&A areas

After you attract sufficient traffic to your site, you may want to set up a question-and-answer (Q&A) or Frequently Asked Questions (FAQ) area on your site. Visitors to your site can ask questions — providing you with keyword-laden questions in many cases — and you can answer them.

A number of free and low-cost software tools automate the creation and management of these Q&A areas. Search for *faq web software* and you'll find them.

Message boards

Message board areas can be quite powerful, in more than one way. Setting up a message board — also known as a forum or bulletin board system (BBS) — allows site visitors to place keywords in your site for you! A message board often draws traffic, bringing people in purely for the conversation.

Do you own a site about kayaks? As you sleep, visitors can leave messages with the word *kayak* in them over and over. Does your site sell rodent supplies? While you go about your daily business, your visitors can leave messages containing words such as *rodent, mouse,* and *rat.* Over time, this process can build up to thousands of pages with tens of thousands of keywords.

BBS systems — even cool ones with lots of features, such as the ability to post photos — are cheap — often free. They're relatively easy to set up, even for low-level geeks. Don't underestimate this technique: If you have a lot of traffic on your Web site, a BBS can be a great way to build huge amounts of content. Search for terms such as *bbs software* and *forum software*.

Blogs

Blogs are sort of like diaries. (The term is a derivation of *Weblog.*) These systems allow people to write any kind of twaddle — er, musings — they want and then publish this nonsense — um, literature — directly to their Web sites. My cynicism aside, you *can* find some extremely interesting blogs out there.

In fact, over the past few years, blogs have become important SEO tools — search engines seem to like them and to visit frequently to index them. In fact, Google even owns one of the top blogging-tools companies, Blogger (`http://blogger.com`). (Would you bet that blogs hosted by Blogger are indexed by Google?!)

There are also free and low-cost blog programs that you can install directly onto your Web site. WordPress, for instance (`www.wordpress.com`), is a very sophisticated blog system with free versions, that's relatively easy to install. (For everything you need to know about using WordPress, check out the latest edition of *WordPress For Dummies,* by Lisa Sabin-Wilson.) WordPress is probably the world's most popular blogging system; a survey found that 24 percent of the world's Web sites use WordPress software. Because it is so sophisticated and flexible, many sites that you wouldn't really consider to be blogs use the software. In fact, blogging systems are really CMS — Content Management Systems, software that simplifies the process of creating and managing Web pages.

Also, some blog-hosting services provide a way to integrate pages into your Web site, and blogs can be effective SEO tools, if you can find a way to create enough content. Although many people set up blogs, the number that *maintain* them is far lower!

If you use any tool that allows visitors to post messages on your site, you should monitor and delete inappropriate messages. Many search engine marketers use such tools to post messages (known as *blog spam*) with links pointing back to their sites.

Blogs can be quite useful for search engine optimization, but I don't think blogs are an SEO magic bullet, as some people have suggested. Blogs are a way to get more content onto your site, and the pages may get reindexed frequently (though there may not be much of a difference between the speed of indexing of "blog" content and other content as there used to be). They also have tools that interlink blogs, so if you run an active blog, you can get links back to your site. However, the big problem with blogs is that someone must have the time to write frequently, the inclination to write frequently, and the ability to write well and to write what people want to read. This is often a tall order!

A Word about Duplicated Content

The idea behind *duplicated content* is that search engines don't like the same content appearing in different places; after all, why would they want to provide people with lots of different ways to get to the same information? As a Google employee stated on the Google Webmaster Central blog (`http://googlewebmastercentral.blogspot.com`):

> *Our users typically want to see a diverse cross-section of unique content when they do searches. In contrast, they're understandably annoyed when they see substantially the same content within a set of search results.*

What does Google do about duplicated content? In general, it tries to eliminate copies. For instance:

> *. . . if your site has articles in "regular" and "printer" versions and neither set is blocked in robots.txt or via a noindex meta tag, we'll choose one version to list.*

A lot of paranoia exists about duplicated content; people talk about how sites can get themselves banned for using duplicated content. Most of this talk is gross exaggeration because sites often have good reasons to have duplicated content. Perhaps you're running news feeds from a popular central source or using press releases about events in your industry. It wouldn't make sense for search engines to penalize people for such innocent uses. Thus, as this Google employee stated,

> *In the rare cases in which we perceive that duplicate content may be shown with intent to manipulate our rankings and deceive our users, we'll also make appropriate adjustments in the indexing and ranking of the sites involved. However, we prefer to focus on filtering rather than ranking adjustments . . . so in the vast majority of cases, the worst thing that'll befall webmasters is to see the "less desired" version of a page shown in our index.*

Read those comments carefully and you'll see that they are directed toward duplicate content *on your own site*; in days past, a common SEO trick was to create a single page of content, then make hundreds of copies, thousands even, each slightly different. So, for instance, you might have essentially the same content, but "customized" for thousands of different cities. The search engines didn't like that kind of "duplicate content" game.

The issue of the same content appearing on multiple sites is very different, though. In fact, there are various reasons why search engines can't penalize sites for republishing content. Whom will they punish — every site holding the content or all but the first one to publish it? Also, how would they know who was first?

Here's another reason that the search engines can't "punish" sites for duplicated content. Say that I've noticed that your rodent-racing site is coming up quickly in the search ranks, and you've got a lot of excellent, unique content related to the exciting world of racing very small animals. If I were of a nefarious bent (which I'm not, but if I were . . .), here's what I'd do: Build a bunch of Web sites on different servers, but build them anonymously. I'd then "scrape" data from your rodent site and republish it on these other sites, forcing the search engines to penalize you.

In any case, the search engine designers know that there are really good reasons for the same content to appear on different sites; press releases, for instance, are designed for wide dissemination, and why wouldn't a range of sites want to present the same release to their various audiences?

In general, then, the dire warnings about duplicated content are wrong. The main problem using content that appears elsewhere is that the search engines can't rank everyone #1 for the same content, so it has to make a choice.

So what can you do about duplicated content, with articles you get from syndication sites, for instance, or press releases you drop into your site? If you want to make it more likely that the content isn't ignored, mix it up a little: Add headings within the pieces, change a few words here and there, surround it with other information that's unique to your site, and so on. But don't worry about a penalty, because if every site that contains duplicate content were dropped from Google's index, the index would be empty.

Chapter 12

Finding Traffic through Local-Search Marketing

. . . .

In This Chapter

▶ Discovering how local search works

▶ Optimizing your pages for local-search marketing

▶ Submitting to the major local-search systems

▶ Submitting to other local-search systems

▶ Working with the Review sites and Yellow Page sites

. . . .

*I*ncreasingly, the Internet is being used as a tool for finding local resources. You can find not only information or buy online, but you can also find homes for sale in your neighborhood, compare local independent insurance agents, and shop at stores close to you that sell the products you need. Thus, it's increasingly important to keep *local-search marketing* in mind when optimizing for search engines — that is, to target by not only a searcher's keyword but also by the searcher's geographic location (sometimes known as *geo-targeting*). *Local search* is the generic term given to the ability to search for information related to a particular location — a state, a city, or even a zip code.

Why You Shouldn't Skip This Chapter

Wait! Before you skip this chapter because you have a purely online business, you need to understand the *two* basic reasons you should consider local-search marketing:

- ✔ You have a local business.
- ✔ Your prospects — your target customers — search locally.

Say you are a local business. You sell insurance in your town or own a local health-food store or are a personal trainer with clients within a 5-mile radius. Clearly, you don't need to rank well on the terms *insurance, health food,* or *personal training.* You need to rank well on the terms *insurance denver, health food waco,* or *personal training paducah.* There's no point in competing for general terms against hundreds of thousands of other companies when you're interested in a fraction of the searches; in fact, the really good news is that it's much easier to rank for a local term than a nonlocal term. The work required to rank on Page 1 for the term *personal training* will be *far* more than the work required for *personal training paducah.*

But, say you're not a local shop for local people. You sell to anyone, any-where. You may find that the people you want to reach don't search for generic terms — they search for generic terms *in combination with local terms.* You may discover this concept if you do a good keyword analysis, which I describe in Chapter 6. Most people don't search for lawyers, for instance; they search for lawyers in a particular city. They don't search for insurance; they search for insurance in a particular state or city. They don't search for mortgages — they search for mortgages in a particular city.

You may find then, that if you want to reach the largest number of people, you *have* to consider the local aspect even if you sell nationally. Large online busi-nesses targeting home buyers, for instance, often create *local-search — targeted* pages designed to reach people in thousands of different locales.

Understanding Local-Search Marketing's Importance

The local aspect of search is hugely important. Remember, for all the e-commerce hype, e-commerce accounts for only a small portion of the overall economy; in other words, most sales are made *offline.* The Department of Commerce, for instance, estimated that in the fourth quarter of 2014, e-commerce accounted for just 6.5 percent of total retail sales.

So offline sales are still extremely important, but they undoubtedly are often affected by online activities. For instance, research has uncovered these gems about Internet users:

✔ Most are *off-channel, Web-to-shop (W2S),* or *ROBO (Research Online, Buy Offline)* buyers. That is, they research products online before buying offline.

✔ When in the brick-and-mortar stores, almost half of Internet users spend extra dollars on products they didn't research.

✔ More money is spent offline after online research than is spent online after online research.

✔ A study released late in 2011 (GroupM Search & Kantar Media Compete) looked at retail sales in Automotive, Consumer Electronics and Entertainment areas; 93 percent of buyers surveyed had used Web search engines as part of their research process, and most buyers had clicked on organic-search links, rather than PPC links.

✔ The study also found that one of the most popular pages viewed by shoppers was the store-location page, showing that visitors are not doing idle window shopping; they are looking for stores to visit.

✔ Forrester Research estimates that "online influenced offline sales" are over $1 trillion a year.

When you search at a major search engine using keywords that indicate you are probably looking for a local business or service — *mexican restaurant, attorney, pizza*, and so on — the search engines will provide local results; search results pulled out of their local directory, along with a map.

Looking through Local Search

All the major search engines — Google, Yahoo!, and Bing — have local search features, incorporated into their map systems but still accessible from regular search. You can see an example of local-search results, from Google Maps, in Figure 12-1, and in Figure 12-2, you can see the type of results that can be displayed for a particular business.

Local searches are carried out if you include location information in your search: *pizza denver* or *tax attorney rhode island,* for example. However, the local search engines also have a good idea where you are (I explain how next), so for many types of searches, if they think it's a local search they can provide local results even if you don't tell them where you are. Search any of the big three search engines for *pizza,* for instance, and they'll assume that you're likely looking for a pizza place, so they include local search in the results. Search for *car insurance, japanese restaurant,* or *hair salon,* and you'll get local results.

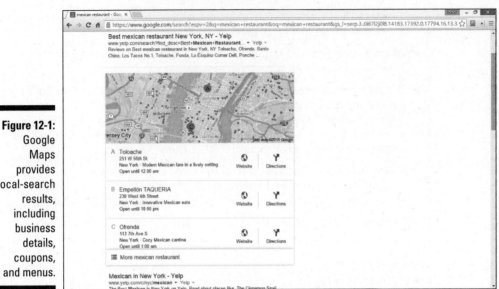

Figure 12-1:
Google
Maps
provides
local-search
results,
including
business
details,
coupons,
and menus.

Figure 12-2:
Detailed
information
is provided
for each
business —
information
that the busi-
ness owner
can add to.

How Does Local Search Work?

Local search is based on several different methodologies, including the science known as *geolocation,* the science of trying to figure out where the heck a computer *is,* geographically speaking. Say, for example, that a computer contacts a search engine and says, "Hi, I'm computer `67.176.77.58`; can you search for information about *rodent racing* and send me the results?" How does the search engine figure out whether that computer is in Colorado and thus wants information about the famous Rocky Mountain prairie dog racing, or is in Florida and is interested in the famous African Gambian pouch rat races?

Well, local search generally works in a few basic ways. Different services use different combinations of these methods.

Search terms

If someone types *dentist new york,* the search engine can be pretty sure that the person is looking for a dentist in New York, not a dentist in Oklahoma City. Simple, eh? I can be in Denver, Colorado, but if I type *dentist new york,* the search engine will display a map of New York.

Partner and localized sites

Search services can guess at a location based on the Web site someone is using. If someone is searching at `www.google.fr`, it's a good bet that the person is in France; if someone searches at `www.yahoo.co.uk`, that person is probably in the United Kingdom. In other cases, partner sites can be even more specific, and related to a particular region or even city.

IP numbers

Internet Protocol (IP) numbers identify computers on the Internet. Every computer connected to the Internet at any moment has a unique IP number.

With information being sent to and fro — from your computer to Web sites and back — there has to be a way for the information to be "addressed" so that various servers on the Internet know where to deliver the information. Thus, every computer connected to the Internet has an *IP number,* or *IP address.*

In some cases, two or more computers share an IP number, as in a situation in which a house or an apartment is using a cable or digital subscriber line (DSL) connection, with several computers connected through a single router; but for the purposes of figuring out location, this information isn't important, of course.

In some cases, computers "own" a particular IP number: Turn the computer off now and turn it on next week, and it has the same number. This is known as a *static IP number*. Often, however, computers share IP numbers. Log out of a dialup account now and in five minutes dial back in, and your computer is assigned a different IP number (known as a *dynamic IP number*). That IP number is shared among many computers, but only one computer can use the number at any particular time.

Take a look at this IP number: `67.176.77.58`. This number uniquely identifies a particular computer in Colorado. If a server sends a page to that address, the page can go to only one place because at that moment only one computer on the Internet is using that number to identify itself. It's like a telephone number. Every telephone in the entire world has a unique number (when you include the country code). Pick up the phone and dial the full number, and there's only one telephone in the world that you can possibly be connected to.

An IP number is a *hierarchical* system. A block of numbers is assigned to a particular organization or company; that organization or company then assigns blocks of numbers to other organizations or companies, which can then assign their numbers to different organizations or companies, or divisions within a company, and so on.

Consider, again, `67.176.77.58`. This number is "owned" by Comcast Cable Communications, a large American cable-TV company. In fact, Comcast has a large block of numbers: `67.160.0.0–67.191.255.255`. Within that large block lies another block that Comcast uses in Colorado: `67.176.0.0–67.176.127.255`. Clearly, `67.176.77.58` lies within this block.

If you want to see this process at work, a number of sites tell you where you are, or at least where they think you are. I just visited IP2Location (`www.ip2location.com`), and it identified my city — though not my exact zip code, and it got my latitude and longitude wrong.

Local-search marketing with IP numbers isn't perfect; it's definitely an imprecise science, for a few reasons:

✔ **You can't assume that a number assigned to a company in a particular area is being used in that area.** It's possible for two computers using two IP numbers that are just one digit apart — `67.176.77.58` and `67.176.77.59`, for instance — to be thousands of miles apart. An IP number block assigned to an organization in one area can be used by many different computers in many different locations. For example, a computer in San Francisco assigned a block of IP numbers may use those numbers for computers in branch offices in San Diego, Oklahoma City, and Seattle.

✔ **Dynamic IP numbers are "here today, there tomorrow."** When you dial into a network and are assigned an IP number, you could be in California while the computer that assigned the number is in Virginia. When you log off and someone logs on and takes your number, the new computer might be in Wyoming. In particular, AOL messes up IP location because it assigns IP numbers to dialup users all around the country.

Still, geolocation is getting better all the time. Although the authorities that assign blocks of IP numbers provide very basic geographic information, this information can then be combined with other clues, such as hostnames. For example, it's possible to trace the path taken by a communication from one computer to another and get the IP numbers and hostnames of the servers between the start and destination computers. Hostnames sometimes contain geographic names that help IP-location systems figure out where they are.

Another clue: Some major Internet service providers (ISPs) assign blocks of IP numbers geographically, so when you crack the code, you can figure out where people using that ISP actually live. Using clues such as these, geolocation engineers at various companies specializing in this science can fairly accurately locate IP numbers.

So the system isn't perfect, but it's close much of the time. In any case, it doesn't usually need to be spot on. If you're searching for pizza in your town, for instance, Google doesn't need to know your exact address; it shows a map with pizza places, and you can zoom in to your specific location if you want.

Google lets searchers actually specify where they are. Click the cog icon at the bottom right of a Google Maps page, or at the top right of a search results page and select Search Settings. Click the Locations link in the left column, and you'll see a box into which you can enter your street address. The only problem is that the vast majority of users don't know about this setting (and it messes up your search results when you travel without remembering to change your location, of course).

There's another way Google figures out your location; by tracking your location on your cell phone, if you're using an Android phone with a Google account set up. Go to `https://maps.google.com/locationhistory/` and prepared to be spooked by what Big Brother knows about you.

Two Ways to Reach People Locally

Let me summarize:

- ✔ Search engines are providing local search services, encouraging people to search locally.
- ✔ People often type location names with their keyword searches.
- ✔ If the searcher doesn't provide a geographic term, but the search engine still thinks it's likely to be a local search, the search engine will "guess" where the searcher is.

Now, it's important to understand that when you do a local search, the major search engines pull data from two main indexes (ignoring the PPC index and the specialized indexes, of course — see Chapter 2). They have the regular organic search results, which are based on the keywords *and*, to some degree, your location. (Even if you don't use a geographic term in your search, Google is likely to find organic pages that it thinks are from businesses in your area.) But it also has a totally separate index to pull from, the Local results, providing the data such as that shown in Figures 12-1 and 12-2.

This type of data is both good and bad. It's good, because it gives you an extra chance of ranking. Perhaps you're not doing too well in the organic results, but you *are* doing well in the Local results, and your site appears high on the page next to the map. Or, if you do a really good job, your business can turn up in the local search results — up by the map — *and* in the organic results, probably lower down on the page (not always; sometimes the map and Local results are displayed before the organic results, sometimes embedded in them). The bad part is that you have more work to do: They are completely different indexes, so you need to do different things to rank well in each one.

So your job, if you want to rank well for local searches, is to know what to do for both of these indexes. I begin with the index I've been telling you about already, the organic-search index, and then I discuss the Local index.

"Localizing" Your Web Pages

I see this all the time with my consulting clients: Web sites that need to rank for local search terms but that haven't the slightest hope of doing so. An example is my rodent-racing client in New York, the owner of the *Big Apple Rodent Racing* track. (Okay, I made up this client, but bear with me.) He came to me saying that he wanted to rank well for *rodent racing new york*, and in fact to rank well for various New York boroughs.

There was one big problem, though. He didn't have a single page with the term *rodent racing* and the name *New York*. The only page that contained *New York* was his Contact Us page, and that page contained only contact information and a map . . . it didn't contain the words *rodent racing*. So my client had not a single page that was a good match for *rodent racing new york*.

So the very first step to take if you want to rank locally is to make sure that you have local terms in your pages. Ideally, have these terms not just in a Contact Us page but on every page.

The problem with putting your location in only your Contact Us page is that while you've probably created dozens, scores, maybe hundreds of lovely keyword-rich pages, you have just removed one of the most important keywords and put it on a separate page. If you want Google to think a page is related to a particular location in addition to finding certain keywords, you need to make sure the location name and keywords appear on the same pages! So, here are a few things you can do:

✔ **Include your full address in your Web pages.** Include your street, city, state, and zip code. Although you can put the address in the footer, ideally it should be near the top of the page somewhere. (If you don't know about prominence, see Chapter 7.)

   If you have more than one address, put all the addresses on each page.

✔ **Include in all your pages the names of all locations you're interested in.** Include a list of city names, for instance, in your footer or in a sidebar, ideally with links to pages with information about each of those cities.

✔ **Create a Contact Us page *for every* location you have.** If you have five office locations, you need five Contact Us pages.

✔ **Put important keywords on your Contact Us pages**.

✔ **Find other reasons to mention the city and zip code in the body of your text.** If possible, put them in <H> tags; use bold font on some of the references, too.

✔ **Include location names in your filenames**. Your URL should contain the name of the location for which you are trying to rank well. So, for instance, instead of yourdomain.com/pizza.html, you could use youdomain.com/pizza-phoenix-az.html.

✔ **Include the city name in your TITLE and DESCRIPTION meta tags.**

✔ **Include city and state names in link text when linking from other sites to yours.** See Chapter 16 for more information.

You should think carefully about what location names are truly important. Different types of searches use different types of location terms. For instance, when people search for *insurance,* they often search with a state name: *car insurance colorado, renters insurance texas,* and so on. For real estate, people usually search with city names or even neighborhood names. For attorneys, people often search using city names but rarely neighborhood names. So you should think about which terms are important and target those terms.

Getting a few keyworded links to your site with the location names in combination with the product or service keywords can be very powerful, so read Chapter 16 carefully. Consider also actually optimizing a few pages for specific locations, using the location and product or service keywords in the <TITLE> and <DESCRIPTION> tags, in H1 headers, several times in the body text, in links to the page, and so on. My rodent-racing client should probably have a page optimized for *New York Rodent Racing,* one for *Brooklyn Rodent Racing,* another for *Manhattan Rodent Racing,* and so on.

Use the Geo meta tags

You might want to also use geo meta tags at the top of your homepage and, if you have multiple locations, place the appropriate tags into each of your contact pages. These tags tell the search engines your exact location. Here's an example:

```
<meta name="geo.placename" content="200 E Colfax Ave, Denver, CO 80203, USA" />
<meta name="geo.position" content="39.740037;-104.984418" />
<meta name="geo.region" content="US-CO" />
<meta name="ICBM" content="39.740037, -104.984418" />
```

Google doesn't use geo tags; Google believes they are not reliable, because they often get copied from one Web site to another or are left in sites being created using page templates, by Web developers who are not paying attention. Reportedly Bing *may* use them, though, as they can be created very quickly and easily, so you might as well do so. There are various geo-tag sites that will create tags for you: You simply provide your location address, and the system will build the tags. Try these sites (or if they are not working search for *geo meta tag*):

✔ www.geo-tag.de/generator/en.html

✔ www.mygeoposition.com

Incidentally, talking of templates, you might also want to check whether your pages contain a content-language tag, like `<meta http-equiv="content-language" content="en-gb">`. You can just remove this; although common, it was never part of the HTTP specification, and had poor browser support. Instead, use the `lang` tag, like this: `<html lang="en-US">`. The first piece (in this case, *en*) specifies the language (English), and the second specifies the country (US). Search for *html language codes* and *2-character country codes* to find the appropriate codes. If these codes are set for a different language or country, you may be telling the search engines that you are outside your actual location.

Google Webmaster (see Chapter 13) also has a Geographic target setting that lets you tell Google what country the site should target and a language setting, too (see the International Targeting settings). Registering for Local Search.

In Chapter 13, you read about how to get your site listed in search engine indexes. Let me quickly cover *another* form of search engine submission here: submitting your business to the search engine's local-search indexes.

First note that your business may turn up in the results even if you take no action. The major search engines pull data from a lot of different sources. If you have a business that has been picked up by some kind of business directory, your business has likely ended up on the local-search indexes of the major search engines. For instance, if your business has a business phone listing, you are almost certainly included.

Being in the index doesn't mean that you can rest on your laurels, though. Just because you are in the index doesn't mean you'll necessarily rank well. In any case, there are *lots* of local-search directories, not just the major ones, so you still have work to do. For instance, Google, Yahoo!, and Bing let you add information about your business directly to the local-search index, increasing the likelihood of being found during a local search and increasing the amount of information that's seen when your information is viewed. Also, you may want to consider the upgrades that some of the search engines sell and that may help push you above your competitors. Table 12-1 summarizes the top three search engines' local-search systems.

A quick word about Yahoo!. As I mention in Chapter 1, Yahoo! gets organic search results (and PPC ads) from Bing. However, Yahoo! still manages Yahoo! Local results itself. That is, the system is separate from Bing, and so your listing in Yahoo! is managed separately from your listing in Bing.

Table 12-1	The Big Three Go Local	
Site	*Description*	*URL*
Google Maps/ Google My Business	Free, including the ability to add video and pictures; if you have more than ten locations, you can submit a data file. To the user, the service appears to be called Google Maps. However, in communications with businesses, Google is branding the service *Google My Business*.	`https://www.google.com/business`
Yahoo! Local	Free or $9.95 per month if you want to add pictures, a "tagline," and a business description.	
Bing Places	Free, including photographs.	`https://www.bingplaces.com`

Grabbing control of (or adding) your business listing

In Table 12-1, in the previous section, I provide the URL of each local service's "ground zero," where you can go to start a new listing or take control of your current listing. You can also start a different way: at the search engine itself. Starting at the search engine shows you where you already stand in the local results, and from there you can grab control of your current listing or add a new one.

1. **Go to the search engine and search for your product.**

   For instance, if you own a pizza parlor, search for *pizza* along with your town's name (just to make sure that Google searches the correct locale).

   If you see your business listed, that's great!

2. **If you don't see your business listed, see whether it's on the full page of results.**

   You should see a link to more local results. Google, for instance, at the time of writing, has a link under the local results that says <u>More</u> or sometimes <u>More Results Near [Location]</u> or <u>Map Results</u>, or you can click the map if one is shown.

3. **If you still can't find your business, add your business name to the search and search again.**

   Search *Roddy's Rodent Pie Shop pizza denver*, for instance.

4. **If you're still not there, try searching for the business name and location, with no product or service keyword.**

   Search *Roddy's Rodent Pie Shop denver*, for instance.

5. **If you're still not there, your business probably isn't listed, so go to the appropriate link in Table 12-1 and add your listing.**

   If you do find your business, though, you need to find your way to the expanded data (see Figure 12-3 for an example). Click various places on the listing; if you end up in your business's Web site, click the browser Back button and come back . . . try clicking something again. These systems all work a little differently, and differ across time, too. (At the time of writing, on Google you can click anything over the listing except the links; on Bing click anywhere except on the URL in the listing; and on Yahoo! click anywhere on the listing and you'll see the expanded data.)

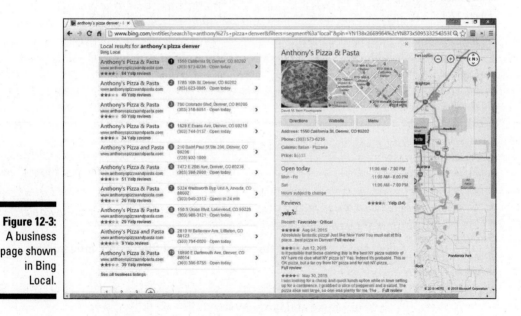

Figure 12-3: A business page shown in Bing Local.

Take a look at what's on your business page — a little sparse? Don't worry, you'll be able to change that soon. You need to look for a way to grab control of your business.

6. **Look for a link or button that says something like <u>Is this your business? Verify your listing</u>; <u>Do you own this business?</u>; or <u>Are you the business owner?</u> (see Figure 12-4) and then click it.**

   You're on your way to taking control of the listing.

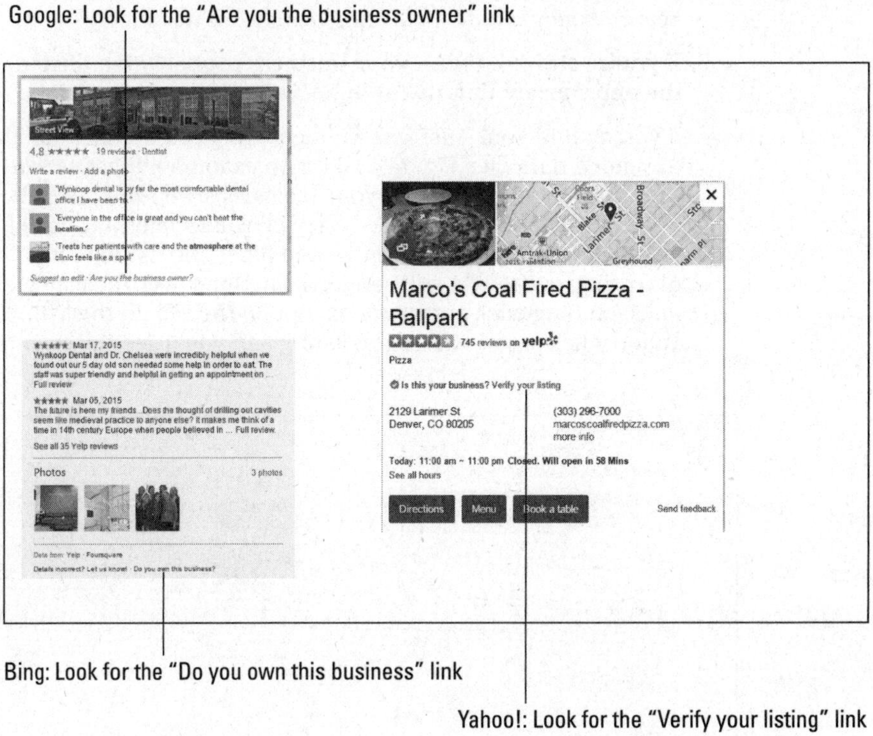

Google: Look for the "Are you the business owner" link

Figure 12-4:
Somewhere,
somehow,
you can
take control
of your busi-
ness listing.

Bing: Look for the "Do you own this business" link

Yahoo!: Look for the "Verify your listing" link

The sort of information you provide depends on which system you're submitting to, of course.

7. **Select some kind of business category and then enter information such as these elements:**

   • Your street address

   • Your phone and fax numbers

   • A link to your Web site

   • A business description

   • The payment methods you accept

- Your operating hours

- The year your business was established

- The languages spoken by your staff

- The brands you sell

- Photos (of anything: your staff, your location, your products, and so on)

- Videos

I recommend that you add as much as possible. Add as much text — with keywords, of course! — as many product and brand names, as many photos as you can, as many videos as possible. Adding keywords helps your listing become a match for more possible search phrases, and in any case, adding content to your listing may give your listing a little oomph in the search results.

The major systems, such as Google, require, not surprisingly, some kind of verification that you really are authorized to manage the business listing. They typically do this authorization by either phone verification (they send a code to your business phone, which you must then enter into the Web account) or they send a postcard containing a code to your place of business. After you log back in to the system and enter the code, your information is accepted, and your changes will go live. (In other systems, such as the ones I talk about next . . . well, there seems to be a degree of trust about who you are.)

Google is now allowing business owners to post "live" to their business listings: messages about special promotions, new products, or whatever else you think might be useful to customers. You can also find a Google certified photographer to come to your location, photograph your business, and submit the photographs to Google My Business (http://www.google.com/maps/about/partners/businessview) and even request a Street View photography session of your business; this is intended for businesses that have large properties that Google Street View camera cars can't reach, such as pedestrian malls, amusement parks, college campuses, race tracks, bike paths in parks, and so on (http://maps.google.com/help/maps/mapcontent/streetview). You can even submit interior maps of large buildings; you may have noticed that many malls, airports, department stores, and even theaters now display interior floor plans — showing each individual store within a mall, for example — on Google Maps (see https://www.google.com/maps/about/partners/indoormaps).

Google also pulls data about businesses from other locations. For instance, if you post events to Eventbrite.com and Eventful.com, your events may probably end up in your business listing. (Of course, both accounts need to have the exact same business name and address to make sure Google can match them up.)

Increasing the odds

Grabbing control of your listing is a great start and may even be a factor that helps your site rank a little higher. But what can you do to increase the odds that your site will rank well in the local results? Here are a few ideas:

✔ A huge part of the local-ranking algorithm is based on your location; it's harder to rank for *shoe shop denver* if your shoe shop is somewhere in a suburb. Although many businesses can't do anything about this, some service businesses actually get a mailbox as close to the center of town as possible and register that address as a business location. (It can't be a Post Office box; you need a mail box that you can register as a "suite number.")

✔ Get more local directory listings, from other business directories and Yellow Page sites, as I explain later in this chapter.

✔ Get links from various other sources directly to your Web site, especially with good location keywords in them (see Chapter 16).

✔ If you have multiple addresses, get multiple business listings.

Keep an eye on your local listings, to make sure things aren't getting changed. Google has some real bugs in its Google Places service. If you respond to reviews, the responses sometimes disappear; competitors may post bad reviews; if you've changed your address recently (the last couple of years), you may find your address changing back to the old one, and so on. (See the section "The Other Side of Local: Review Sites," later in this chapter.)

Finding More Local Systems

More local search systems are out there — many, many more. You may want to use a listing service to submit your data en masse to many of these directories. These services gather information about businesses and then distribute that information to dozens of different Web sites, such as Internet Yellow Page sites; various business directories such as MerchantCircle and HotFrog; map companies such as MapQuest; search engines; and review sites (such as Yelp).

Be careful with this strategy. Make sure to use a tool that will allow you to post your information to several of these in one go (I cover some in this chapter.) You'll want to have a place you can come back to in the event you need to update or modify your contact information. If your location changes and you have listings created for both the new and old location, you could be hurting your local search ranking.

These services often also distribute data to Google, Yahoo!, and Bing, but that doesn't mean you shouldn't take control of your listings on those services. You should, in fact, because these services don't provide the search engines with as much information as the search engines allow you to upload directly. Also, it can take a couple of months for the data to work its way across the distribution network.

These services distribute to numerous other local search systems, such as iBegin, InfoUSA, InsiderPages, Judy's Book, Kudzu, Localeze, MerchantCircle, MojoPages, Superpages/Switchboard, and YellowPages.com. It's less important to contact these services directly, so you might just let a service submit data to these places.

One of the oldest of these services is Universal Business Listings (UBL; www.ubl.org). UBL currently has around 150 services on its distribution list, and has packages beginning at $79 a year.

Yahoo! even has one of these distribution services, *Yahoo! LocalWorks* (https://smallbusiness.yahoo.com/localworks), though it's on the pricey side, currently set at $30 a month to distribute to 50 directories. There's also Yext (www.Yext.com), which works with around 40 directories for $200 a year and up, and Synup (www.synup.com), which charges a monthly fee per directory (it has around 200), but also provides access to 50 directories for free.

You may want to compare options; these services come with such features as review reports (showing you reviews about your business being posted to these directories), reports showing you where you are already listed, and automatic upload of photos and videos.

Why do you need to be in all these directories? You'll get links back to your site, and links are always good, especially from "trusted" sources, as many of these local directories are (see Chapter 16). In addition, some of these local directories sometimes come up in the search results, giving you another opportunity to be found even if *your* site hasn't come up on the results for a particular search (or even if it has; see the Part III WebExtra, *Grab More Page One Listings Using this Sneaky Technique*, for a discussion of how to get multiple links on a single search-results page that lead to your site).

And another reason to get into as many directories as possible is that the major search engines are developing partnerships with many different types of local information companies, such as local directories, review sites, menu and coupon services, and so on.

Google, for example, has partnered with various different directory sites to provide reviews to Google Maps: sites such as UrbanSpoon.com, Yelp.com, OpenTable.com, Gayot.com, Zagat.com, Menutopia.com, Dimmi.com.au, and others.

In other words, the major search engines are pulling local data from a large variety of sources, and those sources vary between search engines, locations, and subjects. Do a few searches for your particular phrases and locations and figure out who's feeding data to whom. Then go to those sources and see how you get listed.

If I ran a restaurant, for instance, I would want to get my menus into Zagat, Menutopia, and MenuPix.com; submit a listing to CitySearch; and figure out how to get reviews into Wcities.com, Zagat, 10Best.com, ViaMichelin, Gayot, and the local papers' Web sites. Also, though of course I don't condone this type of behavior, let's be honest: Some of your competitors are dropping fake reviews into review sites, to prime the data pump, as it were. But I come to that subject in a moment.

Don't Forget Local-Local Directories

Don't forget local directories that perhaps don't feed data to the major search engines but that are still likely to be important in their own right. For instance, if I owned a restaurant in Denver, I would want to know how to get a review into *5280* magazine, which maintains a popular restaurant guide at www.5280.com/restaurants. You get a link to your Web site, which the search engines like (see Chapter 16), and because it's a popular site for locals looking for good eats, you will probably get real, live traffic, not just search engine traffic.

Yet another important category of local directories is what I call "local-local" directories. So far, I've looked at just the "local" directories, which cover the entire nation, or even multiple nations. But there are also "local local" directories that cover one particular locale.

For instance, if I had a business in Philadelphia, I'd be checking into sites such as these:

- www.visitphilly.com
- www.infoaroundphilly.com
- www.philadelphia-city-directory.com
- www.philadelphia.com/places

I'm sure there are others I haven't found in my rather quick search. Again, getting listed in these sorts of directories is good because

✔ You'll get links to your site, and search engines love links (or rather, they reward you for links; see Chapter 16).

✔ These directories will come up in local searches now and then, providing another avenue for people to find your site.

✔ These directories may have a few loyal users who go there looking for businesses.

The Other Side of Local: Review Sites

There's a very important aspect that you have to know about many of these local sites: the reviews. Plenty of these sites allow anyone to post a review about your service. If you never have disgruntled customers and always have ecstatic clients, that's great. But how many businesses can say that? See Figure 12-5, for instance. How would you like these reviews about your business? There's nothing to complain about "I really loved the service," but how about "Horrible experience" or "Hit or miss at best"?

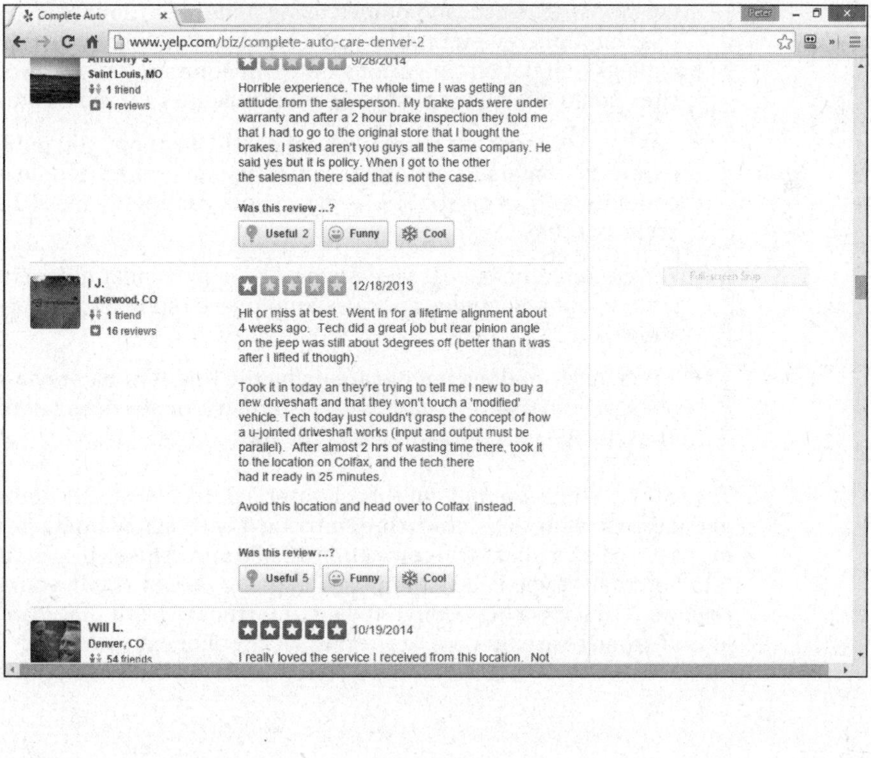

Figure 12-5: Would *you* like these reviews pointing to *your* business?

And how about that psycho competitor? Think he might post bad reviews about your business just to get one over on you? It happens all the time.

Why is it important to have good reviews? A few reasons.

- I don't know for sure, but the number of reviews, or your review star rating, *may* have some effect on your ranking in the search engines local results. It's clearly not "best reviewed sites get ranked first," but the ranking algorithm may at least take reviews into consideration to some degree.

- When a potential customer has to decide which business's site to click, which one do you think will get the click? The business with 10 reviews and 1.5 stars, or the 5-star business with 50 reviews?

- To dilute any bad reviews you get. One or two bad reviews mixed in with a bunch of good reviews probably doesn't do a lot of harm.

Now, it's true that sometimes bad reviews are warranted. But it's also true that sometimes

- A single disgruntled customer can start a feud, posting terrible reviews everywhere he can, sometimes using multiple accounts so that he can post multiple reviews to the same service. Remember, as the search engines pull data from various different sources, bad reviews at several sites could all end up posted on your business's Google listing.

- Angry customers are more likely to complain about you publicly than happy customers are to praise you. Anger energizes people more than contentment, so one or two angry clients can totally mess up your review profile.

- People sometimes post fake reviews — in particular competitors, of course, but sometimes angry ex-employees (spouses, business partners, and so on).

- Some unscrupulous people are using the threat of bad reviews as a form of extortion, trying to get money, products, or services out of businesses in exchange for not posting bad reviews.

True Story: While working on this chapter, I got a call from a dental surgeon in California, who asked for help removing a bad review from his site. He told me that he has a client who owes him $8,000 and refuses to pay; the client told him that "if you keep calling me I'm going to ruin you in your online reviews . . . I have a big family!" It's an unfortunate truth that many unscrupulous customers are now using reviews as a tool of extortion.

So it's essential, even if your business is totally dedicated to customer service, that you keep control over the reviews process, and you do that by making sure that people who like you post reviews. Even if you have a few bad reviews, having enough good reviews will dilute the bad ones.

Go check your business in the local listings. Do you have bad reviews pulling your star rating down? If so, what can you do about it? There are two approaches: Get the reviews removed or dilute the bad reviews.

Removing bad reviews

Can you get rid of bad reviews? Probably not — well, sometimes. It's extremely hard to get bad reviews removed from these review sites. The review sites themselves, in most cases, are protected from prosecution for libel or slander, so your threats probably won't help! On the other hand, Yelp.com — one of the most important review sites — has been sued by a group of small businesses for extortion, the argument being that Yelp's sales staff offers to remove bad reviews if a business pays for advertising. If, however, you have reason to believe the reviews are part of some kind of feud against you, or if they clearly violate the review site's policies, you *may* be able to get them removed, but you would have to have a pretty good argument. (In the case of removing bad reviews from the major search engines, it helps if you have personal contacts inside the companies; if, for instance, you are spending tens of thousands of dollars a month on PPC, you might get some assistance!)

One of my clients was being harassed by a crazy competitor, who was posting bad reviews to Google Maps. I complained to Google, and, after months and several complaints, they removed one of the fake reviews . . . but not the other, which was just as obviously fake.

To complain to Google about a review, log into your Google Places account, then go to your listing page in Google Maps, and use the Flag as inappropriate icon by the review (a little flag picture). This may not get their attention. So, after you've waited a while, log in to your Google Places account, select Help (top right), and look for the Contact Us area; you should find a link that says something like My Listing Has Incorrect Information. You can use this system to contact Google. After you've had a contact from Google once, you'll have an e-mail address you can use next time!

Most review sites allow you to respond to reviews, by the way. You should always respond to bad reviews and (politely!) give your side of the story; apologize for dropping the ball, if necessary. Research shows that such responses can soften bad reviews, limiting the damage to your business.

Diluting bad reviews

By far the easier process is to dilute the reviews — that is, to make sure you have enough *good* reviews to overwhelm the bad ones. (Of course, this doesn't work for you if everyone hates your business!) In fact, if you have a large number of good reviews, with a few bad reviews, that's fine; nobody expects perfection. Getting lots of good reviews will, over time, bring your star rating up and make those pesky bad reviews less obvious. It doesn't necessarily take much time. You can often turn things around in a month or two — I've seen a business go from 2.5 stars on Google to 5 stars in about six weeks.

So, how do you get those reviews? Ask your clients! Perhaps give out cards (maybe to the clients who are most clearly happy with your service) asking them to review your site at Google, Yahoo!, Yelp, and so on. (Most won't, but some will.) Perhaps you could have a computer terminal actually at the point of sale and ask people whether they would write a review right there and then. Many reviews are now being posted from smart phones, so if you build strong rapport with customers, you may be able to get them to post reviews right away — especially your "locals" or regular customers (if they keep coming back, presumably they like you!). Remember, it doesn't always take a lot of reviews to make a difference, so a little work here and there can really help.

One more thing: You can never get started creating positive reviews too early! If you have few (or no) reviews, a single bad review can cause huge problems. So it's a good idea to "inoculate" your business against bad reviews *before* you get them, by building up good reviews *now!*

Identifying important review sites

Which review sites are most important? Clearly, the major search engines themselves are very important, perhaps the most important. But the other review sites that are important to you will depend on your business. For general retail, Yelp.com is hugely important. For many types of service business, Judy's Book (www.judysbook.com) is critical. Medical clinics need to look into Vitals.com and HealthGrades.com. If you're in the travel business — hotels and restaurants, for example — TripAdvisor.com is essential. Other popular sites include Kudzu.com, Local.com, and MerchantCircle.com.

Here's how to figure out what review sites are really important to you. Search for businesses in your industry in Google and look at their reviews. Each review shows which review site it was pulled from; you'll want to be reviewed in those sites.

Working with the Yellow Pages

Another form of directory to be considered is the Yellow Page Web sites, which are sites created by the old Yellow Pages companies. The Yellow Page business is in serious trouble, and by now, the Yellow Page companies must be worried.

Historically, the (paper) yellow page business has been incredibly profitable; the biggest companies make billions of dollars each year, with profits of many hundreds of millions. They're real cash cows, but they're being steamrolled by the Internet.

Millions of computer-literate, Internet-loving people never pick up a Yellow Pages book or, perhaps, pick one up just once or twice a year, compared with several times a month in the pre-Internet days. The number of people who use the book is declining precipitously as local searches move online. More and more, I hear from my small-business friends that they are giving up on advertising in the Yellow Pages. One friend, the owner of a small gym, stopped paying for Yellow Page ads probably a decade or more ago, telling me that "they just don't work anymore"; he gets more business through his Web site than he ever did from the Yellow Pages.

The Yellow Page companies are definitely in trouble, but they do have one big advantage: *feet on the street.* They have huge armies of salespeople talking to businesses every day, and they've used this sales force to continue selling paper ads as well as to sell businesses *online* Yellow Pages ads.

You rarely hear much about the Yellow Pages sites in discussions about online search, but, of course, they *are* search systems — search directories, in effect. But how important are they?

`YellowPages.com`, probably the most important Yellow Page site, used to claim to have 170 million searches a month . . . a few years ago, I saw it was claiming 100 million a month; more recently, I saw a statement that it has 70 million users a month: a drop in the ocean when compared to the 21 billion searches a month considered in the comScore study I look at in Chapter 1.

Table 12-2 shows the largest Yellow Page sites and their Alexa traffic ranks, indicating the sites' overall popularity (the Global Rank). Notice that the most popular of these sites, YellowPages.com, had an Alexa.com rank of 743 when I checked. Compare that with Google (1), Yahoo! (4), Bing (23), and Ask.com (41). (Alexa.com, an Amazon site, provides popularity information about Web sites.) Just for fun, I've included the ranks from the last time I revised this book; you can see that yellow-page sites are definitely in decline!

Many other Yellow Page sites are not *really* Yellow Page sites. The term *Yellow Pages* is an old term — about 130 years old — and it's not a copyrighted term. Thus, anyone can set up a Web site and call it a Yellow Pages Web site, and many people have done so (see, for instance, YellowUSA. com and MagicYellow.com). What I'm talking about here are the genuine Yellow Pages sites, owned by the real Yellow Pages companies — the guys who dump those huge, yellow books on your doorstep that you immediately throw into the trash (or, one hopes, the recycle bin).

Table 12-2	Largest Yellow Pages Sites	
Site	*URL*	*Alexa Rank (2012 Rank)*
AT&T YellowPages.com	`www.yellowpages.com`	908 (743)
SuperPages	`www.superpages.com`	5,624 (2,006)
Yellowbook.com	`www.yellowbook.com`	20,137 (5,082)
Dex	`www.dexknows.com`	15,407 (5,376)
Yell.com (in the UK)	`www.yell.com`	3,774 (3,129)
Yellow.com	`www.yellow.com`	148,465 (24,978)

According to Alexa, 908 sites are more popular than YellowPages.com, including a whole bunch you've probably never heard of. Google Singapore is more popular than all of these sites. (Singapore has a population of 5 million, by the way.) Even My Web Search (`www.mywebsearch.com`), a search engine that nobody seems to have heard of, is more popular than all of these sites but YellowPages.com.

These sites are, quite simply, not particularly popular and get relatively very few searches.

That's not to say you shouldn't be in the Yellow Page sites. You absolutely should if you can get in for free (*maybe* if you have to pay), and there are several ways to do that:

- ✔ **Get a business phone line.** A business line costs more than a residential line, but you get your free listing in the local Yellow Pages book, which also gets your listing in the online Yellow Pages. As with the book, this is just a simple listing with no extras.

- ✔ **Sign up directly through the Web site.** Some Yellow Page sites allow businesses to create free listings directly through their Web sites. Look for an Advertise With Us link or similar.

✔ **Buy a listing or ad through your local Yellow Pages rep.** This is the same guy selling you space in the paper book.

✔ **Submit to to a directory listing service.** UBL, for example, distributes its data to a number of Yellow Page sites, such as `SuperPages.com`, `Verizon.com`, `YellowPages.com`, and `DexKnows.com`. (I discuss UBL and other such services earlier in this chapter.)

The real question, though, is whether you should *pay* to be in the Yellow Pages, and that's much harder for me to answer. The real disadvantage is that it's expensive, sometimes very expensive.

Do the Yellow Pages work? Let's just say that it's a matter of record that many businesses are unhappy with the results of advertising in the online Yellow Pages. That doesn't mean that *no* companies are *happy* with the service, though.

I recommend that if your company already buys Yellow Pages ads and your business is *location specific* — that is, you're trying to attract buyers in a particular area — you should carefully research using the Yellow Pages. Talk to your rep. The rep should be able to tell you how many searches are carried out in the company's online Yellow Pages, in a particular category and a particular region, each month. With that information, you may be able to decide whether purchasing an ad makes sense. However, based on what I have learned from customers of yellow page sites, I would recommend that you take with a grain of salt what you may be told by yellow-page salespeople about how much traffic you are likely to get from an online yellow-page ad and the value of that traffic.

The online Yellow Pages companies sell a variety of services, such as the following:

✔ A link from the listing in the online Yellow Pages to your Web site. However, in most cases, the search engines do *not* recognize it as a link to your site. Some of these directories use *nofollow* links, or they may use redirect links that forward people to your site through the Yellow Page's server. (See Chapter 16 for information on links that are not really links.)

✔ An e-mail link.

✔ A page with detailed information, such as a map to your location, information about your products and services, payment options, and so on.

✔ A link to a picture of your ad that appears in the paper Yellow Pages.

✔ A pop-up promo box that appears when someone points at an icon and that can be modified through an online-management system.

✔ A link to a coupon that customers can print.

Part III

Adding Your Site to the Indexes and Directories

 Visit www.dummies.com/extras/seo for great Dummies content online.

In this part . . .

- ✔ Mapping your site
- ✔ Registering with search engines
- ✔ Appearing in specialized registries
- ✔ Selling in retail marketplaces
- ✔ Visit www.dummies.com/extras/seo for great Dummies content online

Chapter 13

Getting Your Pages into the Search Engines

You built your Web pages. Now, how do you get them into the search systems? That's what this chapter and Chapter 14 explain. In this chapter, I talk about how to get your pages into search engines, and in Chapter 14, I explain how to list your site with search directories.

Search engines can find out about and index your site in essentially three ways:

✔ Links pointing to your site

✔ Simple link-submission pages

✔ Sitemap submissions

The most important of these is the first — links pointing to your site lead the search engine to it. The second is worthless. And the third is very important and comes with a number of ancillary benefits. In this chapter, I tell you about these strategies one by one.

Linking Your Site for Inclusion

In Chapters 16 through 18, I talk about the importance of — and how to get — links pointing from other sites to yours. The more links you have pointing at your site, the more important the search engines will think your pages are.

Links are also important because they provide a way for search engines to find your site. Without links, you *might* get your site into search engine indexes, but chances are, you won't. And being included in the most important index — Google's — is much quicker through linking than through registration. I've had sites picked up and indexed by Google within two or three days of having put up a link on another site. If you simply submit your URL to Google (the next method I look at), you may have to wait weeks for it to index your site (if it ever does).

But one or two links sometimes aren't enough for some search engines. They often are for Google: If it sees a link to your site on another site that it's already indexing, it will probably visit your site and index it, too. But other systems are far choosier and may not visit your site even if they do see a link to it. So the more links you have pointing to your site, the better. Eventually, search engines will get sick of tripping over links to your site and come see what the fuss is all about.

It's all about links. The search engines believe that they can maintain the quality of their indexes by focusing on Web pages that have links pointing to them. If nobody points to your site, the reasoning goes, why would the engines want to index it? If nobody else thinks your site is important, why should the search engines? They would rather find your pages themselves than have you submit the pages.

Simple Link Submissions to the Major Systems

The top two search engines — Google and Bing — provide a very simple way for you to tell them where your site is. Submit your site for free on these pages:

- **Google:** `https://www.google.com/webmasters/tools/submit-url`
- **Bing:** `http://www.bing.com/toolbox/submit-site-url`

Google actually provides a similar method, from within the Google Webmaster account (which I talk about in the next section). The Webmaster account has a Fetch as Googlebot tool (under the Crawl menu). You can use this tool to have Google pull a page and show you the code it has crawled. You can then click the Submit to Index button to submit that page to the Google index. Still, it doesn't guarantee that Google will index the page you submit, though it might be worth trying if you have some particular pages on your site that you can't seem to get indexed.

How about Ask.com? It offers no way to submit your Web site. It relies on its searchbots to find pages through links.

However, now that I've given you these links for submitting your site's pages, let me say one more thing: *Don't bother.*

Using these submission pages is unnecessary and may not even work. As Google says, "We don't add all submitted URLs to our index, and we cannot make predictions or guarantees about when or if submitted URLs will appear in our index." Bing doesn't bother saying anything beyond "Submit Your Site to Bing."

I don't bother submitting URLs to search engines using these simple URL submission pages. But I want you to be aware of them because these submissions are one of the biggest scams in the history of SEO (a business that is rife with scams). Hundreds of submission services convinced many thousands of Web site owners to pay to have their sites submitted to the search engines, often repeatedly. It was a totally pointless waste of money.

You don't need to use basic URL submission. You need links to your site, and you should submit a sitemap, which I cover next.

There is one context in which "submitting" a site to the search engines does make sense, though: in the case of businesses submitting their information to the local-search systems. I cover this subject in Chapter 12.

Submitting an XML Sitemap

I *do* recommend one form of site submission. It isn't a replacement for pointing links to your site, but it can, in some cases, improve indexing of your site. I'm talking about creating XML sitemaps, submitting them to Google and Bing, and making it easy for other search engines, such as Ask.com, to find the sitemap on their own.

In 2005, Google introduced a new XML-sitemap submission system and was soon followed by Yahoo! and Bing (and now, of course, Yahoo! and Bing have partnered, so they act as one system). In Chapter 7, I recommend creating an HTML sitemap page on your site and linking to it from the homepage. The sitemap is a page that visitors can see and that any search engine can use to find its way through your site.

Sitemap, schmitemap

Don't think that creating an XML sitemap is a magic trick guaranteed to get your site indexed. I've seen, for example, Yahoo! (in the pre-Yahoo!/Bing partnership days) pick up the sitemap file, put it into the search results, come by and pick up 3 pages from the index, ignore the other 20, and leave a whole bunch of old, nonexistent pages in the index. I've seen Bing apparently pay little attention to a sitemap. On the other hand, I've also seen Yahoo! pick up hundreds of thousands of pages on a large site soon after finding multiple XML sitemaps. The sitemap may help, but you have no guarantee whether or when the search engines will use it. So don't think of the sitemap as an alternative to the hard work of creating links to your site.

But an *XML* sitemap is different: It's a special file placed on your site that contains an index to help search engines find their way to your pages. You create and place the file and then let the search engine know where it is. This hidden file (visitors never see it) is in a format designed for search engines. I think it's worth your time to create this file because doing so is not a huge task and *may* help, particularly if your site is large. Also, after you've submitted a sitemap and "verified" your submission, the search engines give you lots of interesting information about your site.

In Google's words, "Using sitemaps to inform and direct our crawlers, we hope to expand our coverage of the Web and speed up the discovery and addition of pages to our index." If I can help Google by getting it to index my site more quickly, well, that's fine by me.

What does this sitemap file look like? Take a look at Figure 13-1.

Don't worry: XML sitemaps are easy to create; I show you how in the next section.

These sitemaps are typically named `sitemap.xml` (though different names can be used) and placed into the root directory of the Web site — in the same directory as the home page.

Creating your sitemap

What if you own a small site, though, and have limited technical skills? No problem: Plenty of free and low-cost sitemap-creation tools are available. Firstly, many CMS systems can automatically create XML sitemaps; if you use WordPress to create your site, for example, you can find a number of plugins that, among other SEO functions, create sitemaps for you. You can find "extensions" and "modules" that create sitemaps for Joomla and Drupal systems, too, and probably many, if not most, CMS systems these days. Even simple site builders, such as GoDaddy's Website Builder, have functions to automatically create XML sitemaps.

Figure 13-1:
A small XML
sitemap.

If your site does not have some kind of built-in sitemap module, there are other options. If you're the proud owner of a large, sophisticated, database-driven site, it's probably a job for your programmers; they should create or find a script that automatically builds the XML sitemap.

You can also find a variety of scripts and tools that will create XML sitemaps for you; just search for *create xml sitemaps*. Note that many of the tools call themselves *Google sitemap* creators, because Google was the first search engine to use sitemaps. All you need, however, is the basic Google XML sitemap format for all the other search engines, so if it creates a "Google Sitemap" it will work fine.

Some of these programs run on your computer, some require installing on your Web server, and some are services run from another Web site. You can find a large list of these sitemap generators here:

`code.google.com/p/sitemap-generators/wiki/SitemapGenerators`

Google itself created a Sitemap Generator program (https://code.google.com/p/googlesitemapgenerator), which you can install on your Web server. It's no longer maintained, but still available (it's a Python script, so if you don't know what that means and don't have a geek who does, consider creating the file another way).

My favorite sitemap generator for small sites is XML-Sitemaps.com. You simply enter your domain name into a Web page, and it spiders your site, creating the sitemap as it goes, up to 500 pages. If your site is bigger, you can get the service to install a script on your Web server for $20 (assuming that your server can run PHP scripts). They also have a service for a monthly fee in which they automatically create a sitemap and periodically update it, and they host the sitemap on their servers; all you need to do is point to the sitemap. (I'll explain how you tell the search engines where the sitemap is in a moment. The sitemap itself does not have to hosted on your site.)

Sitemap files can be as large as 10MB and contain as many as 50,000 URLs. If you need to exceed either limit, you must create multiple sitemap files and a sitemap index file that refers to the individual sitemap files. Your XML Sitemaps can also be compressed in the .gz file format so that they transfer more quickly to the search engine. For specifics of the sitemap protocol — which you generally don't need to know — see www.sitemaps.org.

Submitting your sitemaps

You can tell search engines about your sitemaps in three different ways:

- ✔ Submit a sitemap through the search engine's Webmaster account.
- ✔ Include a line in the robots.txt file telling a search engine where the file is.
- ✔ Ping the search engines.

The last method is pretty much optional. You should definitely submit your sitemap to Google and Bing and use a robots.txt file.

Submitting using the Webmaster account

You should set up an account on both the major systems (Google and Bing; Ask.com doesn't currently have Webmaster accounts, and Yahoo!'s data comes from Bing, so Yahoo! no longer has a Webmaster system) and submit your Web site's XML sitemap. Then review the various tools that are available. Here's where you can find the Webmaster areas and sitemap-submission pages:

✔ **Google:** `www.google.com/webmasters`

✔ **Bing:** `www.bing.com/toolbox/webmaster`

You don't need a separate account on each system for each Web site you own — you can submit multiple sites through each account, though the number of Web sites that you can manage through each account is limited (Bing limits the number of sites to 125 sitemaps; for Google, it's 1,000 . . . enough for most people!).

However, in some cases, Web site owners don't want search engines to know that their sites are associated; for instance, if a site owner has three sites, all of which rank on the first page for important keywords, he may not want it to be obvious that all sites are owned by the same person. In such a case, of course, the owner would set up separate accounts for submitting each sitemap.

Here's the basic process you use at all these services:

1. **Set up an account.**

   In each case, you have to set up a password-protected account.

2. **Add the URL of your Web site.**

3. **Tell the search engine where the sitemap is.**

   You provide the URL that points to your sitemap; the search engine checks to see whether it can find the file.

4. **Verify your site.**

   You can verify your site in several ways:

   • *You may use a special meta tag that you add to your home page* (something like `<meta name="google-site-verification" content="1bkH4kUFdeKgcMhxOj8e06-7faFDZqAnS2jvGUDITRg" />`). See Figure 13-2.

   • *You can choose to get a verification file, a small text file, that's stored on your server.* For instance, Google provides you with an `.html` file that you can download and place in your site. The file contains a single line of text, something like this: `google-site-verification: googlec4b99698d01b26f2.html`.

   • *You can choose to add a record — a snippet of information — to your domain name's DNS information.* Don't try this unless you're sure you know what you are doing.

- *Google Webmaster also allows you to verify your site by associating it with your Google Analytics account (see Chapter 24).*

- *Google Webmaster also allows you to verify by associating with your Google Tag Manager account (a system used for managing JavaScript tags).*

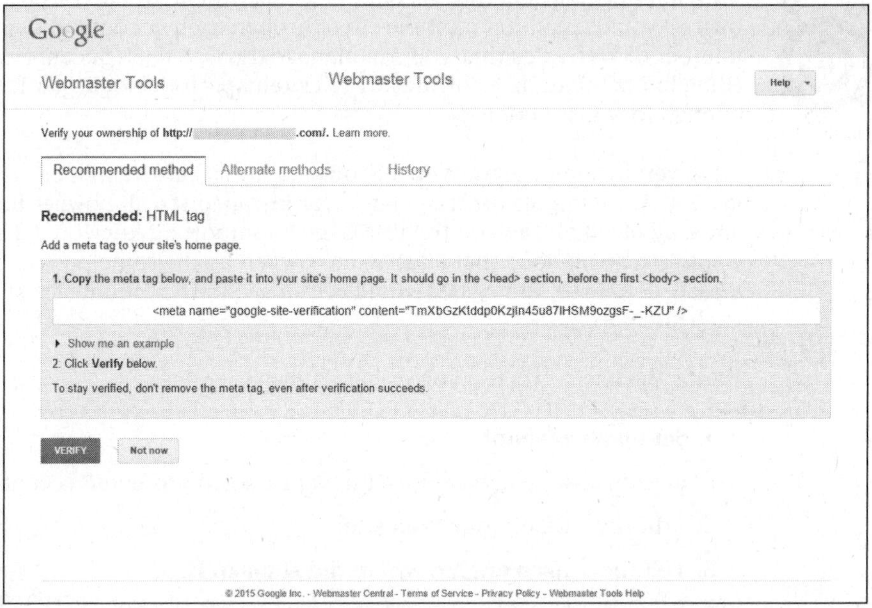

Figure 13-2:
Verifying ownership of a Web site in Google Webmaster Tools.

5. **Tell the search engine that you have used one of these methods, and ask it to "verify" the file.**

   The search engine then checks to see whether the file, meta tag, or DNS record is present (or Google checks to see whether your site contains the correct Google Analytics code). If the search engine finds what it's expecting, it assumes that you must own or have control over the specified site, and thus is willing to provide you with more information about the site.

Each system is different, so I can't go into detail about how each works (though I look at Google Webmaster account in detail later in this chapter). Spend a little time digging around and you'll soon figure it out. Remember, the basic process is to add your site URL, add your sitemap URL, and then verify or authenticate.

Using the robots.txt file

You need a `robots.txt` file in the root directory of your Web site, with the following line inside it:

```
Sitemap: http://www.yourdomain.com/sitemap.xml
```

The URL should point to your sitemap, of course. The URL tells the search engines that don't provide a Webmaster account — such as Ask.com — where your sitemap is, so you'll want to do this even though you're submitting your site through the Google and Bing Webmaster account.

Pinging search engines

Pinging a search engine means sending a message to the search engine telling it where a sitemap is, and telling it that the sitemap has changed. At the time of writing, you can ping Google and Bing; Ask.com took down its ping service some time ago.

You can see this process in action for yourself. Create a sitemap and then change the following URL to show the path to your sitemap:

```
http://www.google.com/ping?sitemap=http://www.yourdomain.com/sitemap.xml
```

Copy and paste this URL into a browser and press Enter, and you receive this response from Google:

Sitemap Notification Received

Your Sitemap has been successfully added to our list of Sitemaps to crawl. If this is the first time you are notifying Google about this Sitemap, please add it via `http://www.google.com/webmasters/sitemaps` *so you can track its status. Please note that we do not add all submitted URLs to our index, and we cannot make any predictions or guarantees about when or if they will appear.*

These are the sitemap-submission URLS; put the full URL to your sitemap, including `http://`, after the = sign:

```
http://www.google.com/ping?sitemap=
http://www.google.com/webmasters/sitemaps/ping?sitemap=
http://www.bing.com/webmaster/ping.aspx?sitemap=
```

You can manually ping sites each time the search engine is updated. If you have a programmer build your sitemaps automatically by pulling data from a database, the programmer should add a ping function to ping the search engines each time the sitemap is updated. And, some sitemap-creation programs that you can buy have built-in ping functions; the version of the XML-Sitemaps.com program that you install on your server can automatically ping for you.

Are sitemaps bad? I've heard the argument that sitemaps are bad because you might rely on the sitemap rather than create links to your site. This bizarre argument is similar to the one that airbags are bad because you might rely on them rather than driving safely. Sitemaps are *good*. But they're not a substitute for links pointing to your site. You still need links, and many of them.

Using Webmaster tools, too

As the previous section notes, the two top search engines — Google and Bing — provide Webmaster accounts through which you can submit your sitemap and provide various tools related to your sitemap and your Web site. You need to verify that you own or manage the site (through the authentication or verification process I mention earlier), then submit a sitemap. You'll be provided with some very useful information and tools to influence how your site appears in the search results.

Right now, Google has the best tools and statistics associated with its Webmaster account (see Figure 13-2). Table 13-1 explains some of these tools.

Table 13-1	Google's Webmaster Tools
Tool	*What It Does*
Dashboard	The "front page" where you'll see summary information related to messages, crawl errors, search analytics, and sitemaps.
Messages	This is where you can see messages you may receive from Google, including information about SEO problems.
The Search Appearance Menu Click the little i icon at the end of the menu name to see an image showing you the different elements of a search result and how you can influence each one.	
Structured Data	Provides information about any "structured data" you have entered into your Web pages (see Chapter 8 for more information).
Data Highlighter	Information about using the Data Highlighter tool to tag information, as an alternative to using structured data (again, see Chapter 8).
HTML Improvements	Problems Google may have found on your site, such as duplicate, long, or short meta description tags, and missing, duplicate, long, short, or noninformative `<TITLE>` tags, and nonindexable page content.
Sitelinks	Lets you tell Google not to use particular pages as Sitelink pages (discussed in Chapter 24).

Tool	What It Does
The Search Traffic Menu	
Search Analytics	Indicates which search queries most often returned pages from your site and which ones were clicked, along with other metrics related to how your site performs in search.
Links to Your Site	Shows links from other sites pointing to your site, indicates which page inside the site they point to, and what keywords are used in the links (an excellent tool!).
Internal Links	Shows links between pages within your site.
Manual Actions	A very important tool, this one! Provides information from Google if your site has been manually penalized.
International Targeting	Allows you to specify what language and country you want to target.
Mobile Usability	Contains information about how your site performs on mobile devices (smart phones); see Chapter 7.
The Google Index Menu	
Index Status	Shows you information about the number of pages indexed by Google on your site, and pages blocked by `robots.txt` or robots meta tags (see Chapter 3, and the `robots.txt` Tester, in this table)
Content Keywords	Keywords that Google found while crawling your site and believes are significant, giving you an idea of what Google thinks of your site.
Blocked Resources	Information about components of your site that may be blocked.
Remove URLs	Lets you remove pages from the Google index.
The Crawl Menu	
Crawl Errors	Shows problems that Google found while crawling your site.
Crawl Stats	Information about how quickly and how often Google crawls your site (see Figure 13-3).
Fetch as Google	Lets you get Googlebot to fetch a page from your site so you can see it how Googlebot sees it.
`robots.txt` Tester	Lets you create and test a `robots.txt` file to make sure that your `robots.txt` file isn't blocking areas of your site accidentally.
Sitemaps	This is where you test and submit a sitemap; Google will tell you when it processed it, if it found any errors, and how many pages it found within the sitemap.

(continued)

Table 13-1 (continued)

Tool	What It Does
URL Parameters	Lets you tell Google to ignore certain URL parameters; a way to eliminate duplicate pages in the Google index.
Security Issues	Information about malware on your site (which might happen if your site has been hacked).
Other Resources	Links to a variety of tools: the Structured Data Testing Tool, Markup Helper, and Email Markup Tester (Chapter 8); Google My Business (Chapter 11); the Google Merchant Center (Chapter 15); PageSpeed Insights (Chapter 7), along with links to Google's hosting service and tool for building a search box to add to your site.

Google also has some important settings hidden away in the Settings menu; the little cog button on the top-right of the page:

Webmaster Tools Preferences	Set up email preferences for Webmaster messages; what types and where they go.
Site Settings	Tell Google to assume that yourdomain.com points to www.yourdomain.com; you can also slow the rate at which Googlebot crawls your site (not recommended, let it rip!).
Change of Address	Allows you to redirect one domain to another, telling Google that, for instance, you're changing the domain name you use for your Web site.
Google Analytics Property	Allows you to link your Google Webmaster and Google Analytics accounts, so that you can see Webmaster info in the Analytics reports (see Chapter 24).
Users	Allows you to provide access to your Webmaster account to other users. (Web designers, for instance. You should *never* let a Web designer set up your Webmaster account; the site owner should have control over the account and provide access when needed to designers and developers.)
Verification Details	Displays a verification report, showing information about when Google attempted to verify the site ownership, if it succeeded, and the email addresses of the verified owners.

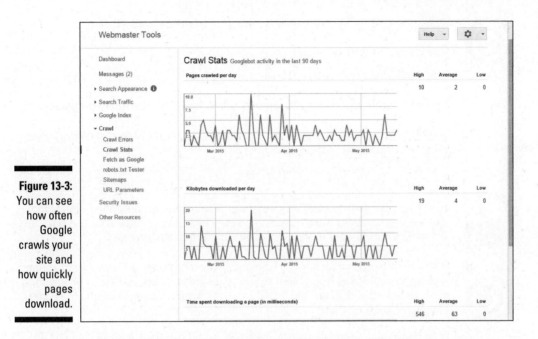

Figure 13-3:
You can see
how often
Google
crawls your
site and
how quickly
pages
download.

This is pretty nifty stuff, eh? Sitemaps are great for big sites; they can really help with indexing. But even if you have a *small* site, submitting and verifying a sitemap is a great way to get some very useful information about your site. (Actually, strictly speaking, you can create a Webmaster account for your site, verify the site, and then access this information even if you haven't submitted a sitemap. However, if you're going to all that trouble, you might as well spend a few minutes with a tool such as XML-Sitemaps.com and submit the sitemap as well.)

Submitting to Secondary Systems

You can also submit your site information to smaller systems with perhaps a few hundred million pages in their indexes — and sometimes far fewer. The disadvantage to these systems is that they're seldom used, compared to the big systems discussed earlier in this chapter. Many search engine professionals ignore the smaller systems altogether. On the other hand, if your site is ranked in these systems, you have much less competition because they're so small.

These secondary systems may be worth submitting your site to:

- **ExactSeek:** www.exactseek.com/add.html
- **Gigablast:** www.gigablast.com/addurl

You can find more, including regional sites, listed on the following pages:

- www.searchenginewatch.com/article/2067248/Guides-To-Search-Engines
- http://dmoz.org/Computers/Internet/Searching/Search_Engines

Some smaller search engines encourage you to pay for a submission. Don't. Unless you know for sure otherwise, you can safely assume that the amount of traffic you're likely to get probably isn't worth the payment.

If you plan to submit your site to many search engines, you may want to use a programmable keyboard or a text-replacement utility or macro program, such as ShortKeys (www.shortkeys.com), which can make entering repetitive data much quicker:

- **Programmable keyboard:** You can assign a string of text — a URL, an e-mail address, and so on — to a single key. Then all you need to do, for instance, is press F11 to enter your e-mail address. The old Gateway AnyKey keyboard, which you can sometimes find on eBay, is great (if it's still functioning); I've also used the Corsair K95 with some success.

- **Text-replacement utility:** Replace a short string of text with something longer. To enter your e-mail address, for instance, you might type just *em*.

A few sites require that you submit your site with a username and password. Most sites require at least an e-mail address; some also require that you respond to a confirmation e-mail before they add your site to the list. *Don't use your regular e-mail address!* Use a throwaway address because you'll receive a lot of spam.

Is it really worth submitting to these secondary search engines? As I mention in Chapter 1, somewhere around 95 percent of all search results are provided by the major search engines, so submitting to the secondary search systems may not be worth the trouble. I think it's one of those "Well, I've got the time, so I might as well do it" kind of things.

Using Registration Services and Software Programs

You can also submit your pages to hundreds of search engines by using a submission service or program. These services used to be very popular, though they are definitely dying out. Search for *search engine submission* and you'll find both Web-based services and software.

You may find free services, but some are outdated, running automatically for a number of years now and not having kept up with changes on the search engine scene.

Many free services are definitely on the *lite* side. They're provided by companies that hope you'll spring for a fee-based full service.

Some submission services also combine search engine registrations with directory registrations, sometimes along with link packages. (I discuss directory registrations in Chapter 14.) By providing links pointing to your site, they can guarantee that your site will be picked up by the major search engines; it's not the submissions to the search engines that are doing the work — it's the links!

Note also that some submission services increase their submission counts by including all services that are fed by the systems they submit to. Some submission services inflate their numbers by including search engines that don't even exist any more. In fact, I feel that some (many?) submission services are little more than scams, charging in some cases very high monthly fees for what's really a service with relatively few benefits.

A few submission software programs are available as well, such as Submit Wolf (`www.trellian.com/swolf`). The big advantage of these software programs is that you pay only once rather than pay every time you use a service.

You actually have a couple of reasons to use these automated tools. You may get a little traffic out of these small search engines, but don't bank on getting much. In many cases, though, the systems being submitted to are not really search engines — they're search *directories,* and being listed in a directory may mean that major search engines pick up a link pointing to your site. I talk more about submitting your site to search directories in Chapter 14, and you discover the power of linking in Chapters 16 through 18.

Chapter 14

Submitting to the Directories

. . . .

. . . .

In Chapter 13, you look at getting your site into the search engines. In this chapter, you look at getting your site into the search *directories*. Submitting to directories can be a great way to get links.

The world's most important directory recently closed down, and the other major directory is incredibly frustrating to work with, even though it's free. However, you may find lots of other, smaller directories you may want to register with.

Pitting Search Directories Against Search Engines

Before you start working with directories, it's helpful to know a few basics about what directories are — and aren't:

- ✔ Directories don't send searchbots out onto the Web looking for sites to add (though they may send bots out to make sure that the sites are still live).

- ✔ Directories don't read and store information from Web pages within a site.

✔ Because directories don't read and store information, they don't base search results on the contents of the Web pages.

✔ Directories don't index Web pages; they index Web sites. Each site is assigned to a particular category. Within the categories, the directory's index contains just a little information about each site — not much more than a URL, a title, and a description. The result is a categorized list of Web sites — and that's really what the search directories are all about.

A few years ago, Yahoo! was based around its directory. In fact, Figure 14-1 shows an example of what Yahoo! looked like early in 1998 (courtesy of a wonderful service called the Wayback Machine at www.archive.org).

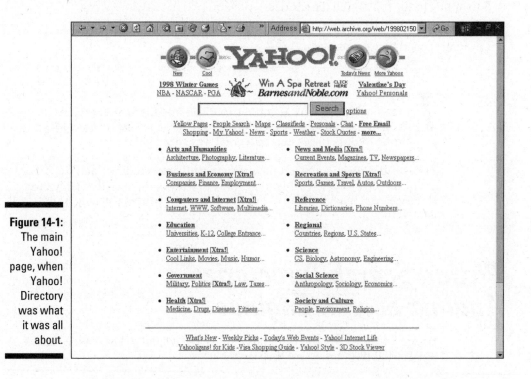

Figure 14-1:
The main Yahoo! page, when Yahoo! Directory was what it was all about.

The idea behind Yahoo! was a categorized directory of Web sites that people could browse. You could click links to drill down through the directory and find what you needed, similar to flipping through a Yellow Pages directory. Although you could use the search box to peruse categories, site titles, and site descriptions, the tool was nothing like the Yahoo! search index of today, which can hunt for your term in billions of Web pages.

But Yahoo! made an enormous mistake. In fact, the image in Figure 14-1 is from a time when Yahoo! was at its peak, a time when most of the world's Web searches were carried out through Yahoo.com — just a few months before Google began full operations. Yahoo! evidently hadn't realized the weaknesses of the directory system until it was too late. These weaknesses include the following:

- **Directories provide no way for someone to search individual pages within a site.** The perfect fit for your information needs may be sitting somewhere on a site that is included in a directory, but you won't know it because the directory doesn't index individual pages.

- **Categorization is necessarily limited.** Sites are rarely about a single topic; even if they appear to be, single topics can be broken down into smaller subtopics. By forcing people to find a site by category and keyword in a very limited amount of text — a description and title — the directories are obviously very restrictive.

- **Hand-built directories are necessarily limited in size.** Hand-built directories, such as Yahoo! Directory and the Open Directory, add a site to their directories only after a real live human editor has reviewed the site. With hundreds of millions of Web sites, a human-powered system can't possibly keep up.

- **Hand-built directories get very dated.** Directories often contain some extremely old and out-of-date information that simply wouldn't be present in an index that is automatically recompiled continually. (Yahoo! *spidered* the sites — that is, sent out searchbots to look through the sites — in its index for broken links and dead sites, but if the site's purpose had changed, Yahoo! didn't always notice.)

The proof of directories' weaknesses is in the pudding: Google took over and now is the dominant search system on the Web. (To be fair, Yahoo! helped Google by integrating Google results into Yahoo! searches, although in the summer of 2004, it dropped Google and began using its own index — then in 2010, Yahoo! dropped its own index and began using Bing's data.)

In fact, Yahoo! no longer even has a directory — it closed the directory late in 2014.

Why Are Directories So Significant?

If Yahoo! Directory has closed, and if most people have never heard of the world's second most important directory (the Open Directory Project at www.dmoz.org), why do you care about them? They may be useful — though far less so than they were in the past — for a number of reasons:

- ✔ Links in directories help provide context to search engines. If your site is in the Recreation: Pets: Rodents category in the Open Directory Project, for instance, the search engines know that the site is related to playing with rodents. The directory presence helps search engines index your site and may help your site rank higher for some search terms. Last time I looked, Google still had almost three million Open Directory Project pages indexed.

- ✔ Links, as you see in Chapters 16 through 18, are very important in convincing search engines that your site is of value. It's sometimes possible to get links from hundreds of search directories, on pages indexed by the major search engines.

- ✔ The Open Directory Project feeds results to other Web sites; at one point hundreds of other sites. Now, not so many. A link from the Open Directory Project may show up as a link indexed on some other sites, too.

The Open Directory Project used to be a force to reckon with. Data from this system was widely spread across the Internet and has been used by major search systems. Yahoo!, for instance, once used data from the Open Directory Project, and until 2011 even Google maintained a directory (at http://dir.google.com), based on Open Directory Project data (which, incidentally, is owned by AOL/Netscape).

Submitting to the Search Directories

Chapter 13 has what some may find an unusual message: "Sure, you can submit to the search engines, but it may not do you any good." Search engines really like links to your site, and having links to your site is often the best way to get into the search engines.

However, the search directories won't find you unless you submit to them. And you can forget automated submission programs for many directories; submissions must be entered into the Open Directory Project by hand, for example.

Submitting to the Open Directory Project

Yes, the Open Directory Project is free, and yes, you can submit very quickly. But the problem is that there's no guarantee that your site will be listed. I've seen sites get into the Open Directory Project within a week or two of submission, and I've seen others that waited months — years! — without ever getting in. Additionally, the submission forms sometimes don't seem to work. Unfortunately, the Open Directory Project — DMOZ, as it's known to search geeks — has more work to do than volunteer editors to do it (each submission has to be reviewed), and although it invites people to become editors, its editor-recruiting process actually discourages editors. Consequently, it's hard to get into the directory.

But don't give up yet. A listing in the Open Directory Project is a great thing to have if you can get it. As I tell my clients, submitting takes only a few minutes, so you might as well try, even if the chance of getting in is low. It's like a free lottery ticket. Here's how to submit:

1. **Read the editor's guidelines at** `http://dmoz.org/guidelines/describing.html`.

   If you know what guidelines the editors use, you may be able to avoid problems. It's hard to get into the directory, so you may as well give yourself the best chance of getting in.

2. **Go to** `www.dmoz.org`.

   The Open Directory Project home page appears.

3. **Find a suitable category for your site.**

4. **Click the <u>Suggest URL</u> link at the top of the page.**

5. **Follow the (fairly simple) directions.**

You simply enter your home page's URL, a short title, a 25 to 30-word description for the site, and your e-mail address. That's it. Then you wait.

Nevertheless, understand that the editors at DMOZ don't care about your site, they care about the directory. In fact, read the DMOZ forums at `www.resource-zone.com`, and you find that the attitude tends to be "tell us about your site, then go away and forget about it." All sorts of factors are working against you:

- ✔ 8,000 editors are managing more than 700,000 categories.

- ✔ Many small directories might only be reviewed by an editor every six months — or far less frequently.

- ✔ The editors regard a six-month wait, or longer, not particularly excessive.

- ✔ In some cases, editors may even ignore submissions. As one editor explained, "There is no obligation to review them in any order nor is there a requirement to review them as a priority. Some editors find it more productive to seek out sites on their own and rarely visit the suggested sites."

As another DMOZ editor succinctly explained it, DMOZ is "very much like a lottery." The fact is, as important as DMOZ is, you may never get into this directory! If you really, really want to get in, you might consider posting in the DMOZ forums, where you can ask real, live DMOZ editors what's going on www.resource-zone.com. Or do as a number of site owners have done; submit to DMOZ to become an editor. Once in, things get much easier! Still, I think that's probably overkill these days, as the directory doesn't have distribution it used to have.

Finding Specialized Directories

For just about every subject you can imagine, someone is running a specialized search directory. Although specialized directories get very little traffic when compared to the big guys, the traffic they do get is highly targeted — just the people you want to attract. Such directories are often very popular with your target audience.

Here's an example of how to search for a specialized directory. Suppose that you're promoting your rodent racing Web site. Go to Google and type *rodent racing directory*. Hmmm, for some reason, Google doesn't find any directories related to rodent racing. Strange. Okay, try *rodent directory*. Now you're getting somewhere! I did this search and found several useful sites:

- ✔ **ThePetDirectory.us:** You can advertise in this directory. A link would be nice, though I'm not sure it's worth the price (sometimes it accepts free listings). I discuss that a little later in the section "You don't have to pay." (I don't regard rodents as pets; racing rodents are working animals.)

- ✔ **NetVet's Electronic Zoo** (http://netvet.wustl.edu): This is a big list of links to rodent-related sites, though mostly related to research (the Digital Atlas of Mouse Embryology and the Cybermouse Project, for instance). It's got a good PageRank, too, PR6, so links from here would be valuable. *And* it's on an .edu domain, which is valuable (see Chapter 16). Perhaps you can suggest that your site is related to research into cardiovascular performance of rodents under stress.

- ✔ **Rodent Resources at the National Center for Research Resources:** Hmmm, this is another rodent research site, but with an Alexa traffic rank of 357 and a PageRank of 8, getting listed in this directory would be very useful. (Maybe it's time to apply for a research grant.) Also, because it's at http://ncrr.nih.gov, which is a government domain, links would be valuable (see Chapter 16).

✔ **The Rodent Breeders List** (`http://AltPet.net/rodents/breeder.html`): This directory strikes me as one of those "not very pleasant, but somebody's got to do it" things. (How do you breed rodents, anyway? Very carefully I assume.) Still, if you breed rodents for your races, you may want to get onto this list.

When you do a search for a specialty directory, your search results will include the specialty directories you need, but mixed in with them, you may also find results from the Open Directory Project. If you want, you can clear out the clutter by searching like this:

```
rodent directory - -inurl:dmoz.org
```

This search phrase tells Google to look for pages with the words *rodent* and *directory* but to ignore any pages that have `dmoz.org` (the Open Directory Project) in their URLs.

Finding directories through DMOZ

You can use other methods to track down specialty directories. In fact, as you get to know the Internet landscape around your business, you'll eventually run into these directories. People mention them in discussion groups, for instance, or you find links to them on other Web sites.

I used to like browsing for these directories in the major directories — Yahoo! and the Open Directory Project. Of course, now the Open Directory is the only one of the two left. It has many directory subcategories, though. It doesn't have one for rodent racing, which apparently gets no respect, but it certainly lists many directories in other categories.

To find directories in DMOZ is to go to the DMOZ.org and browse for suitable categories for your Web site. Each time you find a suitable category, search the page for the word *directory* to see if the page includes a link to a Web Directory or Directories subcategory. You can also use the search box; search for *haunted houses directory,* for example. You might also use synonyms; the term *guide,* for example, is a good one. DMOZ has a category called *Society: Holidays: Halloween: Haunted Attractions: Guides and Directories*, for example, in which it currently has links to eight such guides.

When you find a directory, see what's in it. Don't just ask for a link and move on. Dig around and see what you can find. The directory contains links to other sites that may also have their own directories.

Getting the link

After you've found a directory, you need to get the link back to your site. In some cases, you have to e-mail someone at the directory and ask. Many of these little directories are run by individuals and are often pretty crudely built. The problem you may run into is that it may take some time for the owner to get around to adding the link — after all, the directory is just a hobby in many cases.

Some directories have automated systems. Look for a <u>Submit Your Site</u> link, or maybe <u>Add URL</u>, <u>Add Your Site</u>, or something similar. The site may provide a form in which you enter your information. Some directories review the information before adding it to the directory, and in other, less common, situations, your information may post directly to the site.

By the way, some of these directories may ask you to pay to be added to the directory or give you preferential treatment if you pay.

Should you pay?

Generally, no.

Why not?

Look, it sometimes seems as though everyone's trying to get you to pay these days. Every time you try to get a link somewhere, someone's asking for money. For example, I recently ran across a portal with all sorts of directories that wanted me to pay $59 (*regularly* $99, though I'm not sure what or when *regular* is). That gets you into the index within seven days and gets you preferential placement.

Of course, that means this directory must have had listings over which I could have preferential placement; in other words, I *could* get in free. I scrolled down the page a little and found the free Basic Submission.

I recommend that you do *not* pay for these placements, at least to begin with. In most cases, they simply aren't worth spending $60, $100, or more for the link. It's worth spending a few moments getting a free link, though. If a site asks you to pay, dig around and see whether you can find a free placement link. If not, just move on. If the site can guarantee that you'll be on a page with a high PageRank, the fee may be worth it. (See Chapter 16 for more information about PageRank.)

However, here's another reason to be wary of paying for directory placements. Google has stated that if a directory adds some kind of value — if the payment is for review, not placement, so there's a chance you won't be accepted . . . that is, if the directory has the last say over the link text rather than simply accepting whatever keywords you request — then Google will accept the directory and give value to the links. If, on the other hand, the directory is a simple "pay us and you're in, and by the way, which keywords do you want in your links" type of directory, it may regard the links as no better than purchased links. (See Chapter 17 for an explanation of why the search engines don't like purchased links and what they do about it.)

At some point perhaps, it might be worthwhile to _consider_ thinking about paying for such placements, but generally, only if you know that the site is capable of sending you valuable traffic or providing valuable links.

You don't have to pay

Luckily, you may find that some of the best directories are free. Take, for instance, the model rocket business. Hundreds of model rocket sites, often run by individuals or families, are on the Web. (See the site shown in Figure 14-2.) Many of these sites have link pages. Although these sites don't get huge numbers of visitors, they _do_ get the right visitors (people interested in model rockets) and often have a pretty good PageRank. Most of these sites will give you a free listing, just for the asking. Look for a contact e-mail address somewhere.

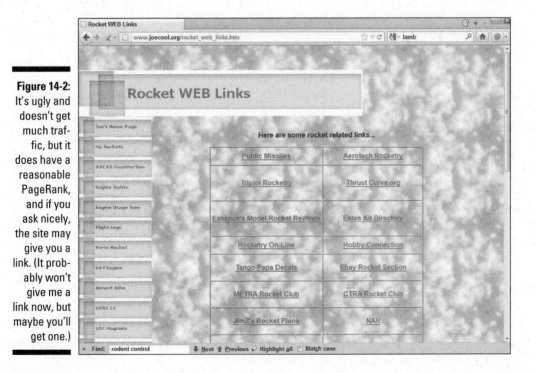

Figure 14-2:
It's ugly and doesn't get much traffic, but it does have a reasonable PageRank, and if you ask nicely, the site may give you a link. (It probably won't give me a link now, but maybe you'll get one.)

Using "Local" Directories

There are also many *local directories* — directories of businesses sorted geographically. These local directories are often good places to get listed. They're easy to get into and can provide more site categorization clues for search engines, and they often have a high PageRank.

However, this is a subject on its own, so I cover it separately. See Chapter 12 for more information.

Chapter 15

Product Search: Remember the Shopping Directories and Retailers

●●●

In This Chapter

▶ Finding the product directories

▶ Working with classified-ad sites

▶ Selling directly from third-party merchant sites

▶ Creating your datafeed files and managing your data

●●●

*I*n Chapter 1, I look at *where* people search, focusing on the major search engines, of course, but also giving you a little teaser: "Many, perhaps most, product searches actually begin in sites such as Amazon, eBay, and Craigslist," I write in Chapter 1, referencing you to this chapter.

So what's this all about? It's simple. In this chapter, you discover that many, even most, product search results don't come from the major search engines' organic-search indexes. If you sell products and you're focusing only on the major search engines, you're making a big mistake.

So read on and find out where people are searching and how you can get your products and links back to your Web site in front of people when they search.

Understanding Where People Search for Products

Back in 2010, comScore estimated that for every two searches carried out on the major search engines (Google, Yahoo!, Bing, Ask.com, and associated sites), one search was being carried out on various other sites, such as YouTube, Facebook, Craigslist, eBay, and Amazon. Combined, comScore estimated, more than 1.5 billion searches were carried out on Craigslist, eBay and Amazon combined. In other words, for every ten searches at the major search engines, a search occurs on one of those three commercial sites.

But things are getting worse, and it's been reported in the press that Google is worried about this trend. Google makes money from selling ads, some of the most valuable ad space is for commercial searches, and, as *Business Insider* reported late in 2012, "What Googlers worry about in private is a growing trend among consumers to skip Google altogether, and to just go ahead and search for the product they would like to buy on Amazon.com, or, on mobile in an Amazon app." . . . then, late in 2014 Business Insider reported that the trend continued, with searches going through Amazon increasing dramatically year over year, with many of the searches being carried out very quickly on mobile devices. Do you see where I'm heading? Almost all Amazon and eBay searches are *product* searches, and a huge proportion of Craigslist searches are for products, too. (Craigslist is also the world's most popular "personal ads" site, with *50 billion* pageviews a month.)

Consider also that many other product indexes exist. How many people search at Buy.com, Overstock.com, PriceGrabber.com, and other similar shopping and price-comparison sites? What about the other "classifieds" sites, such as ePage.com, BackPage.com, and eBayClassifieds.com?

Here's what you can know about searches:

- ✔ Most searches at product retailers, and many searches at classified-ad sites, are for products.
- ✔ Most searches at the major search engines are *not* for products.

That's right. Most searches at the major search engines are not product related; they are homework related, news related, celebrity related, politics related, Kim Kardashian and Iggy Azalea related. Sure, the major search engines' 21 billion searches a month is huge, but it covers all aspects of life, not just making purchases. comScore, in fact, believes that Amazon alone gets three to four times as many product-related searches as Google does. (And note that the major-search-engine searches number has not grown significantly in the past few years, perhaps only a billion searches a month increase in three or four years.)

The simple truth is that *most product-related searches are being made outside the major search engines!*

But wait, there's more! The major search engines have their own product indexes. For instance, in Chapter 2, I discuss various indexes maintained by Google: the PPC index, the organic-search index, and the local-search index, and the *Google Product Listings* index. In Figure 15-1, you can see an example; I searched for *binoculars,* and Google displayed some binoculars from its product index, along with a link for <u>*Shop for binoculars on Google*</u>. Yahoo! and Bing also provide shopping results, too.

Figure 15-1:
Google
Product
Search
results.

So, imagine the following scenario: You sell rodent-racing products, such as harnesses, timers, gates, and the like. You've done a great job getting into the organic-search indexes — most importantly, Google's and Bing's (and, therefore, Yahoo!'s) — and you rank well when people search for your products. But you still have one big problem. Most of the search results being presented to your prospective clients don't come from the organic-search indexes; rather, they come from Amazon's index, or Craigslist's, or eBay's, or even one of the major search engine's product search indexes: Google Product Listing Ads, Pricegrabber, Bing Product Ads, or Pronto.com.

The simple truth is this: If you sell products, you *must* consider the product indexes! (And, if you sell services, you *must* consider at the very least Craigslist, and potentially other service-oriented directories or classified sites.) These directories generally expect you to pay, though not all do; Craigslist, for instance, is free for most ads. In general, the ones that *do* expect you to pay charge only when someone clicks a link to visit your site, or even when a sale is made, so these directories may be worth experimenting with, too. There are, in effect, three different types of indexes:

- ✔ **Simple product indexes:** You list your product in the index, and, with luck, when people search for products like yours, your products pop up, the searchers click, and they arrive at your site.

- ✔ **Classified-ad sites:** You periodically post ads about your products, with links back to your site.

- ✔ **E-commerce sites:** With this type of index, you are putting your products into someone else's store — eBay, Etsy, or Amazon.com, for instance. In some cases, it may not even be obvious to buyers that they're buying from a third party; they put your product into the merchant's shopping cart and pay that merchant. Then you ship the product . . . or, as I describe later in the section "Working with Amazon," in some cases, the merchant may stock and ship your products for you.

By the way, you have another advantage to being in these additional indexes, owing to the fact that results from these indexes often turn up in regular search results. The major search engines obviously integrate their own product index results into their organic-search results. But they also index Craigslist, eBay, Amazon, and most, if not all, of the sites discussed in this chapter. So you get yet another chance (maybe several chances) to rank well in the organic search results.

The following sections look at each of these in turn.

Working with the Product Indexes

The Product Indexes are a simple concept. You get your product listed, so when people search, your product may come up. Just as there is in a search engine's regular search results, there will be a link to your site. In fact, as you've seen, the results may be inserted into the regular search results.

Following is a bunch of product indexes that you might want to check into. Clearly, the most important ones are the indexes used by the major search engines. Go to each one and try to find information about signing up and uploading your data. In some cases, that process is simple — the directory wants you to join, so you find a link that reads something like <u>List Your Products</u> <u>Sell on Our Site</u>, or <u>Information for Merchants</u>. Look in the page footer; you'll often find it there. Sometimes, you have to dig a little deeper because the information is not clearly visible; you may need to use the <u>Contact Us</u> link and ask someone about signing up.

- ✔ **Google Product Listing Ads:** www.google.com/intl/en_us/ads/shopping
- ✔ **Yahoo! Shopping & PriceGrabber.com:** www.pricegrabber.com
- ✔ **Bing Product Ads:** http://advertise.bingads.microsoft.com/en-us/product-ads
- ✔ **Amazon Product Ads**: www.amazon.com/ProductAds
- ✔ **Become:** www.become.com
- ✔ **Shopping.com/DealTime.com/Epinions.com:** www.shopping.com
- ✔ **BizRate & Shopzilla:** www.shopzilla.com
- ✔ **NexTag:** www.nextag.com
- ✔ **Pricewatch (for computer equipment):** www.pricewatch.com

These systems expect you to pay if you want to play — generally, you pay each time someone clicks a link to your site. The shopping and price-comparison sites that let you list for free are rapidly disappearing; Google's system used to be free, for instance, though now it's incorporated into its PPC system.

Most systems charge per click, but provide bidding systems that help determine your position on search results pages. (As you may expect, merchants with the highest bids are listed first on the page.)

What will you pay for the *cost-per-click (CPC)* systems?

✔ In most cases, CPC systems don't charge a listing fee.

✔ You have to begin by funding your account — typically $50 to $250, which goes toward paying for your clicks.

✔ You pay each time someone clicks your link. Clicks vary in price, generally, from 10 or 15 cents up.

✔ In systems that accept bids, there's a minimum click rate, but the actual rate is dependent on how many people are bidding and their pain threshold; in some cases, clicks could even cost several dollars.

✔ You may be charged other fees, such as a fee to place a store logo next to your listing. (Some of the CPC systems give these logos to the highest bidders free.)

I don't have the space to go into the whole concept of cost-per-click or pay-per-click advertising, but here's a little advice: Be careful! Many people lose a lot of money on the PPC-advertising systems, and there's no reason you can't lose money on these product-directory CPC systems, too.

The product-directory systems probably provide better leads than the more general PPC systems, but nonetheless, you must be careful — you must track results — to ensure that you're not spending more on your clicks than you are making on your sales.

Google Product Listing Ads

Google Product Listing Ads (www.google.com/intl/en_us/ads/shopping) is Google's product directory. It's been incorporated into the main Google site for years now and has hundreds of millions of products in the index. I'm sure you've seen Google Product Search, even if you don't realize it. Search, for instance, for *buy vitamin d* at Google, and Google will display a box of product results, along with a <u>Shop for buy vitamin d on Google</u> link. Click this link, and Google takes you to the full Google Product list. The links under the pictures go to specific product pages. Click one of these links, and you see something similar to that shown in Figure 15-2.

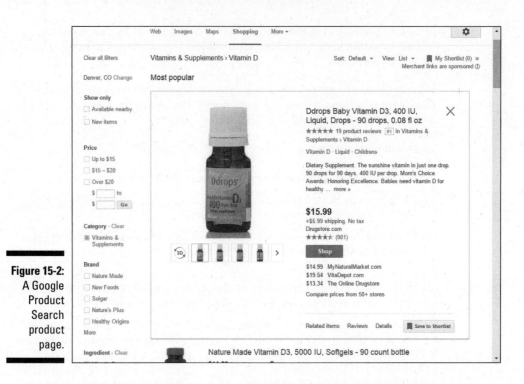

Figure 15-2:
A Google
Product
Search
product
page.

Getting into Google Product Search is easy, but it's no longer free (as it was for a number of years); these days, it's part of Google's PPC system. Just go to http://www.google.com/shopping and click the <u>Information For Merchants</u> link to find instructions. You can submit a *datafeed* file — a simple text file containing the product data (which I discuss later in this chapter). In addition, if you have programmers working on your site, they can use a Google API (Application Programming Interface) to feed data to Google.

Google Product Search doesn't display a lot of information about each product, so it doesn't require much information from you. You provide a link to the information page on your site, a link to an image of the product, the name and description, a price, and a category. Additionally, you can fill various optional fields, such as author name, model number, size, style, weight, and so on.

Yahoo! Shopping, PriceGrabber, and PrecioMania

Early in 2010, Yahoo! Shopping dumped its own shopping directory and went into partnership with PriceGrabber (www.pricegrabber.com) and its Spanish-language *hermano* PrecioMania (www.preciomania.com).

PriceGrabber was already a major shopping index in its own right; it currently claims that it "drives over $1 billion in annual sales for our retailer partners."

PriceGrabber has been a significant shopping directory for a long time because it feeds data to various other shopping directories — over 400 different Web sites — and with the Yahoo! partnership, it feeds to one of the world's most important shopping directories.

The end result? When you search at Yahoo!, it finds the product you're looking for. When you click the link to the product page, Yahoo! finds merchants that sell the product (see Figure 15-3).

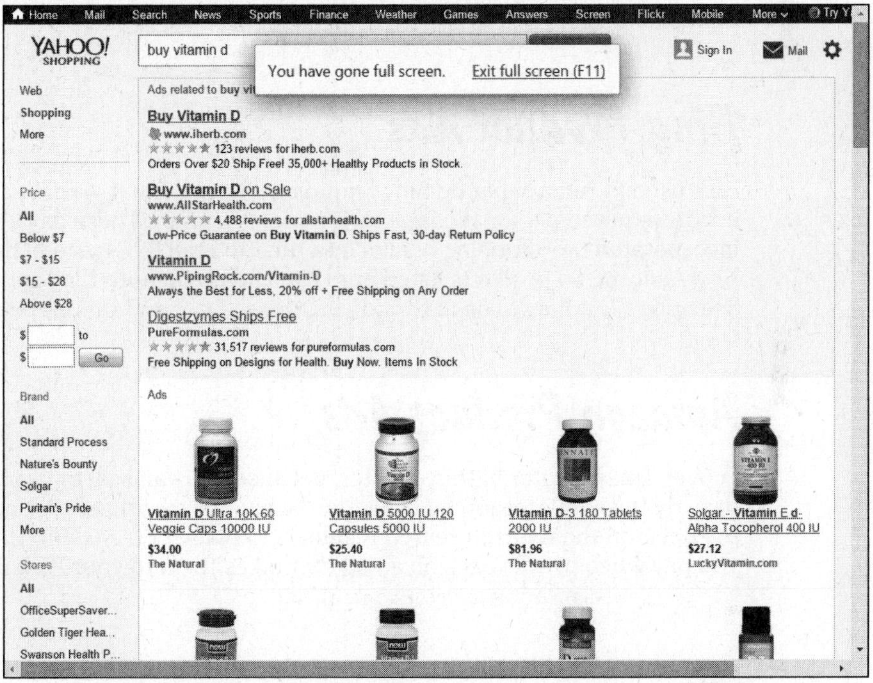

Figure 15-3: You can find links to merchants on the product page.

So how much does all this cost? That depends on the product category. Unlike some systems, Yahoo! and PriceGrabber charge a fixed fee per click that varies among categories; other systems charge a fee that depends on bidding, as the CPC systems do.

For instance, here are a few click prices:

Appliances	$0.65 - $0.85
Books	$0.35 - $0.45
Computers	$0.45–$1.15
Electronics	$0.65–$1.15
Furniture	$0.45–$0.75
Magazines	$0.75-$0.85
Sporting Goods	$0.40 - $0.50
Video Games	$0.35 - $0.60

Yahoo! also incorporates product ads from the *Yahoo Bing Network,* the partnership created when Yahoo! agreed to use Bing's search results on the Yahoo.com site.

Bing Product Ads

Bing used to run a separate Bing Shopping system, and it wasn't easy to get into; it required personal contact with a sales person. These days, they have incorporated the shopping results into their overall PPC system, the *Yahoo Bing Network.* So products listed here can end up on both Bing and Yahoo!. See `http://advertise.bingads.microsoft.com/en-us/product-ads`.

Amazon Product Ads

I cover Amazon later in this chapter, because you can sell your products directly through Amazon by using the Amazon Marketplace. But another way to appear in the Amazon search results is to place PPC ads into the system; you pay when people click on an ad that takes them to your Web site. See `http://www.amazon.com/ProductAds`.

Shopping.com

Shopping.com, owned by eBay (and found on the Web at `www.shopping.com`, of all places) is also a pretty important (that is, popular) shopping directory, with around 100 million viewers a month, thanks to its relationship with eBay, partnerships with major sites such as CNET, and operations in the UK, Australia, Germany, and France. It also charges by the click, and each category has a minimum rate.

Figure 15-4 shows the Digital Cameras page, a subcategory of Electronics.

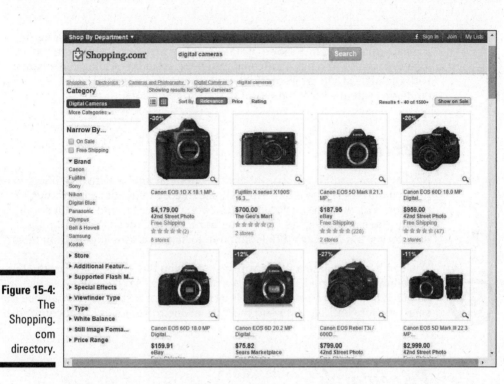

Figure 15-4:
The
Shopping.
com
directory.

BizRate & Shopzilla

BizRate and Shopzilla (www.shopzilla.com and www.bizrate.com) are two popular pay-per-click sites with common ownership. In addition, Shopzilla owns another *seven* different shopping sites, including six in France, Germany, and the United Kingdom: Beso.com, PrixMoinsCher.fr, SparDeinGeld.de, Shopzilla.co.uk, Shopzilla.de, Shopzilla.fr, and Bizrate.co.uk.

Mergers

Shopping.com was formed by a merger of DealTime and Epinions, the most popular product-comparison sites on the Web, and all three sites, Shopping.com, DealTime.com, and Epinions.com, are now owned by eBay, as part of the eBay Commerce Network. Getting into Shopping.com gets you into all three sites, and in some cases onto eBay.com itself.

As with Shopping.com, these services charge a minimum fee per category, typically ranging from $0.35 to around a dollar, an extra $0.10 if you have a logo with the product, and the final rate dependent on bidding. Merchants with the highest bid are listed first, until the visitor re-sorts the list, a common system with a number of these shopping sites.

NexTag

NexTag (www.nextag.com), yet another popular site — with 30 million visitors a month — is also a CPC site with a category minimum and bidding for position. You don't pay a setup fee, but you do have to fund your account before you can get started. That's the norm with all these CPC shopping directories, but NexTag's $150 minimum to start is a little higher than most.

You can load data into a Web-form system if you have only a few products. If you have more, you'll want to use a datafeed file. NexTag will take any datafeed file; if you create one for Pricegrabber, for instance, you can use the same one for NexTag. Just send the Yahoo! one to your NexTag account manager, and he will handle it.

Pricewatch

Pricewatch (www.pricewatch.com) isn't well known outside geek circles, though it claims to be "The Web's very first price comparison site"; it's been in business since 1995. Many people in the computer business use Pricewatch to buy their hardware after checking pricing at the site; the site used to be limited to computers, peripherals, and accessories, though it has branched out in recent years. Hey, even UNIX geeks have lives beyond technology . . . well, some of them do.

This crude system (shown in Figure 15-5) appeals to UNIX geeks in particular. It's fast and has few graphics on the search page (or even on the results pages in most cases).

The Pricewatch folks claim to serve over 400 million pages each month, so if you have products in their categories, you may want to look into working with them.

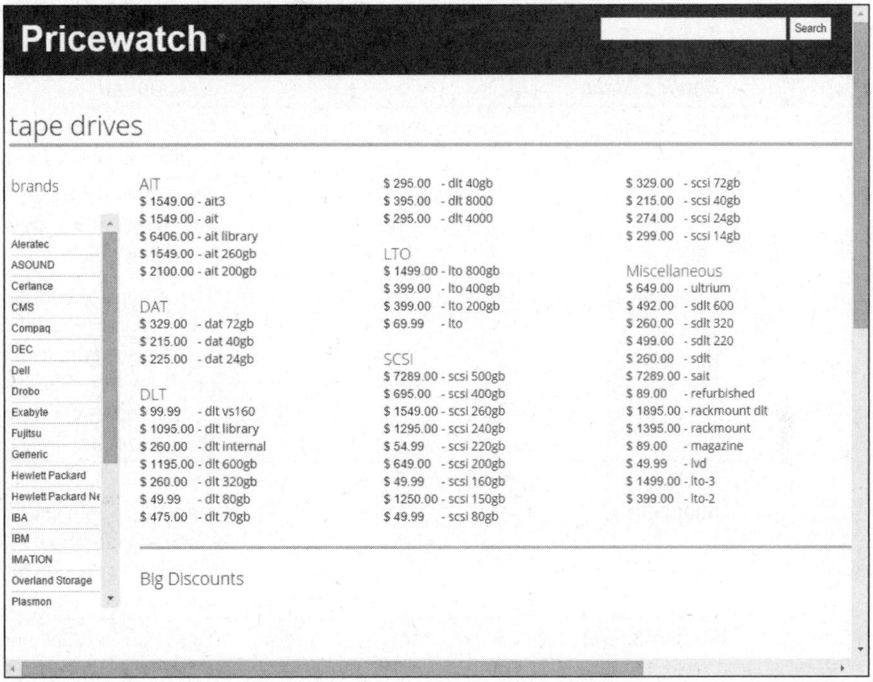

Figure 15-5:
Pricewatch,
a UNIX
geek's
dream
shopping
directory.

Exploring More Shopping Services

Yep, there's more, plenty more. Table 15-1 offers a quick rundown of some other places where you can list your products.

Table 15-1	**Shopping Services**	
Service Name	*URL*	*Description*
AOL Shopping	`http://shopping.aol.com`	A very exclusive property; if you want to work with AOL Shopping, you have to negotiate directly.
Become	`www.become.com`	Created by the founder of mySimon, once a big name in product search.
Best-Price, BuyCheapr	`www.best-price.com,` `www.buycheapr.com`	Two comScore top-10 product-comparison sites. However, these are basically affiliate sites with no way to submit your products.

(continued)

Table 15-1 *(continued)*

Service Name	URL	Description
CoolSavings	www.coolsavings.com	Definitely a smaller site; it claims a million visitors a month.
Dogpile	http://dogpile. pricegrabber.com	This popular "metasearch" site uses PriceGrabber for its shopping results.
mySimon	www.mysimon.com	This company was an early and popular product-comparison site. Now it gets its nontech products from Shopping.com and its tech products form CNET's Shopper.com.
PayPal Shopping	www.paypal-shopping.com	This is a comScore top-15 shopping site. (It claims 1.5 million visitors a month.) Call the PayPal merchant services team for information.
PricingCentral	www.pricingcentral.com	This is a product "meta search" site; search here, and it pulls up links to various shopping directories.
Shop.com	www.shop.com	Originally designed for catalog companies to sell their wares online, this site is looking for merchants with more than 100 consumer-oriented products. See http://www.shop.com/AboutHowToAdvertise-t.xhtml.
ShopLocal	www.shoplocal.com	Claims to have 6.5 billion page views a year. Mostly works with major retailers, so if that doesn't describe you, you may have problems.
Shopmania	www.shopmania.com	Another free-site-turned-PPC.
Smarter	www.smarter.com	Ranked as one of the top-10 product-comparison sites by comScore. Clicks start at 15 cents.

The Classified-Ad Sites

Craigslist.com is, of course, the monster, the newspaper killer, of the classified-ads world. You'd never know it from just looking at the site — to call it "minimalist" is being kind — but this site has over 50 billion page views a month. Each month, over 60 million Americans visit Craigslist one or more times, almost 1 American in 5. Alexa ranks Craigslist as the world's 61st most popular Web site, and America's 11th most popular. Ignore Craigslist at your peril!

It's not alone, though. There are a couple more "significant" classified sites. Significant is in quotation marks because, well, those other sites pale in significance next to Craigslist; nonetheless, some do get significant traffic. I show the following sites' Alexa rankings to give you an idea:

✔ **BackPage.com:** 427 (U.S. ranking)

✔ **eBayclassifieds.com:** 4,591

Perhaps I missed some, but I'm not aware of any other important classified sites. It just shows you the state of the classified-ad biz. Craigslist dominates! (At least in the United States. In the U.K., for instance, most people have never heard of Craigslist, and the big player is probably GumTree.com, which is the U.K.'s 28th most popular site.)

How, then, do you use these sites? You post your products in the listings, with links back to your site. The links won't help you from a search engine ranking standpoint; these are nofollow links (see Chapter 16). And you should check the rules because you can't just go in and post a thousand ads or you will get blocked. But many businesses promote their products and services very successfully through these classified-ad sites — in particular Craigslist — because they get so much traffic. In fact, there are thousands of "Craigslist businesses," probably tens of thousands, small companies that generate significant business through Craigslist, often without any other online presence or marketing mechanism: plumbers, electricians, car mechanics, vehicle chop shops, and so on.

By the way, you may run across lists of classified-ad sites, or services that purport to post you to hundreds, nay, thousands, of classified-ad sites (I just saw one promising to post me in 7,000 sites). These are probably not worth your time. Only a very small number of viable classified-ad sites exist.

Working with E-Commerce or Merchant Sites

The last type of product index I want to discuss are the indexes maintained by e-commerce or merchant sites that allow third parties to sell products through their stores; these are often known as "e-commerce marketplaces" these days.

The two most important, of course, are eBay.com and Amazon.com. eBay's entire business model is based on helping people sell their stuff, whether that stuff amounts to a single item or thousands of items. (Don't think of eBay as just an auction site, by the way. Most products sold through eBay these days are fixed price.)

As for Amazon.com, it had people fooled for a few years into thinking that its business model was acting as an online retailer, selling its own stuff, but Amazon's business model, it turns out, is just selling stuff, whoever's stuff that stuff may be. A large part of Amazon's business, certainly more than a quarter of it, is not selling its own stuff but rather selling stuff provided by thousands of other merchants. You could, perhaps, be one of those merchants.

Why bother? If you already have a store on your Web site, why work with other stores? Because most people looking for products won't find your site; they'll go through product sites. Amazon gets hundreds of millions of searches a month, and some of those are for your products, but you're not getting the sale unless you're working with Amazon. Many of these sites, including Amazon, have automated "related items" systems built into them that will display your product to someone who may have just placed an order for a product that's related or complimentary to yours. This can drive a huge amount of new business to your store.

Are there other such sites, beyond Amazon and eBay? Well, there's Overstock. com, with its tens of millions of visitors each month; you can talk to that company about selling products in its catalog, or quickly set up an account to sell through its Auction site. Another site is Half.com, an eBay-owned, fixed-price retail site that's worth checking into. Even Sears.com and BestBuy.com are "marketplaces." There are others, but these few are the biggies.

Working with eBay

eBay is the world's second most popular e-commerce site (after Amazon), although more dollars are spent on eBay than Amazon. It gets around a billion searches a month.

eBay is not just an auction site, though. It hosts thousands of stores, many of which sell fixed-price goods in addition to taking part in auctions. eBay is part of the overall marketing strategy of many different companies. I have one client, for instance, who has his own e-commerce Web site that ranks very well in organic searches and who has an eBay store, too (and who runs Craigslist ads constantly). I don't go into detail about working with eBay; that's a book by itself. But you may want to consider looking into eBay for your own business.

Working with Amazon

Go to Amazon.com and find the <u>Sell On Amazon</u> link at the bottom of the page. This takes you to an overview of how to sell products on Amazon. There are essentially two programs. If you expect to sell fewer than 40 products a month — or if you just want to get your feet wet — you'll want to use the basic plan, which charges no listing or monthly fee. However, on this plan, you'll pay an additional 99 cents per sale, over and above the regular fees — a percentage commission, and a variable closing fee. Larger merchants can pay a $39.99 per month fee and avoid the 99 cents per sale.

If you want to get an idea of the overall fees for your products, see the calculator at `https://sellercentral.amazon.com/gp/fbacalc/fba-calculator.html`.

Amazon also provides a *Fulfillment By Amazon* service that is real eye-opener for many merchants. Amazon will stock and ship your products for you, at really great prices. Whether the order comes from your own Web store, from eBay, from Amazon, or wherever else, Amazon can handle the shipping for you. (Note, though, that it has two shipping-rate schedules: one rate for orders generated through Amazon itself, and a higher rate schedule for orders that from other sources.)

This actually gives you a real advantage when selling your products through Amazon, as your products are treated exactly as though they were being sold by Amazon itself. In particular, buyers get free shipping on your products through its Amazon Prime program. (Amazon provides free shipping on most orders over $35 and free 2-day shipping on any order for Prime members). You can actually price your products higher than your competitors do and still have an overall lower price; because Amazon ranks products in its list of vendors by total price, including shipping, your product will rank higher than your competitors'. You'll still have to pay a fee to Amazon to ship your product, but because Amazon is so incredibly efficient at shipping, that fee will be pretty low.

Amazon is actually out hunting for people to sell products. It has staff looking for successful Web sites with large catalogs of products that are not well represented on Amazon in order to recruit them. (One of my clients was recently recruited and now has thousands of products selling through Amazon.) Check into it; you may be glad you did!

Managing Your Data

To work with the product indexes and e-commerce sites, you need to figure out how to manage your data — that is, all the information about your products. You'll probably need a data file (often called a *datafeed*) containing information about your products. This can be a simple text file carefully formatted, using the correct layout. A datafeed allows you to quickly upload hundreds, even thousands, of products into the directories within minutes.

Although the datafeed file can be a simple text file, creating it is a little difficult for some people. Of course, if you have geeks on your staff, they can handle it for you. The ideal situation is one in which all your product data is stored in a database that is managed by capable, knowledgeable people who know how to export to a text file in the correct format. All you do is give them the data file specification from the shopping directory, and they know exactly what to do. If that's your situation, be happy. If not, I'll help you.

I'm going to explain how to format your data in a spreadsheet program, which is probably the simplest method. If you have a large number of products, you may already have your data in some kind of database format. Unfortunately, you may need to *manipulate* your data — clean it up — before you can use it. I've noticed over the last couple of decades that, for some reason, data is usually a mess — whether the data files were created by small companies or large. Data is often badly formatted — for example, the text files contain the data, but the fields are improperly *delimited* (separated).

I suggest that you use a spreadsheet program to create your data file. Creating the file in a text editor is difficult and error prone, especially if you have a lot of products. Also, remember that each shopping directory is a little different, requiring different information. The spreadsheet file is your source file, from which you can create the various text files as needed.

You may already have a spreadsheet program; Microsoft Excel is hiding on millions of computers around the world, unknown to their owners. (It's part of Microsoft Office. Or you may have Microsoft Works, which also includes a spreadsheet program. Various other database programs are available — StarOffice and AppleWorks contain spreadsheets, too, and you can get a free spreadsheet program at OpenOffice.org, or use Google's Web-based Google

Docs system (`https://docs.google.com`). Microsoft recently released its free Office Web Apps, which includes a pared-down, Web-based version of Excel; see `http://office.microsoft.com/en-us/web-apps`.

You don't need a terribly complicated program, because the work you do with the file is pretty simple. However, you want to use a program that can have multiple sheets open and will allow you to link from a cell in one sheet to a cell in another.

You can also use a database program to manage all this data. It's just simpler in some ways to use a spreadsheet. Of course, you may already have your data in a database, especially if you have a lot of products.

The data you need

Take a look at the type of data you're going to need for your data file. Google Product Listing Ads, Google's shopping directory, requires the following data:

- ✔ **product_url:** A link to the product page on your Web site

- ✔ **name:** The name of the product

- ✔ **description:** A description of the product

- ✔ **image_url:** A link to the image file containing a picture of the product

- ✔ **price:** The cost of the product

- ✔ **category:** The category in which you want to place the product

- ✔ **offer_id:** Some kind of product number, such as a *stock keeping unit (SKU)* or *international standard book number (ISBN)*

Those are the basic fields, but there are others you can include, such as instock, shipping, brand, UPC, manufacturer_id, and so on. Each service is different, of course. (For details, you need to check the particular systems into which you want to load the data.)

Here's my suggestion. Begin by creating a spreadsheet file containing *all* the data you have about your products. At the very least, include this information:

- ✔ Product name

- ✔ Product description

- ✔ Product price

> ✔ Product category
>
> ✔ A URL pointing to the product's page on your Web site
>
> ✔ A URL pointing to the image file that contains a picture of the product on your site

You also want to include any other information you have — ISBNs, SKUs, EANs, media types, and so on. And, keep the file clean of all HTML coding; you just want plain text, with no carriage returns or special characters in any field.

Formatting guidelines

Some of you may have problems with the product URL. If your site is a framed site, as I discuss in Chapter 9, you have a problem because you can't link directly to a product page. Even if you don't have a framed site, you might have a problem or two. I discuss that in the upcoming section "Getting those product URLs."

Each shopping directory varies slightly, but datafeed files typically conform to the following criteria:

> ✔ They are plain-text files. That is, don't save them in a spreadsheet or database format; save them in an ASCII text format. Virtually all spreadsheet programs have a way to save data in such a format (typically as a .csv file).
>
> ✔ The first line in each file contains the header, with each field name — product_url, name, description, price, and so on — generally separated by tabs.
>
> ✔ Each subsequent line contains information about a single product; the fields match the headers on the first line.
>
> ✔ The last line of the file may require some kind of marker, such as END.
>
> ✔ In most cases, you can't include HTML tags, tabs within fields (tabs usually separate fields), carriage returns, new line characters within fields, and so on — just plain text.

Creating your spreadsheet

Take a look at Figure 15-6. This is a simple spreadsheet file containing a number of data fields; it's an example data file from Google Product Search. Each row in the spreadsheet is a product, and each cell in the row — each field — is a different piece of information about the product.

Figure 15-6:
A sample datafeed spread-sheet.

File	Edit	View	Insert	Format	Tools	Data	Window	Help	_ ₽ ×

	A	B	C	D	E
1	code	product-url	name	price	shopping-category
2	p12-x	http://www.yourstore123.com/1.html	American Pride Polo Shirt	25	Apparel
3	w345	http://www.yourstore123.com/2.html	Women's Overalls	39.95	Apparel
4	f45	http://www.yourstore123.com/3.html	Carrot Cake	29.95	Flowers, Gifts and Registry > Gourmet and F
5	f46	http://www.yourstore123.com/4.html	Apple Pie	19.99	Flowers, Gifts and Registry > Gourmet and F
6	hg202	http://www.yourstore123.com/5.html	Replacement Blade of Cof	12.95	Home, Garden and Garage > Appliances
7	12kn	http://www.yourstore123.com/6.html	PowerMax Juicer	129.95	Home, Garden and Garage > Appliances > S
8	f235	http://www.yourstore123.com/7.html	Soft Recliner	399.99	Home, Garden and Garage
9	p3002-x12	http://www.yourstore123.com/8.html	Litter box - Gray	14.95	Home, Garden and Garage
10	3exe345	http://www.yourstore123.com/9.html	Handheld power drill	89.95	Home, Garden and Garage

Although the final product will be a text file, you want to save the spread-sheet file in a normal spreadsheet file format. When you're ready to upload data to a shopping directory, *then* you save it as a text file.

Getting those product URLs

To do this spreadsheet business right, you need the URL for each product's Web page. If you don't have many products, this is easy — just copy and paste from your browser into the spreadsheet. If you have thousands of products, though, it might be a bit of a problem! If you're lucky and you have a big IT budget or some very capable but cheap geeks working for you, you don't need to worry about this. Otherwise, here's a quick tip that might help.

Many companies have a source data file that they use to import into an e-commerce program. For this to be useful to you, figure out what page number the e-commerce program is assigning to each product. For instance, one e-commerce system creates its URLs like this:

```
http://www.yourdomain.com/customer/product.php?productid=18507
```

Notice that the `productid` number is included in this URL. Every product page uses more or less the same URL — all that changes is the `productid` number. So here's one simple way to deal with this situation. Suppose you have a data file that looks similar to the one in Figure 15-7, in which you have a product ID or code in one column and an empty column waiting for the URL pointing to the product page.

Here's how to get these URLs into your product listing:

1. Copy the blank URL into all the URL fields.

   Copy the URL without the product ID in it, as shown in Figure 15-8. Some spreadsheet programs try to convert the URL to an active link, one you can click to launch a browser. You may want to leave the URL in that format so that later you can test each link. (*Note:* Working with these active links is often a nuisance because it may be hard to select a link without launching the browser.)

Figure 15-7:
Where do
you get the
URL from?

	File	Edit	View	Insert	Format	Tools	Data	Window	Help	_ 🗗 x

	A	B	C	D	
1	code	product-url	name	price	shopping-categ
2	803341		American Pride Polo Shirt	25	Apparel
3	803342		Women's Overalls	39.95	Apparel
4	803343		Carrot Cake	29.95	Flowers, Gifts
5	803344		Apple Pie	19.99	Flowers, Gifts
6	803345		Replacement Blade of Cof	12.95	Home, Garden
7	803346		PowerMax Juicer	129.95	Home, Garden
8	803347		Soft Recliner	399.99	Home, Garden
9	803348		Litter box - Gray	14.95	Home, Garden
10	803349		Handheld power drill	89.95	Home, Garden

Figure 15-8:
Place a
blank URL in
the column
and then
copy the
product
code from
the code
column to
the end of
the URL.

	File	Edit	View	Insert	Format	Tools	Data	Window	Help	_ 🗗 x

	A	B	C	D	
1	code	product-url	name	price	shopping-categ
2	803341	http://www.yourdomain.com/customer/product.php?productid=	American Pride Polo Shirt	25	Apparel
3	803342	http://www.yourdomain.com/customer/product.php?productid=	Women's Overalls	39.95	Apparel
4	803343	http://www.yourdomain.com/customer/product.php?productid=	Carrot Cake	29.95	Flowers, Gifts
5	803344	http://www.yourdomain.com/customer/product.php?productid=	Apple Pie	19.99	Flowers, Gifts
6	803345	http://www.yourdomain.com/customer/product.php?productid=	Replacement Blade of Cof	12.95	Home, Garden
7	803346	http://www.yourdomain.com/customer/product.php?productid=	PowerMax Juicer	129.95	Home, Garden
8	803347	http://www.yourdomain.com/customer/product.php?productid=	Soft Recliner	399.99	Home, Garden
9	803348	http://www.yourdomain.com/customer/product.php?productid=	Litter box - Gray	14.95	Home, Garden
10	803349	http://www.yourdomain.com/customer/product.php?productid=	Handheld power drill	89.95	Home, Garden

2. **Do one of the following to copy the number in the code field and paste it onto the end of the matching URL with a single keystroke:**

- *Create a macro.*

- *Use a programmable keyboard.*

I love my programmable keyboard! It has saved me hundreds of hours. A programmable keyboard automates repetitive tasks, allowing you to carry out actions with a single press of a button.

I used to use an old Gateway AnyKey programmable keyboard, which you can occasionally buy at eBay, but they are so ancient know they are rapidly dying out. It's hard to find good programmable keyboards these days, but I recently ran into the Corsair K95 Gaming keyboard which works pretty well, though is more complicated to use than the old AnyKey.

If you don't have a programmable keyboard (and you should have one!), the spreadsheet you're using may have a built-in macro program that allows you to program actions onto a single keystroke. (MS Excel does, for instance.) Another option is to use a macro program that you download from a shareware site. If you have only 20 or 30 products, programmable keyboards and macros don't matter too much. If you have a few thousand products, it's worth figuring out how to automate keystrokes!

Creating individual sheets

After you have all your data in one sheet of the spreadsheet file, you can create a single sheet for each system to which you plan to upload data: one for Google Product Lising Ads, one for PriceGrabber, and so on. (A *sheet* is a spreadsheet page, and all good spreadsheet programs allow you to have multiple sheets.)

Remember, in general each system requires different information, under different headings, and in a different order. So you need to link information from the original sheet to each individual sheet. You don't want to actually copy this information.

Say that you have five shopping directories you're working with and, after you've finished everything, you discover that you made a few mistakes. If you *copied* the data, you have to go into each sheet and correct the cells. If you *linked* between cells, you can just make the change in the original sheet and the other five update automatically.

Here's how this works in Excel. I assume that you have two sheets, one named Yahoo! (with data needed just for Yahoo!/PriceGrabber) and one named Original (containing all your product data). You want to place the information from the *productid* column in the Original sheet into the Yahoo! sheet, under the column named *code*. Here's how you do it in Microsoft Excel:

1. **Click the Yahoo! tab at the bottom of the window to open the Yahoo! sheet.**

2. **Click cell 2 in the *code* column.**

   In this example, this cell is A2, as shown in Figure 15-9.

3. **Press the = (equal) key to begin placing a formula into the cell.**

4. **Click the Original tab at the bottom of the page to open the Original sheet.**

5. **Click cell 2 in the *productid* column.**

   In this example, this cell is A2, as shown in Figure 15-10.

6. **Press Enter.**

   The program jumps back to cell 2 in the *code* column of the Yahoo! sheet, places the data from the Original sheet into that cell, and then moves down to the cell below.

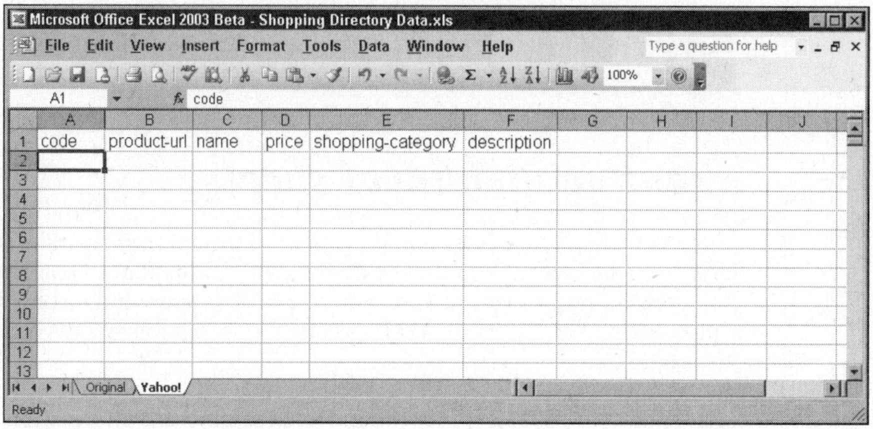

Figure 15-9:
The cursor on cell A2 in the Yahoo! sheet.

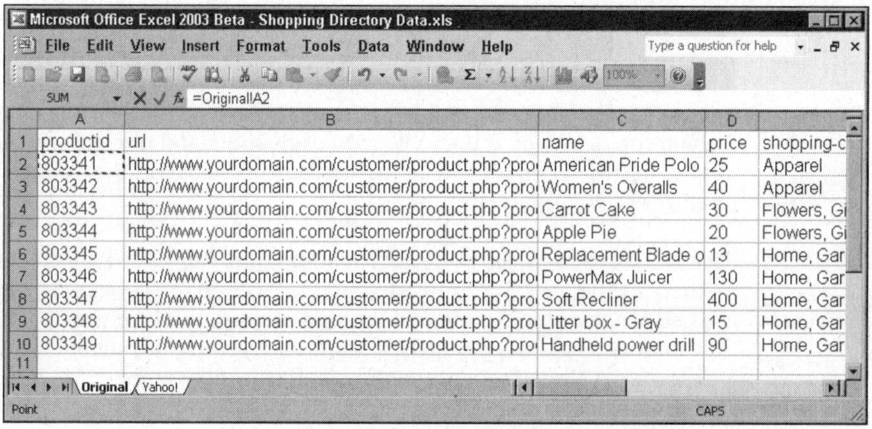

Figure 15-10:
The cursor on cell A2 in the Original sheet.

7. Click cell 2 and then look in the formula box at the top of the window.

You see this formula (or something similar): `=Original!A2`, as shown in Figure 15-11.

This means, "Use the data from cell A2 in the sheet named Original." You haven't copied the data; rather you're linking to the data, so that if the data in A2 changes, so will the data in this cell.

8. With cell 2 in the *code* column of the Yahoo! sheet selected, choose one of the following:

  • *Press Ctrl+C.*

  • *Choose Edit ➪ Copy from the main menu.*

You've copied this data into the Clipboard.

Here's the formula pulling data from Cell A2 in the Original sheet.

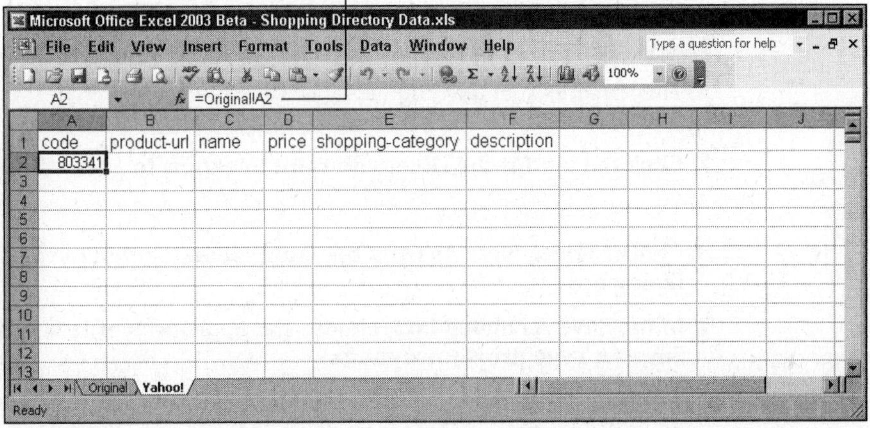

Figure 15-11:
Cell A2 in
the Yahoo!
sheet
contains
=Origi-
nal!A2.

9. **Press the down arrow (↓) to select the cell below.**

10. **Hold the Shift key and press PgDn multiple times, until the cursor has selected as many cells as there are products.**

    For instance, if you have 1,000 products, you want the last selected cell to be cell 1001. (Remember, the first cell contains the header, *code*.)

11. **Choose one of the following:**

    • *Press Ctrl+V.*

    • *Choose Edit ⇨ Paste from the main menu.*

    The cursor jumps to cell 2 again, and data from the Original sheet — from the appropriate cells — now appears in the cells below cell 2.

12. **Press the Esc key to stop copy mode.**

The cells are now linked. If you change data in a *productid* cell in the Original sheet, it changes in the appropriate *code* cell, too.

Repeat this process for all the columns you need and for all the different sheets you need, and you're ready to export your text files.

Creating and uploading your data files

After you've created your sheets, you can export the text files you need to give to the shopping directories. Each spreadsheet program works a little differently. With some programs, you may find an Export command; in

Microsoft Excel, you use the Save As command. Here's how to export the text files from Excel:

1. **Save the spreadsheet file in its original spreadsheet file format.**

   This ensures that any changes you've made are stored in the original file.

2. **Click the tab for the sheet you want to export to a text file.**

   That sheet is selected.

3. **Choose File ⇨ Save As from the main menu to open the Save As dialog box.**

4. **In the Save As dialog box, choose the appropriate file type from the Save As Type drop-down menu.**

   You generally need to select a text format, such as *CSV* (*Comma delimited;* `*.csv`) or *Text* (*Tab delimited;* `*.txt`). Check the shopping-directory specifications, as some may accept other formats.

5. **Provide a filename in the Name field.**

   For example, use Yahoo! if you're submitting to Yahoo!, and so on.

6. **Click OK.**

   You see a message box saying that you can't save the entire file. That's okay; all you want to do is save the selected sheet.

7. **Click Yes.**

   Now you see a message box telling you that some features can't be saved as text. That's okay; you don't want to save anything fancy, just text.

8. **Click Yes.**

   That's it. You've saved the file. It's still open in Excel, with the other sheets, so I suggest that you close the file. (Excel will ask again if you want to save the file — you can just say No.)

   If you want to export another text file, reopen the original spreadsheet file and repeat these steps.

If you want, you can open the file in a text editor like Notepad to see what it really looks like.

After you've created the text file, you're ready to upload it to the shopping directory. Each directory works a little differently, so refer to the directory's instructions.

These data files expire. That is, some of these product-listing systems require that you periodically upload data to make sure it's up to date. Check each system carefully and remember to upload the latest data file before it expires or when you have any important changes.

Multichannel, automated data management

There are, of course, tools that you can use to do some of the work for you. Search Google for *product data feed* or *feed management,* and you find companies advertising a variety of products and services. SingleFeed.com, for instance, can help you feed data to 19 different systems, including Google Product Listing Ads, Bing, Become, NextTag, Shopzilla, and PriceGrabber. Plans start at $99.99 a month.

GoDataFeed.com works with a huge list — more than 60 sites, including not only product indexes and e-commerce systems but also coupon sites, review sites, and affiliate networks. You get all this for $149 a month (or $50 a month for a very limited starter plan).

There are also sophisticated services, such as ChannelAdvisor.com and Mercent.com, which charge hundreds, if not thousands, of dollars a month but provide much more sophisticated services, including PPC-campaign management, inventory management, accounting integration, shipping management, and so on. I should also mention SellerEngine.com, RePriceIt, and AppEagle, very affordable software programs designed to help you manage Amazon.com sales; Zoovy.com, which works with Amazon, eBay, PriceGrabber, and multiple Web stores; Fillz.com, a product designed mainly for selling books, movies, music, and games, so it works with Amazon, Barnes and Noble, and various other media stores; and Monsoonworks.com, another sophisticated system that works with media, textbooks, and consumer goods.

If you have an e-commerce store, then you may want to look into a system that integrates into your store; in other words, manage all your data in one place — your e-commerce store — and push the data from the store into the product feeds. For example, GoDataFeed integrates into e-commerce systems such as Magento, BigCommerce, Shopify, and 3D Cart; if you are using the X-Cart e-commerce system, the publisher, Qualiteam, has an add-on module that feeds data to five different systems.

Whatever your products, companies are out there that want to help! So you really should consider working with these other channels. It's where the searchers are!

Part IV
After You've Submitted Your Site

Visit www.dummies.com/extras/seo for great Dummies content online.

In this part . . .

- ✔ Understanding how search engines calculate value
- ✔ Getting other sites to link to you
- ✔ Getting great links
- ✔ Connecting to social networks
- ✔ Displaying video
- ✔ Deploying in the face of disaster
- ✔ Visit `www.dummies.com/extras/seo` for great Dummies content online

Chapter 16

Using Link Popularity to Boost Your Position

*T*housands of site owners have experienced the frustration of being unable to get search engines to index their sites. You build a Web site, you do your best to optimize it for search engines, you "register" with the search engines, and then nothing much happens. Little or no traffic turns up at your site, your pages don't rank well in the search engines, and in some cases you can't even find your pages in the search engines. What's going on?

Here's the opposite scenario: You have an existing site, one that's been around for a while but with few links pointing to it, and finally find a few other sites to link to it. You make no changes to the pages themselves, yet all of a sudden, you notice your pages jump up in the search engines.

There's a lot of confusion about links and their relationship to Web sites. Many site owners don't even realize that links have a bearing on their search engine positions. Surely, all you need to do is register your page in a search engine and it will be indexed, right? And isn't "content King"? Nope. This chapter takes the confusion out of links by showing you how they can help, and what you need to know to make them work.

Why Search Engines Like Links

A little over a decade or so ago, pretty much all you had to do to get your site listed in a search engine — and maybe even ranked well — was register with the search engine. Then along came Google in 1998, and all that changed. Google decided to use the links from other Web sites as another factor in determining whether the site was a good match for a search. Each link to a site was a vote for the site, and the more votes the site received, the better a site was regarded by Google.

Google: All about links

In fact, Google's original name was *BackRub*. No, really. Check out Google's own corporate history (www.google.com/corporate/history.html):

> *1996: Larry and Sergey, now Stanford computer science grad students, begin collaborating on a search engine called BackRub.*

> *1997: Larry and Sergey decide that the BackRub search engine needs a new name. After some brainstorming, they go with Google.*

BackRub? As in *backlinks*, links pointing to a Web page. And as in "you rub my back, and I'll rub yours," I think, if the original logo is anything to go by. You can see that in Figure 16-1, and again (*no, really*), this is the actual original BackRub/Google logo.

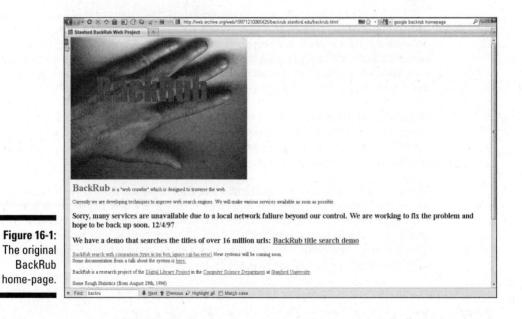

Figure 16-1: The original BackRub home-page.

The founders of Google came up with the original name for a good reason; the original project was all about linking. The research project that led to Google was, according to Wikipedia, "focused on the problem of finding out which Web pages link to a given page, considering the number and nature of such backlinks to be valuable information about that page."

So there you have it. Google was revolutionary *because of the weight given to links*. Google changed the game totally, and now all major search engines look at links to learn about the referenced pages.

Links: The gift that keeps on giving

Links pointing to your Web pages do several things for you:

- ✔ **Links make it easier for search engines to find the page.** As the searchbots travel around the Web, they follow links. They index a page, follow the links on that page to other pages, index those pages, follow the links on those pages, and so on. The more links to a page, the more likely the page is picked up and indexed by search engines, and the more quickly it happens.

- ✔ **Search engines use the number of links pointing to a page as an indication of the page's value.** If lots of pages link to your page, search engines place a greater value on your page than pages with few links pointing to them. If you have lots of links from sites that are themselves linked to by many other sites, search engines conclude that your site must *really* be important. (Google calls this value the page's *PageRank,* but Google isn't the only search engine to use links as an indication of value; Yahoo!, for instance, before the Yahoo!/Bing partnership, was using something called *Web Rank,* and Bing has *Page Score.*)

- ✔ **The more links, the more of your site is likely to be indexed.** The more links, the higher the individual pages' PageRanks (or equivalent), the more important the search engine believes your site is . . . the more of the site is likely to get indexed, and the more frequently.

- ✔ **Links provide information to search engines about the page they're pointing to.** The link text often contains keywords that search engines can use to glean additional information about your page. The theme of the site pointing to your site may also give search engines an indication of your site's theme. For example, if you have links from hundreds of rodent-related Web sites, and those links have rodent-related keywords in them, it's a good bet that your site has something to do with rodents.

- ✔ **Links not only bring searchbots to a page, but may also bring people to the page.** The whole purpose of your search engine campaign is to bring people to your site, right? Sometimes people will actually click the links and arrive at your site; people often forget that in the SEO world!

Links are very important. Sometimes they mean the difference between being indexed by a search engine and not being indexed, or between being ranked well in a search engine and barely being ranked at all. In this chapter, I delve into this subject, a topic broadly known as *link popularity,* to give you a good understanding of what links from other sites pointed to yours is all about. Then, in Chapters 17 and 18, you discover how to get other sites to link to yours.

Backlinks are an integral part of the optimization of your Web site. A *backlink* — this may surprise you — is a link back to your site. Search engines look at backlinks to figure out what your site is about and how important it is. Links aren't something detached from your site; they're an integral part of your site.

Think of your Web site in terms of a regional map. Your site is the major city, and backlinks are the roads bringing traffic into the city. A geographer looking at the map wouldn't regard the city and roads as separate entities; they're all part of the same economic and social system. So don't think of the links pointing to your site as something "out there" — they're a critical part of your site.

Search engines are trying to figure out what site or page is the best match for a search. As you discover later in this chapter, search engines use links as one way to determine this. As with content, though (discussed in Chapter 11), using the number of links to and from a site to measure significance is an imperfect method. A page can conceivably be the best page on a particular subject, yet have few links to it. Just because I publish a page today doesn't mean it's worse than a page that was published five years ago and now has many links to it. However, search engines have difficulty figuring out what the searcher needs, so they have to use what information is available to them. Using links is a way of recruiting Web site owners to help point out useful sites and pages. The strategy is imperfect, but that's the search engine world you're living in.

Understanding Page Value and PageRank

Search engines assign a value to your site based on the links pointing to it. The most popular term for this kind of ranking is *PageRank,* which Google uses. The *PageRank* is a value that Google gives to a page, based on the number and type of links into the page.

PageRank is mentioned frequently in the search engine optimization field for several reasons:

✔ Google is the world's most important search engine and will remain so for the foreseeable future.

✔ You can find out any page's PageRank — or at least a general indication of the relative PageRank, as I explain soon — using some kind of browser plugin. The Google toolbar — available for Internet Explorer (see `http://toolbar.google.com`) — shows you the currently loaded page's PageRank, for instance. If you're using a browser that can't use the Google toolbar — such as the most recent version of Firefox — there are various other SEO toolbars that can show you PageRank.

✔ We also have a basic idea of how PageRank is calculated. Sergey Brin and Lawrence Page, founders of Google, published a paper about the algorithm while at Stanford University. The algorithm used by Google now isn't the same as the one they originally published, but the concepts will be similar.

Having said all that, at the time of writing, the PageRank displayed in the Google toolbar and other PageRank tools is extremely out of date. While Google still uses PageRank internally for ranking, Google hasn't been updating the data source used to display PageRank to the public. The last time it was updated was December of 2013 — they used to update the information several times a year. However, the PageRank indicator is still in the Google toolbar, and comments by various Google employees indicate that, while there is much opposition to publishing the information, some employees also believe it's useful to show the public how "important" a Web site is. (Why not publish it? Many in Google feel that site owners should not be focusing on PageRank; they should focus more on creating good content.)

So is Google giving up on displaying PageRank for good? Perhaps, perhaps not. Maybe it will revive, or maybe PageRank indicator will disappear from the toolbar.

Although this section focuses on PageRank, other search engines use similar rankings, and the things you do with links that boost your PageRank also help boost your site with other search engines. I'll look at PageRank "alternatives" later in this chapter.

Pulling rank

By the way, you can be forgiven for thinking that the term *PageRank* comes from the idea of, well, ranking pages. Google claims, however, that it comes from the name of one of the founders of Google and authors of the original PageRank document, Larry Page. (The other founder is Sergey Brin.) The truth is probably somewhere in between, an amusing pun. Otherwise, why isn't it the PageBrinRank?

PageRank — One part of the equation

The PageRank value is just one part of how Google determines which pages to show you when you search for something. I want to stress that point because so many people get really hung up on PageRank. A low PageRank is often an indicator of problems, and a high PageRank is an indicator that you're doing something right, but PageRank itself is just a small part of how Google ranks your pages.

When you type a search term into Google and click Search, Google starts looking through its database for pages with the words you've typed. Then Google examines each page to decide which pages are most relevant to your search. Google considers many characteristics, such as what the <TITLE> tag says, how the keywords are treated (are they bold, italic, or in bulleted lists?), where the keywords sit on the page, and if keywords in links are pointing to the page (in links both outside the site and within the site). Google also considers PageRank. Clearly, a page with a low PageRank could rank higher than one with a high PageRank in some searches. When that happens, it simply means that the value provided by the high PageRank isn't enough to outweigh the value of all the other characteristics of the page that Google considers.

I like to think of PageRank as a tiebreaker. Imagine a situation in which you have a page that, using all other forms of measurement, ranks as well as a competitor's page. Google has looked at both pages, found the same number of keywords in the same sorts of positions, and thinks both pages are equally good matches for a particular keyword search. However, your competitor's page has a higher PageRank than yours. Which page ranks higher in a Google search for that keyword? Your competitor's.

Many people claim that site owners often focus too much on PageRank (that may be true) and that, in fact, PageRank isn't important. But PageRank (or something similar) definitely *is* a factor. As Google has said:

> *"The heart of our software is PageRank™, a system for ranking web pages developed by our founders Larry Page and Sergey Brin at Stanford University. And while we have dozens of engineers working to improve every aspect of Google on a daily basis, PageRank continues to provide the basis for all of our web search tools."*

So, Google claims that PageRank *is* in use and *is* important. But you need to keep its significance in perspective. It's still only part of the story.

It all comes down to what the searcher is searching for. A page that ranks well for one keyword or phrase may rank poorly for another. Thus, a page with a high PageRank can rank well for some keywords and badly for others.

The PageRank algorithm

I want to quickly show you the original PageRank algorithm; but don't worry; I'm not going to get hung up on it. In fact, you really don't need to be able to read and follow it, as I explain in a moment. Here it is:

PR (A) = (1 − d) + d (PR (t1) / C (t1) + . . . + PR (tn) / C (tn))

Where:

PR = PageRank

A = Web page A

d = A damping factor, usually set to 0.85

t1. . .tn = Pages linking to Web page A

C = The number of outbound links from page tn

I could explain all this to you, honestly I could. But I don't want to. Furthermore, I don't have to because you don't need to be able to read the algorithm. For instance, do you recognize this equation?

$$F = G\ \frac{m_1 \times m_2}{d^2}$$

Don't think you can kid me. I know you don't know what this is. (Well, okay, maybe you do, but I'll bet over 95 percent of my readers don't.) It is the Law of Universal Gravitation, which explains how gravity works. I can't explain this equation to you, but I really don't care because I've been using gravity for some time now without the benefit of understanding the jumble of letters. The other day, for instance, while walking down the street, someone shoved a flyer into my hand. After walking on, glancing at the flyer, and realizing that I didn't want it, I held it over a trash can, opened my hand, and used gravity to remove it from my hand and deposit it into the trash can. Simple.

Getting details

If you want all the nasty, complicated details about PageRank, you can find a number of sources of information online. One description of PageRank that I like is at the WebWorkshop site (`www.webworkshop.net/pagerank.html`). This site also provides a calculator that shows you the effect on PageRank of linking between pages in your site.

You might also see the Wikipedia article on the subject (`http://en.wikipedia.org/wiki/PageRank`), or get the lowdown on PageRank from the horse's mouth: Read *The PageRank Citation Ranking: Bringing Order to the Web* by Sergey Brin and Lawrence Page, the founders of Google. Search on the document's title at Google.

Rather than take you through the PageRank algorithm step by step, here are a few key points that explain more or less how it works:

- ✔ **As soon as a page enters the Google index, it has an intrinsic PageRank.** Admittedly, the PageRank is very small, but it's there.

- ✔ **A page has a PageRank only if it's indexed by Google.** Links to your site from pages that have not yet been indexed are effectively worthless, as far as PageRank goes — actually, as far as *any* linking benefit goes. If it's not in the index, it can't confer any kind of benefit to your site.

- ✔ **When you place a link on a page, pointing to another page, the page with the link is voting for the page it's pointing to.** These votes are how PageRank increases. As a page gets more and more links into it, its PageRank grows.

- ✔ **Linking to another page doesn't reduce the PageRank of the origin page, but it does increase the PageRank of the receiving page.** It's sort of like a company's shareholders meeting, at which people with more shares have more votes. They don't lose their votes when they vote; next time a meeting takes place, they have just as many votes. But the more shares they have, the more votes they can place.

- ✔ **Pages with no links out of them are wasting PageRank; they don't get to vote for other pages.** Because a page's inherent PageRank is not terribly high, this isn't normally a problem. It becomes a problem if you have a large number of links to dangling pages of this kind. Though rare, this could happen if you have a page that many external sites link to that then links directly to an area of your site that won't benefit from PageRank, such as a complex e-commerce catalog system that Google can't index or an external e-commerce system hosted on another site. Unless the page links to other pages inside your Web site, it won't be voting for those pages and thus won't be able to raise their PageRank.

- ✔ **A single link from a dangling page can channel that PageRank back into your site.** Make sure that all your pages have at least one link back into the site. This usually isn't a problem because most sites are built with common navigation bars and often text links at the bottom of the page. Of course, the links have to be readable by the search engines (see Chapter 9).

- ✔ **The page receiving the inbound link gets the greatest gain.** Ideally, you want links into your most important pages — pages you want ranked in search engines. PageRank is then spread through links to other pages in the site, but these secondary pages get less boost.

It's important to understand that Web sites don't have a PageRank; Web pages have a PageRank. It's possible for a site's home page to have a high PageRank, for instance, while its internal pages rank very low.

Here are a couple of important implications from this:

- ✔ **You can vote large amounts of PageRank through your site with a single link.** A page with a PageRank of 5 can pass that to another page as long as it doesn't split the vote by linking to other pages.

  When I use the term *pass,* I use it in the sense of passing on a virus, not passing a baton. Linking from page A to page B passes PageRank from A to B in the same way that person A may pass a cold to person B. Person A doesn't get rid of the cold when he passes it to B; he's still got it. Likewise, page A still has its PageRank when it passes PageRank on to page B.

- ✔ **You can ensure that PageRank is well distributed around your Web site by including lots of links.** Linking every page to every other page is the most efficient way to ensure even PageRank around the site.

Measuring PageRank

How can you discover a page's PageRank? You could install the Google toolbar into your browser; go to `www.toolbar.google.com`. If it's not available for your browser, you might install a different toolbar — you can find various toolbars that provide PageRank in your browser's add-ons library. (As mentioned earlier, at the time of writing this data is very out of date.)

Each time you open a page, the toolbar will load the page's PageRank, as shown in Figure 16-2. In the case of the Google toolbar, if the bar is all gray, the PageRank is 0. If it's all green, the PageRank is 10. You can estimate PageRank simply by looking at the position of the green bar, or you can mouse-over the bar, and a pop-up appears with the PageRank.

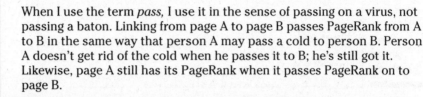

If the PageRank component isn't on your toolbar, click the Adjust Toolbar Options button on the right side of the bar to open the Toolbar Options dialog box; click the Privacy tab, click the Use PageRank check box, and then click the Save button.

If you don't want to install a toolbar, you can still check PageRank. Search for the term *pagerank tool* to find various sites that allow you to enter a URL and get the PageRank.

It's important to understand that as far as PageRank goes, *zero is not zero, and ten is not ten.* Although commonly referred to as *PageRank,* and even labeled as such, the PageRank value provided by PageRank tools and services is not the page's actual PageRank. It's simply a number indicating the approximate position of the page on the PageRank range. Therefore, pages never have a PageRank of 0, even though most pages show 0 on the toolbar, and a page with a rank of, say, 2 might actually have a PageRank of 25 or 100.

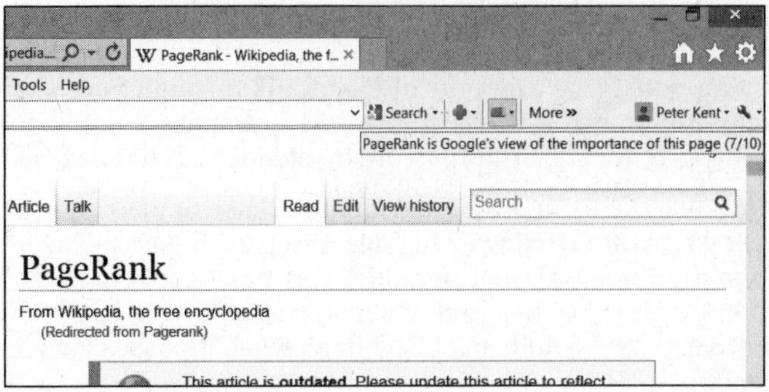

Figure 16-2:
The PageRank bar on the Google toolbar shows PageRank.

The true PageRank scale is probably a logarithmic scale. Thus, the distance between PageRank 5 and 6 is much greater than the difference between 2 and 3. The consensus of opinion among people who like to obsess over such things is that PageRank is a logarithmic scale with a base of around 5 or 6; some people believe it's more likely base 8, or perhaps higher.

Suppose for a moment that the base is actually 5. That means that a page with a PageRank of 0 shown on the toolbar may have an actual PageRank somewhere between a fraction of 1 and just under 5. If the PageRank shown is 1, the page may have a rank between 5 and just under 25; if 2 is shown, the number may be between 25 and just under 125, and so on. A page with a rank of 9 or 10 shown on the toolbar most likely has a true PageRank in the millions. With base 5, for instance, the toolbar PageRank would represent a true PageRank, as shown in Table 16-1.

Table 16-1	**Pure Conjecture — What Toolbar PageRank Would Represent if PageRank Were a Logarithmic Scale Using Base 5**
Toolbar PageRank	*True PageRank*
0	0–5
1	5–25
2	25–125
3	125–625
4	625–3,125
5	3,125–15,625
6	15,625–78,125
7	78,125–390,625
8	390,625–1,953,125
9	1,953,125–9,765,625
10	9,765,625–48,828,125

The maximum possible PageRank, and thus this scale, continually changes as Google recalculates PageRank. As pages are added to the index, the PageRank has to go up. Periodically, Google recalculates PageRank Web-wide, and PageRank drops for many sites, perhaps most.

How can you be sure that the numbers on the toolbar are not the true PageRank? The PageRank algorithm simply couldn't work on a scale of 1 to 10 on a Web that contains billions of Web pages; it just wouldn't make sense. It's not logical to assume that sites like Yahoo! and Google have a PageRank just slightly above small, privately owned sites. I've had pages with ranks of 6 or 7, for instance, whereas the BBC Web site, one of the world's 70 most popular Web sites according to Alexa, has a PageRank of 8 or 9. It's not reasonable to assume that its true PageRank is just 50 percent greater than pages on one of my little sites.

Here are two important points to remember about PageRank values provided by these toolbars and services:

✔ Two pages with the same PageRank may actually have a very different true PageRank. One may have a PageRank that is a quarter or a fifth of the other, perhaps less.

✔ It gets progressively harder to push a page to the next PageRank on the toolbar. Getting a page to 1 or 2 is pretty easy, but to push it to 3 or 4 is much harder (though certainly possible). To push it to the higher levels is very difficult indeed — 8 or above is rare.

Leaking PageRank

It's possible for PageRank to *leak* out of a site, despite the fact that pages don't lose PageRank when they link to other pages. Here's how: Each time you link from one page to another, the origin page is voting for the recipient page. Thus, a link from one page in your site to another page in your site is a vote for that other page. If you link to a page on another site, you're voting for another site's page rather than your site's page.

Suppose that you have a page with a PageRank of 10,000, and it has 40 links on it. Each link is getting a PageRank vote of 250 ($250 \times 40 = 10,000$; this is a simplification, the actual calculation of share is more complicated). Now suppose that half the links on the page are external. In that case, you're taking 5,000 votes and pointing to pages out of your site rather than inside your site. So PageRank leaks in the sense that the PageRank of some pages in your site is lower than it could be.

Generally, you should worry more about getting backlinks to your site from appropriate Web sites than about how much PageRank is leaking through your outgoing links. You can build PageRank quickly by using the techniques in Chapters 17 and 18, and in most cases, worrying about outgoing links won't save you much PageRank. Still, you can do two simple things to help reduce rank leak:

✔ If you have a page with lots of outgoing links, make sure that it also has links to the other pages in your site. You'll be splitting the vote that way between outgoing and internal links, rather than passing all of it on through outgoing links.

✔ Ideally, you want the page with the external links to be one with a low PageRank, reducing the outgoing votes. You can do that by minimizing the number of links from other pages on your site into the link page.

This is a concept called *pagerank sculpting*, which seems overkill and which Google recommends against and tries to mitigate. For instance, at one point you could use the `rel="nofollow"` link attribute (see the section "Identifying nofollow links," later in this chapter for information) so that outgoing links don't pass on PageRank this saves the PageRank for other, internal links. However, Google now accounts for that by reducing the "votes" by the percentage of nofollow links in the page. The links won't pass votes (PageRank) anymore, nor will their "share" be handed over to the other, follow, links to be passed on. To think of this another way, the nofollow links still "use up" the votes, they just don't pass them on, like a ballot that hasn't been submitted.

There are other theories on how Google figures out which pages rank above others. One is the PigeonRank system described by Google in a technical document that you can find in Google's technology area. Google suggests that "low-cost pigeon clusters (PCs) could be used to compute the relative value of Web pages faster than human editors or machine-based algorithms. By collecting flocks of pigeons in dense clusters, Google is able to process search queries at speeds superior to traditional search engines, which typically rely on birds of prey, brooding hens, or slow-moving waterfowl to do their relevance rankings." Find details at www.google.com/technology/pigeonrank.html. No, really.

PageRank Alternatives

As I mention earlier, at the time of writing Google has not updated the PageRank numbers shown in the Google toolbar (and other PageRank tools) in a long, long time. And it may never do so again.

However, there are similar concepts used by various SEO companies. They're similar measures of value based on links pointing to Web pages. For instance, the link analysis tool Majestic SEO (see Chapter 17) has something it calls Citation Flow (a measure based on the number and value of incoming links, something Majestic as described as "correlating to PageRank") and Trust Flow (this is closer to the TrustRank concept; see later in this chapter).

Another major SEO company has a value it calls MozRank ("Pages earn MozRank by the number and quality of other pages that link to them. The higher the quality of the incoming links, the higher the MozRank.").

So PageRank will continue to be used by Google, although it may not be visible for much longer (and is out of date anyway). But alternatives exist.

Page Relevance

The problem with PageRank is that it's independent of keywords. The value is a number derived from links pointing at a page with no relation whatsoever to a specific keyword. A page may have a high PageRank, but that doesn't mean it's the type of page you're looking for when you search for a particular keyword.

Thus, search engines add something else to the mix: *relevance* or *context*. The major search engines are attempting to do this sort of analysis by matching keywords. In effect, search engines are trying to create a context-sensitive PageRank or *topic-sensitive* PageRank. A topic-sensitive PageRank is dependent on a particular topic. Instead of counting any and all links, only links from relevant Web sites are included.

Page relevance is harder to measure, though. The concept of page relevance is that a link from a page related in some way to your page is more valuable than a link from an entirely unrelated page. A link to your rodent-racing site from a Web site that is also related to rodent racing is more valuable than, say, a link from your Aunt Edna's personal Web site.

One way search engines are probably trying to do this is by using directory listings, such the Open Directory Project (see Chapter 14), to provide some context. Because Web sites listed in a directory have been categorized, it gives search engines a starting point to figure out what keywords and sites relate to what categories.

This discussion is getting complicated now, and you really don't need to know the details. However, if you want to read a little geek stuff related to relevance or context, search for a paper, "Topic-Sensitive PageRank," by Taher Haveliwala of Stanford University.

My feeling is that this sort of technology isn't as advanced as many believe or as advanced as search engines want you to believe. Still, people in the search engine business swear that links from related sites are more valuable than links from unrelated sites. To be more precise, links from sites that a search engine thinks are related are more valuable than those from sites that a search engine thinks are unrelated. Because the technology is imprecise, search engines don't always get it right. The fact is that no search engine really knows for sure if one site is related to another; it can only guess. As with everything else, relevance is just one ingredient in the mix.

Consider this example. Say you own a rodent-racing Web site. Among the links pointing to your site is one from a blog owned by an insurance agent. Now, most of the content on that site is related to the insurance business, but it just so happens that the owner is also a big fan of rodent racing. So is that link a relevant link? Of course it is! It's from an insurance site but is placed there for good reason by someone who loves your site. That's the real thing, the kind of link Google wants to see.

So don't let anyone tell you that links from "unrelated" or "nonrelevant" sites have no value. A link from an unrelated site helps search engines find your pages, boosts PageRank, can provide information about what your site is about (if you have good keywords in the links, which I discuss later in the chapter), and may even bring visitors to your site. These links just won't have the extra boost provided by relevance, but that doesn't mean they have no value.

Hubs and Neighborhoods

Having said that relevance may be overrated, I still do recognize that relevance can be useful (it's just not everything). The ideal link is one from a related Web site, not just any old Web site you can convince to link to you. The most powerful *link hubs* — networks of interlinked Web sites — are those that are tightly focused on a particular topic. Search engines respect that, want to uncover such situations and rank the target sites more highly, and are probably getting better every day at doing so.

Search engines are looking for what may be thought of as Web *neighborhoods, communities,* or *hubs* — groups of Web sites related to a particular subject, and the sites that appear to be most central to it. If you're positioned in the middle of a *cloud* — a web of Web sites related to a particular subject — that's a good thing.

Imagine a chart showing the world's rodent-racing Web sites and their connections. In this chart, little boxes represent the Web sites and lines show links between the sites. (Figure 16-3 gives an example of such a chart.) Some of the boxes seem to be sitting by themselves — very few links are going out, and very few are coming in. Other boxes have lots of links going out but few boxes linking back. Now imagine your rodent-racing site. It's a hub with many links going out, and many links coming in. That would look pretty important on a chart. Don't you think search engines would find that interesting? In fact, search engines are trying to figure out this sort of thing all the time. Therefore, if you can build links to turn your site into a hub, that's a great thing! (That doesn't mean that all you need to do is build lots of pages with outgoing links, by the way — far more important are the incoming links.)

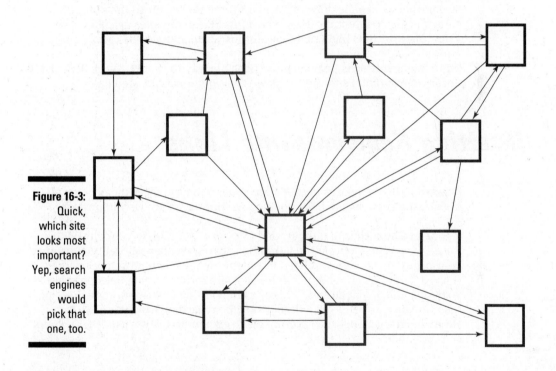

Figure 16-3:
Quick, which site looks most important? Yep, search engines would pick that one, too.

Trust in TrustRank

Yet another ranking concept: TrustRank. The idea, from a document written by Yahoo! search engine researchers, is that a small set of "seed pages" is selected manually; someone manually creates a list of Web sites and pages that are likely to be reputable pages that can be trusted.

Then computers measure how far each site is from the seed site, in the sense of how many links away it is. Sites linked to directly from the original list of trusted sites are assumed trustworthy, and sites they link to are probably reasonably trustworthy, and so on. The farther a site is from the trusted sites, the lower the site's TrustRank.

The basic principle, then? Links from reputable sites are likely to be more valuable than links from sites that are not so clearly reputable. A link from CNN.com, for instance, is likely to count for more than a link from TheKentFamilyNewsService.com. (A link from CNN.com is likely to bring much more traffic from people actually *clicking* the link, too, which, people sometimes forget, is the original purpose of linking.)

Links from `.edu` (education) and `.gov` (government) Web sites are also likely to be more valuable because such sites are less easily manipulated for SEO purposes. Google doesn't present TrustRank values to the public; it's something used internally. However, some SEO companies calculate a trust value; Majestic SEO has Trust Flow, for instance, and Moz has MozTrust.

But remember, this is just one more possible way to weight pages. It certainly doesn't mean that a site can't rank well without lots of trusted links.

Inserting Keywords into Links

As Chapter 6 makes abundantly clear, keywords in your pages are very important. But keywords *outside* your pages can also affect the page results. That is, the keywords in links pointing to your pages are very important.

If you have hundreds of links around the world pointing to your site, with the words *rodent racing* in the links, then search engines will get the idea that your pages are somehow related to rodent racing. It actually makes a lot of sense if you think about it. If hundreds of site owners create links pointing to your site, and, in effect, say, "This site I'm pointing to is about rodent racing," then Google is being given a darn good clue regarding what your site is about. In effect, Google has recruited site owners to tell it what other owners' sites are about.

From the horses' mouths

Read this from the founders of Google, Sergey Brin and Lawrence Page:

✔ ". . . anchors often provide more accurate descriptions of web pages than the pages themselves . . . This idea of propagating anchor text to the page it refers to was implemented in the World Wide Web Worm [a search engine that pre-dates Google] especially because it helps search non-text information, and expands the search coverage with fewer downloaded documents. We use anchor propagation mostly because anchor text can help provide better quality results."

The Anatomy of a Large-Scale Hypertextual Web Search Engine, 1998

Link text, in geek terminology, is known as *anchor text.* The link tag is an <A> tag, and *A* stands for *anchor.* Thus, if you hang around in geek company, you may hear links referred to as *anchors.* For more on anchors, see the "From the horses' mouths" sidebar.

In other words, Google and other search engines use links to get an idea of what the pages are about. Now, wait a second. This is important. If a link pointing to your site can describe to a search engine what your site is about, you'd better do all you can to make sure the link says what you want it to say! Even if you don't own the site that points to the one you're trying to optimize (or are trying to get another site owner or site manager to link to your site), it's in your interest to get the right keywords into the link.

While you browse the Web, take a close look at links on the sites you visit. Now that you know how critical it is to add keywords to links, you'll see that many links provide relatively little value to the sites they're pointing to. Sure, a bad link is better than no link, but a bad link could be better than it is. Here are some of the problems you'll see:

- ✔ **Image links, including buttons or banners linking to sites:** Search engines can't read images, so they're not getting keywords from them. (You should add keywords to the ALT attributes in the image tag, but search engines may not value ALT text as highly as link text.)

- ✔ **Links containing words that are not useful keywords, such as company names:** In most cases, company names don't help you in search engines. Use the keywords your potential visitors and clients are using.

- ✔ **Combinations of descriptions and *click here* links:** For instance: *For more information on rodent racing — rats, mice, gerbils, and any other kind of rodent racing — click here.* Wow, what a waste! All the keywords are there; they just have no link! Remember, *click here* links are a total waste of hyperlink space.

The Googlebomb lives

Just how powerful is putting keywords in links? Well, consider the *Googlebomb.*

The most famous example is the *miserable failure* Googlebomb from back in the years 2004 to 2007. Back then, if you searched at the major search engines for that term, the #1 result in all three was President George Bush's bio page on the White House Web site.

This feat was accomplished by a small group of people using links in blog pages. Despite the fact that this page contained neither *miserable* nor *failure,* and certainly not *miserable failure,* a few dozen links with the words *miserable failure* in the link text were enough to trick the major search engines.

Eventually (after a couple of years), Google bowed to criticism and changed *something* to ensure that the president's page no longer appeared in the search results. Yahoo! and Bing did *not* make this change, at least at that time, so this particular Googlebomb, paradoxically, only worked on Yahoo! and Bing. Today George Bush's page *still* appears near the top of the first page of results on Bing and its partner, Yahoo! (#2 when I checked just now), but it doesn't for Google.

I'm not sure what Google did to remove the George Bush result. It may have manually removed the site from the results, though it says that it "came up with an algorithm that minimizes the impact of many Googlebombs." Nevertheless, Google didn't completely throw out the concept of using keywords in links to tell it what the site is about. In fact, its statement suggests just that. It "minimized" the impact of "many Googlebombs"; it didn't completely stop them.

How can you be sure? Well, I can prove it to you. Search Google for the phrase *click here*; what comes up near the top? The Adobe Reader download page (`http://get.adobe.com/reader`). Why? Because millions of pages around the world have something like this:

> The following PDF document can be read with Adobe Reader. To download it, <u>click here</u>.

Go look at that page; I've been checking for years, and never have I seen the text "click here" inside the page. Yet it's in the top three (#3 right now, #1 in the past) for that phrase. It's the power of links!

Visit the Googlebomb page at Wikipedia (`http://en.wikipedia.org/wiki/Googlebomb`), where you'll find information about all sorts of fun and interesting Googlebombs.

Note, by the way, that Googlebombing in general works in both Google and Bing (although the Adobe site doesn't come up high for *click here* in Bing, perhaps because they have manually demoted it).

Clearly, the way Googlebombs work has changed over time. Perhaps, for instance, in response to complaints about the original *miserable failure* search, Google changed its algorithm to say something like, "If we see x number of links of type y pointing to the site using keywords that don't appear in the site, then ignore the links."

In any case, though, the fact is the basic principle behind Googlebombing remains valid: Putting keywords in links tells search engines what a referenced site is about, and the more links with keywords the better.

I often have clients ask me why a competitor ranks so well, also stating, "Their pages aren't better optimized than mine. We have more pages, and more pages with the right keywords. . . ." When I do a link analysis (see

Chapter 17), I often discover that the poorly optimized, yet highly ranked, site has a huge number of incoming links, with just the right keywords.

Here's the ideal combination for links and the pages they point to: The keywords in the link match the keywords for which the referenced page is optimized. If you have a page optimized for the phrase *Rodent Racing*, point links with the words *Rodent Racing* to that page.

PageRank versus Keywords

So which is more important, PageRank or keywords in the link? Well, they're both important, and the ideal link is a high-PageRank link with good keywords. But I want to make an important point. Many in the SEO business will tell you that low-PageRank links are worthless, but that simply isn't true. Keywords in links are very valuable because they directly tell the search engines what the referenced page is about. So even low-PageRank links, if they have good keywords in them, can be valuable to you; and high-PageRank links without any keywords are also a good thing.

Get a Good Mix

Although you can't always get what you want—high PageRank links with great keywords in them—that's not so bad. You need a good mix of link types. You want your link profile to look natural, not like it's the product of a highly efficient SEO-based link campaign.

You want a variety of keywords in your links, not all of them using the exact same keywords. You want some follow, some nofollow; some text, some images; some from blogs, some from social-network sites, some from news sites, and so on.

Don't worry too much if all your links are not perfect. Having all the same kind of perfect links doesn't look natural and may cause search engines to downgrade some of the links.

Good Links and Bad

Search engines must regard some types of links as more valuable than others. And it seems very likely to me that search engines will, over time, change how they regard links. They have, in fact, over time devalued certain types of links. For instance:

- ✔ Links inside paragraphs of text are likely regarded as more valuable than links in large lists or links set apart from text.

✔ Search engines could compare incoming links with outgoing links, and devalue a site's links if it appears to do a lot of reciprocal linking from link pages.

✔ Links pointing to a page inside a site might be valued more highly than links to the home page.

✔ Outgoing links concentrated on a few pages might be valued less than links spread around a site.

When site owners figured out that links were valuable, they started playing tricks to boost incoming links to their sites. Some tricks were so egregious that search engines decided they were unacceptable. The trick you hear about most often is the *link farm,* an automated system that allows site owners to very quickly create thousands of incoming links by joining with thousands of other site owners to exchange links. Search engines don't like link farms and will exclude link-farm pages if they identify them. Another trick is to create multiple *shadow domains* or *satellite sites* — groups of small, well-optimized Web sites that redirect traffic into a single site — and link them all into one site.

However, as with much in the search engine optimization business, another myth has arisen. You may hear that if a link is found *to* your site from a link farm, you'll be penalized.

Let me set the record straight: Search engines do not penalize sites for incoming links. They can't, or it would *encourage* dirty tricks. Want to push a competitor's site down so that your site can beat it? Then link to it from as many link farms as you can. Obviously, it wouldn't make sense for search engines to encourage this sort of thing, so links from such pages won't hurt your site — though they won't help it, either.

On the other hand, links *to* such sites really can hurt you. Because you do have control over links from your site to others, if a search engine decides that you are linking to a bad neighborhood, it may penalize you.

The bottom line is that you should avoid working with link farms because they can potentially harm you, and they won't help you, anyway.

Do search engines ever penalize? Sure. However, with billions of Web pages in the large indexes, most penalties are automated (although Google also has a team that reviews sites for spam — often, sites that have been reported). To automate penalties, search engines have to create a very loose system that penalizes only the very worst offenses, or they risk penalizing innocent people. The proof is that if you spend time searching through the major search engines, you'll find many pages that clearly break the rules yet are still included in the indexes. (See Chapter 21 for more information on Google penalties.)

Recognizing Links with No Value

Some links have no value:

✔ If a page isn't in the search-engine index, the links from the page have no value. Search engines don't know about them, after all.

✔ If a page is regarded as a *link farm* (described in the preceding section) or some other kind of *bad neighborhood,* as Google calls it, the search engine may decide to exclude the page from the index, or perhaps ignore the links coming from the page.

✔ Some links to your site just *aren't* links to your site; they appear to be, but they're not. I explain in a moment.

✔ nofollow links are a special form of link that usually don't bring any value. I look at them later in this chapter.

Identifying links that aren't links

How can a link not be a link? I've seen this happen many times. Someone gets a link to his site from another site with a high PageRank, perhaps a perfectly related site, and is excited. That's a great vote for his site, isn't it? Then some jerk, perhaps me, has to burst his bubble and point out that, actually, no, it won't have the slightest effect on his site because it turns out that the link is not a link.

When is a link not a link? In cases such as these:

✔ The link has been created in such a way that search engines can't read it or will intentionally ignore it.

✔ The link points somewhere else, perhaps to a program on someone else's Web site, which then forwards the browser to your site.

Here's an example:

```
http://ad.doubleclick.net/clk;6523085;7971444;q?http://www.yoursite.com
```

This link passes through an ad server hosted by an advertising company called DoubleClick. When someone clicks this link, which may be placed on a banner ad, for instance, a message goes to a program on the `ad.doubleclick.net` ad server, which logs the click and then forwards the browser to `www.yourdomain.com`. You may think this is a link to `www.yourdomain.com`, and it may work like one, but as far as the search engine is concerned, it's really a link to `ad.doubleclick.net`. The search engines may follow the link to your site, but they won't assign any kind of PageRank-type value to the link; they know it is an advertising link that you have paid for. (You learn more about "paid" links in Chapter 17.)

This is also a common situation with affiliate programs through services such as Commission Junction; the links to your site go through the affiliate-service servers first, so they don't count as links to your site. "But can't the search engines figure out the redirect?" I hear you ask. Yes, but there's more to this than meets the eye. One reason search engines probably won't provide any value to redirecting links like this — and Google has stated that it generally doesn't — is that such redirecting links are generally created for commercial purposes (advertising and affiliate programs) and thus are not true "endorsements" of the destination Web page.

Here's another example that was more common in the past than today as search engines have become much better at reading JavaScript: Suppose the person creating a link to your site doesn't want the search engine to be able to read the link. This person may be trying to get as many incoming links as possible while avoiding outgoing links, so she does something like this:

```
<SCRIPT LANGUAGE="JavaScript">
<!--
document.write("Visit <A HREF='http://www.yourdomain.com/'>
Joe's Rodent Racing site here</A>.")
//-->
</SCRIPT>
```

The author is using JavaScript to write the link onto the page. You can see the link, other visitors can see it, and the link works when clicked, but search engines may not read the JavaScript, so they may not know there's a link there. What appears to be a perfectly normal link on a Web page could be invisible to search engines; therefore, it may do your site no good as far as PageRank or any other link-popularity algorithm goes.

Here's another form of link that search engines may not read:

```
<A HREF="#" class=results onclick="window.open('searchresult-
temp1.php?CS=cddzdzdrzfzpzpdc&SRCH=134893378&YD=0.88&RK=
3&PID=16&URL=yourdomain.com','merch','Height=' +
screen.availHeight + ',Width=' + screen.availWidth +
',left=0,top=0,scrollbars=yes,status=yes,toolbar=yes,
directories=yes,menubar=yes,location=yes,resizable=yes',
false)";>Everything About Rodent Racing!</A>
```

This is a real <A> link tag. However, it doesn't use the HREF= attribute to point to a Web page. Rather, it uses a JavaScript onClick event handler to make it work. The JavaScript runs a program that, in this case, loads the page into another window. Again, the link works in most browsers, but search engines may not see it, or not give it value if they see it.

Incidentally, it's also possible to do the reverse: make links appear to search engines to be links to your site when actually they're links to another site. For instance, look at the following link:

```
<A HREF="http://www.yourdomain.com/" onClick="return
rewrite(this);" class="">Joe's Rodent Racing</A>
```

This link starts off well, showing `yourdomain.com` as the page being linked to. In fact, if you took the URL from the `HREF=` and pasted it into a browser, it would work properly. However, when someone clicks the link, the JavaScript `onClick` event handler runs, taking the domain and passing it to a JavaScript function called `rewrite`. Because search engines may not read JavaScript, they may not see what really happens when someone clicks the link. (In this example, the click runs through a program that tracks how many people use the link.) Search engines may think it's a link to your site, and I guess it is in a sense, but it has to pass through a program on a different site first.

Identifying nofollow links

There's a simple way to tell search engines to ignore links; use the `rel="nofollow"` attribute, like this:

```
<a href="http://www.domainname.com/page.html" rel="nofollow">Link Text</a>
```

You can also block all links on a page by using the `robots` meta tag, like this:

```
<meta name="robots" content="nofollow">
```

Tell the search engines not to follow the link — *nofollow* — and what exactly do they do? They ignore the link. It's as though the link were nonexistent. They may not bother following the link to the referenced page, and they don't use the information to index the page. (Even if they follow the link, they won't assign value to the referenced page based on that link.) That is, you get no PageRank, Web Rank, or equivalent benefit, and no benefit from the keywords in the link. (That's the theory, anyway; you can read my alternative theory in Chapter 19.)

More and more sites are using `nofollow` attributes to stop people from placing links purely to help their search engine rank. Here's a classic example: Craigslist. The hugely popular Craigslist.com classified-ad site used to be a great place to put links; businesses would drop ads into the system and include links back to their sites to help boost their search position. So, in 2007, Craigslist decided to put a `nofollow` attribute into all links placed on the site in order to discourage this behavior.

Various browser plug-ins can show you nofollow links. For instance, after installing the Firefox NoDoFollow plug-in you can right-click a Web page and select NoDoFollow, and all the links on the Web pages you view will be colored; follow links will be gray, and nofollow links will be pink. (For this reason, nofollow links are occasionally called *pink links*.)

Recalling a Few Basic Rules about Links

I explain why links are valuable and how they can help boost your position in the search engines. But I cover a lot, so here's a summary:

- Links from sites related to yours are often more valuable than links from unrelated sites. (Because the relevancy software is almost certainly imprecise, this isn't always the case.)

- Links from pages with a high PageRank are more valuable than those from pages with a low PageRank.

- Virtually all incoming links to your site have some kind of value, even if the pages have a very low PageRank or are not contextual. It may not be much of a value, but it's there. (Assuming, of course, that the page with the link is indexed, that the link is not a nofollow link, that it's not a redirect, and so on.)

- The higher the number of outgoing links on a page that has a link pointing to your site, the lower the PageRank transferred to your site. This is because the vote is being shared. Thus, in some cases, a link from a low-PageRank page with no other links may actually be more valuable than a link from a high-PageRank page with many links.

- Links are even more valuable when they include keywords because keywords tell search engines what the referenced site is about . . . even if the link is on a low-PageRank page.

- A link strategy that positions your site as an authority, or a *hub,* in a Web community or neighborhood can be a powerful way to get the attention of the search engines.

- And don't forget that, as discussed in Chapter 7, even *internal links* — links from page to page within your site — are valuable because the keywords in the links tell the search engine what the referenced page is about.

Chapter 17

Finding Sites to Link to Yours

· ·

In This Chapter

▶ Getting other sites to link to you

▶ Finding who links to your competition

▶ Looking at reciprocal link campaigns and much, much more

▶ Buying links — the ins and outs

· ·

*I*n Chapter 16, I explain the value of linking — why your site needs to have *backlinks* (links from other sites pointing to it). Now you have the problem of finding those sites.

Chapter 16 gives you some basic criteria. You need links from pages that are already indexed by the search engines. Pages with high PageRanks are more valuable than those with low PageRanks. Links from related sites may be more valuable and so on. However, when searching for links, you probably don't want to be too fussy to start with. A link is a link. Contrary to popular opinion, links bring value — even links from unrelated sites.

It's common in the SEO business to say that only links from "relevant" sites have value, but I don't believe that's true. How do search engines know which sites are relevant and which aren't? They don't. Sure, they can guess to some degree. But they can't be quite sure. Therefore, my philosophy is that every link from a page that's indexed by search engines has some kind of value. Some will have a higher value than others, but don't get too hung up on relevance. And don't worry too much about PageRank. Sure, if you can go after sites with high PageRanks first, do it, but often it makes sense to simply *go get links* — links with keywords in the text — and not worry too much about the rank of the linking page.

Use this chapter to get links, and things will start happening. Your site will get more traffic, the search engines will pick it up, and you should find your pages rising in the search engine ranks.

Controlling Your Links

Before you run off to look for links, think about what you want those links to say. In Chapter 16, I talk about how keywords in links are tremendously important. The position of a page in the search engines depends not only on the text within that page, but also on text on other pages that refer to that page — that is, the text in the links. In fact, even a link from a low PageRank page can bring real value, if it has good keywords in it.

Converting good links to bad

For instance, suppose your rodent-racing company is called Robertson Ellington. (These were the names of your first two racing rats, and they still have a special place in your heart. And you've always felt that the name has a distinguished ring to it.) You could ask people to give you links like this:

> <u>**Robertson Ellington**</u>
> Everything you ever wanted to know about rodent racing — rodent-racing schedules, directions to rodent-racing tracks, rodent-racing clubs, and anything else you can imagine related to rodent racing.

You got a few useful keywords into the description, but the text in the link itself (known as the *anchor text*) — Robertson Ellington — is the problem. The link text contains no keywords that count. Are people searching for *Robertson Ellington*, or are they searching for *rodent racing*?

A better strategy is to change the link to include keywords. Keep the blurb below the link, but change the link to something like this:

> <u>**Rodent Racing — rats, stoats, mice, and all sorts of other rodent racing**</u>

The perfect link text

Here are some strategies for creating link (or *anchor*) text:

- ✔ Start the link with the primary keyword or keyword phrase.
- ✔ Add a few other keywords if you want.
- ✔ Perhaps repeat the primary keyword or keyword phrase once in the link.

You need to control the links as much as possible. You can do this a number of ways, but you won't always be successful:

✔ Some sites provide Link to Us pages in their Web sites. If this makes sense for your site (it's a site that lots of people are going to want to link to; see later in this chapter for the discussion of *link bait*) provide suggested links to your site — include the entire HTML tag so people can grab the information and drop it into their sites.

   Remember that although links on logos and image buttons may be pretty, they don't help you in the search engines as much as text links do. You can add ALT text to the image, but ALT text is probably not as valuable as link text. Some site owners now distribute HTML code that creates not only image links but also small text links right below the images.

✔ When you contact people and ask them for links, provide them with the actual link you'd like to use.

✔ As soon as someone tells you she has placed a link, check it to see whether the link says what you want. Immediately contact that person if it doesn't. She is more likely to change the link at that point than weeks or months later.

✔ Use a link-checking tool occasionally to find out who is linking to you and to see how the link appears. If necessary, contact the other party and ask whether the link can be changed.

Whenever possible, you should define what a link pointing to your site looks like, rather than leave it up to the person who owns the other site. Of course, you can't force someone to create links the way you want, but sometimes if you ask nicely . . . .

Always use the `www.` portion of your URL when creating links to your site: `http://www.yourdomain.com` and not just `http://yourdomain.com`. Search engines regard the two addresses as different, even though in most cases they are actually pointing to the same page. So if you use both URLs, you are, in effect, splitting the vote for your Web site. Search engines will see a lower link popularity. (See Chapter 16 for a discussion of how links are votes.)

Many sites use a 301 Redirect to point `domain.com` to the `www.domain.com` form. For instance, type **google.com** into your browser's Location bar and press Enter. Where do you go? You go to `www.google.com` because Google's server admins have "301'd" `google.com` to `www.google.com`. If you want to do this on your site, search for the term *301 redirect* for instructions. Also, the Google Webmaster console (see Chapter 13) provides a way for you to tell Google to use www.*yourdomain*.com as the primary address for your site; select Site Settings on the Settings menu and you see the following option buttons:

- ✔ Don't set a preferred domain
- ✔ Display urls as www.*yourdomain*.com
- ✔ Display urls as *yourdomain*.com

You want the middle option, of course. The Google Help text says that "If you specify your preferred domain as http://www.example.com and we find a link to your site that is formatted as http://example.com, we follow that link as http://www.example.com instead."

Google does provide information about links to Web sites in another way; the associated Google Webmaster account (see Chapter 13). However, this is only information for the sites over which you have control. You can't get information about competing sites, which is often very useful; you can find out how your competitors are beating you, and perhaps beat them at their own game.

Doing a Link Analysis

One of the first things you may want to do is find out who is already linking to your site. Or perhaps you'd like to know who is linking to your competitors' sites. The following sections look at how you can find this information.

Google

In theory, Google shows you links pointing to a particular URL. I explain this only because many people know about it, and thus someone at some point will probably tell you to use it. It's pretty worthless, for two reasons:

- ✔ It shows links to a particular page, not to the entire site.
- ✔ It shows *some* of the links to the page, not all.

You have two ways to use this Google search syntax. The Google Toolbar has a Backward Links command; open the home page of the site you want to analyze, click the PageRank button on the toolbar (see Chapter 16), and then choose Backward Links from the drop-down list.

The other way is to simply search for `link:domainname.com` in Google or in the search box in the Google Toolbar. For instance, search for `link:dummies.com`, and, at the time of writing, Google returns 148 results.

These Google methods are not worth the energy you expend to type the command or select from the toolbar. I rarely use them because the information is pretty much useless.

Link popularity software

Numerous sophisticated link popularity software tools are available to run on your computer or as a Web service. However, most have a significant problem; for their data, they rely on information that is initially pulled from the major search engines.

Several take a different approach. Moz Open Site Explorer (`www.opensite explorer.org`), ahrefs Site Explorer (`https://ahrefs.com/site-explorer`), and MajesticSEO (`www.majesticseo.com`) have actually created their own indexes of Web pages, so that rather than asking the major search engines for data, they use their own indexes to find links pointing to your, or your competitor's, site. Moz currently has an index of around 187 billion pages, while MajesticSEO and ahrefs have trillions.

Let's look at `http://dummies.com` again. I found 148 links in pointing to dummies.com using the *link:dummies.com* syntax at Google, as noted earlier. How does that number compare with these three other systems?

- ✔ **Google:** 291
- ✔ **Moz Open Site Explorer:** 511
- ✔ **ahrefs Site Explorer:** 379,733
- ✔ **MajesticSEO:** 1,055,293 current; 2,682,427 including old, deleted links

So if you're looking for the most data, Majestic is definitely the way to go; many people use Moz or ahrefs because they like specific features of those systems, or they find them easier to use, while still reporting a large number of links. If you want to try Majestic SEO, go to `www.majesticseo.com` and enter a domain name into the Site Explorer search box at the top of the page. Notice the Use Fresh Index and Use Historic Index option buttons. You'll probably want to use the Fresh Index, which is the default. If you select the Historic Index, you'll find many old links that no longer exist included in your report. (You are allowed to use it a few times per day before being forced to create an account.)

In Figure 17-1, you can see the first results page. Notice the menu bar immediately above the Trust Flow circle; these options help you find the different categories of information (more than most people need!). Here are some of the things you'll find:

- ✔ **Referring Domains:** The number of domains that have Web pages linking to the analyzed domain, with a breakdown of how many are educational (`.edu`) domains and how many are governmental (`.gov`).

- **External Backlinks:** The number of links from other sites pointing to the domain you specified, with a breakdown of how many are images, how many are nofollow links, how many are educational and governmental, and so on.

- **Top Backlinks:** The links that MajesticSEO thinks are the most valuable.

- **Top Referring Domains:** A list of the domains with the most links pointing to the site.

- **Top Pages:** The most-linked-to pages on the site.

- **Map:** Shows where, geographically, links are coming from.

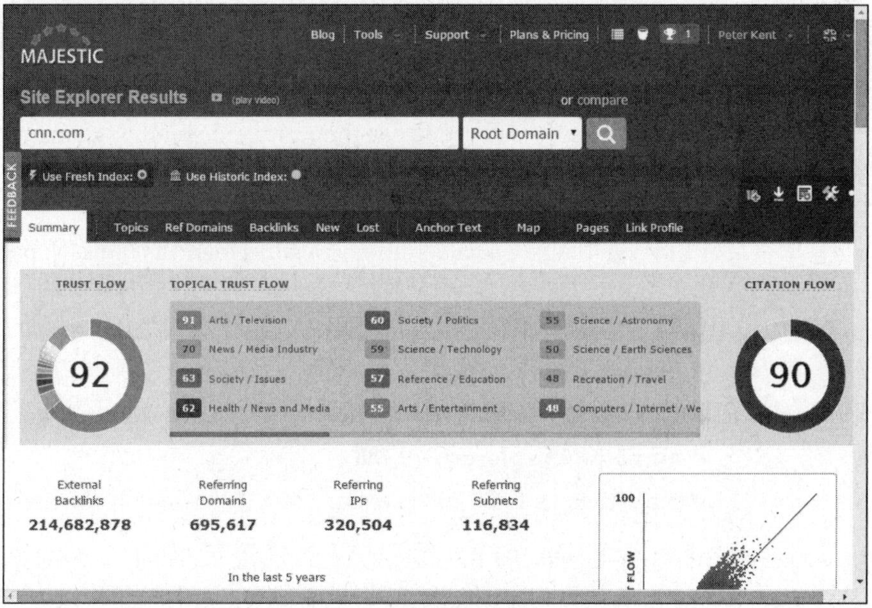

Figure 17-1:
The first results page from MajesticSEO.

And that's just the beginning. Create a full report to find details, and lots of them, including a full list of all the links pointing to the specified site, including where the links is placed, the link text, and the specific page that the link points to.

If you "verify" that you own your Web site (Majestic gives you a file to place in the root of your site), you get free reports about your own site. To check links to other sites, you have to pay. It may be worth signing up for a month to do a good link analysis of competitors.

In fact, one problem with this system, for inexperienced SEO people, is that it has so much data that you don't know where to start. So, what *is* important? Here's what you should care about:

✔ Where do links come from? What sites are linking to yours, or your competitors? You can get ideas for where to ask for links to your site.

✔ What is the anchor text — the text in the links? Links with keywords are powerful. When analyzing competitors, for instance, you can often get an idea of how hard you have to work by seeing how well the links are keyworded; the more links with good keywords, the harder you have to work.

✔ How valuable are the linking pages? What PageRank do they have, for instance? (Majestic doesn't use PageRank but has something similar called Citation Flow; it also has a TrustRank-type metric, Trust Flow.)

Generating Links, Step by Step

Here is a quick summary of various ways to get links; I explain them, and their advantages and disadvantages, in detail in the following sections:

✔ **Register with search directories.** The Open Directory Project and the specialty directories aren't only important in their own right but often also provide links that other search engines read.

✔ **Ask friends and family.** Get everyone you know to add a link.

✔ **Ask employees.** Ask employees to mention you.

✔ **Contact association sites.** Contact any professional or business association of which you're a member and ask for a link.

✔ **Contact manufacturers' Web sites.** Ask the manufacturers of any products you sell to place a link on their sites.

✔ **Contact companies you do business with.** Get on their client lists.

✔ **Ask to be a featured client.** I've seen sites get high PageRank by being linked to from sites that feature them.

✔ **Submit to announcement sites and newsletters.** This includes sites such as URLwire (`www.urlwire.com`).

✔ **Promote something on your site.** If you have something really useful, let people know about it!

✔ **Find sites linking to your competition.** If other sites link to your competition, they may link to you, too.

- ✔ **Ask other sites for links.** During your online travels, you may stumble across sites that really should mention your site, as a benefit to their visitors.

- ✔ **Search for** *keyword add url*. You can find sites with links pages this way.

- ✔ **Contact e-mail newsletters.** Find appropriate e-mail newsletters and send them information about your site.

- ✔ **Mention your site in discussion groups.** Leave messages about your site in appropriate forums, with links to the site.

- ✔ **Promote to blogs.** Blog sites are often well indexed by search engines.

- ✔ **Pursue offline PR.** Getting mentioned in print often translates into being mentioned on the Web.

- ✔ **Give away content.** If you have lots of content, syndicate it.

- ✔ **Apply for online awards.** Sign up for site awards.

- ✔ **Advertise.** Sometimes ads provide useful links.

- ✔ **Use a service or buy links.** Many companies sell links; Google doesn't like this, but at the same time has encouraged it for many years.

- ✔ **Just wait.** Eventually links will appear, but you must prime the pump first.

I'm going to mention a few more things, although these methods are in decline or simply don't work anymore.

- ✔ **Send press releases.** Sending press releases, even if distributed through the free systems, used to work incredibly well.

- ✔ **Make reciprocal link requests.** Asking other site owners to link to you, in exchange for a link to them, was popular for years.

- ✔ **Respond to reciprocal link requests.** Eventually, other people will start asking you to link swap, perhaps.

- ✔ **Use link-building software and services.** Try using a link-exchange program or service to speed up the process.

These link-building strategies are ranked by priority in a very general way. One of the first things you should do is to ask friends and family for links and one of the last is to wait. However, in between these strategies, the priority varies from business to business, or person to person. You may feel that a strategy lower on this list is important to do right away.

The next sections look at each of these link-generation methods. But before I start . . . how quickly should you create these links? Some in the SEO business believe that links shouldn't be created too fast because a sudden huge increase in links to your site looks unnatural. Imagine a situation in which your site gets a link or two a month and then suddenly starts getting several thousand a month — that might suggest something odd going on, eh?

I can't give you a number; I can't say "never create more than x links a month," or "y links a week are far too many." It all depends. It depends on what your site has been doing in the past and how many links it already has. If Wikipedia got a thousand links one day, this might not be at all out of the ordinary. If you got 1,000 links one day, it might be unreasonable. (Wikipedia has literally billions of links pointing to it, so actually 1,000 a day is probably nothing.) Just keep in mind that too fast may look suspicious to the search engines.

Register with search directories

In Chapter 14, I discuss getting links from directories, the Open Directory Project and specialty directories. Links from directories are important not only because people can find you when searching at the various directories but also because search engines often spider these directories.

Google, for instance, still includes hundreds of thousands of Open Directory Project pages, and thousands of different specialty directories. These links are highly relevant because they're categorized within the directories; as you find out in Chapter 16, the search engines like relevant links. Therefore, if you haven't registered with the directories, consider that the first step in your link campaign.

Ask friends and family

Ask everyone you know to give you a link. Many people now have their own Web sites or blogs, Facebook pages, and LinkedIn accounts. Ask everyone you can think of to mention your site. Send all of them a short e-mail detailing what you'd like them to say. You may want to create a little bit of HTML that they can paste straight into their pages. If you do this, you get to control the link text to ensure that it has keywords in it: *The best darn rodent racing site on the Web,* for instance, rather than *Click here to visit my friend's site.*

Ask employees

Employees often provide, by accident, a significant number of links back to their employer's Web site. In particular, employees often mention their employer in discussion groups that get picked up by the search engines. So why not send an e-mail to all your employees, asking them to link to the company's site from their sites, blogs, and various social-networking sites, and to mention you in discussion groups? Again, you might give them a piece of HTML that includes an embedded logo.

Also, ask them to always use a signature with the link when posting to Web-based discussion groups.

Of course, some employers don't want their employees talking about them in discussion groups because they're scared about what the employees will say. If that's your situation, I can't do much to help you, except suggest that you read *Figuring Out Why Your Employees Hate You For Dummies,* by I. M. N. Ogre.

Contact association sites

Association sites are a much-overlooked source of free and useful links. Contact any professional or business association of which you're a member and ask for a link. Are you in the local Better Business Bureau, the Lions Club, or Rotary Club? How about the Rodent Lovers Association of America, or the Association for Professional Rodent Competitions? Many such sites have member directories and may even have special links pages for their members' Web sites.

Contact manufacturers' Web sites

Another overlooked source of links is manufacturers' Web sites. If you sell products, ask manufacturers to place link from their sites to yours. I know one business that sold several million dollars' worth of a particular toy that it got from a single retailer. For several years, the company was the primary seller of the product referenced by the retailer, which at the time didn't sell directly to consumers; the link brought the retailer *most* of its business at the time. The manufacturer is a well-known national company that gets plenty of traffic, and the manufacturer's Web site had a PageRank of 6 on its main page. (See Chapter 16 to see why that's impressive.) The link to the retailer was on the manufacturer's home page, so not only did the link bring plenty of business, but it also got plenty of attention from the search engines.

Contact companies you do business with

Many companies maintain client lists. Check with all the firms you do business with and make sure that you're on their lists.

Ask to be a featured client

While looking at a competitor's Web site for a client, I noticed that the competing site had a surprisingly high PageRank even though it was a small site that appeared to be linked to from only one place, www.inman. com, which is a site that syndicates content to real estate sites. It turned out that the competitor was linked to directly from one of Inman's highest

PageRanked pages. Inman was using the client as an example of one of its customers.

If you're using someone's services — for Web hosting, e-mail services, syndication services, or whatever — you may want to contact the site and ask whether *you* can be the featured client. Hey, someone's going to be, so it may as well be you.

Submit to announcement sites and newsletters

There used to be scores of "announcement" services, Web sites and newsletters that published information about new Web sites. Most have gone.

The only one I'm aware of now is URLwire (`www.urlwire.com`). This service, which has been around since the beginning of the Web, claims to have more than 125,000 readers, of whom 6,500 are journalists and site reviewers who get the e-mail newsletter. It costs $495 (and has for *years*), but the impact can be significant, if you can get accepted. (It doesn't take just anyone; you have to have a good story.) Not only do you get a link from a page with a PageRank of 5, but you probably also get picked up by many other sites and newsletters. (URLWire uses nofollow links for keyworded links, but follow links for the URL link to your site.)

Create a little linkbait

One of the most powerful link-building techniques is to place something very useful on your site and then make sure that everyone knows about it. I've included a little story in the "How links build links" sidebar at the end of this chapter. It shows how links can *accumulate* — how, in the right conditions, one link leads to another, which leads to another, and so on. In this true story, the site had something that many people really liked — a directory of glossaries and technical dictionaries. The site eventually garnered around 200,000, all because the site owner provided something people really wanted and appreciated.

This is something known these days as *linkbait* — something so valuable to others that they link to it. It can be something fun, something useful, something weird, something exciting, something cool, or something important. Just something that provides so much value to other people that they link to it from their blogs and Web sites, from social-media accounts and within discussion forums; something they want to tell others about. Matt Cutts, well-known SEO blogger and Google employee (see Chapter 23), defines link bait as anything "interesting enough to catch people's attention."

Find sites linking to your competition

If a site links to your competition, it may be willing to link to you, too. Find out who links to competing sites and then ask them if they can link to yours. In some cases, the links are link-exchange links (which I look at in the later section, "Make reciprocal link requests"), but in many cases, they're just sites that provide useful information to their readers. If your site is useful in some way, you've got a good chance of being listed.

On the other hand, when you do a link analysis on your competitors, you'll often find that many of the links are *purchased* links, which I talk about later in this chapter, in the "Use a service or buy links" section.

Asking for the link

When you find sites linking to your competitors, you discover that some of them may be appropriate for a link to yours; directories of products or sites, for instance, may want to include you. So how do you ask for the link? Nicely. Send an informal, chatty message. Don't make it sound like some kind of form letter that half a billion other people have received. This should be a personal contact between a real person (you) and another real person (the other site's owner or manager). Give this person a reason to link to your site. Explain what your site does and why it would be of use to the other site's visitors. Yes, this can be time consuming. Nobody I've ever met said that link building is easy.

Ask other sites for links

During your travels online, you'll run across sites that provide lists of links for visitors — maybe your site should be listed, too. For instance, while working for a client that had a site related to a particular disease, I found sites that had short lists of links to sites about that disease. Obviously, my client should also have been in those lists.

Approach these sites the same way you approach the sites linking to your competitors: Send an informal note asking for a link.

Don't forget the blogs, by the way. Blogs exist on virtually any subject, and most bloggers provide links to sites they like, often in the "blog roll" or "favorite sites" box on one side of every page on the blog.

Search for keyword "add url"

Go to Google and search for something like this:

```
"rodent racing" + "add url"
```

Google searches for all the pages with the term *rodent racing* and the term *add url*. You find sites that are related to your subject and have pages on which you can add links, as shown in Figure 17-2. (For some inexplicable reason, you don't find much with *"rodent racing" +"add url"* but you find plenty with, for instance, *"boating" +"add url"* or *"psychology" +"add url"*.)

You can also try these searches:

```
"rodent racing" + "add a url"
"rodent racing" + "add link"
"rodent racing" + "add a link"
"rodent racing" + "add site"
"rodent racing" + "add a site"
"rodent racing" + "suggest url"
"rodent racing" + "suggest a url"
"rodent racing" + "suggest link"
"rodent racing" + "suggest a link"
"rodent racing" + "suggest site"
"rodent racing" + "suggest a site"
```

However, these aren't always high-quality links. Generally, the search engines don't really like this sort of linking, and the word on the street is that links from such pages probably don't have the same value that you get from links that are personally placed. On the other hand, they may be easy to get; it's a tradeoff. Often the pages that appear are directory pages; some may be valuable, some not.

Figure 17-2:
Searching for a keyword or keyword phrase along with + *"add url"* uncovers sites that are just waiting for you to add a link to your site.

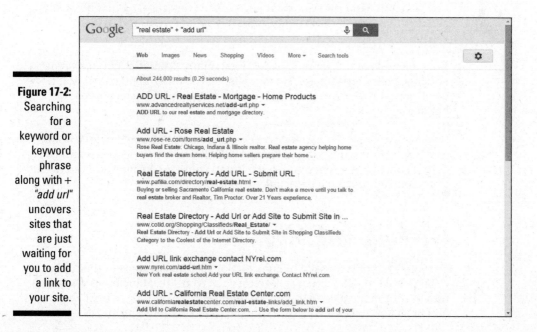

Mention your site in discussion groups

Search engines index many Web-based discussion groups. Whenever you leave a message in the discussion group, make sure that you use a message signature that has a link to your site and also include the link in the message itself.

Sometimes URLs in messages and signatures are read as links, and sometimes they aren't. If you type **http://www.yourdomain.com** in a message, the software processing the message can handle the URL in one of two ways:

- ✔ It can enter the URL into the page as simple text.
- ✔ It can convert the URL to a true HTML link (`<A HREF=" http://www.yourdomain.com"> http://www.yourdomain.com/ </A>`).

If the URL is *not* converted to a true link, it won't be regarded as a link by the search engines.

Another strategy is often employed with discussion groups. Seek out questions that you can answer, answer them, and put keyworded links in your message. For instance, say you have a rodent-racing site; you dig around in the rodent-racing forums, answering questions when possible. Someone asks about where to find scores from recent races, and you respond by saying something like, "Well, I may be biased, but I think my site is the best place to find rodent-racing scores!" (putting a link on rodent-racing scores, of course. Have I mentioned how important keywords in links are?). Don't be pushy and don't just post ads. Provide value in your answers, and (usually) nobody will mind.

Now, a couple of things to consider. First, many discussion groups create nofollow links (see Chapter 16) in posts; on the other hand, many don't. So you'll get search engine value from many of the links, perhaps even most, but not all.

However, you may get *indirect* search engine value from the nofollow links, too. Many of these discussion groups will turn up when people search, so even if someone searches and doesn't find your site, he may find the discussion group and then click the link to your site.

Working with blogs

The Internet holds literally billions of blog pages, and some of them have to be related to the subject served by your Web site. Many blogs allow visitors to respond, and in fact you may find services offering to post responses into blogs for you as a way to create links back to your site.

Don't bother. Apart from the fact that most of these services pollute the blogs with meaningless, worthless messages, most blog software uses nofollow links, so you won't get any value from them.

The best way to work with blogs is to find something the bloggers may be interested in, some kind of PR-story hook, and get them to write about your site.

Pursue offline PR

Getting mentioned in print often translates into being mentioned on the Web. If you can get publications to write about and review your site, not only do many people see the link in print — and perhaps visit your site — but often your link ends up online in a Web version of the article.

Give away content

Many companies have vast quantities of content on their Web sites. It's just sitting there, available to anyone who visits. So why not take the content *to* the visitors before they reach your site? Placing the content on other Web sites is a powerful way not only to build links back to your site but also to get your name out there — to "brand" yourself or your company. I look at this topic in more detail in Chapter 18.

Apply for online awards

This used to be a very popular technique, and there were *many* award sites. It's much less common these days, but I still do see people touting awards they've received now and then; if you get a reward, there's a good chance that the site giving the reward has linked to you.

Advertise

You may want to consider advertising in order to get links to your site. However, you need to consider a couple of issues first:

- ✔ Advertising is often grossly overpriced. It may be much too expensive to justify just for a link.

- ✔ Advertising links often don't count as links to your site. Rather, they're links to the advertising company, which runs a program that forwards the visitor's browser to your site. Search engines won't see the link as a link to your site, or will give the link no value if they recognize it as an advertising link. (See Chapter 16 for more information.)

In some cases, buying ads on a site to get a link does make sense. For instance, if many of your clients visit a particular Web site and you can get a low-cost ad on that site, buying an ad to both brand your company and to get a link that the search engines can read may be worthwhile. And remember that it's a very relevant link because it comes from a site that's important to your business.

Use a service or buy links

I can't stress enough that link campaigns can be very laborious, tedious, and time consuming. That's why many people decide they are better off paying someone to perform the work. Some of these services simply run a link-acquisition campaign for you. Others already have an inventory of ad space on thousands of sites and charge you to place a link on a set number.

One company I've seen is selling almost 800 links for $30 per month. Another company I've seen claims that it can put links on 250 sites for $99. Some companies sell links from pages of a particular PageRank, too. One company, for instance, claims to be able to sell you a link on a PageRank 8 site for $799. (A PageRank 4 page is just $29.)

The vote from a page is shared among all the pages it links to, so the more ads that are sold, the less the value of each ad. You should know exactly what page the link will be placed on, and you should be able to view the page. Consider buying links as a form of advertising that should be evaluated as such. How much of an impact will the ad have on bringing more visitors to your site?

Many, many companies are doing this sort of work. You can find them by searching online (search for *buy links*, *text links*, *purchase links*, *link popularity*, and *link building* at a major search engine) or in the freelancer sites, such as Guru.com, eLance.com, and oDesk.com.

Make sure that you understand what you're getting into. As you've seen, you can use many methods to get links to a site, but they don't all provide the same value. Are you working with a company that can find good links from popular sites that are relevant to yours or a company that uses an automated link-exchange tool to gather links from anywhere it can? There's a real difference! Also, are the links on pages that are actually indexed? In recent years, Google has targeted link "networks" to knock them out of business; such companies are effectively banned from Google, and thus links they places are never seen by that search engine.

Caution! Google doesn't like purchased links!

It's important to understand that Google doesn't like purchased links. In fact, none of the major search engines would be pleased to know that you were buying links pointing to your site. Google even encourages people to report paid links (see www.google.com/webmasters/tools/paidlinks).

On the other hand, the major search engines have actually (albeit indirectly) *encouraged* link buying for years. How? *Many high-ranking sites succeeded thanks to the purchase of links*!

In the past, it was very common, when analyzing clients' competitors, for me to find that the competitors were ranking well thanks to a few hundred, or maybe thousand, purchased links.

That's why people bought links in the past: Because it worked! Furthermore, it's hard for search engines to deal with this problem for a couple of reasons. First, how do search engines know the link is purchased? Yes, there are highly automated systems that place purchased links, and the search engines may be able to find a *signature* — some kind of characteristic that identifies the link as purchased; over the past few years, Google in particular has become really good at identifying sites selling links. However, how will a search engine know whether you ask Fred over at ReallyFastRodents.com, "Fred, if I give you $20 a month, will you link to my site?"

Additionally, if the search engines penalize site owners for purchasing links — well, how much is it worth to you to push your competitor out of the search engines? Sure, *you* may be too ethical to play this game, but plenty of people aren't. So, say you're tired of seeing ReallyRapidRodents.com ranking above your rodent-racing site month after month. Perhaps you could buy a bunch of links pointing to his site, report him to Google, and see Google drop him from the search engine. Therefore, search engines have to be very careful about penalizing sites for buying links. The more likely scenario is that when search engines identify the links as purchased, they downgrade or ignore them, not penalize the referenced site.

Just wait

I'm not really recommending that you sit and wait as a way to build links, but if you're doing lots of other things asking everyone you know for links, getting mentioned in papers and magazines, contacting e-mail newsletters to do product giveaways, and so on — you'll gather links anyway. You've got to prime the pump first; then, things seem to just take off.

Fuggetaboutit

Don't bother getting links in guest books, Free for All pages, and link farms, for the following reasons:

- Many Web sites contain guest book pages, and one early link-building technique was to add a link to your Web site in every guest book you could find. The search engines know all about this technique, so although many guest books are indexed, links from them probably have very little value in most search engines.

- *Free for All (FFA)* pages are automated directories that you can add a link to. They bring virtually no traffic to your site, are a great way to generate a lot of spam (when you register, you have to provide an e-mail address), and don't help you in the search engines.

- *Link farms* are highly automated link-exchange systems designed to generate thousands of links very quickly. Don't get involved with link farms. Not only can they not help you, but also, if you link to one or host one on your site, you may be penalized in the search engines.

Search engines don't like these kinds of things, so save your time, energy, and money. There are a few more things that worked incredibly well in the past, but not so much today.

Send press releases

Press releases were once a very popular way to create links, and they worked incredibly well. They've fallen out of favor, though, because Matt Cutts of Google (see Chapter 23) has stated that you shouldn't expect to get ranking help in the search engines from releases. There's also a persistent (but apparently unfounded) rumor that doing press releases can get your site penalized. I've seen this mentioned in various blogs, but the authors either don't say why they believe this, or link to other pages that also don't provide evidence that it's true.

I can't think of a good reason why the search engines would penalize anyone for doing press releases, but I can think of good reasons why they would devalue any links that appear in the releases. Thus, it's possible that if Google, for instance, finds a follow link in press release on a press-release site, it's not going to give that link any value; if Google can recognize a press release on a non-release site, the links in the release also won't have any value.

Make reciprocal link requests

A *reciprocal link* is one that you obtain in exchange for another. (It's often also referred to as a *link exchange*.) You ask site owners and managers to link to your site, and you in turn promise to link to theirs.

In theory, reciprocal linking helps you in several ways:

- ✔ The search engines see nice, keyworded links coming into your site from appropriate, relevant sites.
- ✔ You link to appropriate, relevant sites, too. (In Chapter 16, I discuss the concept of hubs or value networks.)
- ✔ You may get some traffic through the links themselves (though I doubt you'll get much).

Reciprocal linking is different from asking to be added to a list, although plenty of overlap exists. With the latter, you don't need to offer a link in exchange because the link list is a service to the other site's visitors. However, sometimes site owners respond with, "Sure, but will you link to us, too?" In this case, you've just found yourself in a reciprocal linking position.

Before I go further, though, I need to address a couple issues. First, you may hear that reciprocal linking can get your site penalized — is that true?

If reciprocal linking caused Google to penalize sites, half the Web would disappear. If it's true, why does Google index so many reciprocally linked pages? Why do sites that use reciprocal linking often rank so high? In addition, why would search engines penalize people for using a technique that they have in effect encouraged over the years — a technique so common that, for good or bad, it's part of the landscape of the Web?

Which brings me to the next major question: Does reciprocal linking actually work? My answer is, it certainly used to work, and work well . . . but these days, it has very little value, if any. Reciprocal linking was truly powerful a few years ago; I've seen sites rank first on Google in very competitive markets, based almost entirely on reciprocal linking (and, by the way, at a time when many in the SEO business were saying that reciprocal linking didn't work!).

I wouldn't bother with reciprocal linking today. The only reason I'm mentioning it is that you may still run into reciprocal linking requests.

Also, one of the bad things about traditional reciprocal linking is the *link page,* pages stacked with link after link. Some reciprocal linkers use a more reasoned approach; although they still do link exchanges, they spread the links around the site rather than just dump them onto link pages.

You've undoubtedly seen *links pages* all over the place — pages with titles such as "Useful Links," "Useful Resources," "Visit Our Friends," and so on. These pages never generated much traffic to the referenced Web sites, even in the height of the reciprocal-linking days.

Links pages have the following problems:

- **Search engines downgrade links from such pages.** A link from an ordinary page is likely to be more valuable than a link from a links page.

- **Links pages often have dozens or even hundreds of links on them.** Remember that the more links on a page, the lower the vote for each outgoing link.

If you want to do a little reciprocal linking — perhaps with friends who own sites — the ideal situation would be to

- Scatter links to other sites around your site in locations that make sense.

- Encourage site owners linking back to you to do the same. Start educating the other sites you work with! (In fact, tell them to run out and buy this book; better still, tell them to buy ten copies of this book for colleagues, friends, and family.)

- Avoid having large numbers of links on one page.

Three-way and four-way linking

You may also run into a more complicated form of reciprocal linking. The idea is that instead of linking from site A to site B and back from site B to site A, you create a three- or four-way link, as shown in Figure 17-3. (You may actually see this described as a *one-way link exchange,* but it's the same concept; the site you link to doesn't link back.)

Figure 17-3:
Traditional reciprocal linking (top left). Three- and four-way linking is probably more beneficial.

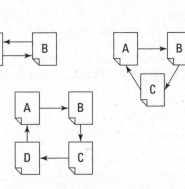

It's easy for the search engines to recognize reciprocal linking. If a search engine sees a link from one site to another and then sees a link coming back, there's a good chance it's a reciprocal link. (I'm sure it's more complicated than this, but the basic principle remains. For instance, does the site have lots of outgoing links, to sites that link back, on the same page?) So it's pretty easy for search engines to recognize reciprocal linking, and because they're aware that such linking is used as an artificial way to boost ranking, they can lower the value of these links.

Say, however, you have a large collection of sites that want to trade links. Rather than have every site link to every other, you might try a more complicated structure where site A links to B, B links to C, and C links back to A, as shown in Figure 17-3. Instead of getting two incoming links, each site only gets one, but it's probably of more value because it's not so obviously a reciprocal link. Or maybe you link site A to B, B to C, C to D, and D to A. In this case, each site gets one link instead of three, but again, the links are likely to be more valuable than simple A-to-B-to-A reciprocal links. Some companies that perform SEO work for large numbers of clients use this technique; for example, some companies with a large number of hosting and Web development clients link between client sites, but not reciprocally. There are also some services that provide three-way linking, but not many, thanks partly to the software complexities involved in managing a three-way process.

Be Careful Whom You Link To!

In general, links to your site can't hurt you. The link may have no value, but it's unlikely to lead to some kind of penalty. It's with *outgoing* links — links from your site to other sites — that people sometimes get themselves into trouble. There are essentially two ways people cause problems:

- ✔ In attempts to get incoming links, they sign up with some kind of Free for All program or link farm. To be part of one of these programs, they have to link to other sites in the program, thus showing the search engines that they are in fact taking part in such link games. As Google puts it, you shouldn't link to "bad neighborhoods."

- ✔ They sign up with a program to sell links to other Web sites on their Web pages. The search engines are getting much better at recognizing this kind of thing, and may penalize the owner of the site selling the links.

How links build links

I want to share a story that provides a wonderful illustration of how a link campaign can work. It shows how you can build links, PageRank, and traffic, all at the same time, the old-fashioned way, using link bait. I found this story in one of WebmasterWorld's discussion groups a few years ago. As the author of the post put it, you should remember how the "Internet started and what it was supposed to be all about: sharing information." The search engines want you to remember this, too.

The story is about an Aussie called Woz. Once upon a time, Woz had a site called Glossarist (it's gone now — this was a long time ago), a directory of glossaries and topical dictionaries. This was a hobby for Woz, and he had done little to promote the site. However, one sunny day — July 26, 2003 — he noticed a 4,000 percent increase in traffic. (For the math challenged among you, traffic on that day was 40 times greater than the day before!) The site had been mentioned in the ResearchBuzz e-mail newsletter and Web site (`www.researchbuzz.com`, which still is around), by the fairy godmother, Tara Calishain. Not surprisingly, ResearchBuzz is a resource for people interested in research. It's the sort of site that would be interested in a directory of glossaries and topical dictionaries.

The very next day, a wonderfully bright and sunny day, Glossarist was picked up by The Scout Report (`http://scout.wisc.edu/Reports/ScoutReport/2001/scout-010727.html`), which, perhaps a little more surprisingly, is a "weekly publication offering a selection of new and newly discovered Internet resources of interest to researchers and educators."

Then on August 9, a *really* sunny day, the site was mentioned in USAToday.com's Hot Sites

(`www.usatoday.com/tech/2001-08-09-hotsites.htm`). I've had one of my sites mentioned in *USA Today,* and believe me, your traffic really spikes when that happens!

By the middle of August, Woz wuz able to identify links from over 200 sites — "libraries and student-resource pages from schools and universities, translation sites, business reference sites, writers sites, information architecture sites, and so on." He also got a lot of traffic from newsletters that had been forwarded from subscribers to friends and colleagues. (Both *ResearchBuzz* and *The Scout Report* are very popular e-mail newsletters.) Not only did site owners find out about him through these e-mails, but many visitors also came to his site through the e-mail links.

All this publicity was great, providing his site with a lot of traffic through those links and making it more likely that his site would be found and indexed by search engines. It also boosted his site's PageRank. By mid-August, the Glossarist PageRank had reached 3; by the end of August, it was 8, which is an excellent PageRank for a hobby site created by a single person without a marketing budget!

By the end of August, Woz had around 300 links. And, as Woz claims, he didn't request a single one of these links. Today? Well, today, many years later, I checked using MajesticSEO and found that throughout the site's history it had around 200,000 links, including more than 3,000 links from `.edu` and `.gov` Web sites.

Don't underestimate the power of this kind of grass-roots promotion. It can be tremendously powerful. One link can set off a chain reaction, in the way that a single link in ResearchBuzz did.

Chapter 18

Even More Great Places to Get Links

*L*inking is tough. It's hard to get the links you need. In the previous chapter, I list a whole bunch of different ways to get links, some of which may work for you and some of which may not. But there's a simple maxim in linking: "You can't have too many links."

Actually, you may reach a point at which you're ranking really well for all the keywords you need to rank for, and you just seem to stick there. I've seen sites that, with very little additional link work, sit at the top of the search results for literally years. But those of you who are not yet in that happy situation still have more link work to do. So, dive right in to this chapter and find out more great places to get links to your site.

Got Content? Syndicate It!

I discuss one aspect of syndication in Chapter 11 — using syndicated content to bulk up your Web site. Now I look at the flip side — syndicating your content to other Web sites and e-mail newsletters. The basic concept? You write something (something interesting or useful or entertaining, I hope) and then provide the information to other Web site owners so that they can post it on their site. In return, you get links from the article back to your site.

These days, this form of content syndication typically is known as *content marketing*; as Wikipedia describes it, "Content marketing is any marketing that involves the creation and sharing of media and publishing content in order to acquire and retain customers." In other words, the basic principle is to create content — articles, videos, "infographics," and so on — and widely distribute them in order to "cast a net" that can catch customers.

So content marketing is not just about SEO; ideally, potential customers will click on the distributed content. It's a tool for engaging the attention of your prospective customers and getting them to take some kind of useful action, such as downloading further information from you, signing up for a subscription of some kind, or clicking a link to go to your Web site.

Of course, the SEO aspects of content marketing are what's important. The SEO aspect is that the content you distribute would have links pointing to your Web site, and the links would help your site rank. This has been a popular link-building strategy for years; creating content (in particular articles), distributing the content widely, and then getting the value of the links pointing from the content to your Web site. Does it still work? It can, though it's not as easy as it used to be.

Some site owners use this form of syndication as the *only* type of promotion they do — and it can sometimes work well. They write articles and distribute them as widely as possible. But many sites already have a lot of content. Why not give it away and use it as a technique to grab more search engine positions, generate links to your site, and brand your site and company?

The Duplicate Content "Problem"

One oft-cited reason for not doing just that? The duplicate-content issue. There's a lot of talk in the SEO world about duplicate content, and much is quite simply wrong. There seems to be a general feeling that duplicate content is "bad," and that having duplicate content on your site will get your site "penalized."

There are two types of duplicate content:

- ✔ Content duplicated within your own site; multiple copies of the same page, for example.

  This a problem, though it's unlikely to get your site penalized. What's more likely to happen is that a search engine may ignore most of the pages and just pick one as the "primary" copy.

- ✔ Content duplicated across multiple sites; the same article syndicated across the Web, for example.

  The idea that content duplicated across multiple Web sites can get a site penalized, thrown out of the Google index even, clearly is nonsense. There are many good reasons for content appearing on multiple sites, as Google is well aware. In the words of one Google article on duplicate

> content, "This article describes how you can use canonical URLs to improve link and ranking signals for content available through multiple URL structures or via syndication. In the world of content management and online shopping systems, it's common for the same content to be accessed through multiple URLs. With content syndication, it's also easy for content to be distributed to different URLs and domains entirely."

Google isn't saying you shouldn't syndicate content, it's just saying that they'd like you to use "canonical URLs" to manage duplicate content. They quite clearly accept content syndication as acceptable; they would just like for you to help them along a little.

The "canonical URL" tells the search engines the "preferred URL" for the content. For example, if you add this to a page within the <head> section

> *<link rel="canonical" href="https://www.yourdomain.com/rodent-racing/ rats -to-watch-in-2015.html" />*

the search engines will assume that the "preferred URL" for this content is the page specified in that tag, regardless of where it found this particular page.

Do you *have* to use a canonical URL? Will you be "punished" if you don't? Know that, as Google says, "While we encourage you to use any of these methods, none of them are required. If you don't indicate a canonical URL, we'll identify what we think is the best version or URL." In fact, even if you use the canonical URL, Google states that it might not use the URL.

So, my first point is that you shouldn't fear duplicate content. It's not the huge danger often claimed (although within a site it can be a real problem; I'm certainly not suggesting it's okay to have a thousand pages with the same content except for switching out a state or city name here and there). The Web is full of duplicated content: press releases, news feeds, and yes, syndicated content. Plenty of Web sites do just fine.

In fact, here's a great example: www.ap.org (AP, the Associated Press). They distribute, among many other forms of content, "thousands of stories in text each day." These articles end up on thousands of Web sites. I searched for a particular quote in one AP story, and found the article in 1,300 Web sites, including sites owned by *The New York Times,* ABC News, Yahoo! News, *The Washington Post,* and the *Daily Mail.*

Were those pages using the canonical URL? Yes, but not to point back to AP.org, but to point to the primary location for the article *in their own Web sites!*

How badly has syndicating content hurt the Associated Press? Well, it certainly doesn't seem to be hurting with Google. Google still indexes AP.org (more than 13 million pages when I looked); it has a PageRank of 9 (admittedly an out-of-date measurement — see Chapter 16), and Google News accepts AP articles distributed by hundreds of different news sources.

So content marketing — syndicated content, as it used to be widely known — can be used without harming you.

However, my second point is that even if you are worried about syndicated content, you don't have to have the *same* article you have on your own site distributed widely. The article can be modified in various ways to make it different. It's much easier to modify an existing article than write a new one. You can take an existing article, add a few things, remove a few things, change titles and subheadings, modify a few paragraphs here and there . . . and you have a new article.

By the way, another huge advantage to using syndication is that the links you get back to your site are from relevant sites. Remember, the search engines like *relevant*. If you write articles about rodent racing and get them posted on other sites, what are those other sites likely to be about? Quite likely, rodent racing.

Four syndication technologies

Before I explain how to distribute these articles, you need to know a little geek stuff related to the technology used to syndicate content. You can syndicate content in basically four ways. Two of these methods are good, but two of the methods may not help you with search engines. Use the wrong methods, and it doesn't matter how widely you distribute your content; there's a good chance it won't bring any search-engine benefit. (It could still bring traffic through the links in the articles, though.)

The following list details the four main syndication technologies:

✔ **Browser-side inclusion:** Many syndicators employ browser-side content inclusion through the use of JavaScripts; a *JavaScript* in a Web page pulls the article off the syndicating site. The problem is that the Web browser runs the JavaScripts when the page loads. Searchbots, however, don't always run JavaScripts. It's true that in recent years Googlebot has begun reading JavaScripts, and is now very good at doing so. But it's unclear how well Bing reads JavaScript, and (as explained in Chapter 9) Bing even states that you shouldn't rely on them reading it; as for other, less-important search engines, you should assume the same. In which case, although site visitors will see the links (and some may click), you won't get the benefit of the link popularity in the search engines that are not reading JavaScript.

✔ **Hosted content:** Some content syndicators, generally those *selling* content, host the content on their own servers, and the sites using the content link to it. The content *appears*, to the visitor to one of the sites using the content, to be sitting on that site, but, in fact, it's on the content-company's domain. The problem with this method is that if you host content for, say, 50 sites, you don't get the benefit of 50 links in the search engines. Rather, the search engine sees that you have the same article 50 times and ignores 49 of them.

- **Manual inclusion:** This method works well for search engines; they see the content and the links to your site. The people you give the content to essentially copy and paste the content into their sites.

- **Server-side inclusion:** You can do server-side inclusions a number of ways, such as by using INCLUDE commands, running PHP or ASP scripts (server-side scripts), or using RSS feeds. The advantage is that the search engines *will* see your content and the links back to your site. The disadvantage is that the methods are more complicated to use than either manual or browser-side inclusion.

To ensure that search engines see links to your Web site, I recommend that you don't use the first or second methods. That leaves the last two, of which the third, manual inclusion, is easiest and by far the most common.

It's possible to make a JavaScript-style syndication give you at least one link that is readable by all search engines. Typically, syndicators ask users to drop a piece of JavaScript into their pages. Of course, you can ask them to drop a piece of HTML that includes a JavaScript inside, along with a link outside the JavaScript. For instance, rather than use

```
<SCRIPT LANGUAGE="JavaScript" src="http://www.ronaldsrodents.com/content/
        article.js"></SCRIPT>
```

you can use

```
<SCRIPT LANGUAGE="JavaScript" src="http://www.ronaldsrodents.com/content/article.
        js"></SCRIPT><P><STRONG>Article provided by <A HREF="http://
        ronaldsrodents.com>Ronald's Racing Rodents</A>. Visit us for more
        great articles on rodent racing.</P>
```

Getting the most out of syndication

If you intend to syndicate your work, consider the following points when creating your articles:

- Every article should contain your site name near the top of the article. When possible, you should also put a site logo near the top and include a link on the logo back to your site.

- Try to work a link to your site into the body of the article. You can do it a couple times, maybe, but don't overdo it. Perhaps link to another article on your site for more information. Make sure that the link text has useful keywords. (Note, however, that most syndication services don't allow links in the body; I look at syndication services in a moment.)

✔ At the bottom of the article, include an attribution or bio box, including a keyworded link back to your site and a logo with a link on it.

If you have a lot of traffic to your site, and plenty of content that you can share and think that people may want to use, set up a library on your Web site where people can access the articles. In the library, you should post certain conditions:

✔ Consider putting limits on the number of articles that can be used without contacting you first. For example, site owners can use up to five articles, and if they want more, they must get permission.

✔ State clearly that you retain copyright of the article and make clear the following conditions:

- *The user cannot change the content.*

- *All logos, attributions, copyright notices, and links must remain.*

- *Links must remain as standard HTML <A> tags and cannot be converted to another form of link.*

Or perhaps you could simply announce on your site that you have content available, and have site owners contact you to discuss what they'd like to use.

Article libraries: Getting the word out

When you have your articles ready, you need to get them into the hands of people who can use them. One very popular strategy in the past is the article libraries. It could possibly still be used today.

There are actually hundreds of article libraries in which you can post your articles, but these are generally of low value. They *used* to bring two benefits. First, the article sits in the article library, which may be indexed by the search engines (many are), and thus the links to your site will be picked up by the search engines. Second, if you're lucky, the article will be picked up by site owners who need content for their sites; if so, your article then appears in *those* sites, gets indexed by the search engines, and provides more value.

In the past, this strategy worked very well for marketers. However, these article libraries often are of very low value these days. They became full of low-quality "spammy" articles, and the search engines definitely devalued them. But the search engines often still index them — at the time of writing, Google has almost 2,000,000 articles indexed on Amazines.com (Bing seems to like the article libraries less than Google). It might be worth sending a few quick articles out through this channel to get a few quick (though perhaps low-value) links.

Here are just a few of these article libraries:

- www.amazines.com
- www.articlealley.com
- www.articlecity.com
- www.articlesbase.com
- www.ezinearticles.com
- www.freesticky.com
- www.goarticles.com

Who will write your articles?

Of course, you come to the old question: Whom can you get to do this work? Perhaps you can write these articles yourself. Perhaps an employee in your company fancies himself an author. Or perhaps you can hire someone.

It's off to Guru.com, eLance.com, or oDesk.com you go, where you'll find countless people willing to write articles for you for $10 to $20 an article — some of whom can even speak a few words of English! Still, you're not looking for poetry or Nobel-prize-winning literature; you're looking for short articles with good keywords in them, and you really can find people who can write short articles — 500 to 700 words — very cheaply. (As I explain in Chapter 24, the easiest way to write short articles is to steal them from somebody else, so you may want to look into using Copyscape to check that your "writer" is actually writing.)

 I don't recommend that you use articles from these article libraries on *your* site, nor that you use cheap, barely intelligible articles you've had written by someone who shouldn't be allowed to call himself a writer. Garbage content on your site can hurt you in the search results.

Syndicating Outreach

The form of syndication I've just described is, let's face it, low quality, and search engines are starting to give less weight to them. If you read some of the articles in the article libraries I point you to, you know that many of the articles are written by people who are not English speakers or not writers. They are, to speak bluntly, terrible. No, really, *absolutely terrible*. Of course, what do you expect a $10 article to look like? I'm betting that Salman Rushdie and Scott Turow are not writing these articles as a side business.

These are articles written for one purpose only: to get links. In many cases, all you can expect the article to simply sit in the article libraries and never be syndicated to other Web sites; you are in effect buying the value of the links from the article libraries themselves. (The better your articles, of course, the more likely they are to be picked up from the libraries and placed into other Web sites.)

There used to be another channel for articles: the high-quality article sites. These sites required you to submit for approval before being able to submit articles. Furthermore, some of these sites even allowed you to create articles that included follow links. Such sites include Examiner.com (but they switched to follow links), Suite101.com (gone), AssociatedContent.com (also gone), Helium.com (yep, gone as well), and various others.

With this avenue pretty much gone (you may still find such sites, but they seem to be falling out of favor), how do you use content syndication to get more valuable links?

One way is to reach out to sites and bloggers asking if you can write for them. This might be termed "guest blogging," and that form of syndication, like so many other SEO techniques, has gotten a bad name in recent years. You may even hear the same old stories: Google doesn't like guest blogging, guest blogging will get you penalized, and so on. But what Google doesn't like is the low-quality, automated, spammy form of guest blogging in which in effect article owners are paying to have low-quality articles placed on blogs in order to point links back to their Web sites.

In fact, in a long article on the horrors of guest blogging, Matt Cutts of Google (see Chapter 23) made these comments ("I'm not trying to throw the baby out with the bath water. There are still many good reasons to do some guest blogging [exposure, branding, increased reach, community, etc.]. . . . And there are absolutely some fantastic, high-quality guest bloggers out there. I changed the title of this post to make it more clear that I'm talking about guest blogging for search engine optimization (SEO) purposes. I'm also not talking about multi-author blogs. High-quality multi-author blogs like Boing Boing have been around since the beginning of the web, and they can be compelling, wonderful, and useful."

It's the spammy garbage that Google objects to: "a bunch of low-quality or spam sites have latched on to 'guest blogging' as their link-building strategy, and we see a lot more spammy attempts to do guest blogging. Because of that, I'd recommend skepticism (or at least caution) when someone reaches out and offers you a guest blog article."

If you can produce high-quality, useful, interesting articles that bloggers might be interested in carrying (and, sure, might just happen to contain a couple of useful links to your site!), personal outreach to a few bloggers might be a good way to get your content out there.

Syndicating Utilities and Infographics

A number of companies do a tremendous job at building truly huge numbers of incoming links by giving away Web utilities and, more frequently these days, infographics. The basic concept is that you create something useful and let people place it on their Web site if they include a link back to your site.

Here's an example. You may remember those dreadful page counters at the bottom of many Web pages, a number showing how many people had visited the page (and essentially say to visitors, "the owner of this site is an amateur")? Many of those page counters were given away to create links back to the site that was giving them away. The code provided to people placing them on their sites included a small piece of text with a nicely keyworded link, and I've seen this strategy work very well. Sometimes the counter linked back to the site giving away the counter; sometimes it linked back to a completely different site and promoted a different site owned by the owner of the counter site or perhaps a site the owner had been paid to promote.

A strategy involving giving something away can work in many different ways with a little imagination. Whatever you give away — clip art, videos, flash animations, calculators — make sure you include links back to your site. For instance, your rodent-racing site could distribute a utility for handicapping mice and rats. (I don't mean to damage them physically; I mean to calculate the race handicap — *what do you think I am!*) The utility would have a link back to your site — nicely keyworded — providing you with lots of great backlinks for search engines to read.

These days, a really popular "giveaway" is the Infographic; very tall (you have to scroll to see them all), cool, informational graphics, full of interesting statistics bundled into an attractive graphical package (see Figure 18-1 for an example). The idea is that people pick up these things and post them in their Pinterest account, on their blog, in their social-networking account, and so on. You? Well, you get a link or two back to your site, because you provide a piece of code that people can use to embed the image, like this:

*<a href="http://yourdomain.org/blog/2016/02/winning-the-rodent-race/"><img src="http://yourdomain.org/blog/wp-content/uploads/2016/02/rodent-race.jpg" alt="Winning the Rodent Race [Infographic]" border="0" /></a>
Via: <a href="http://www.yourdomain.org/">Rodent Racing for the Masses</a>*

If you're interested in this kind of link building, spend a little time in research; there's an art to launching a widget or infographic. And one more thing: What does Google say about getting links from these things?

Well, as with many aspects of link building, Google feels it's been overdone, and they're right. In particular, they don't like the idea of companies selling link space in widget and infographic code, as does happen sometimes. It used to be popular for companies to build and distribute widgets of various kinds for the simple purpose of selling links in the embed code to third parties (it often worked very well as an SEO link-building technique). I think this happens far less often with Infographics. They tend to be more promotional PR techniques, often used for pushing a Web site's "brand."

Figure 18-1:
An info-graphic in Infograph icsArchive. com, a library of infographics.

But here's what Matt Cutts (Chapter 23) has said about links in these things; he complained about the "spammy" widgets and infographics (in particular when the link points back to a third party rather than the widget originator, or when the anchor text "really keyword rich"), and recommends the use of nofollow links. He also stated that "I would not rely on widgets and info-graphics as your primary way to gather links" and that "I would not expect a link from a widget to necessarily carry the same weight as an editorial freely given where someone is recommending something and talking about it in a blog post."

And More Link-Building Ideas . . .

A few more ideas for building links:

- ✔ Carry out traditional PR (public relations) campaigns, targeting blogs and newsletters, to promote your site. You need a good "story," but if you contact enough sites, you can get people to talk about you.

- ✔ Dozens of "Question and Answer" sites exist, such as BlurtIt.com, Askville, Yahoo! Answers (`http://answers.yahoo.com`), Answers. com, and so on. Some have follow links; some have nofollow links. Some SEO people seek out questions about their sites and answer them, including a link to their site, of course.

- ✔ Keep your eyes open and do a few link analyses on your competitors (see Chapter 17) now and then; you'll be surprised at some of the link tricks you can learn from competitors.

The search engines — in particular Google — have dramatically improved their ability to sniff out bad links, such as links that have likely been paid for. For this reason, I have been telling my consulting clients for several years that link building is moving toward the PR — Public Relations — model. Instead of playing "link games," you should be thinking about how you can get people interested in talking about your Web site. To paraphrase Matt Cutts, how you can get them to create "editorial [content] freely given where someone is recommending something and talking about it in a blog post [or other form of Web site]."

These are the very best form of links. That doesn't mean there's no role for other forms — such as infographic links that we just looked at — it just means other forms of links won't be as valuable as "the real thing."

The nofollow Curse

A quick note about the `nofollow` tag I mention earlier and in Chapter 16. This tag — `rel="nofollow"` — tells search engines to ignore a link. Ironically, while the link seems to tell search engines not to follow the link, they may actually follow to see where it goes; but it also, in effect, tells them not to give any credit to the referenced Web site. That is, a link to your site, with `rel="nofollow"` in the link, is as good as no link at all from a search engine ranking perspective; nothing's passed on. No PageRank, no TrustRank, no equivalent value. This tag was created to stop *blog spam*. When blogs first became popular, many people, trying to push their sites up in the search engines, were visiting blogs and posting messages in the blog with links back to their sites, solely to boost their sites in the search engines. Thus, blogs became inundated with absolute garbage. You could even hire foreign companies to place links in blogs for you or buy programs that hit thousands of blogs in a few hours. (Still can.)

So, the major search engines came together to figure a way to put a stop to it. They figured that if blog spam had no real benefit, it would stop. Therefore, nofollow was born.

What's happened over the last few years though is that, gradually, other sites have started using the nofollow tag. Wikipedia used to be a great place to put links back to your site until it started coding every link with nofollow. Craigslist, too, was a very popular place to post ads with links back until it began using nofollow.

So, if you discover a good place to put links to your site, first check to see whether the links are genuine links; that is, make sure they don't have nofollow in the link itself, or nofollow in a meta tag at the top of the page. Second, check periodically. A site that allows regular follow links today may not tomorrow.

That doesn't mean you should never place a link if you're only going to get a nofollow. There may still be value in the link . . . hey, you might get people clicking on it. And having a few nofollow links is a good thing; it makes your overall "link profile" look more natural. But it does mean that you probably won't want to invest major time and resources into a campaign that only garners nofollows.

Who's Going to Do All This Work?!

Wow, finding sites to link to yours is a lot of work. It's very LTT (laborious, tedious, and time consuming). It's also not, shall I say, high-rent work. How do you get all this done? Assuming that you're not using a link-acquisition firm, here are some options:

- ✔ Do you have kids? If not, get some. It's a little drastic, but after you've spent a week or two doing this stuff, it may not seem so bad.
- ✔ Do your neighbors or employees have kids?
- ✔ Do your siblings have kids? Do your kids have kids?
- ✔ Local schools and colleges definitely have kids, so you may want to find one or two who will do a few hours of work each evening.
- ✔ Check out one of the online talent sites — Guru.com, eLance.com, and oDesk.com, for example. They have lots of folks just waiting to tackle jobs like this.

You can decide what kind of link campaign you want to run, come up with a step-by-step plan, then set your new employees loose.

Chapter 19

Social Networking — Driven by Drivel

. . . .

In This Chapter

▶ Understanding social networking

▶ Avoiding the hype

▶ Reaping the SEO benefits of social networking

. . . .

*I*s there a place for social networking in a book on SEO? Well, to some degree, yes. But I don't go into great detail about social networking, because many of the benefits (when there are benefits) are not related to SEO. Social networking can be used in various ways to market a product or service, or an associated Web site, but that's not all about SEO.

Just What Is Social Networking?

Before I go any further, I should answer a basic question: What *is* social networking?

A *social-networking service* is one that helps people communicate together and share information quickly. Consider for a moment a basic, informational Web site. Clients come to the site, read about the products or services being promoted by the site, perhaps take some kind of action — make a purchase, sign up for a newsletter, or whatever — and go away. The communication flow is all one-way.

Of course, you could add two-way communication to a Web site — a chat system that allows customers to chat online with customer-service staff, for instance. But it's still fairly limited communication.

A social-networking service, though, provides multichannel communications. Members of the service's "community" can communicate with any other member who wants to communicate. Facebook, the world's largest social-networking service, claims to have almost a billion users *each day*, with 1.44 billion active user accounts. If Facebook were a country, it would be the world's most populous nation. Any of those 1.44 billion members can communicate with any other member, assuming the other member is interested in communicating.

Social networking is more than just "communicating," though. Social network sites often encourage people to set up their own minisites or profiles, on which they can post information about themselves, such as photos and messages. They can search for and connect with other members with similar interests, or members they know out in the real world.

The social-networking landscape is large and amorphous. You can certainly argue that discussion groups are part of social networking, and there are many tens of thousands of discussion groups. Blogging is also often considered a part of social networking. But various other things often are bundled in with social networking systems, such as Skype and Whatsapp. However, I think of these more as communication tools, not as true social-networking systems. (I believe that they more correctly come under the heading of *social media* — communications tools for ordinary people that may be used in a "social network context.")

I think one important characteristic of true social-networking sites is that they make publishing easy for people with no technical skills. All of a sudden, through the power of social networking, virtually anyone can be an online publisher, rather than merely a consumer of online information.

Social networking is a relatively new term; even most of today's Facebook members probably didn't know the term until relatively recently. (Facebook didn't open to the public until September 2006.) But social networking is actually an old concept, going back to the late 1970s or early 1980s. Online services such as CompuServe might be thought of as proto-social-networking services, allowing one-to-one communication between members, group communications in forums, the sharing of digital materials (text documents, images, software), and so on. (As a sociological concept, the term *social networking* goes back to at least the early 1970s.)

Today, though, what are the really important social-networking sites? The four most important, in North America, are definitely Facebook, Twitter, LinkedIn, and Google+.

Twitter has around 300 million individual users *tweeting* (that is, for those of you who have been held hostage in a cave somewhere, sending short Twitter messages) around 500 million times a day. (Is Twitter *really* a social-networking service? Yes, because it *allows* multichannel communication. However, the majority of Twitter users never send a message; they use it to *receive* information, so for most users, it could be argued, it's really more of a message-delivery service than a social network.)

Then there's Google+. Launched in 2011, it's a slick Facebook competitor that has suffered from Facebook burnout (who needs *another* social network when you're already wasting too much time on the ones you have?!) but also benefited from the power of brand Google. Within six months, Google+ had grown to 90 million members, eventually reaching around half a billion users; still not much more than a third of Facebook's membership. But from an SEO perspective, it's not just numbers that count. Google+ can be, as you see later in this chapter, an important factor in SEO regardless of the size.

Many other social-networking services exist, of course. Here are a few of the biggies in North America:

- **MySpace:** Perhaps 50 million users, defying the odds and actually *growing* while most pundits said it would soon be dead; it used to be the world's #1 social-networking site before a dramatic decline. Many teenagers use MySpace until they decide they're too embarrassed to hang out with the kids and switch to Facebook.

- **LinkedIn:** A business-networking site (based on the "six degrees of separation" concept), with over 300 million users and growing.

- **Pinterest:** Over 70 million active members and growing rapidly among female users. Pinterest lets you organize and share beautiful things (primarily images) you find on the Web.

- **Flickr:** A photo-sharing network with almost 100 million users.

There are many, many social-networking sites, including "social-bookmarking" sites (such as Delicious and Stumbleupon), sites related to particular interests, sites designed to help people find old friends (Classmates.com, for instance), and so on.

Beware the Social-Networking Hype

Social networking, properly used, can most definitely be a very valuable marketing tool. Having said that, I want to warn you that there's a lot of social-networking hype out there, and it's easy to get swept up into social networking only to find you have wasted a lot of time and money.

First, consider that social networking will work better for some companies than others. For instance, take Twitter. This service can be a great way to communicate with people for some businesses. ShopAtHome.com has around 267,000 followers of its Twitter feed. This company provides shopping discounts, so a Twitter feed is a natural fit for it; people like deals! Groupon, a "deal of the day" service, has dozens of separate feeds, one for each city it works in; the GrouponChicago feed currently has over 50,000 followers.

But what about a company that provides air-conditioning installation service? How many people want to hear from it every day? I'm not saying that it's not possible for such a company to benefit from a Twitter feed, but I am saying that the chance it will benefit from a Twitter account is much lower (okay, almost nil).

Also, social-networking campaigns need to be well thought out and well managed. Plenty of companies are happy to take your money for setting up some kind of generic, "me, too" social-networking system that hasn't a hope in Hades of working.

Here's an example. Way back when — say, eight or ten years ago — I would hear from new clients who said things like, "My friend Joe [my nephew/the last SEO firm I worked with/and so on] told me that if you want to do business online, you *must* have a MySpace account." I even heard this from real estate agents. (My answer? "Oh, are you selling houses to 13-year-olds?") It was complete nonsense, of course, but the hype was strong, too powerful for many businesses to resist, and led to millions of dollars of waste.

So before you let someone talk you into a social-networking campaign, make sure you understand exactly how it would work. Why will people join your group or subscribe to your Twitter feed? What do you expect them to do? How will you communicate with them? How will all of this benefit you?

Before anyone accuses me of being "against" social networking, let me just reiterate. Social networking *can* work well, at least for the right companies that have all their ducks in a row. However, I'm pretty certain that most dollars spent on social networking are wasted.

The Drivel Factor

If you don't know this already, you need to learn quickly. Most — the vast majority — of social networking is *drivel*. (Drivel: senseless talk; nonsense; saliva, drool; to talk nonsense; to talk senselessly.)

Do I have to prove this, or can you take it as a given? Okay, here's an example. Pear Analytics did a study of randomly selected public Twitter messages and found that

- 40.6 percent were "pointless babble."
- 37.6 percent were "conversational messages."
- 8.7 percent were "pass along" messages, those useful enough to have been forwarded by another Twitter user.
- 3.6 percent were information about news from the mainstream media.

- ✔ 5.9 percent were company self-promotion.
- ✔ 3.9 percent were spam.

What is "pointless babble"? You know the type of message: *I want to eat cereal, but I'm out of milk!!!* or *Where has that postman got to?!* — the sort of thing that burns up perfectly good electrons for no good reason.

Taken together, then, the pointless babble, conversational messages, and spam comes to around 82 percent of all messages.

The challenge for the marketer is to somehow cut through the drivel and find the value.

The SEO Benefits of Social Networking

Because this is a book on SEO, I want to get back to that subject: How can social networking help your SEO efforts? There are essentially four ways:

- ✔ **Link benefit:** Links from social-networking sites can, in some cases, help boost your pages in the search engines.

- ✔ **Search engine real estate:** As the search engines index some social-networking pages (and Tweets), being in social-networking sites gives you another online location, another possibility for being found by the search engines.

- ✔ **Promotional benefit**: The whole point of a social networking campaign is to promote your site or business; doing so puts it in front of people and builds awareness. The more aware people are of your site, the more links you're going to get.

- ✔ **The social networking sites *are* search engines:** What's a search engine? A site where people search. And people search on social-networking sites.

Getting links through social-networking sites

You find out about the value of links in Chapters 16 through 18. Well, Google has indexed over 5 *billion* Facebook pages, and many of those pages contain links to the page owners' Web sites.

Here's the problem, though. These links are nofollow links (see Chapter 16), so, in theory at least, they have no link value. Twitter also uses nofollow links, as does MySpace and many other social-networking sites.

So, do those links have any value? In Chapter 16, I told you *no*. In this chapter, I'm suggesting a theory. I don't know whether this is true, but . . . what if the search engines *do* sometimes read nofollow links? After all, what is the point of nofollow links? The original purpose was to stop people from spamming blog comments by telling the search engines not to follow the links and thus removing an incentive for blog comments. But the purpose of nofollow was not really to stop search engines indexing links — that was just a mechanism to discourage spam.

Now, imagine that you are a search engine programmer. You want as much information as you can get to help you rank pages. Aren't all those links on social-networking sites useful? After all, Google was based on the concept of examining links to learn about referenced sites. In the pre-social-networking days, Google recruited a relatively small number of site owners to tell them which sites were important.

Now, with the barriers to entry being much, much lower for social networking and social bookmarking — it's much easier to set up a Facebook, or MySpace, or Digg account than to build a Web site — Google has a much larger army of site reviewers to help it figure out how to rank Web sites. There are quite simply many more social-networking accounts than there are conventional Web sites.

So you, the search engine programmer, know that all this great information is out there to . . . but wait! They are nofollow links! Do you decide not to use the links?

To make nofollow links accomplish their original purpose, search engines don't have to ignore the links; it's good enough if people *think* the search engines ignore the links. But perhaps they don't. Perhaps they do read those links to extract this vast amount of useful information.

That's just a theory; again, I don't know whether it's true. I can tell you that under the commonly accepted nofollow theory, many social-networking links have no SEO value. On the other hand, if my unproven theory is correct, these links *do* have SEO value. (And remember, links have value in their own right; sometimes people click them!)

You can find conflicting information on this issue if you care to search and see what the search engines say. Certainly, both search engines have said in the past that they do use social-networking data. For example, Bing has stated that "We do look at the social authority of a user. We look at how many people you follow, how many follow you, and this can add a little weight to a listing in regular search results," and Google has said that "we do use it as a signal. It is used as a signal in our organic and news rankings." As for the specific question of "do you ignore nofollow links or not," note that, in the early days, the social networks did not use nofollow links. If the search engines found those links useful in the early days, they might not have simply stopped using them for ranking just because the networks started nofollowing them.

My personal belief? Social networks *can* help your search engine ranking. How do you generate links from social-networking sites? By engaging your community. If you have a strong social-networking community, you can use various techniques to encourage members to create links to your Web sites, on their own Web sites, their blogs, their social-networking profiles, and so on.

Grabbing search engine real estate

Another way that social networking can help you — perhaps — is to grab *real estate* in the search results — that is, when someone searches for your keywords, your site comes up in the search results *and* some of your social-networking profiles come up in the results, or the profiles of others who are linking to you come up in the results.

In practice, grabbing real estate is harder than it seems, because social-networking pages themselves are not given much weight by the search engines. How do I know that? Because they don't often come up in the search results.

You can find significant exceptions, though. For instance, search for the name of a band or musician, and you may see their Facebook page appear in the results. When searching for individual's names, LinkedIn.com pages often come up pretty high in the results.

Still, if you want to grab real estate through social networking, the way to do it is to create various social-networking accounts for your site or business, and then ensure they have lots of links pointing to them, containing the correct keywords, of course (see Chapters 16 to 18).

Promotional Benefit

As I mention elsewhere, the best links are real links. To paraphrase Matt Cutts again, what you need is links in "editorial [content] freely given where someone is recommending something and talking about it in a blog post" or some other form of Web site.

Thus, as I mention elsewhere (Chapter 18), SEO linking is moving toward a PR model: You promote your site, business, or product, and people write about you — and link to you — because there's a real story to be told.

Social networking can be a huge part of a PR campaign, a way to reach the masses, and to encourage the masses to talk about you. It's a way to get people to mention you in their blogs, to help journalists to discover you and write about you in magazine, news, and newsletter sites, and so on. So social networking can be a hugely important tool for many businesses to promote themselves and, almost coincidentally, end up with links that promote their Web sites.

The social-networking sites are search engines

The major social networking sites are also major search engines, with billions of searches a month; in fact, Facebook alone gets more searches each month than Ask.com.

So, social-networking sites *are* search engines. Now, it's true that many of these searches are for people, but many will be for interests and products, too. So another SEO reason for a social-networking strategy is that you have a chance of coming up in the many social-networking site searches.

The Google+ Factor

Google+ is Google's social-networking site. After failing with Orkut (most Americans have never even heard of Orkut), Google started over and tried again. For a while, Google seemed to be really getting somewhere, with 90 million members in the first few months, but it was never able to beat Facebook at its own game. It's still one of the world's most important social networks, though.

One reason for its success — and one reason why it's so important to SEO — is that Google is working to integrate Google+ pages into the search results themselves. In fact, Google+ is being integrated into the entire Googlesphere; one example is that Google integrated businesses' Google+ pages into the search results. (Any "local" business really *must* have a Google+ page. See Chapter 12.)

Social Networking — A Book in Itself

Social-networking marketing is a big and complicated subject that deserves a book of its own. I outline in general terms how social networking can be used to help your site from an SEO perspective, but social networking is a form of marketing by itself, independent of any SEO benefits you may derive from it. So I leave it there and move on, in Chapter 20, to a related subject: using video for SEO purposes.

However, to find out more about using social networking for your business, see *Social Media Marketing For Dummies,* 3rd Edition, by Shiv Singh and Stephanie Diamond (published by John Wiley & Sons, Inc.) and *The Digital Handshake: Seven Proven Strategies to Grow Your Business Using Social Media,* by Paul Chaney (also published by Wiley).

Chapter 20

Video: Putting Your Best Face Forward

....

....

Most people don't generally think of video sites as search engines, but for the last few years, that's just what the largest video site has become. YouTube has billions of searches every month — more, in fact, than Yahoo! or Bing. You might think of YouTube as the world's second largest search engine.

At the time of writing, YouTube was reporting that it has a *billion* users, viewing 4 billion videos every day. Three hundred *hours* of video is being uploaded every minute.

Video is big. But how do you use it from a search engine perspective? This chapter tells you about the SEO benefits of working with video, the best ways and places to upload video, and how to do so most effectively.

The SEO Benefits of Video

So how can you benefit, from an SEO perspective, from video? In these ways:

- ✔ **Providing content on your site that search engines like:** That's the theory, anyway, but the reality is a little different, as I detail in a moment.

✔ **Getting listed in more search engines — the video search engines:** YouTube is a hugely important search engine. So getting videos into YouTube (and other video-search sites) gets you into the video-search game.

✔ **Grabbing search engine real estate:** This is in some ways more important because Google likes to insert videos into its search results, as you can see in Figure 20-1.

Figure 20-1:
Video inserted into the Google search results.

Videos on your site

The most obvious benefit to putting videos on your site, from an SEO perspective, is that it provides content that the search engines like, and you'll often hear that as a reason given for using video on your site. The reality is a little different; videos are *not* particularly good search engine fodder, although you can improve that situation a bit. The proof of the pudding is in the eating, they say; when videos are embedded into the search results, they are almost always from major video sites, such as YouTube.com and Vimeo.com.

Ah, I can hear someone in the back mumbling, "But Google listens to the videos and transcribes them!" That's true, or at least was for a while. In fact, if you go to YouTube.com and view a video (YouTube is owned by Google, by the way), look for a little CC button in the bottom-right corner of the video player. (It may or may not be there — one of those "here today, gone tomorrow" things.) If it *is* there, then click the button, and you can play the audio with "closed caption" transcription shown at the bottom of the video.

Automated transcriptions are problematic, though. Here's a transcription I got from YouTube some time ago. See whether you can figure out what this is all about:

> But this is not something audiences for instance and decision on right this second and faint dot com and their pretty amazing yes I always wanted only a lot some may still a year maybe a favorite and your ratings are important they help determine the top ten finalists I think answer is get your friends and family behind and if you think that there's a great privilege to you they say let's everybody was the standard and so then check out those the is a great great great and if you get Iraq ice-cold can separate store

Believe it or not, this is a transcription of a promotional video from Coca Cola's Fanta soft drink, promoting a contest to find the fourth "Fantana girl." What, you didn't get that? I must admit that I've seen better transcriptions than this, but the system is definitely not perfect.

So, if you think that the search engines will listen to and transcribe your videos into something that might actually help you, think again. Not this year, anyway, or the next.

Is Google trying to transcribe the videos it finds on the Web at present? I don't know, but even if it is, don't expect a video sitting on your site to do you much good from an SEO perspective, unless you help it along a bit. Like this:

- ✔ **Label it.** Create a nicely keyworded label or short description of the video; use an `<H>` tag in the HTML around this label.

- ✔ **Describe it.** Include a longer description, again with good keywords.

- ✔ **Transcribe it.** Do a *real* transcription and post the transcribed text on the page. Services exist that can do this for you very affordably and pretty efficiently.

- ✔ **Name it.** Use keywords in the video's filename and URL.

- ✔ **Link to it.** Create links, on your site and others, to the video page, using keywords and the term *video* in the link. This is very important; providing links into the video page can help a lot.

- ✔ **Tag it.** As usual, use keywords (including the word *video*) in your page's `<TITLE>` tag and `DESCRIPTION` tag.

- ✔ **Add to it.** Add other keyworded content on the page, especially if the transcription is short.

- ✔ **Submit it.** You can include video content in your sitemap (which I discuss in Chapter 13) or create a special mRSS (media RSS) feed, providing the video title, description, a thumbnail URL, and so on. Some video experts believe that submitting both a regular sitemap and an mRSS sitemap is a good idea. You can find details about both in the Google Webmaster Help information.

Use the word *video* throughout; remember, you're trying to tell the search engines that this is a video. Don't overdo it, but you can use the term *video* in the `<H>` tag, the description, the filename, links, `<TITLE>` tag and `DESCRIPTION` meta tag, and so on.

Don't use pop-up video players; embed them into the page. If you do use pop-ups, the danger is that the video isn't found by the search engines, especially if the pop-up is generated by JavaScript. Also, the video may be "orphaned" in the search results, much the same way as framed pages become orphaned (as I describe in Chapter 9).

You might also allow other people to embed your video into their sites; this can help create links back to the video, assuming that people actually take you up on the offer.

Have you heard about Google TV (https://www.android.com/tv/)? No, it wasn't the huge success everyone thought it would be, but it's still around, renamed Android TV. The basic idea: a television search engine. Imagine your TV set getting TV from wherever you normally get it (cable, satellite, or over the air) *and* connecting to the Internet. Add a search engine — Google, of course — and now you can search and find exactly the show, documentary, funny video, or whatever, and view it from wherever it may be.

Now, because of this, Google is getting more serious about indexing video on the Web. In particular, Google is eager to get your video-sitemap data. As Mr. Google SEO, Matt Cutts (see Chapter 23) said a while back, "If you tell us where your videos are, we will try to index them a little bit harder. For example, if you think about things like Google TV. . . it's in everybody's interest that all the videos that are on the Web be able to be very discoverable and very searchable." Google *wants* your video, so make it easy for Google to get it.

Playing the video search engine game

If you go to the trouble of creating videos, why not distribute them as widely as possible, on as many video sites as possible? Remember, these are search engines, too, so being present when someone searches for your keywords would be good. As Woody Allen said, "Eighty percent of success is showing up," and if you're not in the video sites, you're not showing up. So, here are a few tips for you on uploading your videos:

- ✔ **"Watermark" your videos.** Now and then you'll find videos, on the video-upload sites or perhaps embedded into someone's Web site, with no identifying information in the video itself. You need to make sure your videos stand alone as a marketing tool for your site, so *watermark* the videos with your site's domain name — at the very least at the beginning and end of the video, but ideally on every single frame so that no one can view the video without knowing where it comes from. (If you have videos that are not watermarked, you can use the Annotation tool on YouTube to overlay text onto the video. Oh, use keywords when you annotate, too!)

- ✔ **Provide plenty of keyworded descriptive info.** The video-upload services provide space for you to supply a title, description, and keywords (or tags). Use them and use them fully — by entering a long description with plenty of keywords, for instance.

- ✔ **Include a link to your Web site.** Put it in the URL field if the service provides one, or the description if it doesn't. You want people to be able to find your site, after all. Note, however, that most video sites provide nofollow links (see Chapter 16 for details on nofollow links), so you won't get rank-boosting value in the search engines from them.

- ✔ **Put your domain at the top of the description, in particular on YouTube.** YouTube hides your video description, except for the first line, so to ensure that people see your site's URL, you need to put it on the first line.

- ✔ **Encourage your consumers or social fans to comment on your videos (ideally, to leave a video comment).** In addition to leaving a regular comment below a YouTube video, you can also leave a video comment there as well. Google may like these comments, perhaps because the fact that it requires more effort suggests it may be more reasoned and useful.

- ✔ **Include a transcript or caption file.** YouTube allows you to upload time-coded captions or a plain-text transcription file. (You have to upload the file first, view the file in your Uploaded Videos area, and then click the Captions button.) Google will probably read these files.

There are literally dozens of video hosting sites to which you can upload your videos. You can find a good list at `http://en.wikipedia.org/ wiki/List_of_video_hosting_websites`. Of course, it'll take you, um, forever to upload to all of them. So you should consider using a video-upload service, which works by having you load the video once into the distribution service so that the service can then upload to a variety of different sites. For instance, OneLoad (`www.oneload.com`) will upload your video to over 20 different services (up to ten times a month for free). Another distribution service is TrafficGeyser.com, which can upload to a similar number (and has some other advantages, which I discuss in a moment).

Incidentally, the ranking of videos on the upload sites is not just a matter of keywords and links to the page. On YouTube, for instance, other aspects may be taken into consideration, such as

- The number of times the video is viewed
- The ratings given to the video by viewers
- The number of times the video was shared
- The number of comments
- The number of people subscribing to the video publisher's channel after viewing the video
- The number of times the video is embedded into viewers' own Web sites

Trying to make your video go viral? Understanding the preceding list will provide clues to how to make that happen! (Of course, you also need something that's viral quality, not just your last Disney vacation video.)

Grabbing search engine real estate

So, you've got your videos uploaded to the video-upload sites. You now have a chance of being found in what are, in effect, video search engines. But as the search engines index some of these video sites, you also now have a chance of your videos turning up in the regular search results (refer to Figure 20-1).

But there is a bit more to the game, if it's played right. If you want to encourage the search engines to rank your videos well, you really need links pointing to the videos. That's right, you need to create links from various places to the video-upload sites; as Chapter 16 notes, links help pages rank, so it makes sense that your videos on a video-upload site might need a few links to help them rank. TrafficGeyser.com actually automates this process, uploading videos to the video hosting services *and* posting links to the videos on social-networking sites.

Chapter 21

When Google Bites Back: A Guide to Catastrophe

*I*magine that Google decided it didn't want to play with you anymore. Imagine an enterprise rolling along nicely, bringing in plenty of business on the Web, perhaps even most or all of its business, and most of that business came through the search engines, when, all of a sudden . . . the site just drops in the search results. All of a sudden, you can't find your site anywhere through any of the great keywords for which you were ranking well.

A frightening thought, eh? But it happens, and it has happened to many. Why? And what can you do about it? Well, that's the subject of this chapter, which gives you a look at what search engine penalties are all about, how to avoid them, and what to do if the worst happens.

How, and How Much?

There are, in a broad sense, two types of penalties, and Google can impose them in two ways. The types of penalties are as follows:

✔ **Total:** Your site is completely dropped from the search engine. It's no longer in the index, and the search engine will probably stop visiting your site. (This is often called *de-indexing* or a *ban*.) Assuming that you've been penalized (and, as I discuss a little later in the section "Is It Really a Penalty? A Little Analysis," your site can be dropped for reasons other than a penalty), you've *really* annoyed Google!

✔ **Partial:** Your site is still in the search engine, but it just doesn't seem to be ranking well; plus, some other symptoms are appearing (which I discuss in the upcoming section "Is It Really a Penalty? A Little Analysis") that also suggest a penalty. But the site is still in the Google index, and Google even returns periodically to crawl more pages. This is still bad, of course, but not as bad as a total ban. Google's saying, in effect, "We don't like what you've done, but we're willing to give you another chance." *Phew!*

Imposing a penalty

By the way, a partial ban probably has different grades, different "levels" of penalty. In fact, the SEO community has come up with all sorts of names, such as a *–30 penalty* (Google adds 30 positions to your site every time it comes up in the search results, pushing it down three pages); a *PageRank penalty* (Google reduces your PageRank); a *–950 penalty* (you drop so far that you just can't be found); and so on. Google almost certainly has some kind of obscenity filter that is intended to drop porn sites from the regular results and that says, in effect, "We're not going to drop you from our index because you haven't necessarily done anything wrong, but we don't want your site coming up for regular search results." These penalty types are conjecture, though — Google doesn't state what the penalties are, beyond saying, in effect, "Yes, we penalize, and we have different grades of penalty."

Now, the two processes by which a penalty can be imposed are the following:

✔ **Algorithmically:** The Google "algorithm," the complex piece of software that evaluates sites and decides how to rank them, has found something on your site egregious enough to penalize your site.

✔ **Manually:** Google has a "*webspam* team" that employs real, live human beings to examine Web sites. If the team finds something it doesn't like, it can impose a penalty, known as a *manual action*.

Relatively few sites actually get penalized; in fact, if you pay attention during your travels around the Web, you'll find all sorts of sites that really should be penalized. These are sites that play all sorts of nasty SEO tricks yet somehow are still in the index. Why?

First, with a trillion or so pages in the Google index, there's simply no way to manually examine all of them for spamful intent. On the other hand, to automatically or algorithmically apply penalties, search engines have to create a very loose system that penalizes only the very worst offenses or they are bound to penalize innocent sites. I know that Google's search engine engineers are trying to not penalize innocent parties. This fact is obvious because so many indexed pages clearly break the rules.

On the other hand, having said that . . . Google has become much better at analyzing sites in recent years, and finds and penalizes sites much more easily. In particular, it has in recent years been getting quite good at identifying networks of sites in the business of selling links (see Chapter 17) and dropping them from its index.

The Google spam team

I know a little about the spam team, too, by the way. I know, for instance, that you can submit sites to be checked for spam. If you have a competitor that is quite clearly playing significant SEO tricks that "break the rules," you can actually tell Google (and the other search engines) about that site (take a look at www.google.com/webmasters/tools/spamreport).

I also have an idea of what the spam team does, partly from the "leaking" in 2007 of the *Google Spam Team Quality Rater Guidelines*, a PDF document that apparently provides information to team members on how to examine a site to see whether it's playing unacceptable SEO tricks. This leaked book is generally accepted in the SEO community as being genuine, and if you do a search (at Google!) for that title, you may still be able to find it. Reportedly, a 2011 version was leaked, too, though that leak was quickly plugged by Google. It makes fascinating reading, at least for search geeks. (Actually, Google has two spam-related teams. It has a search-quality team, which examines search results to see how well the Google algorithm is working and provide feedback that is used to improve the algorithm. But it also has a *webspam* team that examines spam in order to manually block bad pages.)

Here's what worries me about the webspam team: How often does it make mistakes? Everyone makes mistakes, of course, and plenty of those mistakes are made during work hours. (Have you worked in corporate America? Let's face it — it's not exactly a mecca of efficiency and competence.) A simple statistical analysis indicates, in fact, that people make somewhere around 30 percent of all their mistakes during working hours. And, just perhaps, tomorrow one of those mistakes will be made by the Google webspam team, and your site (or mine) will be hit with a penalty.

So, from the perspective of the site owner with the "damaged" site, two big questions are of concern:

✔ Has the site been penalized? It may seem obvious — the site has disappeared, so obviously it has been penalized — but the situation is actually more complicated than that.

✔ If so, then what can be done about it?

So, start at the beginning and first determine whether your site has *really* been penalized.

Is It Really a Penalty? A Little Analysis

It may seem counterintuitive, but just because your site appears to have been penalized doesn't mean that it has. In fact, it seems to me that in most cases when a site owner thinks his site has been penalized, it really hasn't. You see, when your site drops in the search results, a number of reasons could be behind it. A few (I'm sure there are more) are as follows:

- ✔ You've done something to damage your site, telling Google not to index it anymore.

- ✔ Someone else, perhaps a hacker, has done something to damage your site.

- ✔ Google has changed its algorithm, and all the great little SEO tricks you were using in the past no longer work, so your site is dropping in the ranks.

- ✔ Google is in the middle of an upheaval, and your site is dropping for no particular reason and will probably come back in a few days . . . and then perhaps drop again and come back later.

- ✔ You really have been penalized. Google's algorithm has identified something it doesn't like in your site.

- ✔ You really have been penalized. A Google webspam team member has seen your site (perhaps because it was reported by a competitor), didn't like something you were doing, and penalized the site.

Before you can figure out which of these possibilities is true, you have to determine what is really going on with your site. "It's dropped in the search results" isn't enough; you need more detail.

Here are a few things to consider when trying to figure out whether your site has been penalized:

- ✔ Does your Google Webmaster console contain a message?
- ✔ Is the site still indexed?
- ✔ Has Google flagged your site as "suspicious"?
- ✔ Has the number of pages in the index significantly changed?
- ✔ What happens when you search for your domain name?
- ✔ What happens when you search for the domain name minus the TLD (Top Level Domain; the .com piece, for instance)?
- ✔ What happens when you search for a text string in your <TITLE> tag?

✔ What happens when you search for a text string in your home page?

✔ Is Google still crawling your Web site?

✔ Have you used a Penalty Checker?

In the following pages, I look at each of these items.

Does your Google Webmaster console contain a message?

There are a few criteria that suggest whether your site has been penalized, but there's a really quick check that will short-circuit this process if your site *has* been the subject of a manual action. Follow this process if, for whatever reason, you think your site has been penalized.

Log into your Google Webmaster account (see Chapter 13) and check whether Google has sent you a message about a problem in your site. There is a Messages area in Google Webmaster, but this is mostly used for status messages these days. (Google also sends messages to sites that have been hacked, or even sites that are running old server software that leaves them open to being hacked.)

Open up the <u>Search Traffic</u> menu, and click on the <u>Manual Actions</u> link; this is where you find information about manual-action penalties, if any, applied to your site. These may be split into Site-wide and Partial matches; problems that apply to your entire site, and problems that apply only to a part of your site (so Google may penalize your entire site, or only certain parts).

These are the types of problems that Google lists:

✔ **Unnatural links to your site:** Bad links pointing to your site, such as paid links (but see my discussion of this subject in Chapter 18)

✔ **Unnatural links to your site — impacts links:** This means that Google found bad links pointing to your site, but that they are "penalizing" the links; that is, reducing the value of the links, but not penalizing your site itself. Of course, devaluing the links can cause search-rank drops, because they are no longer providing ranking value.

✔ **Unnatural links from your site:** This is more of a problem. Google has found bad links *from* your site to others.

✔ **Hacked site:** Your site has been hacked and contains malware of some kind (I discuss this problem in this chapter).

✔ **Thin content with little or no added value:** Google has found content it believes to be garbage; perhaps you picked up something from one of those article libraries!

✔ **Pure spam:** Google has found total garbage, such as "as automatically generated gibberish, cloaking, scraping content from other websites, and/or other repeated or egregious violations of Google's quality guidelines."

✔ **User-generated spam:** Google has found what it believes to be spammy content and links created by users of your site, such as spam links in forum messages.

✔ **Cloaking and/or sneaky redirects:** Google has found that you are using cloaking or sneaky redirects (see Chapter 10).

✔ **Hidden text and/or keyword stuffing:** Google has found that you are using hidden text or keyword stuffing (see Chapter 10).

✔ **Spammy freehosts:** Your site is on a hosting service that has a very high percentage of spam Web sites (see Chapter 7).

✔ **Spammy structured markup:** You are using structured markup (see Chapter 8), but appear to be playing various tricks; perhaps marking up content that is not visible to the user, for instance.

Nothing there? That may not mean you're in the clear. You may have been penalized *algorithmically* rather than being the subject of a "manual" action. If there *is* something here, though . . . well, now you know what is going on. Later in this chapter, I show you what to do next.

Is the site still indexed?

Go to Google and ask it how many pages are indexed, like this:

```
site:domain.com
```

For instance, if you type `site:cnn.com` into Google and press Enter, Google displays a list of pages from cnn.com and shows a number at the top, under the search box. It will be something like `About 3,380,000`.

Now, say that you do this for your site, and it comes back with a list of pages. That's good news; clearly you haven't been hit with the most serious penalty. You may still have been partially penalized, though.

However, say Google returns a message like this:

```
Your search - site:domain.com - did not match any documents.
```

Now you know that you have definite problems. Has the site been penalized? Perhaps, but before you can say for sure, you have to rule out other possibilities.

Has Google flagged your site as "suspicious"?

If your site is no longer indexed, Google may have found some kind of *malware* on the site, bad software such as Trojan horses or viruses. This sometimes happens when a site has been hacked. So, try this little check. (In fact, try it even if the site *is* still indexed; doing so takes only a moment.) Type the following into your browser's Location bar and press Enter:

```
www.google.com/safebrowsing/diagnostic?site=yourdomain.com
```

Google will return a page telling you whether your site is listed as suspicious (see Figure 21-1). If so, there's your problem! You need to figure out what's on your site that Google doesn't like and get rid of it. By the way, in the response page, if your site is not infected, you may see something like this:

```
Google has not visited this site within the past 90 days
```

Just ignore this line; it does *not* mean that your site has not been indexed for 90 days. (It's probably referring to the bots that are sent out to examine a site for malware.)

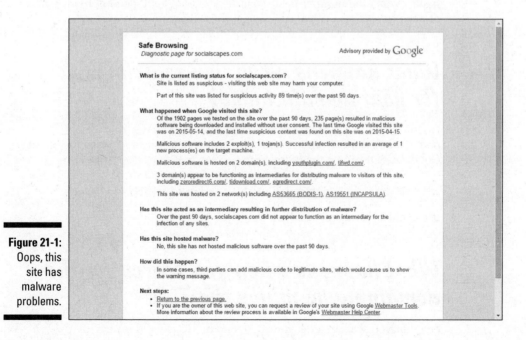

Figure 21-1: Oops, this site has malware problems.

However, even if your site passes this test, there could still be problems. Sometimes Google displays a small *This site may be hacked* message in the search results, under the Web page's title, even if the site passes this *safebrowsing* test.

If you see this message — or even if you don't, but still are trying to track down your site's problem — go into Google Webmaster, and click the Security Issues menu link on the left. If Google has found problems, you find information here. You also find links to information on how to fix the problem, and how to request a review of your site in order to remove the "may be hacked" message.

Has the number of pages in the index significantly changed?

If your site *is* still indexed, how many pages does Google say it has in the index? Has it dropped considerably? If so, this fact doesn't mean anything in isolation. Google's index numbers fluctuate a lot of time, after all. However, if you come back a few days' running, or over a couple of weeks, and the number seems to be in free-fall, you may have a problem. On the other hand, even if the number is fairly solid, you could still be under some kind of penalty.

What happens when you search for your domain name?

Go to Google and search for your exact domain name in this format: *domainname.com*. What happens? Does Google return pages from your site? Good. Does it return the following?

```
Your search - domainname.com - did not match any documents.
```

If so, that's bad. Really bad.

What happens when you search for the domain name minus the TLD?

Say that you searched for your domain and Google did return the page. In that case, you might try searching for the domain name without the TLD (Top Level Domain); that is, don't search for `domainname.com` but search for `domainname` instead.

Don't bother if your domain name is a short, common term. But if it's a string of two or three terms, in a sequence that is unlikely to appear except in your domain name, then Google should bring up your site. If it doesn't, that's not good.

What happens when you search for a text string in your <TITLE> tag?

So, things are going okay so far; or maybe you've got bad news, but you want a little more confirmation. Copy a line of text from a `<TITLE>` tag in a page on your site that you know to be indexed.

Next, search for that term like this:

```
site:domainname.com "The text from the title tag"
```

Does Google find this? It should find it if the page you picked is definitely in the index and you typed it all correctly. Okay, now search for the string of text, in quotation marks, *without* `site:domainname.com` in front of it.

Google now doesn't find it? If you pick a distinct enough phrase, very few pages should come up in the results, perhaps even fewer than ten, so you should be able to find the results if they're there. If Google *doesn't* return it — wow, that's bad.

What happens when you search for a text string in your home page?

You can try a similar test by searching for a particular string of text that you know is in a page that is definitely in your site. First, test like this:

```
site:yourdomain.com "The text from the home page"
```

When the page appears in the search results (and if it doesn't, that's very unusual, and very, very serious; are you sure you entered the text correctly?), you'll see that your search string is shown in the search box. Just delete the `site:yourdomain.com` piece and press Enter to search again.

If you get a `No results found for` message at the top of the page, or if that message doesn't appear, but you just can't find your page in the search results, that's a serious problem.

Is Google still crawling your Web site?

Here's another thing to check while you're in the Webmaster account: Is Google still crawling your site? Go to the Webmaster account home page and click the name of your site. The site's Dashboard page appears. Click the <u>Crawl</u> menu link and then the <u>Crawl Stats</u> link. If you're lucky, a page with information like that shown in Figure 21-2 appears. If not, your site is no longer being crawled; in other words, the Googlebot is no longer visiting your site and downloading pages. That's what we in the SEO business call *A Very Bad Thing.*

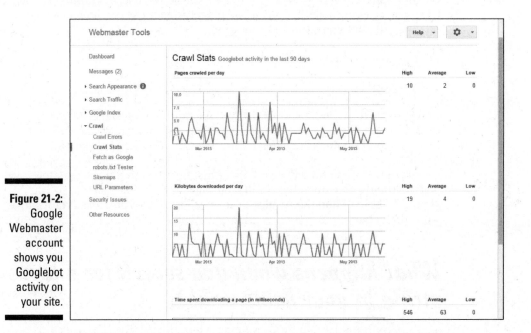

Figure 21-2: Google Webmaster account shows you Googlebot activity on your site.

Still, even if Google *is* still crawling your site, it doesn't mean you have not been penalized. You may have a partial penalty, and Google is waiting for you to fix the problems.

Try a penalty checker

For further confirmation, you may want to try a "Google penalty checker"; you can find one by doing a search. The tool creators generally don't tell you exactly how they determine whether your site has been penalized; they probably just run through some of the tests that I have looked at in this chapter already. Still, they may provide a little confirmation of what's going on, a sort of "second opinion." (See Figure 21-3.)

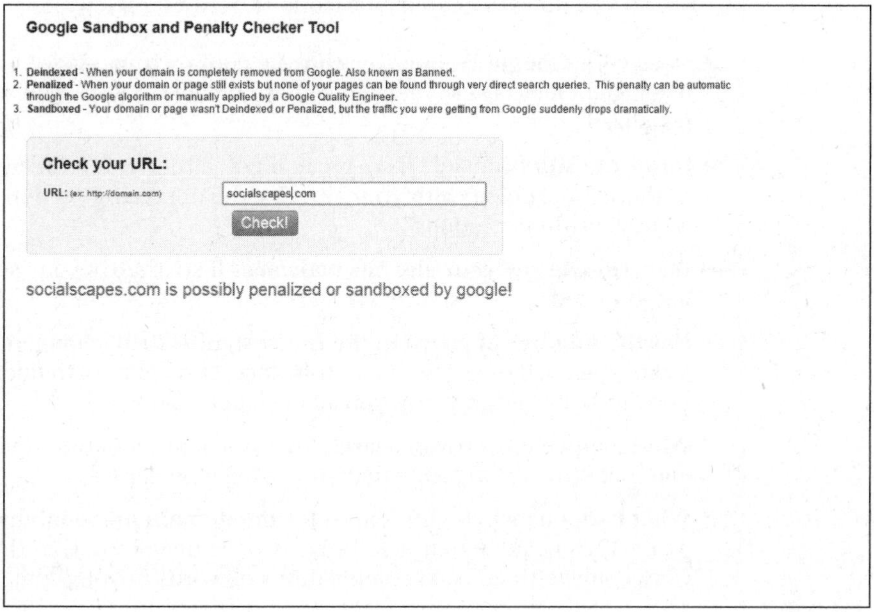

Google Sandbox and Penalty Checker Tool

1. **Deindexed** - When your domain is completely removed from Google. Also known as Banned.
2. **Penalized** - When your domain or page still exists but none of your pages can be found through very direct search queries. This penalty can be automatic through the Google algorithm or manually applied by a Google Quality Engineer.
3. **Sandboxed** - Your domain or page wasn't Deindexed or Penalized, but the traffic you were getting from Google suddenly drops dramatically.

Check your URL:

URL: (ex: http://domain.com)   [socialscapes|.com]

[Check!]

socialscapes.com is possibly penalized or sandboxed by google!

Figure 21-3:
The Li'l
Engine
Google
Penalty
Checker in
action.

You may get different results from a penalty checker than you get when you perform these checks yourself; for instance, things may still look bad to you — Google won't return your site in the result when you search for text in your home page's `<TITLE>` tag or page content, perhaps — and yet the penalty checker says there's no penalty. That result *may* be because of the difference between Google data centers; different locations get results from different Google data centers, and it takes time for changes to propagate all the way across all data centers.

Some of these penalty checkers are no good; I've seen one that says Google. com is penalized, and you may get a negative result in one checker and a positive result in another (so you may want to try a few). But some seem okay; perhaps they're getting better in general. Still, they don't have any secret channel to Google; they're just using the sorts of checks I describe here.

Pulling It All Together: Have You Been Penalized?

So what do you do with all this information? Here's a review.

- ✔ **Does your Google Webmaster console contain a message?** Clearly, if you get a message saying you've been penalized, well, you've been penalized!

- ✔ **Is the site still indexed?** If so, great; if not, either you've been penalized or there's a problem with your site. See the upcoming section "Dealing with Algorithmic Actions"

- ✔ **Does Google say your site has malware?** If so, there's your problem. If not, proceed.

- ✔ **Has the number of pages in the index significantly changed?** If so, not a good sign. On the other hand, this number does tend to fluctuate in Google, so it doesn't prove you've been penalized.

- ✔ **What happens when you search for your domain name?** If you can't find it, it strongly suggests that you've been penalized.

- ✔ **What happens when you search for the domain name minus the TLD?** Again, if you can't find it, you've likely been penalized. (But this search works only with unusual combinations of words in your domain name.)

- ✔ **What happens when you search for a text string in your <TITLE> tag?** Yet again, if Google doesn't return your site, you've likely been penalized.

- ✔ **What happens when you search for a text string in your home page?** Again, if your site isn't in the search results, you've probably been penalized.

- ✔ **Is Google still crawling your Web site?** If so, that's a great sign; you may still be penalized, but you've got another chance. If not, you've quite likely been penalized badly.

- ✔ **Try a penalty checker (or a few).** The penalty checker says what it says; it's just another bit of information, one way or the other.

So, what can you do now?

- ✔ **If you got a manual action message:** Read what Google is telling you and follow the instructions! You'll get specific instructions in the Manual Actions area of your Webmaster account, even a video in some cases, telling you what you need to do.

✔ **If you are no longer indexed, and Google has stopped crawling your site:** You need to check to see whether your site is "damaged" in some way (see the upcoming section "Dealing with Algorithmic Actions") and then, if everything seems okay, consider what you may have done to be banned. (On the other hand, you probably know whether you've been playing egregious SEO tricks; you may not know whether a company you hired to work on your site has, though.)

✔ **If you are still indexed okay, but all indications suggest that you've been penalized:** See the "Digging Your Way Out of the Hole" section, later in this chapter.

Of course, another possibility is that you don't seem to have been penalized but your site is not ranking well for your keywords. This scenario could be the case for one of two reasons:

✔ **Google is in the middle of some kind of update.** This happens now and then. Sites jump up and down in the search results for a period of a few days or even weeks, and then things settle down to more or less where they were before.

✔ **Google has changed its algorithm, and your site no longer appears to be a good match for your keywords.** In other words, the content and links that you had before worked okay, and now Google has adjusted its algorithm so that they don't. For instance, many people have been hit over the years by adjustments in the algorithm related to reciprocal linking. Although reciprocal linking used to be very powerful, now it's pretty weak, and therefore many sites relying on that technique don't rank well anymore. Then there's the more recent Penguin algorithm update that improved Google's ability to recognize purchased links. Sites that used to rank well based on a particular network will drop in the results if that link network is no longer indexed by Google, because they are losing the value of those purchased links. That's not the same as a penalty; it's just that the trick you *used to* employ no longer works.

Dealing with Manual Actions

If you have a Manual Action message, you are lucky. You can just follow the instructions provided in the linked Help information; you may even find a video. If Google is complaining about links pointing to your site, it wants you to do two things:

✔ Remove the links

✔ Disavow the links

Removing bad links can often be pretty difficult; if an SEO firm your company used years ago placed these links, for instance, good luck figuring out how to get them removed!

As for "disavowing" the links — telling Google that you don't want the links to be used when assessing your site rank — that's much easier to do, but I would recommend that you do not do this unless you have found a Manual Action message, or if you are absolutely sure that you are being penalized for having bad links pointing to your site. I personally would also not use the Disavow Links tool if I got an *Unnatural links to your site — impacts links* message in the Manual Actions area; as described earlier in this chapter, this means Google has found some bad links that it is going to ignore, but it won't penalize your site.

If you decide to use the Disavow Links tool, follow these steps:

1. **Download all the links pointing to your Web site that Google has indexed.**

   You can find this information by clicking the Search Traffic link in Webmasters console, then clicking the Links to Your Site option.

2. **Review the downloaded file, then remove all the links that you *don't* want to disavow.**

   The file now contains the list of links you want to disavow.

3. **Upload the edited file to Google.**

Reconsideration requests

After you fix the problems, you can file a *reconsideration request*. There's a link in the Manual Actions area of your Webmaster account. You can state what happened and what you've done. Explain, for instance, if an SEO firm you used did some bad things, or if something you did may have been misinterpreted by Google.

Provide as much information as possible. If Google is complaining about links, even if you haven't been able to get all the garbage links removed you should explain how much *incredible effort* you have put into getting them removed (right? . . . you know, you've tried over and over to get to the root of the problem and just can't get them removed . . .). Google provides a document and a video explaining what it wants you to do when submitting a reconsideration request, which you should definitely refer to before doing the request; explain what the problem was, what you've done to fix it, what the final result was, and then, be contrite! *Sorry, it won't happen again, I swear!*

Pyschological warfare?

I believe there's an element of psychological warfare going on in the area of links. Google's representatives have stated that they do everything they can to avoid innocent Web sites being penalized for having bad links pointing to them, yet at the same time Google says that sites could be penalized for having bad links pointing to them. Those two statements are hard to reconcile; if my competitor's site can be penalized for bad links pointing to it, then can't I just pay a firm a few hundred bucks to point the spammiest possible links at the site? *Yes*, says Google! . . . *No*, says Google!

I can't help feeling that Google is attempting to *scare* Webmasters into two things. First, not creating spammy links pointing to their sites; second, telling Google where the spammy links are! If Google sends thousands of "bad link" messages to Webmasters and encourages them to use the Disavow Links tool, and if thousands of Webmasters send Google, via the Disavow Links tool, thousands of text files containing information about millions of bad links . . . that's fantastic information for Google!

And the proof is in the pudding. Over the last few years, Google has become *much* better at identifying sites that are in the business of selling links. In fact, I wish Google had been doing something like this — Manual Action messages and the Disavow Links tool — years ago (Google's Matt Cutts has stated that they made a mistake in letting the "spammy links" problem go on too long). For years, by default, Google *encouraged* Webmasters to buy links of various kinds, it *encouraged* the creation of spammy links. Creating spammy links *worked*, so an entire industry grew up to help Web sites rank well by creating garbage links. If your competitor was beating you in the search ranks by buying links . . . well, if you can't beat 'em, join 'em!

Today, I think that some of the action around links is more intended to scare you and elicit information about bad links than it is really related to a direct penalty. If you receive a Manual Action message about links, has a penalty really been applied? Or is Google just fishing for information? In some cases, I think it may be the latter.

Dealing with "Algorithmic Actions"

What if you have no Manual Action message? What if you have gone through all the checks in this chapter and are *sure that* your site has been penalized? You're working blind, in effect. Even if you fix the problems there's no reconsideration request available to you; that's reserved for manual actions. All you can do is fix the problems and wait for Google to reindex your site and (perhaps) remove the penalty.

If you've been dropped from Google's index, the first thing to consider is whether you have, in effect, told Google to drop your site. I've seen this happen on a number of occasions, and the mistake can be minor. A few mistyped characters in your `robots.txt` file, for instance, can tell Google that you don't want to be indexed. (I've even seen a site sabotaged by someone intentionally changing the `robots.txt` file.)

I recommend that you start by checking your `robots.txt` file (see Chapter 7 for more about this file), in particular the Disallow lines. For instance, the following is fine:

```
User-agent: *
Disallow: /includes/
```

On the other hand, the following removes your site from the search engines:

```
User-agent: *
Disallow: /
```

A small, simple mistake, and you're dead in the water!

Google Webmaster account (see Chapter 13) provides some nice tools that help you check your existing `robots.txt` file. First, there's the Blocked Resources report. Click the Google Index menu link, then select Blocked Resources; this report will tell you whether anything on your site is being blocked by `robots.txt`.

There's also the `robots.txt` tester. Click the Crawl menu link and then the `robots.txt` Tester link. This tool lets you enter a particular URL to see whether it's blocked, and also enter the text of your `robots.txt` file and test it. You can even request that Google quickly re-crawl your `robots.txt` file if you've modified it.

Note that you can also block search engines using the `robots` meta tags in individual pages. If, for instance, you have the following:

```
<META NAME="robots" CONTENT="noindex">
```

you've just told the search engines *not* to index that page.

These are the most common problems, although there are other, far less likely, possibilities, such as the server being unresponsive to search engines. (You would have that problem only if you have a particularly incompetent or malicious server administrator, but it definitely happens.) Your Google Webmaster account can tell you if Google's having problems accessing your site; select Crawl and then Crawl Errors.

Digging Your Way Out of the Hole

So, say that you've decided that you have indeed been banned or penalized, but you're not getting a Manual Action message from Google. Reversing a ban may be very difficult, though not impossible; you did something very naughty. A penalty under which you are still indexed, and possibly even crawled by Googlebot, is likely to be less of a problem.

You need to figure out what you did to make Google mad. Note that it *could* be accidental — you did something that Google doesn't like, but you did it innocently. For instance, you may have a medical Web site that contains sufficient density of sex-related terms to trigger a Google obscenity filter. Or maybe you have been using cloaking or hidden text (see Chapter 10) for perfectly good reasons, yet Google has interpreted it as a trick.

Or perhaps you hired a Web-development team that implemented various tricks without your knowledge, or maybe your employer gave you a site to look after long after the tricks were used. Or you might have purchased a domain name that was penalized because of dirty tricks in the past. (Just changing owners isn't enough to automatically lift the penalty; see the discussion of this issue in Chapter 3.)

So, here's what I suggest. You should review various materials and write a list of possible items that Google objects to. Here are a couple of places to check:

- **Google's Webmaster Guidelines** (`www.google.com/support/webmasters/bin/answer.py?answer=35769`): You can ignore much of what's here; you're interested only in things that will be interpreted as mal-intent (such as "sneaky redirects"), not things that simply hurt your search engine ranking (such as poor `<TITLE>` tags).

- **The Google Manual Actions documentatation:** Even if you haven't got a Manual Action message, review the information in this area. It's a great resource, with documents and videos related to all the bad things Google doesn't like.

- **The Google Spam Team Quality Rater Guidelines:** Search for this to see if you can find a copy. Read, in particular "Part 4: Webspam Guidelines," to see the sort of things the spam team is looking for. (Unfortunately, this guide is a few years old.)

You might also go into the SEO forums (see Chapter 23) and ask for help. But be warned: Many of the responses you get will be just plain *wrong!* (In particular, forum members seem to see spam on just about every page they look at.) So sometimes working with the forums can lead you in the wrong direction, and at the least can raise your frustration level during a difficult time.

Finding on-page problems

Start with on-page problems, which are the most likely issues to be causing a penalty. Read through the Webmaster guidelines and Spam Team guidelines and check your site, issue by issue.

Here are the sorts of things mentioned in the Spam Team guidelines:

- ✔ **PPC Pages:** Pages created purely for the sake of placing Google AdSense PPC ads on them, with little or no useful content

- ✔ **Parked Domains:** A Web site that has no real value beyond being a placeholder for sponsored links

- ✔ **Thin Affiliates:** A page that has no purpose but to deliver a visitor to another Web site

- ✔ **Hidden Text and Hidden Links:** Text and links placed on a site so that they are visible to search engines, but not to visitors

- ✔ **JavaScript Redirects:** JavaScript used to automatically redirect someone to another site so that the search engine sees the page content but the visitor doesn't

- ✔ **Keyword stuffing:** A page overstuffed with keywords, often repeated many times

- ✔ **100% frame:** A trick in which the main frame, seen by the search engine, contains one set of content, while another frame, that covers the first one, shows different content to the visitor

- ✔ **Sneaky redirects:** Another redirect trick, in which a page redirects through multiple Web sites, often ending up at a merchant site such as eBay or Amazon

Of course, there are sure to be other things the Spam Team looks at now; this document dates back to 2007. You might also check for outgoing links, in particular these three forms:

- ✔ **Injected links:** Sometimes hackers break into a site and insert hidden links to "bad neighborhood" sites such as link farms.

- ✔ **Sold links:** Did you sign up with a firm that pays you to place links on your site to other sites? You might get penalized for that.

- ✔ **Links to bad neighborhoods:** Have you joined some kind of massive link-exchange program in which you link to a service that automatically creates links to thousands of sites? That could be a problem.

Finding link problems

Next, check your off-page issues — that is, links from other sites to yours. You often hear people in the SEO world talk about these links as a potential problem, but in fact they rarely are. Google has to be very careful about penalizing sites for links pointing to a site, unless it can find links on the site itself pointing back to the bad neighborhoods, as I discuss in the previous section. Otherwise, Web site owners with few scruples would "attack" competitors by linking to their sites from bad neighborhoods in the hopes of getting those competitors kicked out of the search engines.

So consider external link problems, but be aware that in most cases, they're not a problem, unless something indicates a relationship between the two linked sites. (If you have link problems, you've most likely received a message in the Manual Actions area of your Webmaster account, unless your site has "benefited" from a really egregious spammy-link campaign.)

Finding domain name problems

Sometimes a domain name may be damaged goods. For instance, perhaps you purchased a domain name that has been penalized in the past. The site currently contains nothing that is causing problems, but the domain itself has a penalty applied to it that hasn't been lifted.

This isn't the case, of course, if you have owned and operated the domain name successfully and have just been hit with a penalty. If you need to check a domain that you purchased, though, you might look in the WayBackMachine (`www.archive.org`), to see whether it has a record of what the site looked like in the past. Was it a spammy-looking site? Also, search for the domain name in Google and see whether it has been discussed on other Web sites in the past. Finally, you might look at other domains owned by the previous domain owner. Are some of those domains damaged goods, too? In the case of egregious Web spamming, Google may penalize all of a domain-holder's domains at one time.

Sitting and waiting

Having gone through the process recommended in the previous sections, you may end up with a list of items that may be at odds with ranking well on Google. If you're lucky, some are quite obviously a problem; there's hidden text on your pages, clearly intended to be hidden from readers, or someone hacked into your site and injected links to link farms. I call this being lucky because you know the cause of the penalty and can remove it and move on.

More problematic is when you're just not sure. For instance, the Google Spam Team Quality Rater Guidelines talks about hidden text being used to mislead search engines (which it often is) but also says that "hidden text is not considered to be Spam if there is no intention to trick the search engine." So, what happens if you had no intention to trick the search engine? Could the Google staff member be misinterpreting your use of hidden text? (For instance, many sites these days display the first paragraph or two of articles, only displaying the rest if a reader chooses to view it.)

You *can't* submit a request for reconsideration unless you've received a Manual Action message. If you don't have a message, but you're sure you've been penalized, all you can do is fix the problems and wait.

Are there other avenues you can pursue? I have been told by someone who spends good money on PPC that if you have an account manager, that person can sometimes contact the right person at Google to get an answer. On the other hand, I have a client in this happy situation: Despite spending literally hundreds of thousands of dollars on PPC each month, and despite the fact that when he ran into a problem he *did* get answers from Google, those answers were so vague as to be useless. It's next to impossible to get a good, solid, "this is the problem" answer from Google on these issues. (Unless, that is, Google sends a message to you in the Manual Action area describing the problem.)

So, that's it. It's a very scary experience and no really good answers exist. However, for all this talk of penalties, I want to reiterate that you have probably not been penalized. Just because your site has dropped in the search results doesn't mean that you're being punished. In most cases, it means that Google has changed the algorithm it's using and it no longer gives your pages, or the links pointing to your pages, the same weight it did in the past.

If you find all this confusing and frustrating . . . well, welcome to the world of SEO! And perhaps you should start thinking about not putting all your eggs in one basket. A site that relies 100 percent on SEO is at risk. You may want to begin thinking about other forms of online marketing, so your business doesn't live and die based purely on the whims of the major search engines!

Part V
The Part of Tens

In this part . . .

- ✔ Destroying myths
- ✔ Keeping current
- ✔ Taking care of tips
- ✔ Visit `www.dummies.com` for great Dummies content online.

Chapter 22

Ten-Plus Myths and Mistakes

In This Chapter

▶ Understanding common mistakes made by site developers

▶ Deconstructing harmful myths

▶ Knowing the problems that hurt your search engine rank

A lot of confusion exists in the search engine world — a lot of myths and a lot of mistakes. In this chapter, I quickly run through a few of the ideas and omissions that can hurt your search engine positions.

Myth: It's All about Meta Tags and Submissions

This is the most pervasive and harmful myth of all, held by many Web designers and developers. All you need, many believe, is to code your pages with the right meta tags — KEYWORDS and DESCRIPTION, and things like REVISIT-AFTER and CLASSIFICATION — and then submit your site to the search engines. I know Web designers who tell their clients that they'll "handle" search engine optimization and then follow nothing more than this procedure.

It's completely wrong for various reasons. Most meta tags aren't particularly important (see Chapter 7), if they're even used by search engines at all. Without keywords in the page content, search engines won't index what you need them to index. (See Chapter 7.) Submitting to search engines doesn't mean they'll index your pages. (See Chapter 13.) Moreover, what about links? (See Chapters 16 through 18.)

Myth: Web Designers and Developers Understand Search Engines

I'm a geek. I've worked in software development for over 30 years. I still work closely with software developers (these days, mostly Web-software developers) and Web designers; I build Web sites for my clients (so I work with developers and designers on these sites); my friends are developers and designers, and I'm telling you now that most developers and designers do *not* understand search engines to any great degree.

Most Web-development companies these days tell their clients that they know how to handle search engines, and even that they're experts. In most cases, that's simply not true — no more than it's true that I'm an expert in neurosurgery. This makes it very hard for business owners when they hire a Web development team, of course, though I hope this book will help. It will give you an idea of the sorts of questions you should ask your developers so that you can figure out whether they really *do* understand search engine requirements (see also the Web Extra from Part IV, *How to Pick an SEO Firm (Without Getting Burned!)*.

In addition, many Web developers don't enjoy working with search marketing experts. They think that all search engine experts want is to make the site ugly or remove the dynamism. This is furthest from the truth, and Web developers who refuse to work with SEO experts may just be defensive about their lack of knowledge.

Myth: Multiple Submissions Improve Your Search Position

This is perhaps one of the biggest scams in the SEO world; the "submission" service, a promise to "submit" your Web site to hundreds, nay, thousands of search engines.

As far as the major search engines go, multiple submissions, even automated submissions, don't help. Someone recently told me that he was sure it did help because his position improved in, for instance, the Open Directory Project when he frequently resubmitted. This is completely wrong — in the case of the Open Directory Project, there's no way it could possibly help, because all entries have to be reviewed by a human editor, and submitting multiple times is more likely to annoy the editor rather than convince him to let you in! (On the other hand, it's very hard to get into the Open Directory Project these days, so submitting to several, appropriate, categories *may* help.)

Submitting to search engines — requesting that they index your pages — often doesn't get your page indexed anyway. Far more important is a link campaign to get plenty of links to your site (see Chapters 16 through 18). And you should definitely be working with XML sitemaps (see Chapter 13).

Some of these multiple-submission services don't even submit where they claim to submit; on a number of occasions, I've reviewed the "here's where we submit your site to" lists for some of these services and found out-of-business search engines included.

Mistake: You Don't Know Your Keywords

This is also a major problem: The vast majority of Web sites are created without the site owners or developers really knowing what keywords are important. (That's okay, perhaps, because most sites are built without any idea of using keywords in the content anyway.) At best, the keywords have been guessed. At worst — the majority of the cases — nobody's thought of the keywords at all.

Don't guess at your keywords. Do a proper keyword analysis. (See Chapter 6.) I can almost guarantee that two things will happen. You'll find that some of your guesses were wrong — people aren't often using some of the phrases you thought would be common. You'll also discover very important phrases you had no idea about.

Just recently, I talked with a company that ranked *really* well for the keywords it was interested in. The only problem was that there was another group of keywords the company simply hadn't considered, which were almost as important as the ones it had — and for this second group of keywords, it didn't rank at all. So it doesn't matter how well you play the SEO game — if you didn't consider keywords, you might as well not bother.

Mistake: Too Many Pages with Database Parameters and Session IDs

This is a surprisingly common problem. Many, many sites (in particular, sites built by big companies with large development teams) are created with long, complicated URLs containing database parameters or session IDs. (See Chapter 9.)

My favorite example used to be CarToys.com, a large chain of electronics stores. This site had thousands of products but fewer than 100 pages indexed by Google, and most of those were Adobe Acrobat files, pop-up ads ("Free Shipping!"), or links to dynamic pages that wouldn't appear when a searcher clicked a link in the search results. Luckily for CarToys.com, someone at the company figured it all out, fixed the problem, and Google then picked up tens of thousands of pages.

The chance that your site won't get indexed if you have clunky URLs is far lower today than it was in the past. However, there's still a problem. Every URL is a keywording opportunity, a location that search engines give lots of weight to when ranking pages; so if you don't have keywords in your URLs, your site is missing out on a huge opportunity.

Mistake: Building the Site and Then Bringing in the SEO Expert

Most companies approach search engine optimization as an afterthought. They build their Web site and then think, "Right, time to get people to the site." You really shouldn't begin a site until you have considered all the different ways you're going to create traffic to the site. It's like starting to build a road without knowing where it needs to go; if you're not careful, you'll get halfway there and realize "there" is in another direction.

In particular, though, you shouldn't start building a Web site without an understanding of search engines. Most major Web sites these days are built by teams of developers who have little understanding of search engine issues. These sites are launched and then someone decides to hire a search engine consultant. And the search engine consultant discovers all sorts of unnecessary problems. Good business for the consultant; expensive fixes for the site owner.

Myth: $25 Can Get Your Site a #1 Position

You hear a lot of background noise in the search engine business from companies claiming to be able to get your site into thousands of search engines and rank your site well for $25 a month. . . . Or a $50 flat fee . . . or $75 a month . . . or whatever.

The truth is that it's more complicated than that, and everyone I've spoken to who has used such services has been very disappointed. They often don't get into the major search engines at all, and even if they get included in the index, they don't rank well. Search engine ranking is sometimes very easy — but other times it's complicated, time consuming, and tedious. Most of the offers streaming into your Inbox in spam e-mail messages or displayed in banner ads on the Web aren't going to work.

Myth: Google Partners Get You #1 Positions

If you receive a spam e-mail or even a telephone call telling you that the sender has a "special arrangement" with Google and can get you a #1 position within hours or days, delete it; it's nonsense — a scam. It's true that you can buy a top position on Google through its AdWords PPC (Pay Per Click) program, though you'll be bidding against your competitors. In fact, that's what most of these companies do; they quickly set up PPC campaigns for you, though that's generally not clear from their sales pitch. And, while PPC isn't the subject of this book, I'll just say that the campaigns set up by these companies are likely to be slipshod attempts to merely show you top positions, without regard to whether the advertising campaign will actually bring you business.

Mistake: You Don't Have Pages Optimized for Specific Keywords

Have you built pages optimized for your most important keywords? I spoke recently with a firm that ranked pretty well — #5 in the search results — for his most desired keyword phrase, but not well enough (obviously, the site owner wanted #1).

The funny thing was that he was doing very well considering the fact that he didn't have a single page optimized for the keyword phrase he desired. Sure, he had pages close, pages that had the individual words in the keyword phrase scattered throughout the page, but not a single page that was fully optimized for the phrase.

Therefore, think about your most important phrases. Do you have pages *fully optimized* — that is, you have the phrase at the beginning of the `<TITLE>` tag, at the beginning of the `DESCRIPTION` tag, in `<H1>` tags, scattered throughout the page, and so on — for all these phrases? If not, maybe you don't *deserve* the #1 spot!

Mistake: Your Pages Are Empty

This one is a huge problem for many companies; the pages have nothing much for search engines to index. In some cases, the pages have little or no text that a search engine can read because the words on the page are embedded into images. In other cases, the words may be real text but are very few and aren't the right keywords. This is a particular problem for many e-commerce sites, which often just have a short paragraph of information for each product. I encourage clients to find ways to bulk up their pages with more product information, which provides more opportunity for useful keywords in the content pages.

Remember, search engines like — *need* — content. To a search engine, *content* means text that it can read and index. Whenever you provide text to a search engine, it should do the most for you — help you to be found in the search results. And the more content, the better.

Myth: Pay Per Click Is Where It's At

Pay Per Click (*PPC;* the small "sponsored" ads you see at the top of the search-results pages) can be a very important part of a Web site's marketing strategy. It's reliable, predictable, and relatively easy to work with. But it's not the only thing you should be doing. In fact, many companies cannot use PPC because the clicks are too expensive for their particular business model (and click prices are likely to keep rising as search marketing continues to be the hot Internet marketing topic).

The growth in PPC has been partly caused by the lack of search engine optimization knowledge. Companies build a site without thinking about search engines and then don't hire professional expertise to help them get search engine traffic, so they fall back on PPC. Many companies are now spending hundreds of thousands of dollars on PPC each month; they could complement their PPC campaigns with natural search engine traffic for a small fraction of that cost.

The wonderful thing about PPC advertising and SEO is that the two work hand in hand. If you want to know whether a word is important enough to optimize, get a hundred clicks from your favorite search engine through PPC and look at the conversion rates and the return on investment (ROI). Want to expand your PPC keyword list? No problem; look at the words that people are already using to find you as a baseline and grow your list from these words. (For example, if they are using *rodent racing* to find you, buy ads triggered by the words *mouse rodent racing, rat rodent racing,* and so on.) Many companies are using PPC profitably; just don't assume it's the only way to go.

Many companies actually use PPC and SEO in combination. One client of mine has high organic-search positions, yet still buys PPC positions. Overall, he gets more business than he would if he did only one or the other.

Mistake: Ignoring Site Usability and Aesthetics

The changes implemented in Google's Panda update introduced a totally new concept to search marketing. Pre-2011, the major search engines attempted to match search queries with the best page based on page content; essentially the question was, "Does the content in Page A match the search query better than the content in Page B?" With Panda, however, Google moved to the next step and tried to answer the question, "Even if the content is a perfect match, will the searcher *like* this page?"

In other words, a page that is a perfect match as far as the content of the page goes may not be presented to the searcher because of things that Google believes the searcher won't like once arriving at the page — things like too many ads near the top of the page. It's not just Google, either; Bing introduced a similar concept to the Panda update called (more prosaically), *Content Quality*, which looks at Web pages and asks the questions "Is the content useful and sufficiently detailed," and "Is the content well-presented and easy to find."

From the perspective of conversions — converting visitors to customers — usability and aesthetics have always been important. Now, and more so in the future, they are also relevant to reaching visitors, because the search engines are going to pre-approve sites, rather like sending your butler to visit a hotel before you deign to stay there. (You do have a butler, don't you?)

Mistake: Believing Everything You Read

Just because something's "in print" — or on a Web site — doesn't mean it's true! I see all sorts of incorrect information on this subject all the time. This field is full of misinformation, ambiguousness, and outright nonsense. I often hear my clients say, "Well, I read x the other day," and I have to convince them that x is quite simply wrong. It's hard to do, though, because so many people think that if someone said something in a forum, or on a blog, or even in a book on SEO, it *must* be true. Let skepticism be your byword.

When I'm told that something is undoubtedly true, I want to see the evidence. Did Google say it, for instance? If not, and if it doesn't seem to make sense, then it's probably not true.

I'll sometimes check for the veracity of an SEO claim by searching for the concept along with the words *matt cutts*. Matt Cutts is the head of Google's webspam team, and is the *de facto* liaison with the SEO world. He maintains a blog, has published numerous videos (see Chapter 23), and is often interviewed; if I want to get to the truth of a particular SEO claim, I try to find out what Matt has said about the subject. (However, be careful when you read that "Matt Cutts" said something; often, when I trace a claim back to the original Matt Cutts statement, it's very different.)

Chapter 23

Ten-Plus Ways to Stay Updated

*T*he naysayers said it couldn't be done, that a book about search engine optimization couldn't be written because the technology is changing so quickly. That's not entirely true — I wrote the first edition of this book eight years ago, and the basics are still the same: creating pages that search engines can read, picking good keywords, getting lots of links into your site, and so on.

But some details do change. Where are people searching these days? What tricks are search engines really clamping down on? Why did your site suddenly drop out of Google (as many thousands do now and then; see Chapter 21)?

You may also need more detailed information than I can provide in this book. Perhaps you have a problem with dynamic pages and you need to know the details of URL rewriting for a particular Web server, for instance. You need to know where to go to find more information. In this chapter, I provide you with resources that you can use to keep up-to-date and track down the details.

Let Me Help Some More

Visit my Web site at www.SearchEngineBulletin.com. I point you to important resources, provide links to all the Web pages listed in this book (so that you can just click instead of typing them), and provide important updates. I also have bonus chapters on pay per click, copyright law, and Google search techniques.

I also provide consulting services, including phone consultations. I can examine a company's online strategy from not just the perspective of search engines but also a wider view; I've been working online for over 30 years and have experience in Web design, e-commerce and online transactions, traffic conversion, non–search engine traffic generation, and so on. An hour or two of advice can often save a company from the huge expense of going down the wrong path!

The Search Engines Themselves

One of the best ways to find information about search engines is by using carefully crafted search terms at the search engines themselves. Say you want to find detailed information about dealing with session IDs (see Chapter 9). You can go to Google and search for *search engine session id*. Or perhaps you have a problem with dynamic URLs and know that you need to use something called *mod_rewrite*. Go to a search engine and search for *mod_rewrite* or *mod rewrite*. (The former is the correct term, although many people talk of *mod rewrite* in the vernacular.)

It's amazing what you can find if you dig around for a little while. A few minutes' research through the search engines can save you many hours of time wasted through inefficient or ineffective SEO techniques. I suggest you read the bonus chapter, from an earlier edition of this book, posted at www.searchenginebulletin.com and www.dummies.com/go/searchengineoptimizationfd, which explains various techniques for searching at Google. A good understanding of how to use search engines will pay dividends.

Google's Webmaster Pages

Google is happy to tell you what it wants from you and what it doesn't like. No, it won't tell you exactly how it figures out search result rankings, but good information is there nonetheless. It's a good idea to review the advice pages Google provides for Webmasters. You can find them at the following URLs:

- ✔ **Google Webmaster Guidelines:** www.google.com/webmasters/guidelines.html
- ✔ **Google Webmaster Help Center:** www.google.com/support/webmasters

Google's Search Engine Optimization Starter Guide

Late in 2008, Google finally decided, "If we can't beat them, join them," and published its own SEO guide.

It's basic but useful stuff, and I find it particularly handy when I'm arguing with Web developers. For instance, when a Web developer says, voice dripping with skepticism, "Why should we bother using H1 tags; nobody does anymore," I can say quite simply, "Because Google says so," and end the conversation right there.

You can find the guide here:

www.google.com/webmasters/docs/search-engine-optimization-starter-guide.pdf

Bing SEO Tips

You can find information about optimizing pages for submission to Bing (and, through its partnership, inclusion in the Yahoo! search results) at http://onlinehelp.microsoft.com/en-us/bing/gg132923.aspx. You'll find a wide range of information, from how the MSNbot works to how to handle a site move.

Matt Cutts

Matt Cutts is a well-known employee of Google (well known in SEO circles, that is) who works for the Search Quality team. He maintains a blog (www.MattCutts.com/blog) about a wide range of issues, including many related to SEO issues, is frequently interviewed, and has created hundreds of videos on SEO issues (search www.youtube.com/user/GoogleWebmasterHelp for *matt cutts*). There are even Web sites that collect and summarize his words of wisdom, such as www.theshortcutts.com (get it?), and a quick search for any SEO topic, combined with the search term *matt cutts*, will often lead to some really useful information.

I like to use Matt's info to find out the *real* answers; when I hear an SEO tip that I think perhaps is unlikely to be true, yet oft quoted, I sometimes think, "Let's see what Matt has to say on the subject." It's also a great way to deal with uncooperative Web developers and difficult clients who have been hearing some kind of SEO nonsense.

Here's an example. I sometimes hear from clients that "Google doesn't care about links anymore." My answer? "Oh, really? Well, perhaps you should hear what Matt Cutts has to say about that!" (What does he have to say? "I think backlinks still have many, many years left in them. But inevitably what we're trying to do is figure out how an expert user would say this particular page matched his information needs. And sometimes backlinks matter for that.")

Watch out! Just because someone on the Interwebs says "Matt Cutts said *x*" doesn't mean it's true.

In fact, that "many, many years" quote came from a video that was described on TheShortCutts.com with this simple statement: "Will backlinks lose their importance in ranking? Ideally yes, as Google better understands content." Read just the summary, and you could be forgiven for thinking that links are already dropping in importance; if you listen to the video, you get a very different impression. I've frequently seen people misinterpret what Matt says to an even greater degree than this. If I see someone claiming Matt believes something that sounds unlikely to me, I try to dig down until I find the original Matt Cutts video or document. All too often, I find that, in fact, he's said something quite different.

Search Engine Watch

The Search Engine Watch site gives you a great way to keep up with what's going on in the search engine world. This site provides a ton of information about a very wide range of subjects related to not only search engine optimization but also the flip side of the coin — subjects related to searching online. In fact, perhaps this site's greatest weakness is that it provides *so much* information; it's really intended for search engine optimization experts rather than the average Webmaster or site manager. The site is divided into a free area and a paid-subscription area.

Visit the site at www.searchenginewatch.com.

The Official Google Webmaster Help Group

Google Groups hosts a very useful resource, the *Official Google Webmaster Help Group,* which has tens of thousands of members and hundreds of thousands of archived messages. It's a great way to find out what people in the business are saying about, well, just about anything. Find it at www.google.com/support/forum/p/Webmasters.

Here are a couple more great ways to peek into the mind of Google:

- ✔ **Google Webmaster Central Blog:** A very useful site, with information from actual employees of Google providing the Google view of search engine optimization. Visit `http://googlewebmastercentral.blogspot.com`.

- ✔ **Google's Inside Search:** This is really a promotional site targeting Google users rather than the SEO community, but it's a great way to keep up-to-date with new search features as Google introduces them. See `https://www.google.com/insidesearch`.

- ✔ **Google Trends:** This is an analysis of what people are searching for, when, and where. You can find the most popular brand-name searches, charts showing how searches peak for particular keywords during news events or in response to TV shows, the most popular searches for particular men, women, and fictional characters, the most popular movie searches in Australia, the most popular brands in Italy, and so on. Google provides weekly, monthly, and annual reports. Check it out at `www.google.com/trends`.

- ✔ **Google Correlate:** Enter a search term to find frequency over time or by location: `www.google.com/trends/correlate`.

Moz

Moz (originally SEOMoz) is a software company providing SEO tools. The company also maintains a very good blog on SEO issues, and of course learning from other SEOers in the industry is extremely valuable. See `http://moz.com/blog`.

WebMaster World

WebMaster World (`www.webmasterworld.com`) is a very good discussion group, with many knowledgeable people. It'll cost ya, though: $89 for six months, or $149 for a year.

HighRankings.com

Hosted by a search engine optimization consultant, HighRankings.com is a pretty busy forum (free at this time) with discussions covering a wide range of subjects. Check it out at `www.highrankings.com/forum`.

Chapter 24

Ten-Plus Useful Things to Know

In this chapter, I describe a number of useful little things to know, from 301 redirects to Google's enhanced image search; from various information sources to how Google creates multiline search result entries.

Managing Sitelinks (Multiline Search Results)

You've probably seen multiline search results, such as those shown in Figure 24-1.

How does this happen? More important, how can you make it happen for your site?

Google calls these internal site links, um, *sitelinks,* and they're intended to help users find their way into popular pages within a site when they search for that site's domain name. Sitelinks also may appear when Google *thinks* you're looking for that particular site, even though you didn't search for the domain specifically. Search for *dummies,* for instance, and the Dummies.com site appears, with sitelinks; search for *search engine optimization for dummies,* though, and none of the sites in the results, including Dummies.com, have sitelinks.

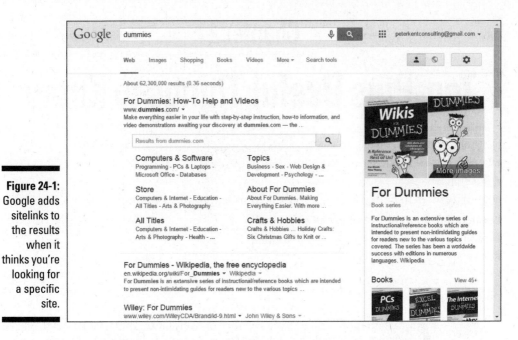

Figure 24-1:
Google adds
sitelinks to
the results
when it
thinks you're
looking for
a specific
site.

Google actually analyzes the site and tries to figure out which pages are significant. At the time of writing, there's no *direct* way for you to tell Google which pages to use (Google said long ago that it may allow Webmaster input in the future, but the future's already here, and Google still doesn't.)

In the early days, Google created sitelinks for only very popular sites, but these days, many, many sites have sitelinks displayed in the search results now and then. So how can you tell Google which pages to use? You do so indirectly, through site structure. Google looks at the site's link structure, and if you have lots of links saying <u>Contact Us</u> that point to a particular page, that page may be picked up for a sitelink. Google may also look at folder structure. If you have a <u>products</u> link pointing to a /products/ folder, it may give even more of a hint. Google also recommends using `alt` attributes to help create sitelinks, so if you have image links to pages you want to appear as sitelinks, remember to include an `alt` attribute in the `<img>` tag.

However, if you're fortunate enough to be in the happy situation of having sitelinks, but don't like one of the pages that Google is using, you *can* tell Google not to use it. Log into your Webmaster account (see Chapter 13), click the <u>Search Appearance</u> link in the left navigation bar, and then click the <u>Sitelinks</u> link. You'll be able to specify the pages you want to "demote" — the ones you don't want appearing as sitelinks. It may take "some time" for the blocked sitelink to no longer be used, and there's an idiosyncrasy you should be aware of. Google says that blocking a sitelink is effective for 90 days after your most recent visit to the Sitelinks page, so you may want to put in your scheduling program a note to revisit every so often.

Adding a Search Box and Your Site Name

Have you noticed that when Google displays sitelinks for a site, it sometimes also displays a search box above the sitelinks, allowing users to directly search within the site? How about the site name that appears in the search results for many companies at the beginning of the URL line? (*Wikipedia > wiki > Rat* instead of the URL *www.Wikipedia.org/wiki/Rat*, for instance.)

How do you get this working for *your* site? First, you need to set up Google Custom Search on your site (see `https://developers.google.com/custom-search`). It's free and pretty easy to set up.

Then, you need to use a piece of structured data markup that tells Google to insert the search box in the results. You can find information on markup, and the particular markup required, in the Google Structured Data Markup page (`http://support.google.com/webmasters/bin/answer.py?hl=en&answer=99170`). As for displaying the site name instead of a URL, you'll find the required code there, too.

Checking Your Site Rank

How do you know how well your site ranks in the search engines? You can go to a search engine, type a keyword phrase, and see what happens. If you're not on the first page, check the second; if you're not there, check the third. Then go back and do it for 50 search terms on several search engines. It will take a while.

Another problem with manually checking position is that if you're logged into a Google account, Google will start "personalizing" your search results to what it thinks is most appropriate for you; you won't see what the average user sees.

Luckily, you can get help. Many programs can check your search engine position for you. You tell the program which keywords you're interested in, which search engines you want to check, and which Web site you're looking for in the search results. Then you let the program do its work.

Traditionally, search engines have "banned" such tools. In theory, if Google notices that a computer is using one of these tools excessively, it may ban search queries from that computer. That doesn't mean it hurts your Web site, of course, because the queries are not coming from your Web site.

On the other hand, Google now provides a special application programming interface (API) that programs such as WebPosition can use to send queries directly to Google, bypassing the search page. Such access *is* okay. (You can find information about Google APIs at `https://developers.google.com/apis-explorer`.) As for WebPosition, it recently changed from Windows-based software that you purchase to a monthly Web service, so the software runs on WebPosition's servers, and accessing the data is its problem, not yours.

You can see a typical keyword report, showing positions for each keyword in several search engines — in this case, produced by WebPosition Reporter — in Figure 24-2. Many other programs can create site-ranking reports for you — both through programs that are installed on your computer and through Web-based services, such as Moz (`https://moz.com/products/analytics`), SEMRush (`http://www.semrush.com/`), WebCEO

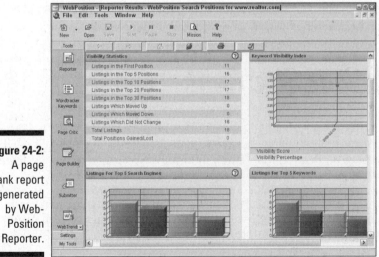

Figure 24-2:
A page rank report generated by Web-Position Reporter.

(www.webceo.com), Authority Labs (www.authoritylabs.com), Rank Tracker (www.link-assistant.com/rank-tracker), and even a few free services, such as GoogleRankings (www.googlerankings.com).

Here's a quick tip for a quick rank check. Go to Google and run a search; then click the little cog icon in the top-right corner of the page, and select Search Settings. Find the Results Per Page slider and move the slider to 100. (You won't be able to do this unless you turn off Google Instant Predictions first.) Click the Save button, and now, each time you search Google, you see 100 search results, so finding your site in the results may be easier.

Ranking Images

Images often appear in search results. Why? How? Well, as usual, it's all about keywords. To encourage the search engines to display *your* images in response to particular keywords, put those keywords in

- ✔ The name of the image file.
- ✔ The image tag's alt attribute
- ✔ The text around the image
- ✔ An H heading tag above and close to the image
- ✔ An image caption

The page should be optimized for the same keyword, too. I'm not sure whether the search engines read images' metadata, but it doesn't hurt to also put the keywords in the metadata. Image metadata is text information embedded into the image file; copyright information, the creator of the image, contact information, and so on. (JPEG and PNG files have this data; GIFs don't.) You can find metadata editors; you can also edit directly from Windows File Editor (right-click, select Properties, then click the Details tab to find the metadata).

Checking for Broken Links

Link checkers are always handy, whether you're interested in optimizing your site for the search engines or not. After you've created a few pages, run a link check to make sure you didn't make any mistakes in your links.

Again, many, many link checkers are available, including paid services, such as LinkAlarm (`http://linkalarm.com`) and SEMRush (`www.semrush.com`), that will automatically check links on your site and send you a report. I sometimes use a little Windows program called Xenu's Link Sleuth, shown in Figure 24-3 (`http://home.snafu.de/tilman/xenulink.html`). It's free, which is always nice! (The creator of Link Sleuth requests that if you like the program, support some of his favorite causes.) This program is very quick — checking tens of thousands of links in a few minutes — and very easy to use. It produces a report, displayed in your Web browser, showing the pages containing broken links. Click a link, and the page opens so you can take a look. You can use the program to check both internal and external links on your site.

Note also that your Web design software package may include a built-in link checker.

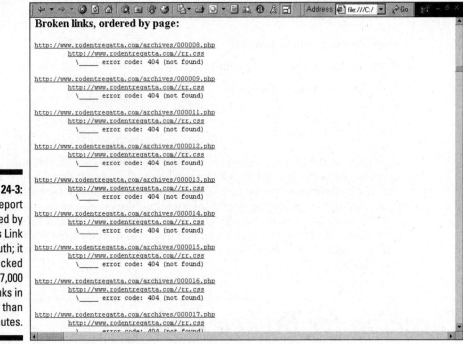

Figure 24-3: A report created by Xenu's Link Sleuth; it checked over 17,000 links in fewer than ten minutes.

Assessing Traffic with the Alexa Toolbar

The Alexa toolbar (`http://download.alexa.com`) can be handy, too. I sometimes use it to assess the traffic of Web sites I may want to work with. For instance, if someone approaches you trying to sell advertising space on a site, how do you know whether it's a good deal? So many sites get almost no traffic that it may not be worth the expense.

The Alexa toolbar can give you a very general idea of whether the site gets any traffic at all; you can view traffic details for the site, such as the *traffic rank,* an estimate of the number of visitors to the site out of every million Internet users, and so on. Reportedly, Alexa's numbers are pretty good for the world's most popular sites, but rather inaccurate for the average site. However, you can still get a general feel. If the site is ranked 4,000,000, you can bet it doesn't get much traffic at all. If the site is ranked 4,000, it's far more popular. Alexa also provides a list of the most popular sites in thousands of categories — a good way to track down affiliates, for instance, or link partners.

Alexa isn't the only company providing this sort of information, though. Sites such as `www.compete.com` and `www.quantcast.com`, popular competitors to Alexa, provide estimates of traffic and rank. (Note, however, that none of these numbers are accurate; they are just estimates.) Also, various SEO browser add-ons include the Alexa ranking numbers on their toolbars.

Installing a Code Reviewer

You may want to install a code-review plug-in in your browser. These tools allow you to quickly analyze a Web site — that is, to look into the site code while looking at the Web page. Right-click a page component and select Inspect Element, and you see the code that creates it — great for seeing exactly how links are coded, for instance. You can also edit code to immediately see how the page would look with modifications.

The Chrome browser has a built-in console for this purpose; if you're using another browser, you might use Firebug (shown in Figure 24-4). While Firebug was originally created for Firefox, there are "Lite" Firebug versions for other browsers (Internet Explorer, Chrome, Opera, and Safari).

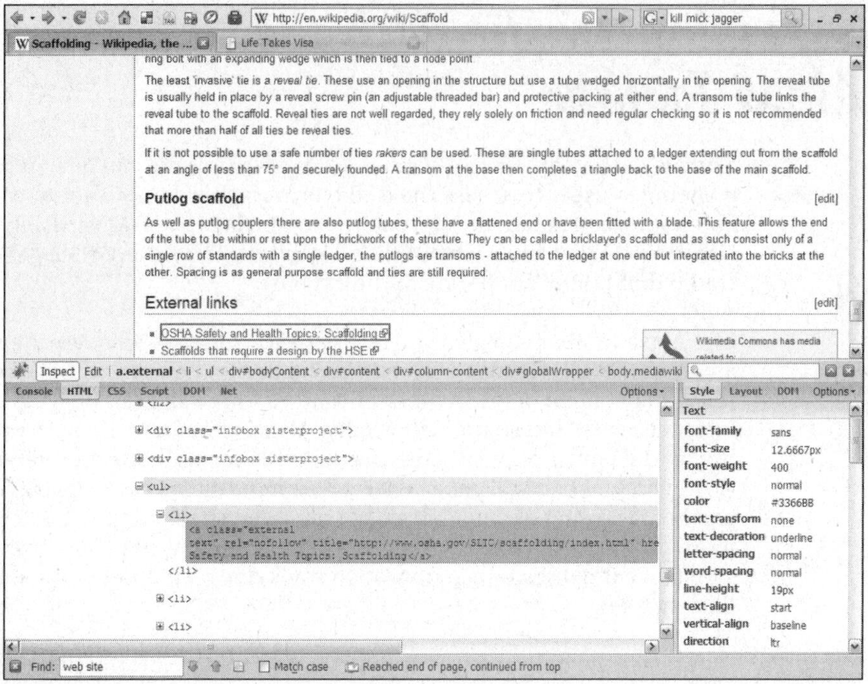

Figure 24-4:
Firebug
is a great
tool for
analyzing
Web pages.

Finding Your Keyword Density

As I explain in Chapter 6, you don't need to get too hung up on keyword density. You can analyze to the *n*th degree, and everyone has a different opinion as to exactly what the density should be. But it's sometimes interesting to check your pages for keyword density, and a few tools are available to help you do so, such as the following:

✔ **SEO Tool's Keyword Density Analyzer:** www.seochat.com/
seo-tools/keyword-density

✔ **Webconf's Keyword Density Tool:** www.webconfs.com/keyword-
density-checker.php

Analyzing Your Site's Traffic

You really should track traffic going to your site. At the end of the day, your search engine position isn't terribly important — it's just a means to an end. What really counts is the amount of traffic coming to your site. And it's important to know *how* people get to your site, too.

There are essentially two types of traffic-analysis tools: those that read server logs and those that tag your Web pages and track traffic by using a program on another server. In the first case, the tool analyzes log files created by the Web server — the server adds information each time it receives a request for a file. In the second type of tool, you have to add a little piece of code to your Web pages — each time a page from your site is requested, the program is, in effect, informed of the fact.

You quite likely have a traffic-analysis tool already installed on your site — ask your server administrator how to view your logs. Otherwise, you can use a tag-based traffic-analysis tool, and these days you don't even have to pay.

Analysis tools show you all sorts of interesting (and often useless) information. But perhaps the most important things you can find are

- How many people are reaching your site, and from what areas
- Which sites are sending visitors to your site
- Which search engines are sending visitors to your site
- What keywords people are using to reach your site
- What pages visitors are exiting from most frequently

You may find that people are reaching you with keywords that you hadn't thought of, or perhaps unusual combinations of keywords that you hadn't imagined. This doesn't replace a real keyword analysis, though, because you see only the keywords used by people who found you, not the keywords used by people who *didn't* find you but were looking for products or services like yours. See Chapter 6 for more information about keywords. (Unfortunately, the keywords information provided in traffic logs was dramatically reduced when Google stopped sending this information to Web servers.)

These days, it seems that almost everyone but the largest companies is using Google Analytics. A few years ago, Google purchased one of the top independent traffic-analysis firms, Urchin, and then started *giving away* traffic-analysis accounts. Visit www.google.com/analytics.

This is a very sophisticated tool, and to fully understand what can be done with the system, you need to spend a few dozen hours with a good book, such as Brian Clifton's *Advanced Web Metrics with Google Analytics* (which I'm mentioning not just because it's published by an imprint of Wiley, the publisher of the fine tome you are currently reading, but because it's a good read, too; well, as good as a book about Web analytics can hope to be; I mean, it's not John Grisham, but still . . . you know what I mean). Still, Google analytics can be set up to run a few minutes and provide useful information "right out of the box."

By the way, you can link your Google Webmasters account with your Google Analytics account, thereby incorporating information from your Webmaster account into your Analytics reports. See Chapter 13 for information about the Webmaster account.

Traditionally, the traffic-analysis companies were big believers in blinding their customers with science. They didn't understand that sometimes less is more and focused on throwing as much complicated information at the client as possible. Things are getting better, though, and Google Analytics isn't too bad. Whatever route you take, you really need to install analytics.

Thanks to Google Analytics, it's now hard for a Web analytics company that targets the small-business market to make it, and some of these firms have died out. You might want to look at www.crazyegg.com, though, which I think has a "we'll survive through the power of *cool*" strategy that seems to be working for it. It's a simple-to-set-up system that provides very cool "overlays," like the one in Figure 24-5. These overlays are *heatmaps* intended to show what page components people are looking at on your site. (Actually they are based on mouse movements, but the company claims that mouse movements can be 88 percent correlated with eye movements.)

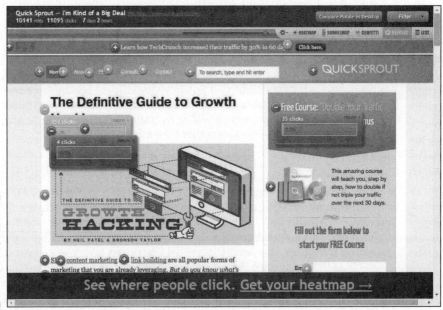

Figure 24-5:
A demo of Crazy Egg's neat traffic analysis overlay.

Tracking Phone Calls

Many companies have a significant problem in tracking business. The business comes through the phone, not through the Web directly. Prospective clients come to the Web site, and then, rather than submitting a lead through a submission form or making a purchase on the site, they pick up the phone.

As an example, doctors' offices and medical clinics are likely to get a very high proportion of phone leads; if a phone number is prominently displayed on the site, most people — perhaps 95 percent or more — will call rather than use the submission form.

How, then, do you track this traffic? Use a call-submission service. Such a service, which can be very affordable, starting at around $10 a month, provides you with a phone number to place on your site. Then it tracks all the calls through the number; some services even record the calls. You get reports showing these calls, of course, but some services can even integrate with Google Analytics, so you can see the number of calls that way, too.

I've used `www.hostednumbers.com`, which is good for small businesses (you can get a single number for $8 a month), but various other services may be more appropriate for larger companies needing more numbers. The company `http://dial800.com`, for instance, provides five numbers for $9 a month.

Really sophisticated phone-tracking services can provide dynamic number assignment. Companies such as Mongoose Metrics, for instance (`www.mongoosemetrics.com`), can automatically assign a number depending on where a visitor comes from. If the visitor *direct loads* your site (that is, types the domain name into the browser's Address Bar), he sees one number; if he arrives by clicking on a PPC ad, he sees another; if he comes from the organic-search results, he sees yet another number, and so on. You can integrate calls into your Google Analytics reports, too. Such services really help you figure out what parts of your marketing (SEO or not) are working and what parts are not. To find these services, search for *phone call tracking*.

Checking for Duplication and Theft

Copyscape (`www.copyscape.com`) is an interesting tool that allows you to see whether anyone has stolen your site content and to see how closely your content matches other sites. For instance, if you're quoting documents or using syndicated content, the less duplication, the better. The concern is that search engines may downgrade pages that they know duplicate other pages, so you don't want your pages to match others too closely.

Enter a URL into Copyscape, and it searches for pages that match the page referenced by the URL, to varying degrees. Copyscape returns the results, and when you click the links, you see the page with the matching text colored and, at the top, a Copyscape banner telling you how many words match.

Here's a particularly useful application for this tool. When you pay for someone to write articles for you, whether for your site or for syndication (see Chapter 18), run the articles through Copyscape. One way to make writing $10 articles profitable is not to write them, so you may find that the writer isn't the writer, but he copies really well. Copyscape can track down this kind of perfidy in seconds. An interesting little toy; experiment and see.

Using 301 Redirects

301 redirects tell search engines that a particular URL really points to another URL. Google uses a 301, for instance, to point `google.com` to `www.google.com`. (Try it; go to `google.com`, and you'll see that the page redirects to `www.google.com`.)

301s are especially useful when moving pages or changing domain names. They're very easy for server administrators; about the only time you have problems with 301 redirects is when your site is a shared hosting account on a Windows server. You should also use a 301 redirect from the non-www version of your domain name; that is, from `yourdomain.com` to `www.yourdomain.com` (if it's good enough for Google, it's good enough for you).

Search for *301 redirect* in Google, and you find plenty of information.

Getting Multiple Results on the Search Results Page

How would you like three, four, five, or more results on the search-results page leading people to your site? It can be done; I've seen it done and done it several times myself.

Getting two results on the first page is common; as you know by now, Google often returns two pages from a single site, one indented below the other. But how about more? People use a couple of strategies to do this:

- ✔ **Create multiple sites:** Some companies create two or more totally independent Web sites in an attempt to grab more "real estate" on the search-results page, and if done right, this strategy can work well. If you want to be paranoid, though, and ensure that the sites are never identified as belonging to the same business, the domain names can't have the same contact information. To this end, many people use a domain-privacy system to block exposure of ownership information. In addition, you need to make sure that the domain names have completely different IP numbers — not just the set of numbers at the end of the full set, but a different "C" block or higher. (The bold number in the following IP number is the C block: 98.137.**149**.156.)

- ✔ **Get into the pages that rank alongside yours:** Take a look at the other pages ranking high for your keywords. If you're lucky, you can get onto those pages. I've seen situations in which numerous other links in the first page of search results point to directories, and you may be able to buy a position in those directories. Another possibility: Affiliate companies that rank well may be willing to sell your products.

- ✔ **Buy a PPC ad:** Many companies rank well in the search engines *and* buy PPC ads. Many searchers go straight to the PPC ads rather than organic results; on the other hand, many ignore the PPC ads and use only the organic results. Thus, many companies decide to cover all bases and position themselves in both areas.

The problem with the first strategy is that you now have two or more sites to work on — which you have to create links to in order to get them to rank well. Still, it's a strategy that does work for companies that do it right.

Here's an example. Search for *free credit report*, and, at the time of writing, you find, among others, these results:

PPC Ads

FreeCreditReport.com

Experian.com

FreeCreditScore.com

Organic Results

AnnualCreditReport.com

FreeCreditReport.com

Experian.com

Six results on one page, five of which link directly to Web sites owned by Experian, and one of which (AnnualCreditReport.com) is owned by another company but that contains a prominent link to Experian.com. I've seen better, though; I've seen as many as seven organic results pointing to the same company through its own sites and directories.

You Need an Attractive Site

This isn't directly related to SEO, but it's so important and is such a big issue with small companies I consult with that I need to mention it. You see, it doesn't matter how well your site ranks: If your site is grotesquely ugly, you're not going to sell much!

I don't understand why people don't get this. I often show clients a competitor's site in one browser tab and their site in another tab. (I use Web meeting software so that we can both see the same thing while talking on the phone.) I jump between the two and ask, "Now, which company would *you* buy from?"

Still, even when someone understands, it's often difficult to find good design. So, here are some tips:

- ✔ Web design is *not* a pure commodity, like sugar or memory chips. Many businesses seem to think that design is design is design, and they buy the cheapest design they can find. You should buy design only from an individual or company that has already created something that looks good.

- ✔ Never buy design from a firm without knowing that it has the designer of the work you liked available for your project. Just because that firm has done good work in the past doesn't mean that it will for you, especially if it assigns a different designer to your project.

- ✔ Here's a great way to find designers: Go to `http://99designs.com` and look at the project winners (99designs.com is a design-contest site with some really great work). Find work you like and then contact the designer directly to discuss your project. Or run a contest yourself to let designers compete for your business.

- ✔ Other places to find designers are Guru.com, eLance.com, and oDesk. com. But, remember, always check designers' portfolio to make sure they really can create a good design for you.

- ✔ Understand that no direct correlation exists between price and quality of graphic design. You can spend a lot of money on garbage or get quality work for very little. (It reminds me of the Pepsi and Nike logos. Pepsi reportedly paid a million dollars for the 2008 redesign of its logo, which looks remarkably like the *old* logo; Nike's swoosh logo cost the company $35.)

✔ Don't get hung up on beautiful Web design. Most companies need *professional,* not *award-winning,* design. Many designers want to create something cool, but what you want is usable — something that looks good and lets people get the task at hand done.

✔ Speaking of usability, few designers understand this concept. You might want to read *Don't Make Me Think,* by Steve Krug (New Riders Press); it's an excellent book on the subject.

✔ Never, never, *never* create a Web design with white text on a black background! (Well, a few headers here or there don't create a problem, but you should *never* do this to body text.) White text on a black background says to people, "Don't read this!" The proof? None of the world's top sites use light text on a dark background. So, if you see a designer who likes this type of layout, move on to someone else.

Here's a great test tool that shows you exactly why you shouldn't do white on black: `www.ironicsans.com/owmyeyes`.

Finding More SEO Tools

If you're looking for more useful SEO stuff, take a look at the following sites:

✔ **SEO Help:** `www.measuring-up.com/seo-reference/seo-resources.html`

✔ **Webconfs.com:** `www.webconfs.com`

✔ **Pandia SEO:** `www.pandia.com/seo-software`

✔ **Moz:** `www.moz.com`

✔ **SEMRush:** `http://www.semrush.com/`

Fixing Your Reputation

I've had a few clients come to me with an embarrassing problem; when people search for their name or business, the search engines return some not-so-pleasant results. This often happens to people who are the subject of lawsuits or criminal prosecutions. (I'm sure that in some cases the problems are well deserved, just as I'm sure that in some cases they are not. I'm not passing judgment here, merely addressing the technical issues.)

For instance, I recently spoke with an attorney who had a very contentious relationship with the judiciary in the city in which she practiced and had been the subject of various sanctions by local judges. When searching for her name, most of the results were newspaper stories about her problems.

How does one deal with such problems? *Reputation management* has become a big business, but I'll tell you essentially the process used by reputation-management firms. In most cases, there is no practical way to "remove" the links in the search results that you object to, so the strategy is to push those links down in the search results, onto the second page at least, if not further.

To do that, reputation-management firms do various things:

- Create links pointing to your Web site — or Web sites if you have multiple — using your name as the keywords in the anchor text, to ensure your site ranks well.

- Create a bunch of small sites about you, perhaps at Linkedin.com, Facebook.com, and other social-networking and directory sites.

- Create links — again using your name as the anchor-text keywords — pointing to these sites.

The plan, then, is to seed the results with a bunch of "friendly" sites, sites you control, and push them up to dominate the search results, thus pushing the bad stuff down.

If you have an unusual name, this is actually quite easy to do. If you have a very common name, or a name shared with someone famous, it's very hard.

I've heard several things about reputation-management firms. I've seen cases in which they've done a good job. I've seen one case, in which the job was actually very easy (an unusual name), in which the firm totally failed to achieve anything. But most disturbingly, there are reports of reputation-management fraud. The claim is that disreputable firms are using complaint sites such as RipOffReport.com and PissedConsumer.com to find companies that have reputation problems and then contacting the firms to offer their services, claiming they can remove complaints from such sites (which they almost certainly can't). As an article posted by RipOffReport.com explains, "Once the Reputation Management SEO company knows who you are and knows that your business is worried about online attacks, they know you are vulnerable. Armed with that knowledge, unscrupulous Reputation Management SEO companies may even engage in digital extortion by threatening to create more false complaints about you unless you continue paying them."

So, there are reputable firms out there, but beware of the scams!

Index

Notes

Notes

Notes

Notes

About the Author

Peter Kent is an e-commerce consultant who specializes in search-engine optimization (SEO). He has provided consulting services to hundreds of companies large and small, including Amazon, Zillow, Avvo, Lonely Planet, and TowerRecords.com. He has worked online since 1984, written about the Internet since 1993, and authored almost 50 books (including dozens of Internet-related books) and hundreds of periodical articles and columns.

Dedication

For Chris. We miss you terribly.

Author's Acknowledgments

I'd like to thank all my clients, who have given me an opportunity to play with search-engine optimization in a wide variety of businesses. I'd also like to thank Amy Fandrei, my Acquisitions Editor, and my editor, Pat O'Brien, for making the process quick and easy. And, of course, the multitude of Wiley staff involved in editing, proofreading, and laying out the book.

Publisher's Acknowledgments

Project Manager: Pat O'Brien

Technical Editor: Tyler LeCompte

Sr. Editorial Assistant: Cherie Case

Production Editor: Kumar Chellappan

pple & Mac

ad For Dummies,
th Edition
78-1-118-72306-7

hone For Dummies,
th Edition
78-1-118-69083-3

acs All-in-One
or Dummies, 4th Edition
78-1-118-82210-4

S X Mavericks
or Dummies
78-1-118-69188-5

logging & Social Media

acebook For Dummies,
th Edition
78-1-118-63312-0

ocial Media Engagement
or Dummies
78-1-118-53019-1

VordPress For Dummies,
th Edition
78-1-118-79161-5

usiness

tock Investing
or Dummies, 4th Edition
78-1-118-37678-2

vesting For Dummies,
th Edition
78-0-470-90545-6

Personal Finance
For Dummies, 7th Edition
978-1-118-11785-9

QuickBooks 2014
For Dummies
978-1-118-72005-9

Small Business Marketing
Kit For Dummies,
3rd Edition
978-1-118-31183-7

Careers

Job Interviews
For Dummies, 4th Edition
978-1-118-11290-8

Job Searching with Social
Media For Dummies,
2nd Edition
978-1-118-67856-5

Personal Branding
For Dummies
978-1-118-11792-7

Resumes For Dummies,
6th Edition
978-0-470-87361-8

Starting an Etsy Business
For Dummies, 2nd Edition
978-1-118-59024-9

Diet & Nutrition

Belly Fat Diet For Dummies
978-1-118-34585-6

Mediterranean Diet
For Dummies
978-1-118-71525-3

Nutrition For Dummies,
5th Edition
978-0-470-93231-5

Digital Photography

Digital SLR Photography
All-in-One For Dummies,
2nd Edition
978-1-118-59082-9

Digital SLR Video &
Filmmaking For Dummies
978-1-118-36598-4

Photoshop Elements 12
For Dummies
978-1-118-72714-0

Gardening

Herb Gardening
For Dummies, 2nd Edition
978-0-470-61778-6

Gardening with Free-Range
Chickens For Dummies
978-1-118-54754-0

Health

Boosting Your Immunity
For Dummies
978-1-118-40200-9

Diabetes For Dummies,
4th Edition
978-1-118-29447-5

Living Paleo For Dummies
978-1-118-29405-5

Big Data

Big Data For Dummies
978-1-118-50422-2

Data Visualization
For Dummies
978-1-118-50289-1

Hadoop For Dummies
978-1-118-60755-8

Language &
Foreign Language

500 Spanish Verbs
For Dummies
978-1-118-02382-2

English Grammar
For Dummies, 2nd Edition
978-0-470-54664-2

French All-in-One
For Dummies
978-1-118-22815-9

German Essentials
For Dummies
978-1-118-18422-6

Italian For Dummies,
2nd Edition
978-1-118-00465-4

e Available in print and e-book formats.

Available wherever books are sold. **For more information or to order direct visit www.dummies.com**

Math & Science

Algebra I For Dummies,
2nd Edition
978-0-470-55964-2

Anatomy and Physiology
For Dummies, 2nd Edition
978-0-470-92326-9

Astronomy For Dummies,
3rd Edition
978-1-118-37697-3

Biology For Dummies,
2nd Edition
978-0-470-59875-7

Chemistry For Dummies,
2nd Edition
978-1-118-00730-3

1001 Algebra II Practice
Problems For Dummies
978-1-118-44662-1

Microsoft Office

Excel 2013 For Dummies
978-1-118-51012-4

Office 2013 All-in-One
For Dummies
978-1-118-51636-2

PowerPoint 2013
For Dummies
978-1-118-50253-2

Word 2013 For Dummies
978-1-118-49123-2

Music

Blues Harmonica
For Dummies
978-1-118-25269-7

Guitar For Dummies,
3rd Edition
978-1-118-11554-1

iPod & iTunes
For Dummies, 10th Edition
978-1-118-50864-0

Programming

Beginning Programming
with C For Dummies
978-1-118-73763-7

Excel VBA Programming
For Dummies, 3rd Edition
978-1-118-49037-2

Java For Dummies,
6th Edition
978-1-118-40780-6

Religion & Inspiration

The Bible For Dummies
978-0-7645-5296-0

Buddhism For Dummies,
2nd Edition
978-1-118-02379-2

Catholicism For Dummies,
2nd Edition
978-1-118-07778-8

Self-Help & Relationships

Beating Sugar Addiction
For Dummies
978-1-118-54645-1

Meditation For Dummies,
3rd Edition
978-1-118-29144-3

Seniors

Laptops For Seniors
For Dummies, 3rd Edition
978-1-118-71105-7

Computers For Seniors
For Dummies, 3rd Edition
978-1-118-11553-4

iPad For Seniors
For Dummies, 6th Edition
978-1-118-72826-0

Social Security
For Dummies
978-1-118-20573-0

Smartphones & Tablets

Android Phones
For Dummies, 2nd Edition
978-1-118-72030-1

Nexus Tablets
For Dummies
978-1-118-77243-0

Samsung Galaxy S 4
For Dummies
978-1-118-64222-1

Samsung Galaxy Tabs
For Dummies
978-1-118-77294-2

Test Prep

ACT For Dummies,
5th Edition
978-1-118-01259-8

ASVAB For Dummies,
3rd Edition
978-0-470-63760-9

GRE For Dummies,
7th Edition
978-0-470-88921-3

Officer Candidate Tests
For Dummies
978-0-470-59876-4

Physician's Assistant Exam
For Dummies
978-1-118-11556-5

Series 7 Exam For Dummies
978-0-470-09932-2

Windows 8

Windows 8.1 All-in-One
For Dummies
978-1-118-82087-2

Windows 8.1 For Dummies
978-1-118-82121-3

Windows 8.1 For Dummies
Book + DVD Bundle
978-1-118-82107-7

Available in print and e-book formats.

Available wherever books are sold. **For more information or to order direct visit www.dummies.com**

Take Dummies with you everywhere you go!

Whether you are excited about e-books, want more from the web, must have your mobile apps, or are swept up in social media, Dummies makes everything easier.

Leverage the Power

For Dummies is the global leader in the reference category and one of the most trusted and highly regarded brands in the world. No longer just focused on books, customers now have access to the For Dummies content they need in the format they want. Let us help you develop a solution that will fit your brand and help you connect with your customers.

Advertising & Sponsorships

Connect with an engaged audience on a powerful multimedia site, and position your message alongside expert how-to content.

Targeted ads • Video • Email marketing • Microsites • Sweepstakes sponsorship

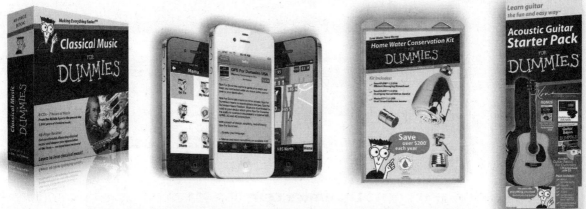